SHINOBU ODA

HEIGHT: 6'1"

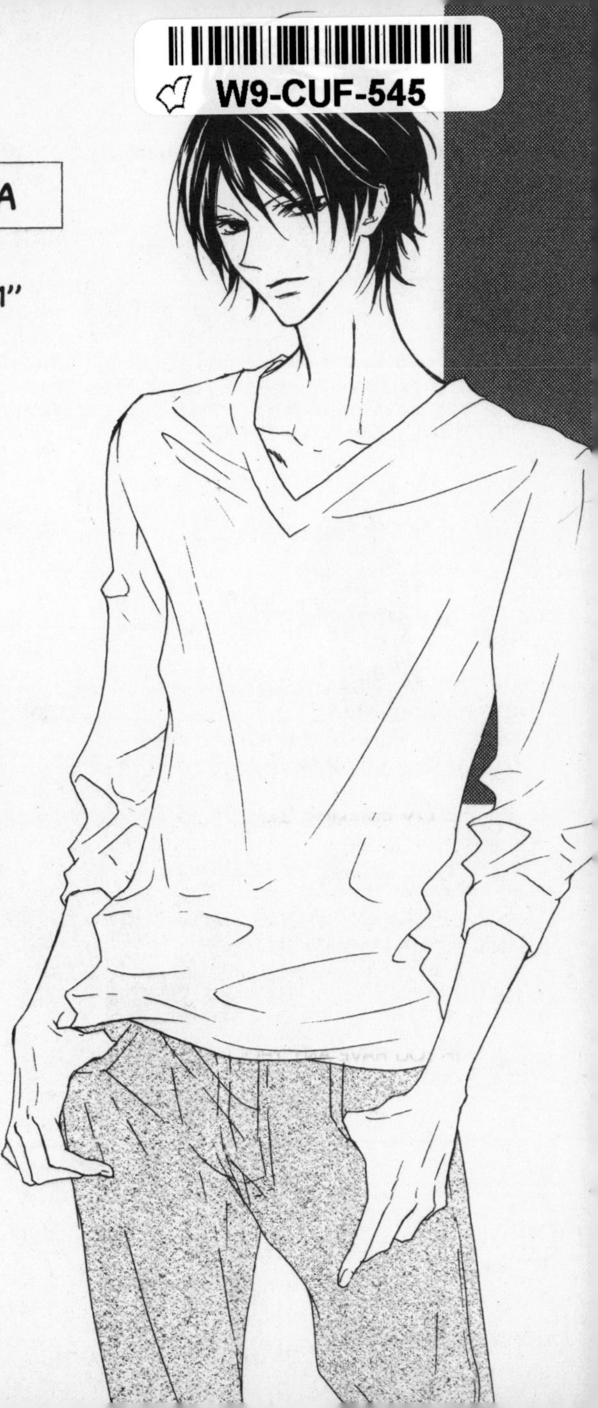

HERE WEARING CASUAL CLOTHES, WHICH YOU DON'T NORMALLY GET TO SEE ON HIM IN THE STORY. I THOUGHT HE'D WEAR KIND OF ROUGH CLOTHES IN HIS OFF-HOURS. IT'S EASY FOR ME TO DRAW HIS HAIR AND SNEERING FACE.

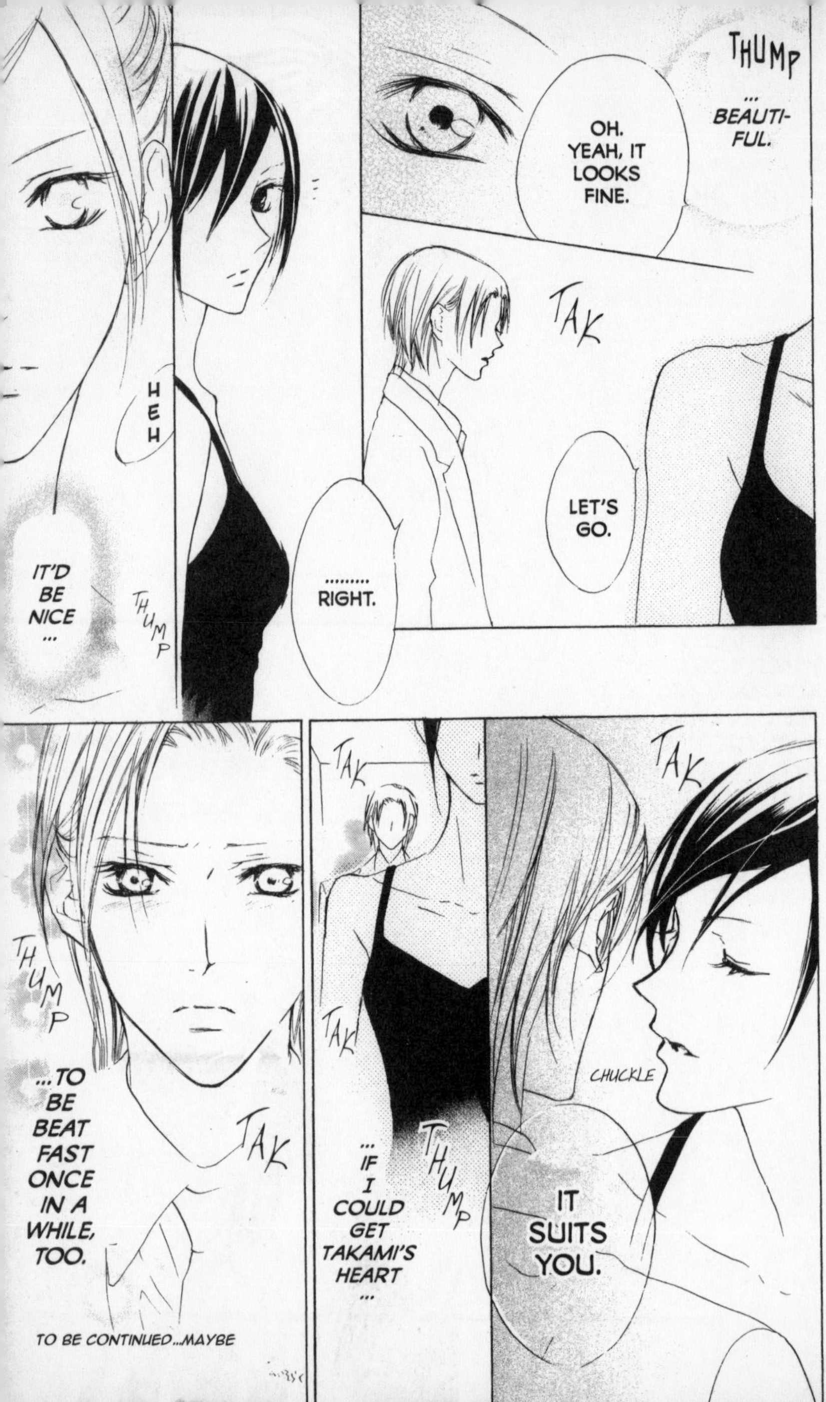
THUMP
...BEAUTI-FUL.
OH. YEAH, IT LOOKS FINE.
TAK
LET'S GO.
.........RIGHT.
HEH
IT'D BE NICE...
THUMP
TAK
CHUCKLE
IT SUITS YOU.
TAK
TAK
THUMP
...IF I COULD GET TAKAMI'S HEART...
THUMP
...TO BE BEAT FAST ONCE IN A WHILE, TOO.
TAK
TO BE CONTINUED...MAYBE

CONTENTS

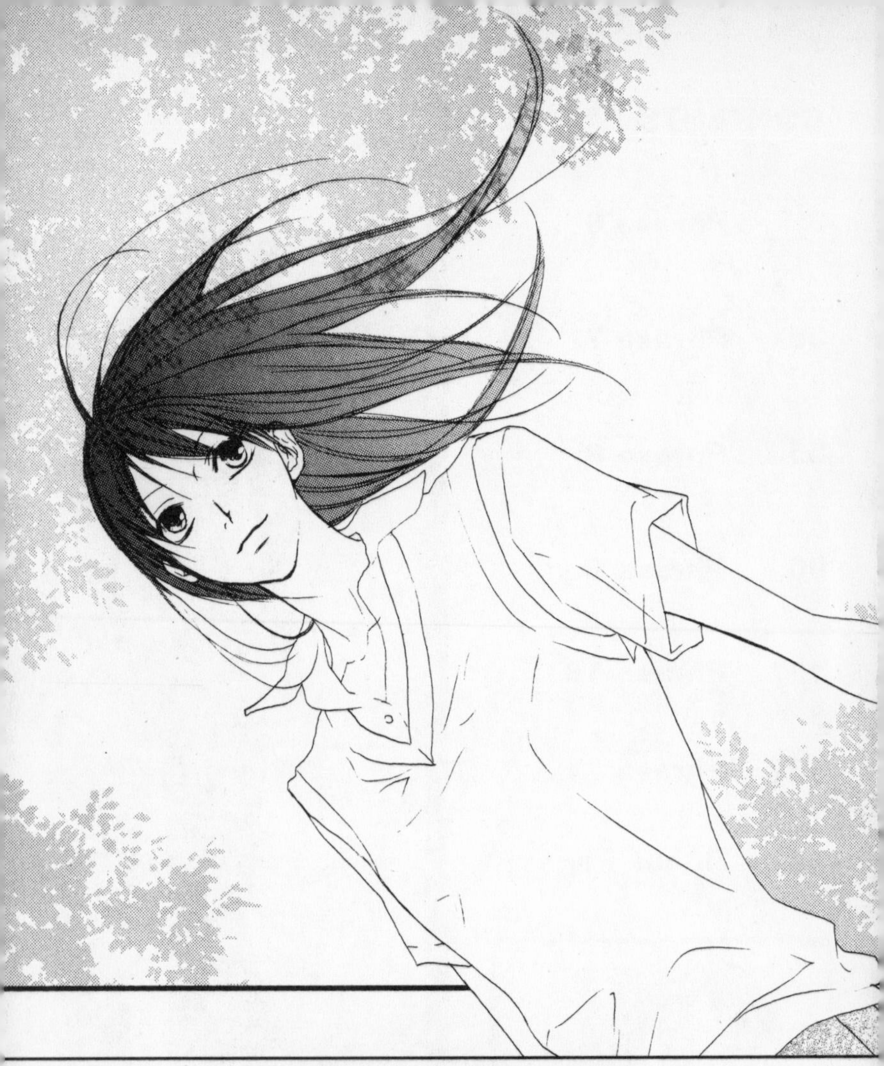

VENUS CAPRICCIO

Volume 2 **By Mai Nishikata**

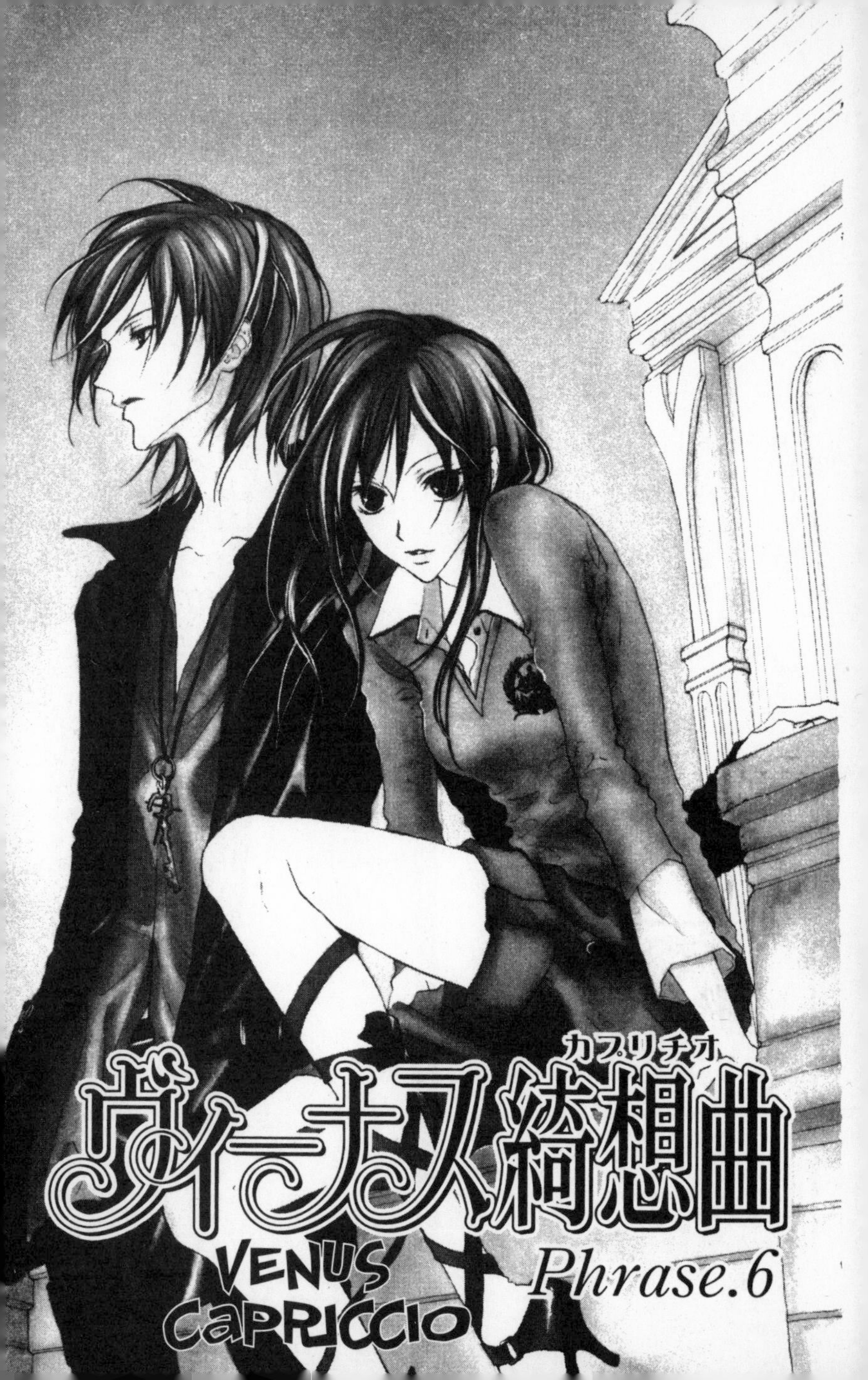
ヴィーナス綺想曲
カプリチオ
VENUS CAPRICCIO
Phrase.6

Don't take your eyes off them!!

TAGLINE MY EDITOR CAME UP WITH WHEN THIS EPISODE WAS PUBLISHED IN THE MAGAZINE. IN ENGLISH AND IN COLOR, IT LOOKED REALLY COOL.

I WANTED TO REPRINT ONE OF MY PRE-INKED PENCIL DRAWINGS HERE.

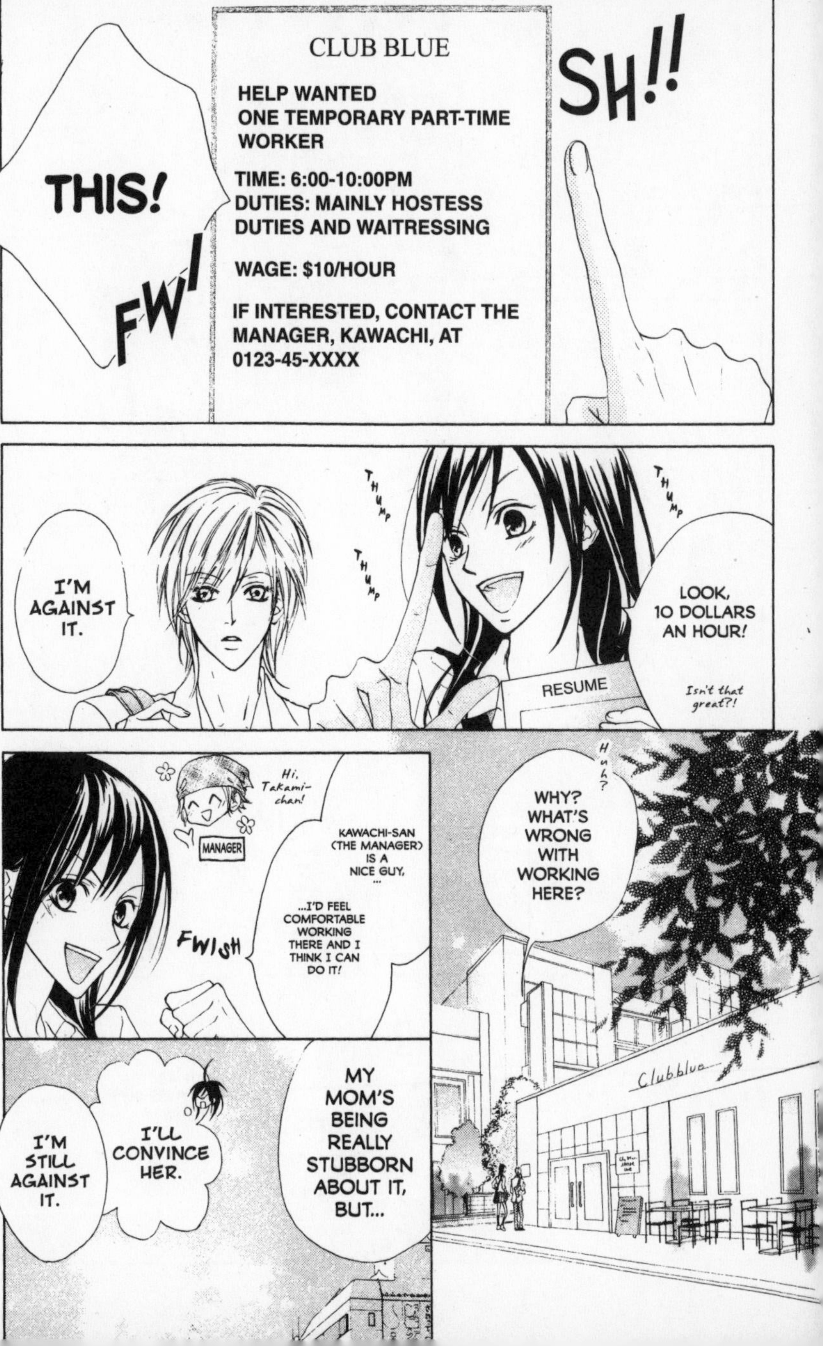
SH!!
CLUB BLUE
HELP WANTED
ONE TEMPORARY PART-TIME WORKER
TIME: 6:00-10:00PM
DUTIES: MAINLY HOSTESS DUTIES AND WAITRESSING
WAGE: $10/HOUR
IF INTERESTED, CONTACT THE MANAGER, KAWACHI, AT 0123-45-XXXX
FWI
THIS!
LOOK, 10 DOLLARS AN HOUR!
Isn't that great?!
THUMP
THUMP
THUMP
RESUME
I'M AGAINST IT.
Huh?
WHY? WHAT'S WRONG WITH WORKING HERE?
Clubblue
KAWACHI-SAN (THE MANAGER) IS A NICE GUY, ...
...I'D FEEL COMFORTABLE WORKING THERE AND I THINK I CAN DO IT!
Hi, Takami-chan!
MANAGER
FWISH
MY MOM'S BEING REALLY STUBBORN ABOUT IT, BUT...
I'LL CONVINCE HER.
I'M STILL AGAINST IT.

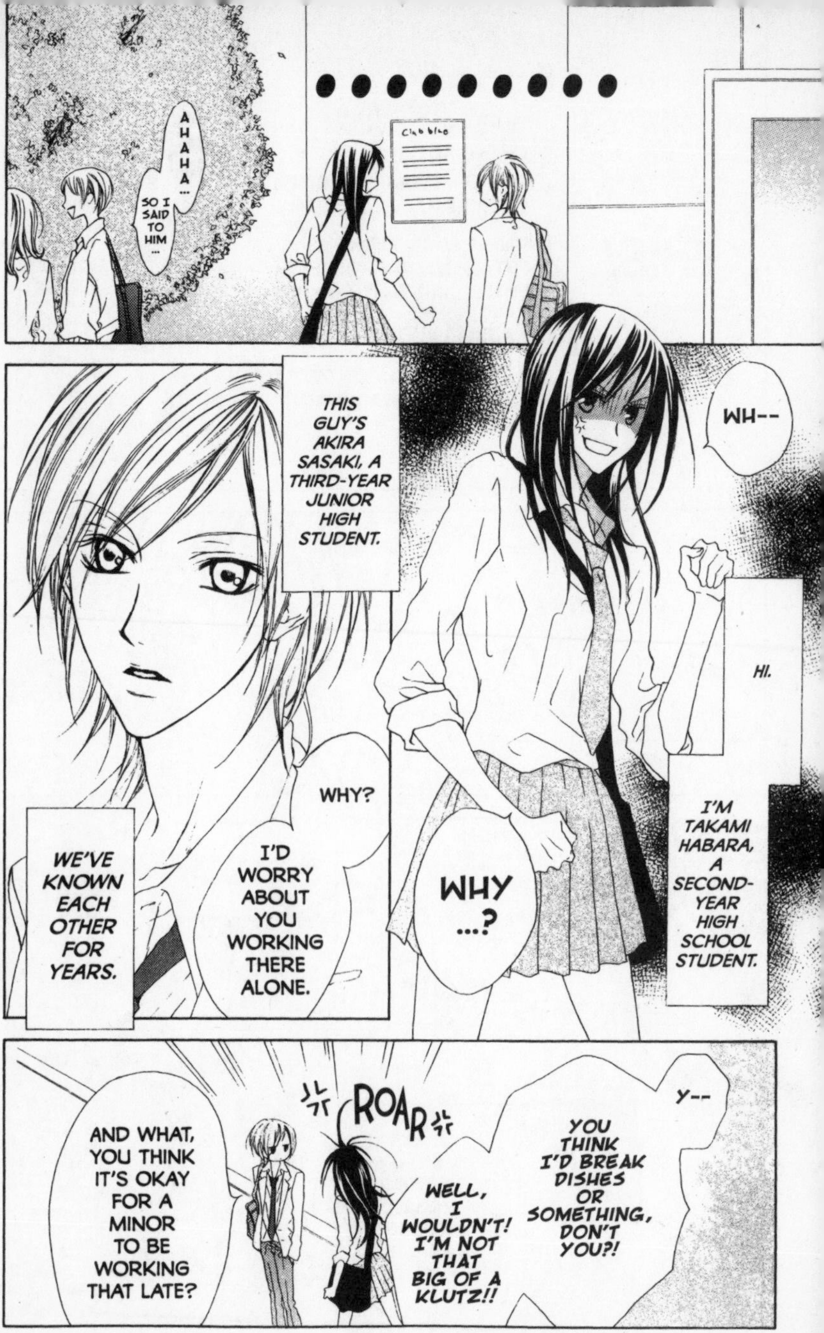
●●●●●●●●●●
AHAHA...
SO I SAID TO HIM...
WH--
HI.
I'M TAKAMI HABARA, A SECOND-YEAR HIGH SCHOOL STUDENT.
WHY...?
THIS GUY'S AKIRA SASAKI, A THIRD-YEAR JUNIOR HIGH STUDENT.
WHY?
I'D WORRY ABOUT YOU WORKING THERE ALONE.
WE'VE KNOWN EACH OTHER FOR YEARS.
Y--
YOU THINK I'D BREAK DISHES OR SOMETHING, DON'T YOU?!
WELL, I WOULDN'T! I'M NOT THAT BIG OF A KLUTZ!!
ROAR
AND WHAT, YOU THINK IT'S OKAY FOR A MINOR TO BE WORKING THAT LATE?

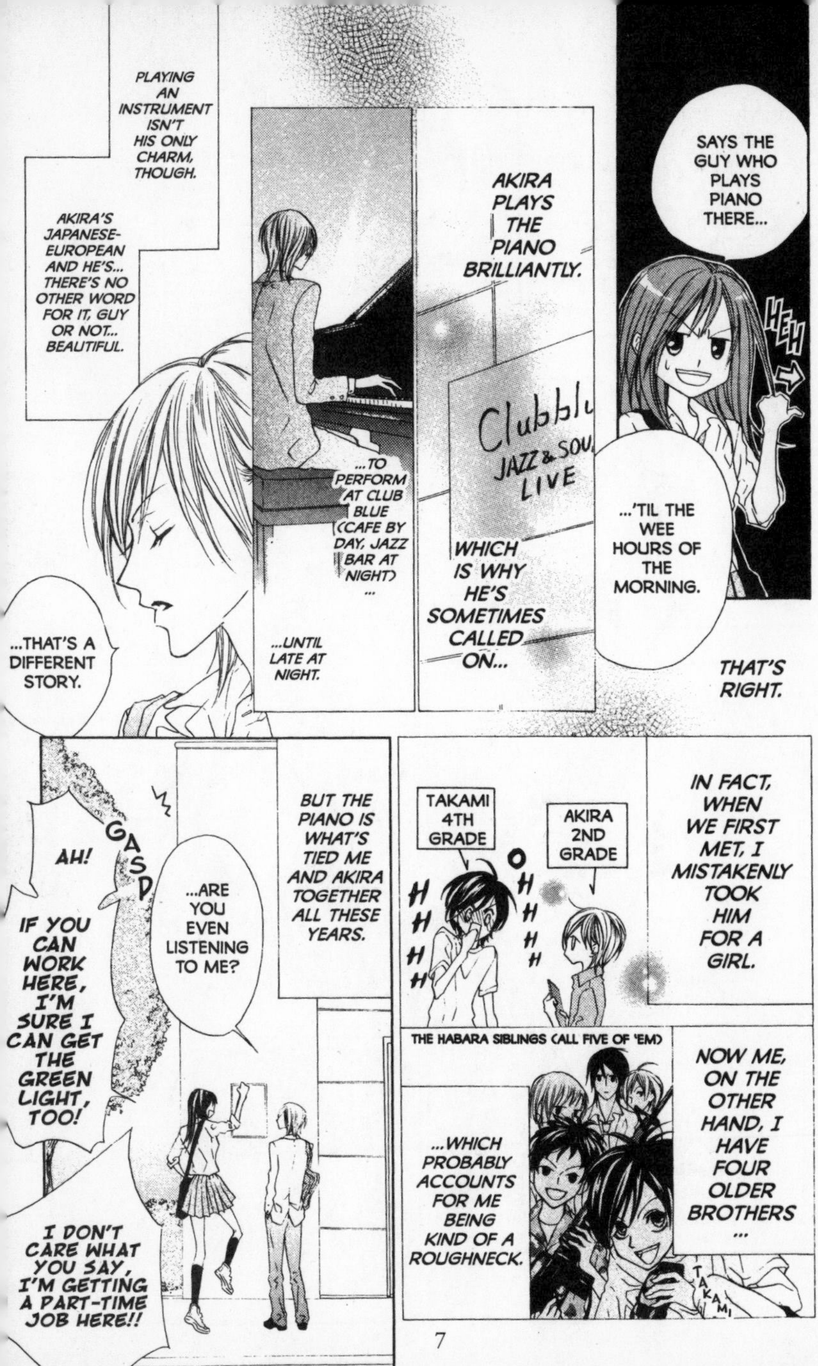
SAYS THE GUY WHO PLAYS PIANO THERE...
HEH
...'TIL THE WEE HOURS OF THE MORNING.
THAT'S RIGHT.
AKIRA PLAYS THE PIANO BRILLIANTLY.
WHICH IS WHY HE'S SOMETIMES CALLED ON...
...TO PERFORM AT CLUB BLUE (CAFE BY DAY, JAZZ BAR AT NIGHT)...
...UNTIL LATE AT NIGHT.
PLAYING AN INSTRUMENT ISN'T HIS ONLY CHARM, THOUGH.
AKIRA'S JAPANESE-EUROPEAN AND HE'S... THERE'S NO OTHER WORD FOR IT, GUY OR NOT... BEAUTIFUL.
...THAT'S A DIFFERENT STORY.
IN FACT, WHEN WE FIRST MET, I MISTAKENLY TOOK HIM FOR A GIRL.
AKIRA 2ND GRADE
TAKAMI 4TH GRADE
NOW ME, ON THE OTHER HAND, I HAVE FOUR OLDER BROTHERS...
THE HABARA SIBLINGS (ALL FIVE OF 'EM)
TAKAMI
...WHICH PROBABLY ACCOUNTS FOR ME BEING KIND OF A ROUGHNECK.
BUT THE PIANO IS WHAT'S TIED ME AND AKIRA TOGETHER ALL THESE YEARS.
...ARE YOU EVEN LISTENING TO ME?
GASP
AH!
IF YOU CAN WORK HERE, I'M SURE I CAN GET THE GREEN LIGHT, TOO!
I DON'T CARE WHAT YOU SAY, I'M GETTING A PART-TIME JOB HERE!!

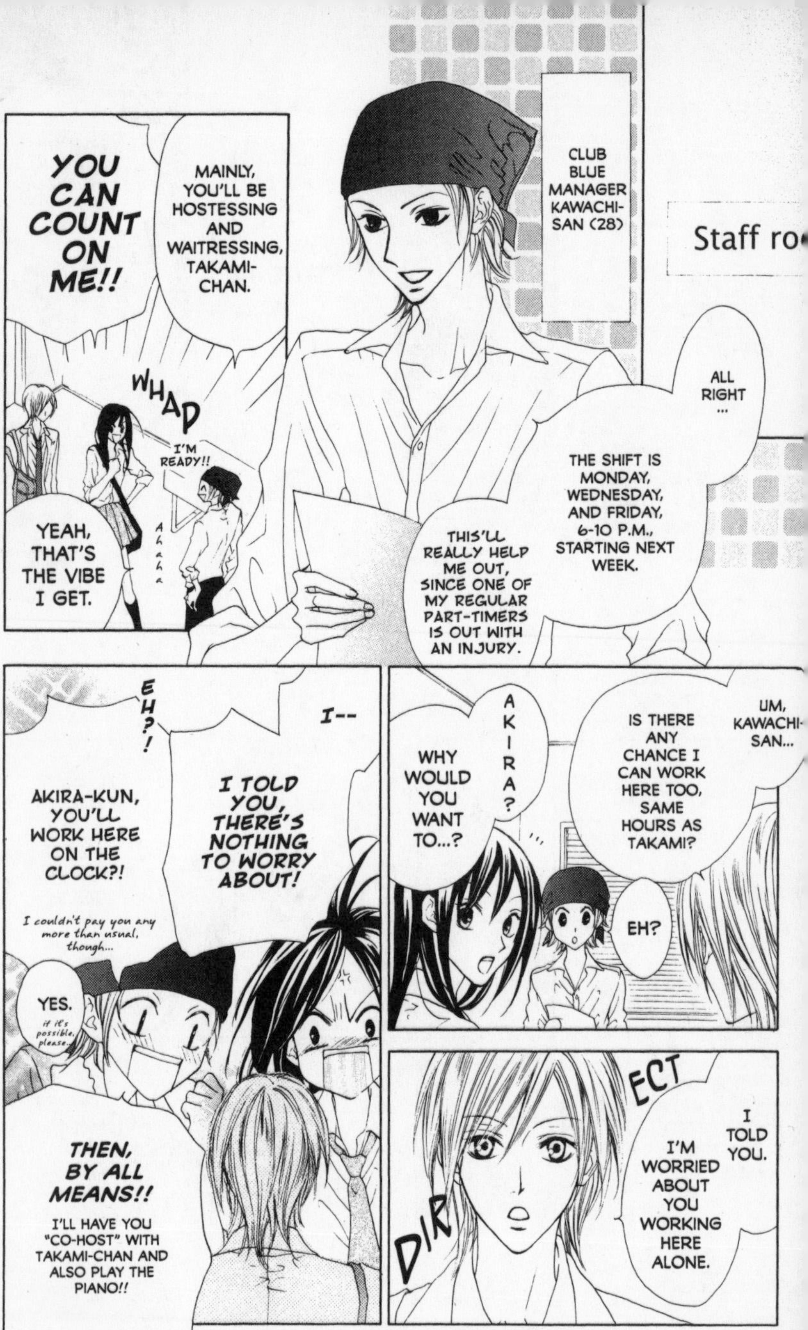
CLUB BLUE MANAGER KAWACHI-SAN (28)
Staff ro
ALL RIGHT ...
THE SHIFT IS MONDAY, WEDNESDAY, AND FRIDAY, 6-10 P.M., STARTING NEXT WEEK.
THIS'LL REALLY HELP ME OUT, SINCE ONE OF MY REGULAR PART-TIMERS IS OUT WITH AN INJURY.
MAINLY, YOU'LL BE HOSTESSING AND WAITRESSING, TAKAMI-CHAN.
YOU CAN COUNT ON ME!!
WHAP
I'M READY!!
Ahaha
YEAH, THAT'S THE VIBE I GET.
UM, KAWACHI-SAN...
IS THERE ANY CHANCE I CAN WORK HERE TOO, SAME HOURS AS TAKAMI?
EH?
AKIRA?
WHY WOULD YOU WANT TO...?
I TOLD YOU.
I'M WORRIED ABOUT YOU WORKING HERE ALONE.
DIRECT
I--
I TOLD YOU, THERE'S NOTHING TO WORRY ABOUT!
EH?!
AKIRA-KUN, YOU'LL WORK HERE ON THE CLOCK?!
I couldn't pay you any more than usual, though...
YES.
if it's possible, please.
THEN, BY ALL MEANS!!
I'LL HAVE YOU "CO-HOST" WITH TAKAMI-CHAN AND ALSO PLAY THE PIANO!!

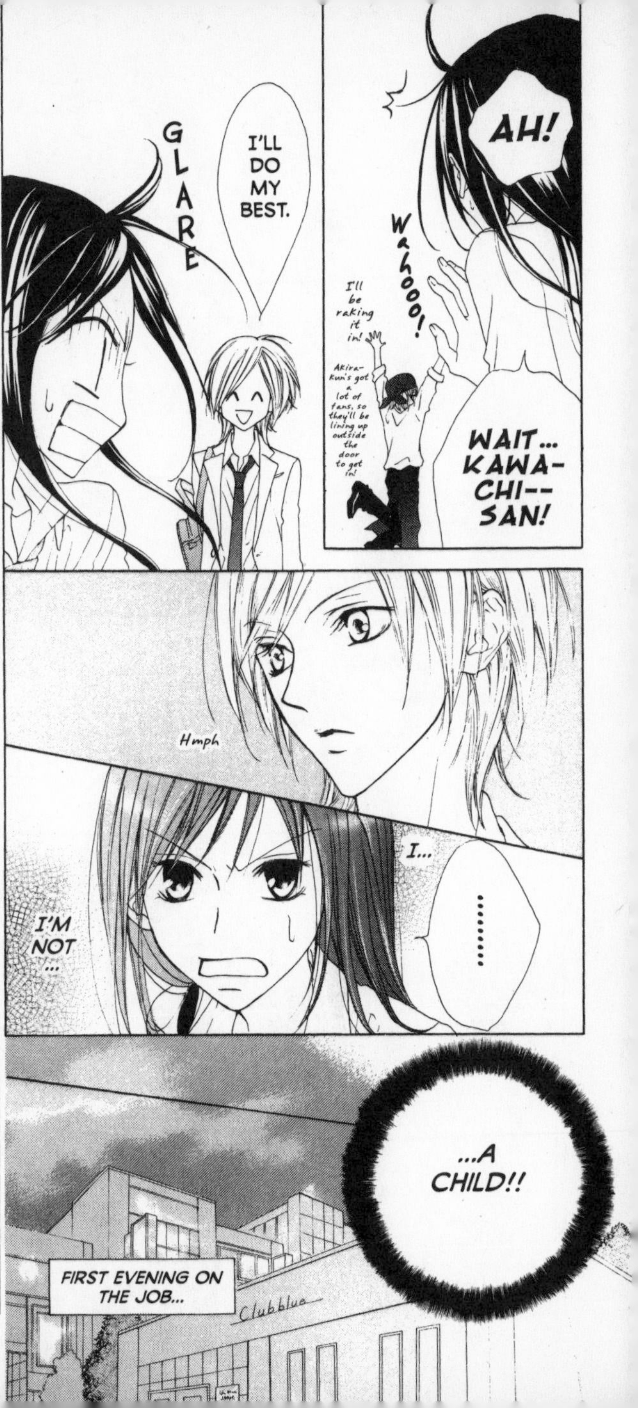

AH!
Wahooo!
I'll be raking it in!
Akira-kun's got a lot of fans, so they'll be lining up outside the door to get in!
WAIT... KAWA-CHI--SAN!
I'LL DO MY BEST.
GLARE
Hmph
I...
....
I'M NOT ...
...A CHILD!!
FIRST EVENING ON THE JOB...
Clubblue

1

HELLO, NISHIKATA HERE!
THANK YOU FOR GETTING VOLUME 2 OF "VENUS CAPRICCIO"!

COMPARED TO THE PREVIOUS VOLUME, THE EPISODES IN THIS ONE HAVE KIND OF A CALMER FEEL TO THEM.

DO I WANNA SAY CALM OR MELLOW? ANYWAY, TAKAMI SEEMS TO FLY OFF THE HANDLE MUCH LESS IN THIS ONE. (LOL).

I'M DRINKING HOT WATER AS I WRITE THIS.

HOT WATER'S TASTY.

WELL, I HOPE YOU ENJOY VOLUME 2 OF VENUS. (IF YOU DO, I'LL BE REALLY HAPPY)!

WILD HAIR

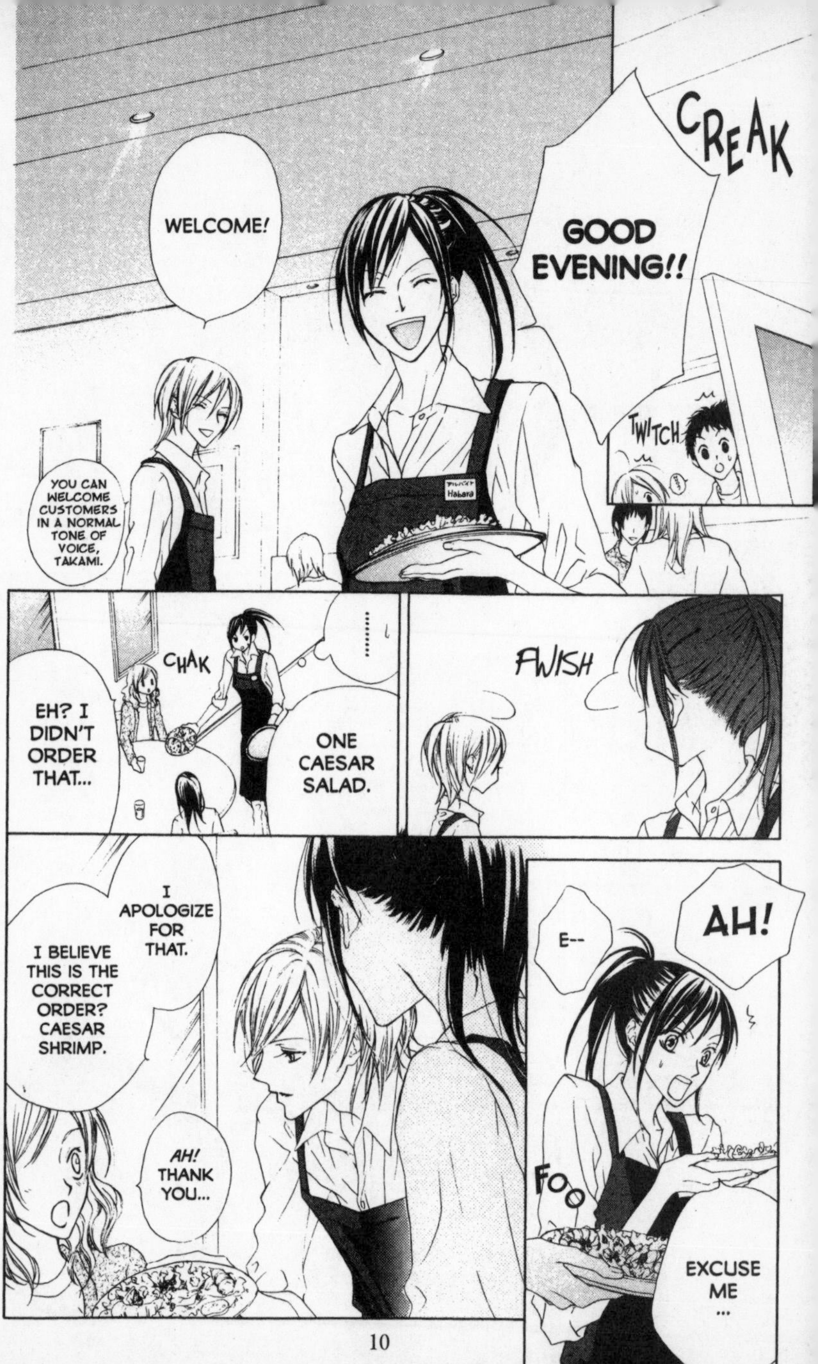
CREAK
GOOD EVENING!!
TWITCH
WELCOME!
YOU CAN WELCOME CUSTOMERS IN A NORMAL TONE OF VOICE, TAKAMI.
FWISH
......
CHAK
ONE CAESAR SALAD.
EH? I DIDN'T ORDER THAT...
AH!
E--
FOO
EXCUSE ME ...
I APOLOGIZE FOR THAT.
I BELIEVE THIS IS THE CORRECT ORDER? CAESAR SHRIMP.
AH! THANK YOU...

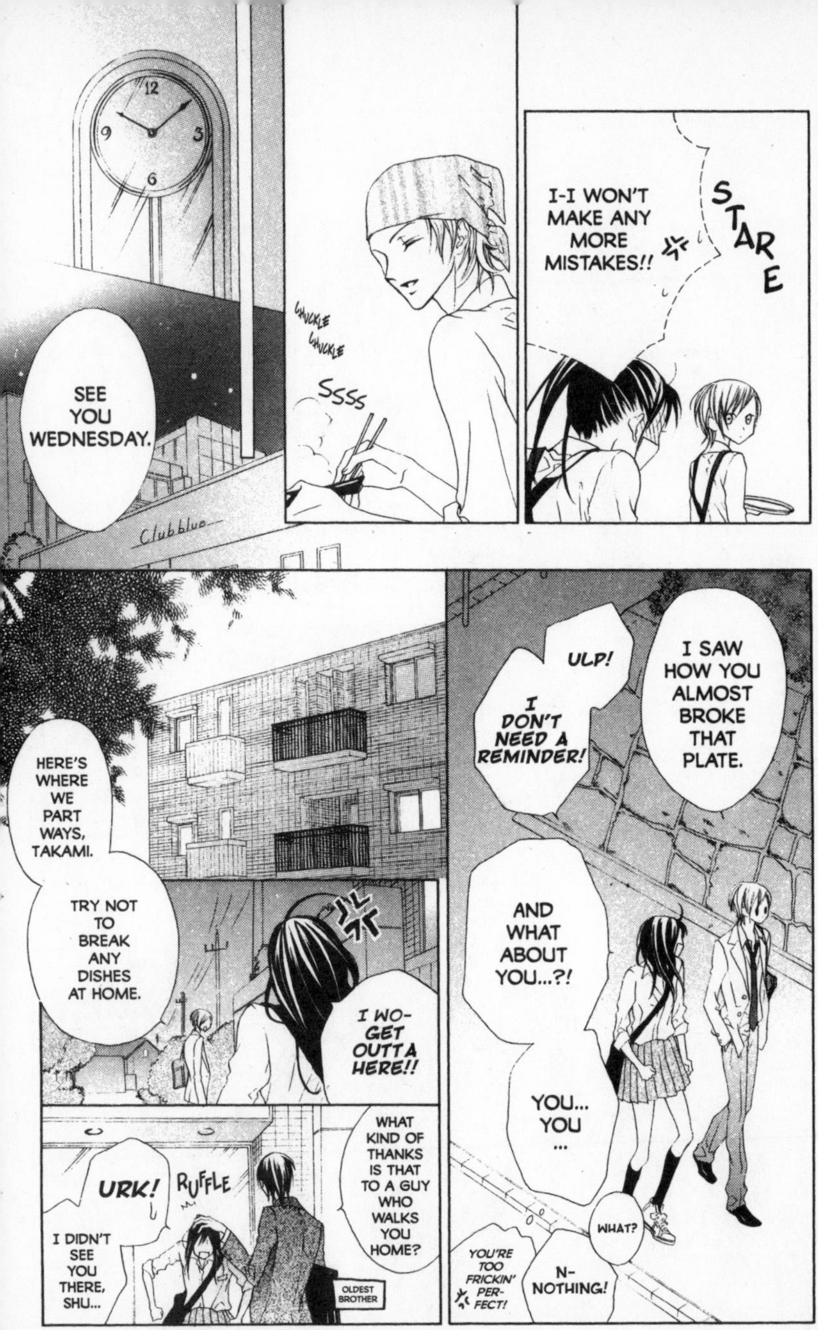
STARE
I-I WON'T MAKE ANY MORE MISTAKES!!
CHUCKLE CHUCKLE
SSSS
SEE YOU WEDNESDAY.
Clubblue
I SAW HOW YOU ALMOST BROKE THAT PLATE.
ULP!
I DON'T NEED A REMINDER!
AND WHAT ABOUT YOU...?!
YOU... YOU ...
WHAT?
N-NOTHING!
YOU'RE TOO FRICKIN' PER-FECT!
HERE'S WHERE WE PART WAYS, TAKAMI.
TRY NOT TO BREAK ANY DISHES AT HOME.
I WO- GET OUTTA HERE!!
WHAT KIND OF THANKS IS THAT TO A GUY WHO WALKS YOU HOME?
RUFFLE
URK!
I DIDN'T SEE YOU THERE, SHU...
OLDEST BROTHER

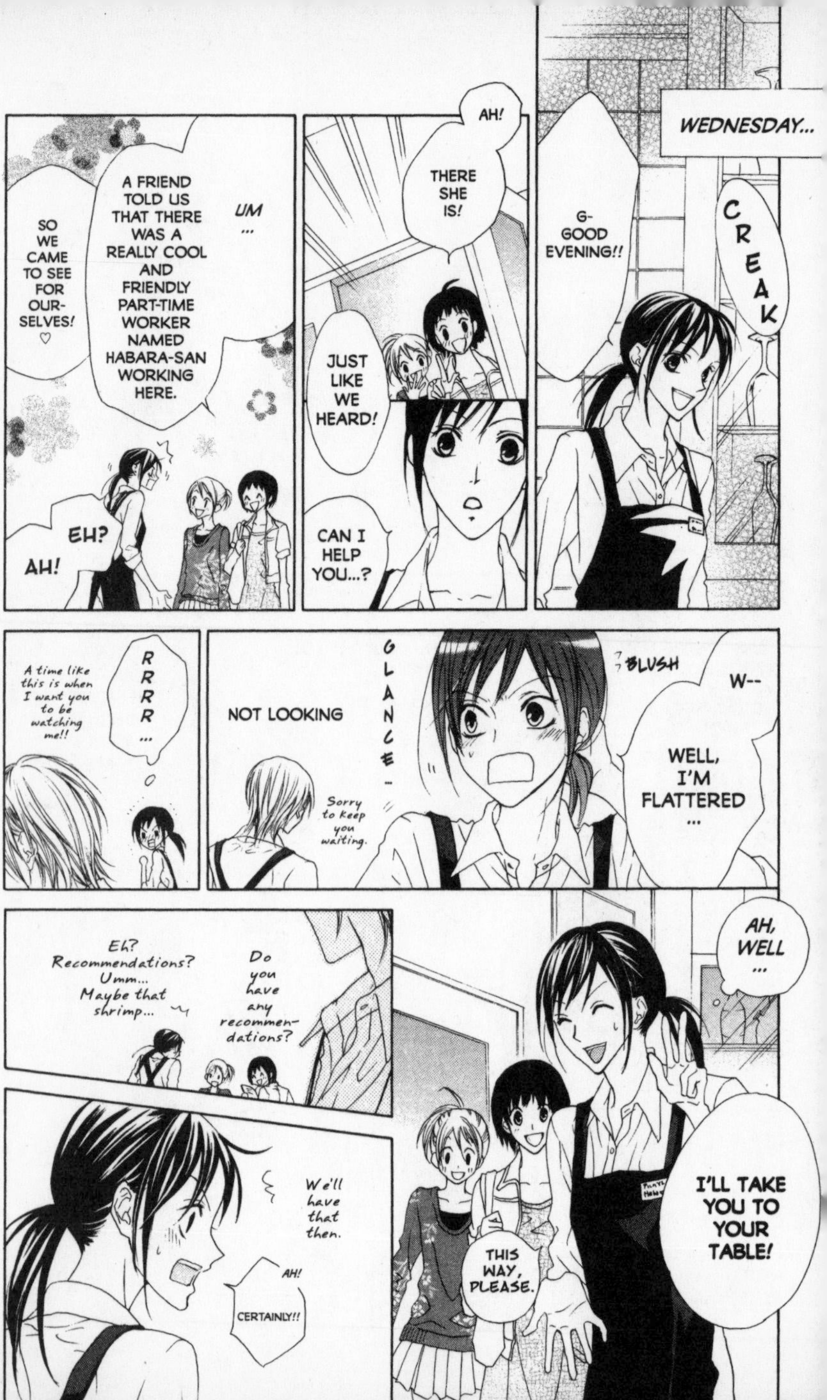
WEDNESDAY...
CREAK
G- GOOD EVENING!!
AH!
THERE SHE IS!
JUST LIKE WE HEARD!
CAN I HELP YOU...?
UM ...
A FRIEND TOLD US THAT THERE WAS A REALLY COOL AND FRIENDLY PART-TIME WORKER NAMED HABARA-SAN WORKING HERE.
SO WE CAME TO SEE FOR OUR-SELVES! ♡
EH?
AH!
W--
WELL, I'M FLATTERED ...
BLUSH
GLANCE ...
NOT LOOKING
Sorry to keep you waiting.
RRRR ...
A time like this is when I want you to be watching me!!
AH, WELL ...
I'LL TAKE YOU TO YOUR TABLE!
THIS WAY, PLEASE.
Do you have any recommen-dations?
Eh? Recommendations? Umm... Maybe that shrimp...
We'll have that then.
AH!
CERTAINLY!!

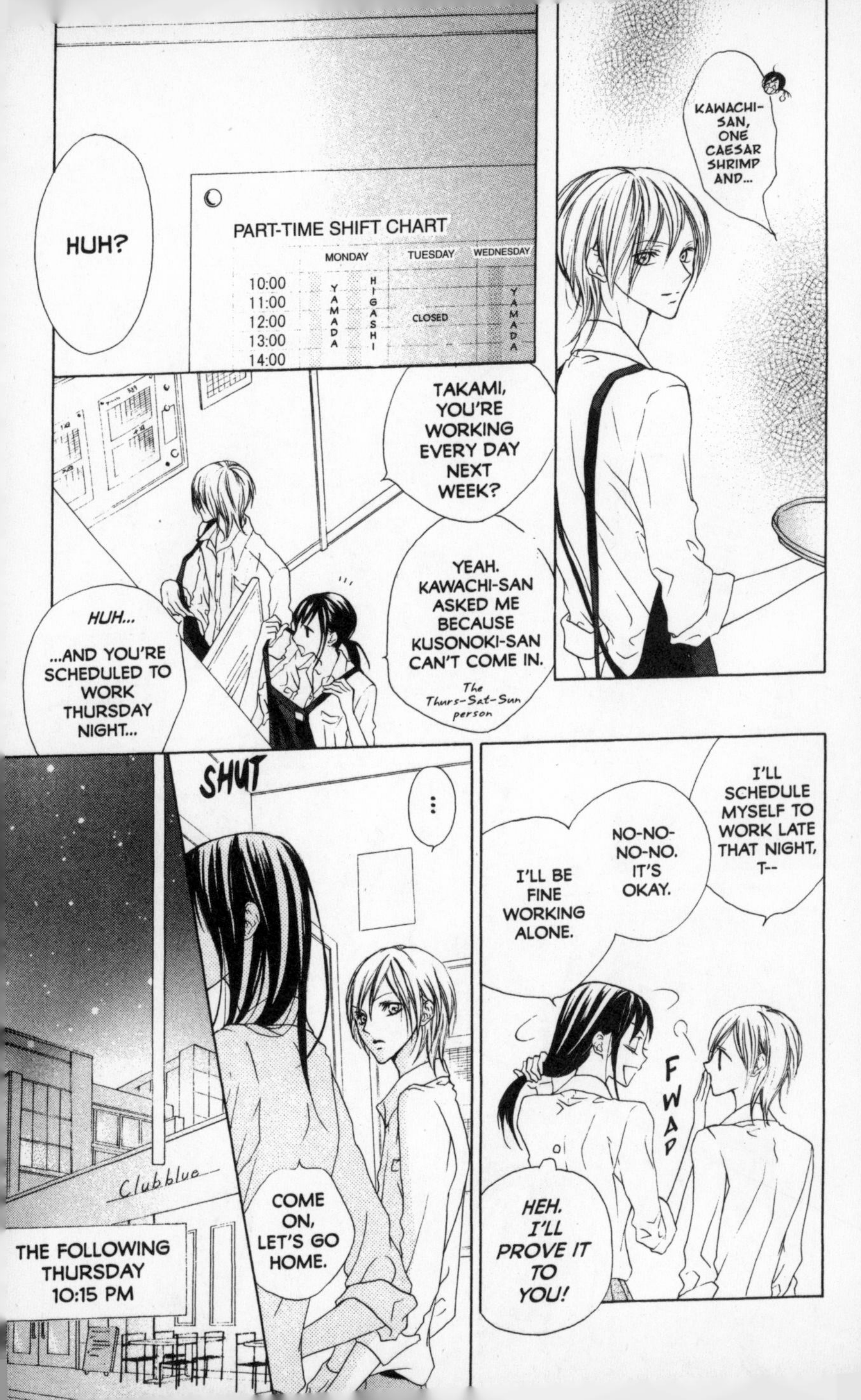
KAWACHI-SAN, ONE CAESAR SHRIMP AND...
PART-TIME SHIFT CHART
MONDAY TUESDAY WEDNESDAY
10:00 11:00 12:00 13:00 14:00
YAMADA HIGASHI CLOSED YAMADA
HUH?
TAKAMI, YOU'RE WORKING EVERY DAY NEXT WEEK?
YEAH. KAWACHI-SAN ASKED ME BECAUSE KUSONOKI-SAN CAN'T COME IN.
The Thurs-Sat-Sun person
HUH...
...AND YOU'RE SCHEDULED TO WORK THURSDAY NIGHT...
I'LL SCHEDULE MYSELF TO WORK LATE THAT NIGHT, T--
NO-NO-NO-NO. IT'S OKAY.
I'LL BE FINE WORKING ALONE.
FWAP
HEH. I'LL PROVE IT TO YOU!
SHUT
...
COME ON, LET'S GO HOME.
Clubblue
THE FOLLOWING THURSDAY 10:15 PM

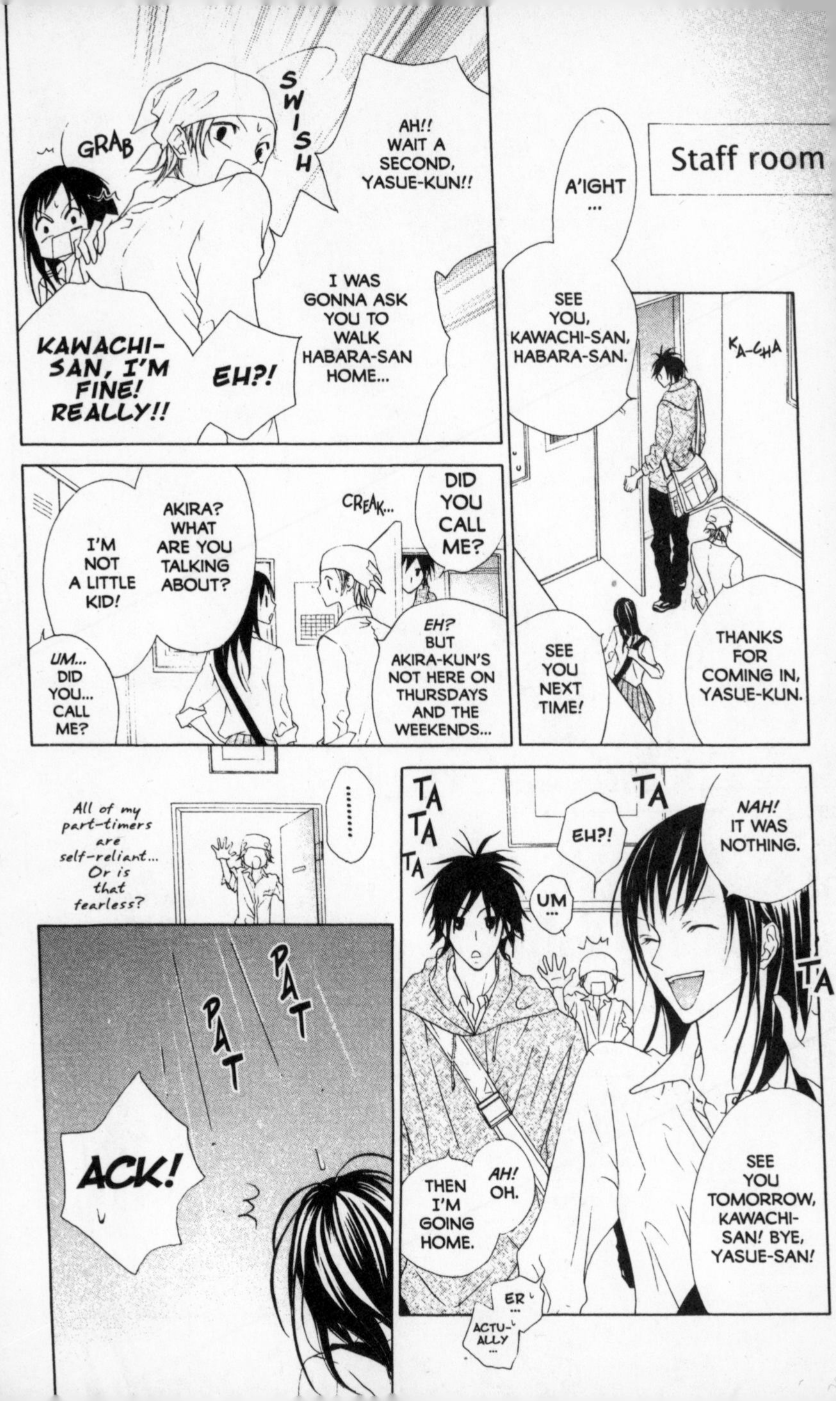
Staff room
A'IGHT...
SEE YOU, KAWACHI-SAN, HABARA-SAN.
KA-CHA
THANKS FOR COMING IN, YASUE-KUN.
SEE YOU NEXT TIME!
SWISH
AH!! WAIT A SECOND, YASUE-KUN!!
I WAS GONNA ASK YOU TO WALK HABARA-SAN HOME...
EH?!
GRAB
KAWACHI-SAN, I'M FINE! REALLY!!
DID YOU CALL ME?
CREAK...
EH? BUT AKIRA-KUN'S NOT HERE ON THURSDAYS AND THE WEEKENDS...
AKIRA? WHAT ARE YOU TALKING ABOUT?
I'M NOT A LITTLE KID!
UM... DID YOU... CALL ME?
NAH! IT WAS NOTHING.
TA
EH?!
TA TA TA TA
UM...
TA
SEE YOU TOMORROW, KAWACHI-SAN! BYE, YASUE-SAN!
AH! OH.
THEN I'M GOING HOME.
ER... ACTU-ALLY...
....
All of my part-timers are self-reliant... Or is that fearless?
PAT
PAT
ACK!

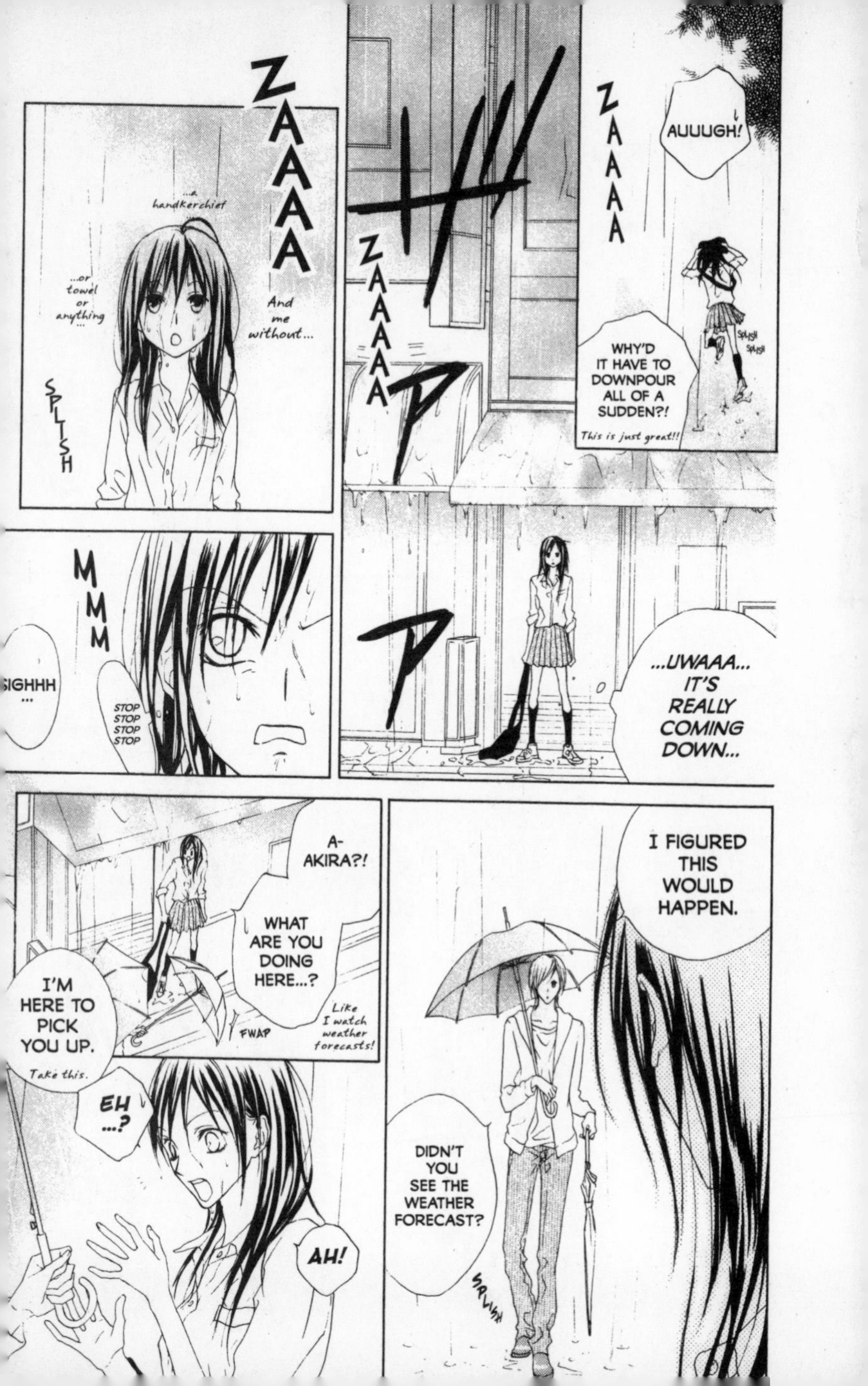

ZAAAA
AUUUGH!
WHY'D IT HAVE TO DOWNPOUR ALL OF A SUDDEN?!
This is just great!!
SPLISH SPLISH
ZAAAA
ZAAAAAA
P
P
...UWAAA... IT'S REALLY COMING DOWN...
ZAAAAA
And me without...
...a handkerchief
...or towel or anything...
SPLISH
MMM
STOP STOP STOP STOP
SIGHHH...
I FIGURED THIS WOULD HAPPEN.
DIDN'T YOU SEE THE WEATHER FORECAST?
SPLISH
A-AKIRA?!
WHAT ARE YOU DOING HERE...?
Like I watch weather forecasts!
FWAP
I'M HERE TO PICK YOU UP.
Take this.
EH...?
AH!

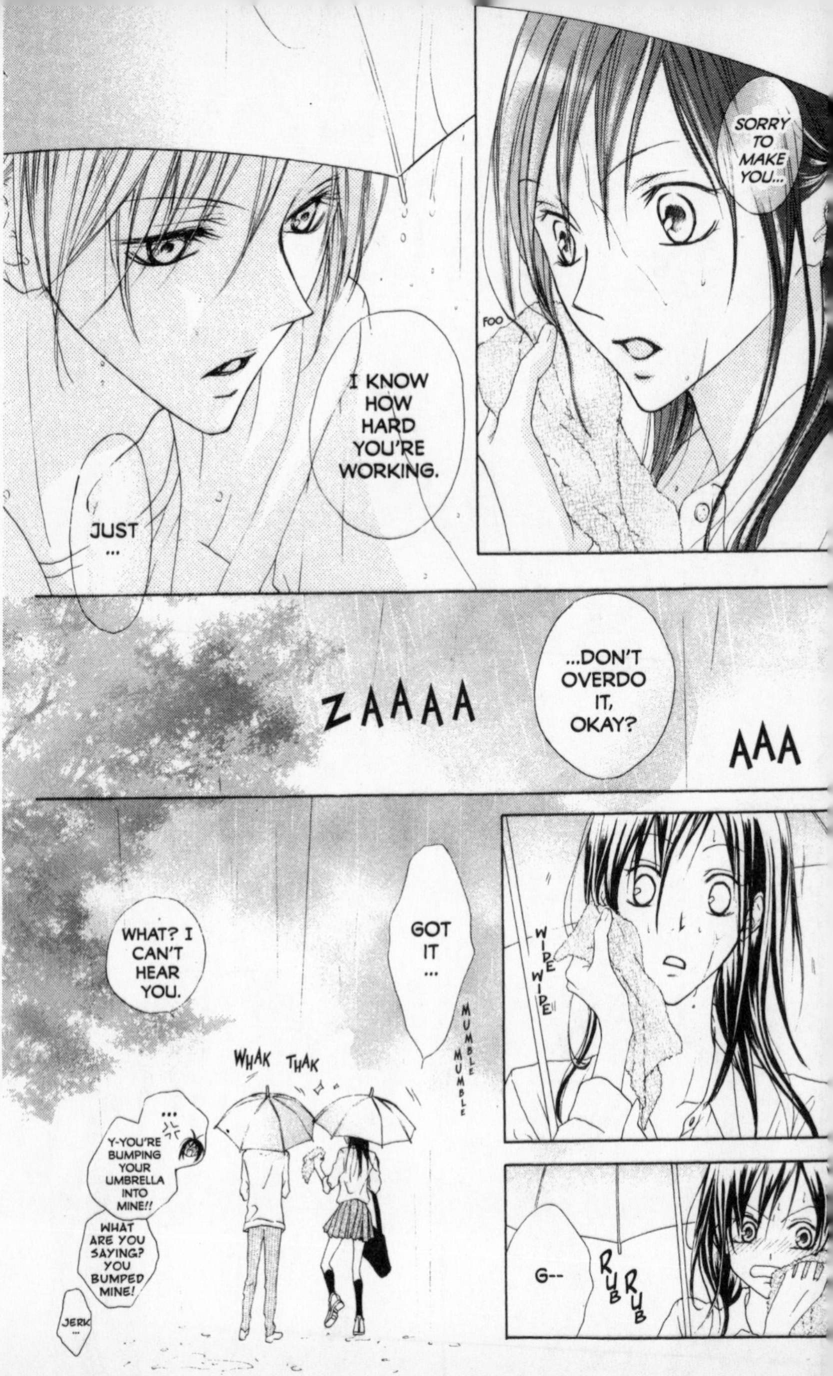
SORRY TO MAKE YOU...
FOO
I KNOW HOW HARD YOU'RE WORKING.
JUST ...
...DON'T OVERDO IT, OKAY?
ZAAAA
AAA
WIDE WIDE
G--
RUB RUB
GOT IT ...
MUMBLE MUMBLE
WHAT? I CAN'T HEAR YOU.
WHAK THAK
...
Y-YOU'RE BUMPING YOUR UMBRELLA INTO MINE!!
WHAT ARE YOU SAYING? YOU BUMPED MINE!
JERK ...

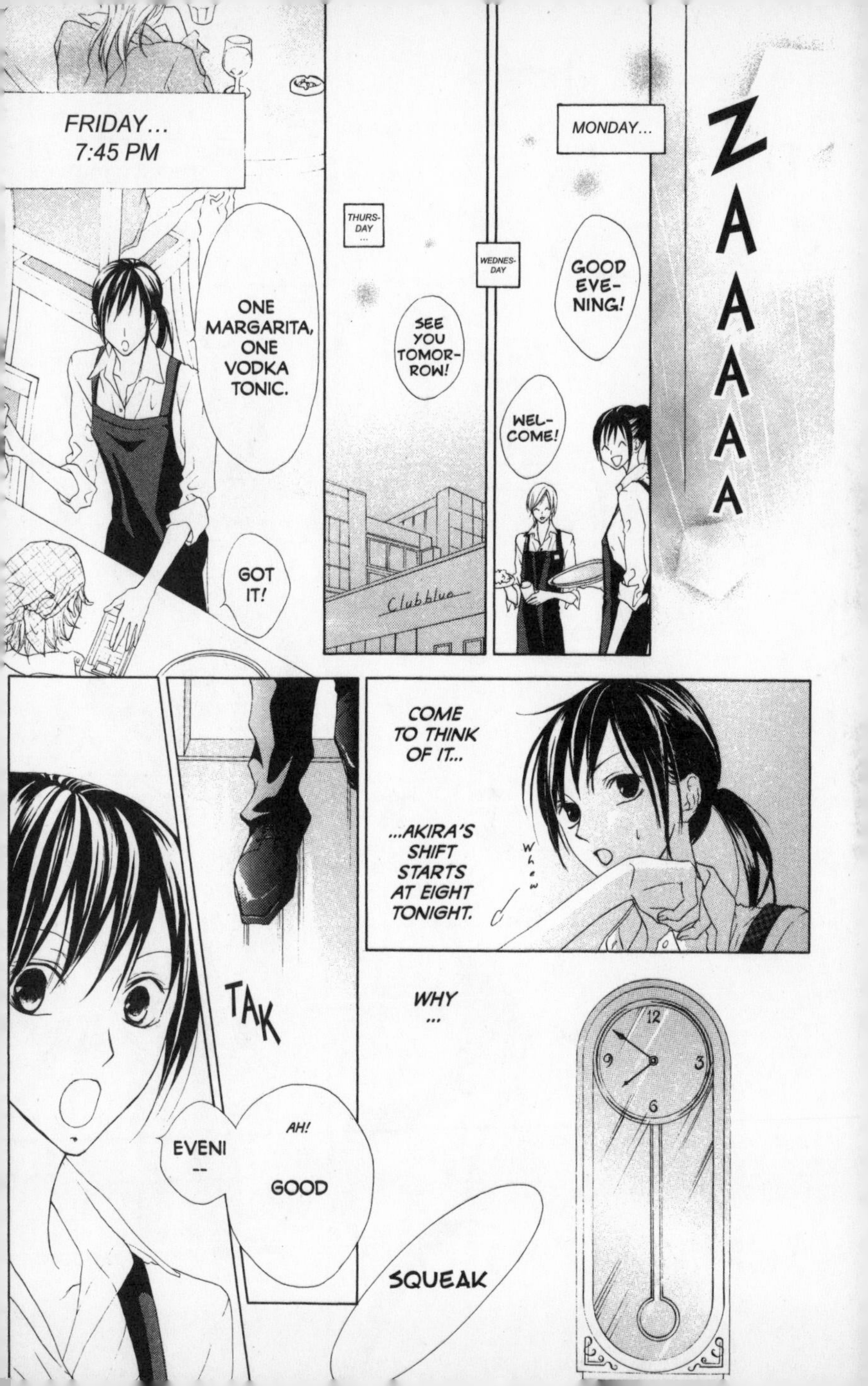
ZAAAAA
MONDAY...
GOOD EVE-NING!
WEL-COME!
WEDNES-DAY
THURS-DAY ...
SEE YOU TOMOR-ROW!
Clubblue
FRIDAY... 7:45 PM
ONE MARGARITA, ONE VODKA TONIC.
GOT IT!
COME TO THINK OF IT...
...AKIRA'S SHIFT STARTS AT EIGHT TONIGHT.
Whew
WHY ...
TAK
SQUEAK
AH!
GOOD
EVENI --

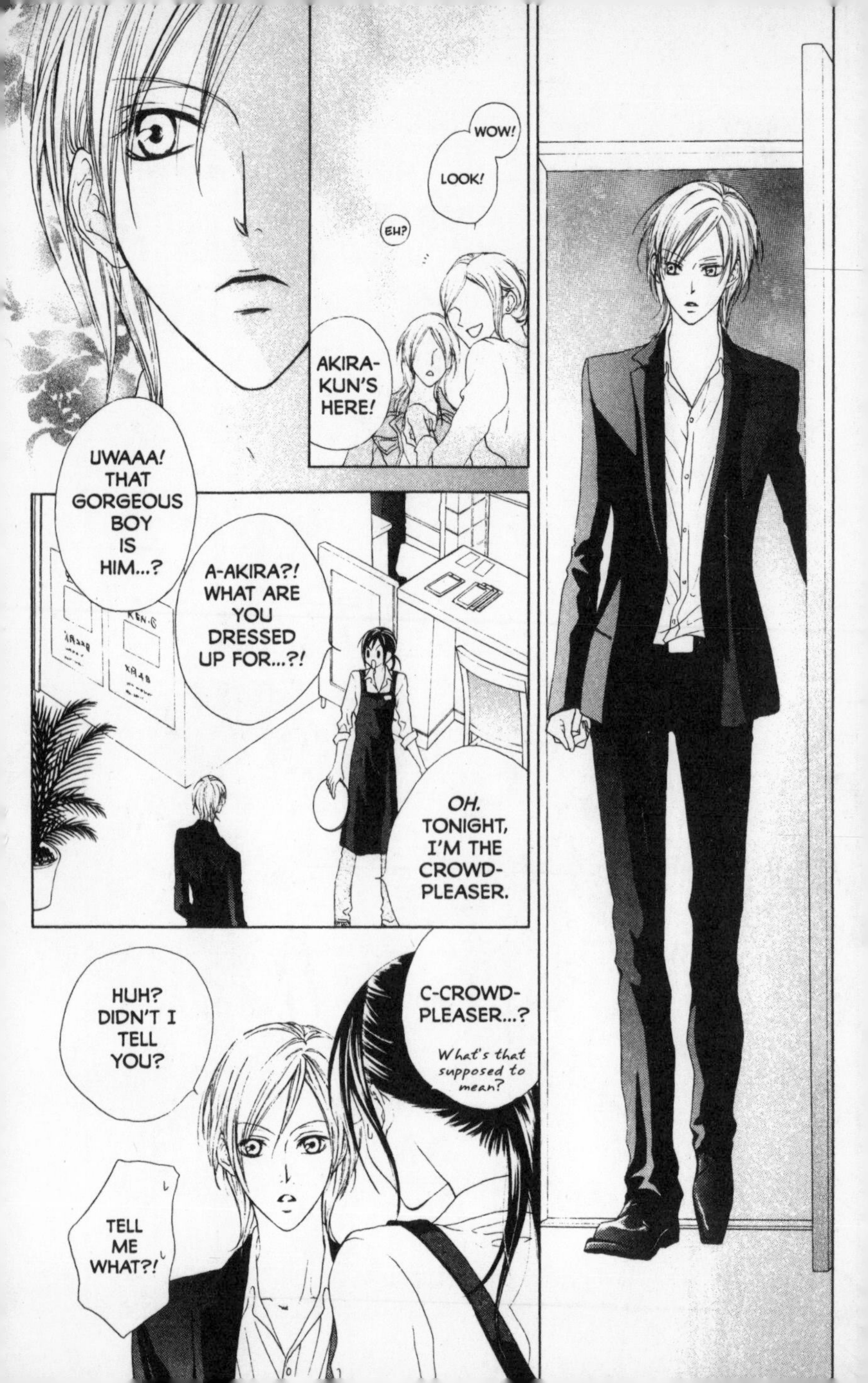
WOW!
LOOK!
EH?
AKIRA-KUN'S HERE!
UWAAA! THAT GORGEOUS BOY IS HIM...?
A-AKIRA?! WHAT ARE YOU DRESSED UP FOR...?!
OH. TONIGHT, I'M THE CROWD-PLEASER.
C-CROWD-PLEASER...?
What's that supposed to mean?
HUH? DIDN'T I TELL YOU?
TELL ME WHAT?!

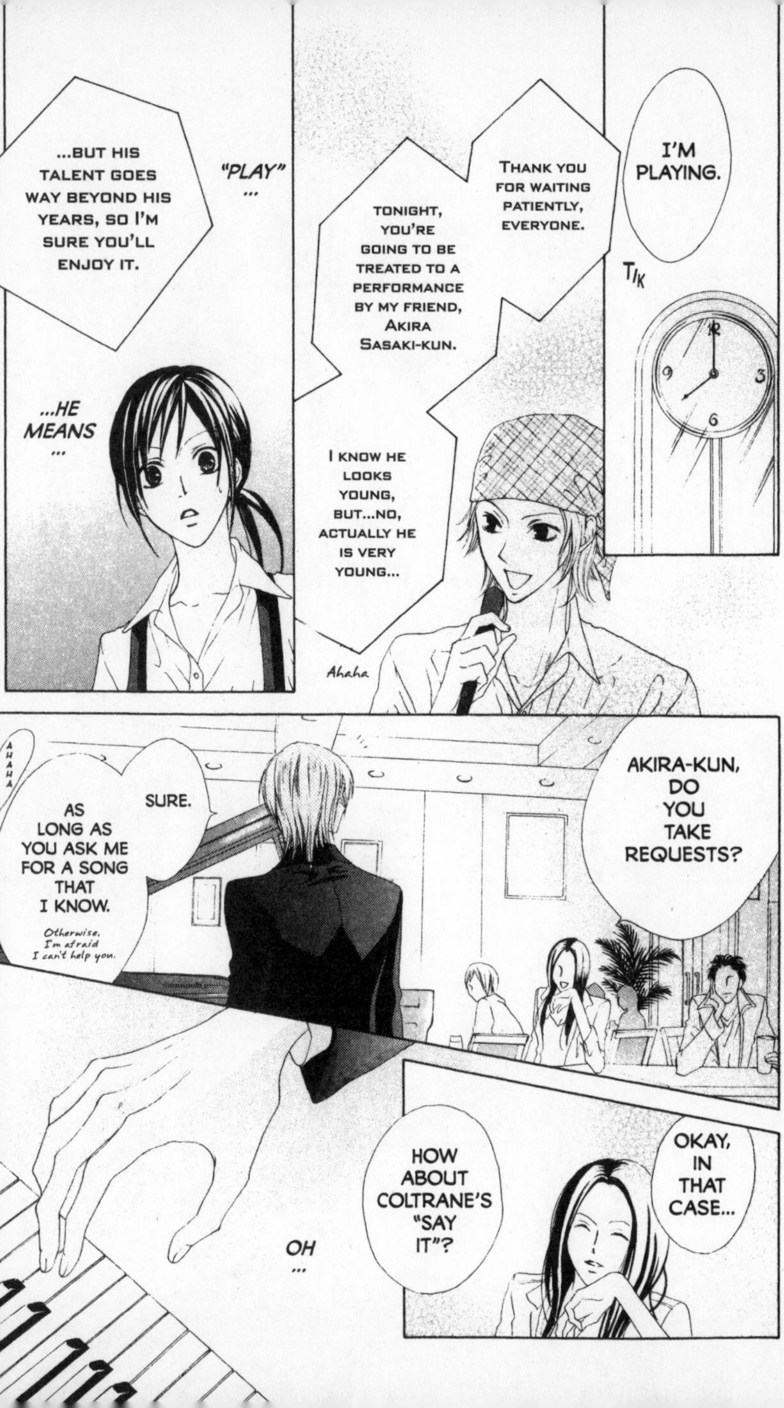
I'M PLAYING.
TIK
THANK YOU FOR WAITING PATIENTLY, EVERYONE.
TONIGHT, YOU'RE GOING TO BE TREATED TO A PERFORMANCE BY MY FRIEND, AKIRA SASAKI-KUN.
I KNOW HE LOOKS YOUNG, BUT...NO, ACTUALLY HE IS VERY YOUNG...
Ahaha
...BUT HIS TALENT GOES WAY BEYOND HIS YEARS, SO I'M SURE YOU'LL ENJOY IT.
"PLAY" ...
...HE MEANS ...
AKIRA-KUN, DO YOU TAKE REQUESTS?
AHAHA
SURE.
AS LONG AS YOU ASK ME FOR A SONG THAT I KNOW.
Otherwise, I'm afraid I can't help you.
OKAY, IN THAT CASE...
HOW ABOUT COLTRANE'S "SAY IT"?
OH ...

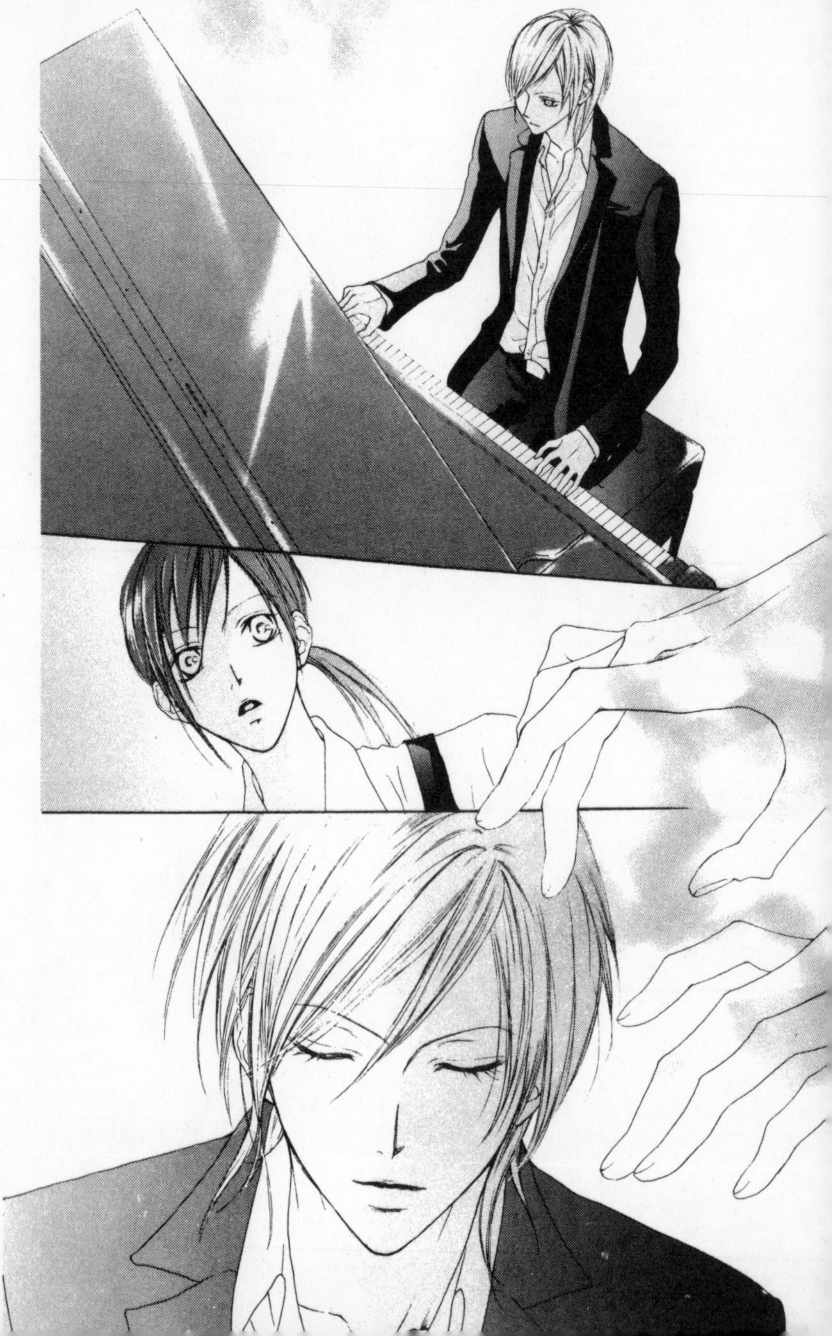

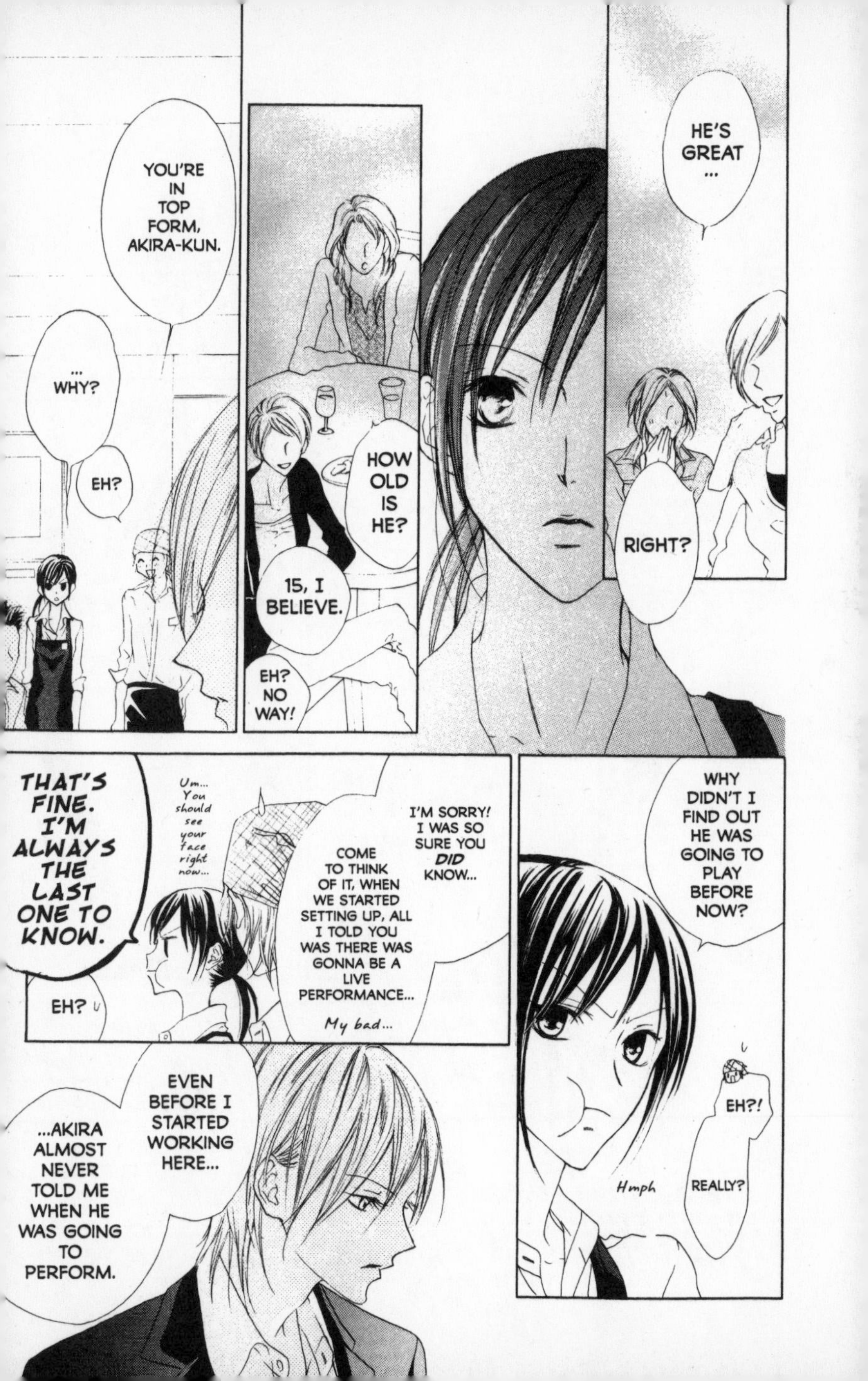
HE'S GREAT ...
RIGHT?
HOW OLD IS HE?
15, I BELIEVE.
EH? NO WAY!
YOU'RE IN TOP FORM, AKIRA-KUN.
... WHY?
EH?
WHY DIDN'T I FIND OUT HE WAS GOING TO PLAY BEFORE NOW?
EH?!
REALLY?
Hmph
I'M SORRY! I WAS SO SURE YOU *DID* KNOW...
COME TO THINK OF IT, WHEN WE STARTED SETTING UP, ALL I TOLD YOU WAS THERE WAS GONNA BE A LIVE PERFORMANCE...
My bad...
Um... You should see your face right now...
THAT'S FINE. I'M ALWAYS THE LAST ONE TO KNOW.
EH?
EVEN BEFORE I STARTED WORKING HERE...
...AKIRA ALMOST NEVER TOLD ME WHEN HE WAS GOING TO PERFORM.

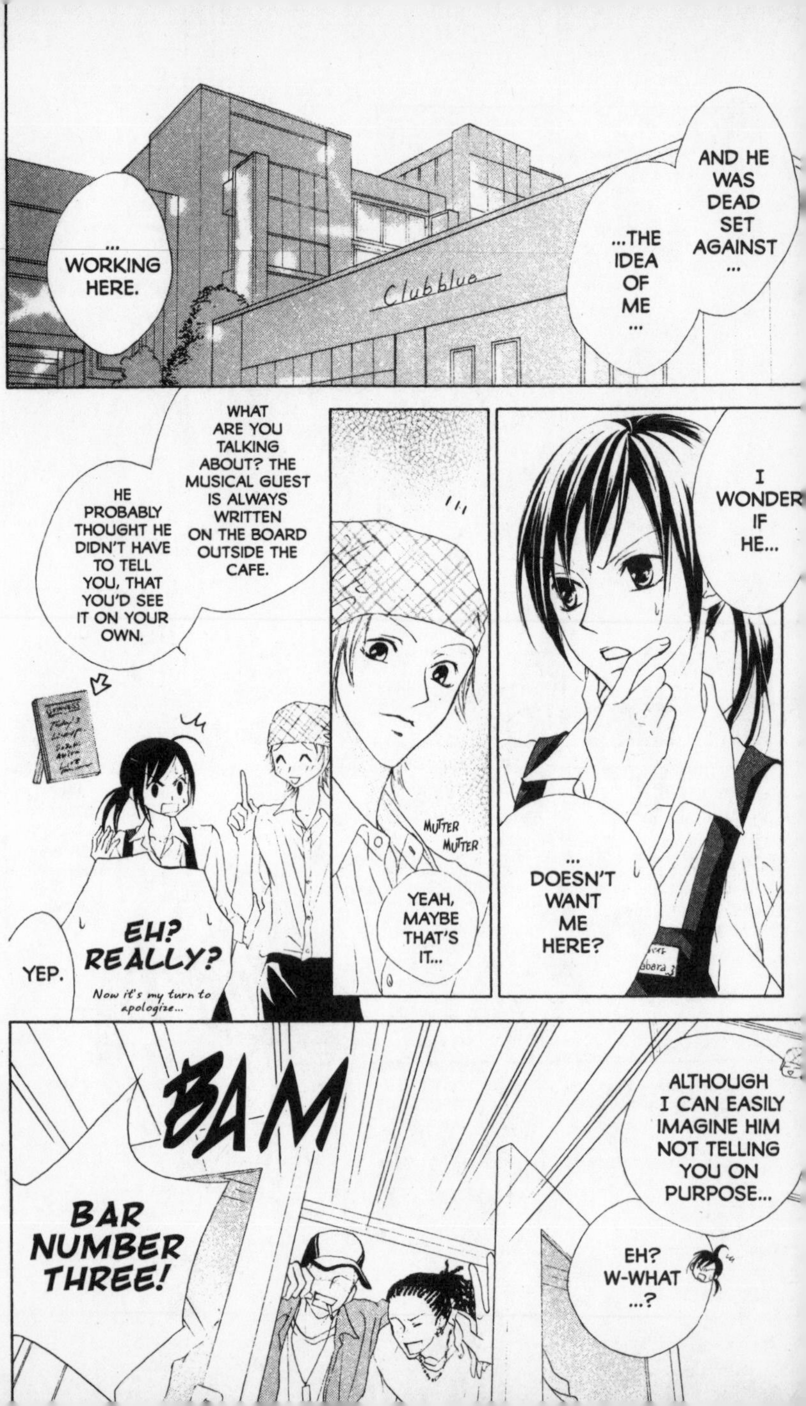
AND HE WAS DEAD SET AGAINST ...
...THE IDEA OF ME ...
Clubblue
... WORKING HERE.
I WONDER IF HE...
... DOESN'T WANT ME HERE?
MUTTER MUTTER
YEAH, MAYBE THAT'S IT...
WHAT ARE YOU TALKING ABOUT? THE MUSICAL GUEST IS ALWAYS WRITTEN ON THE BOARD OUTSIDE THE CAFE.
HE PROBABLY THOUGHT HE DIDN'T HAVE TO TELL YOU, THAT YOU'D SEE IT ON YOUR OWN.
EH? REALLY?
YEP.
Now it's my turn to apologize...
ALTHOUGH I CAN EASILY IMAGINE HIM NOT TELLING YOU ON PURPOSE...
EH? W-WHAT ...?
BAM
BAR NUMBER THREE!

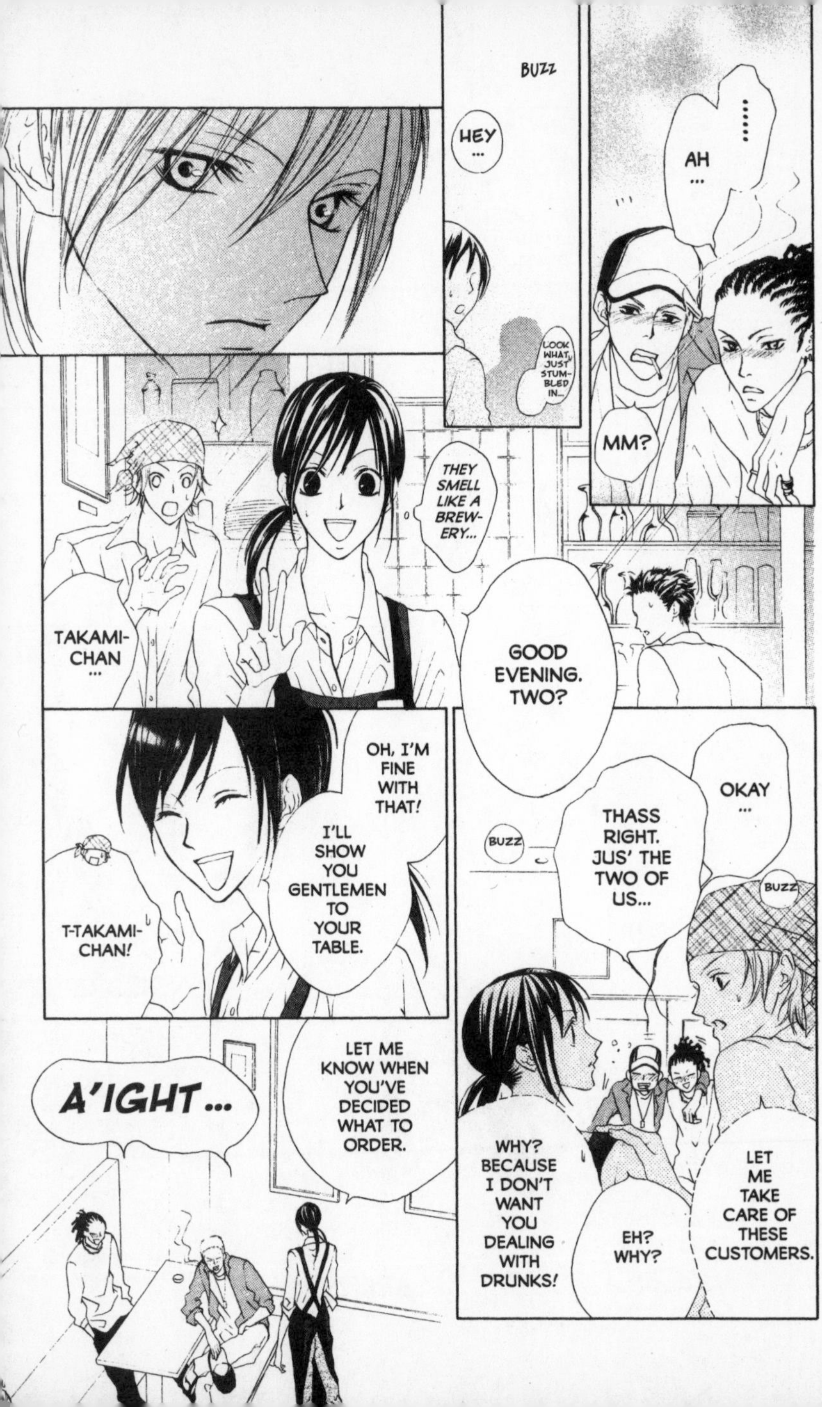
......
AH ...
MM?
BUZZ
HEY ...
LOOK WHAT JUST STUMBLED IN...
GOOD EVENING. TWO?
THEY SMELL LIKE A BREWERY...
TAKAMI-CHAN ...
OKAY ...
THASS RIGHT. JUS' THE TWO OF US...
BUZZ
BUZZ
LET ME TAKE CARE OF THESE CUSTOMERS.
EH? WHY?
WHY? BECAUSE I DON'T WANT YOU DEALING WITH DRUNKS!
OH, I'M FINE WITH THAT!
I'LL SHOW YOU GENTLEMEN TO YOUR TABLE.
T-TAKAMI-CHAN!
LET ME KNOW WHEN YOU'VE DECIDED WHAT TO ORDER.
A'IGHT ...

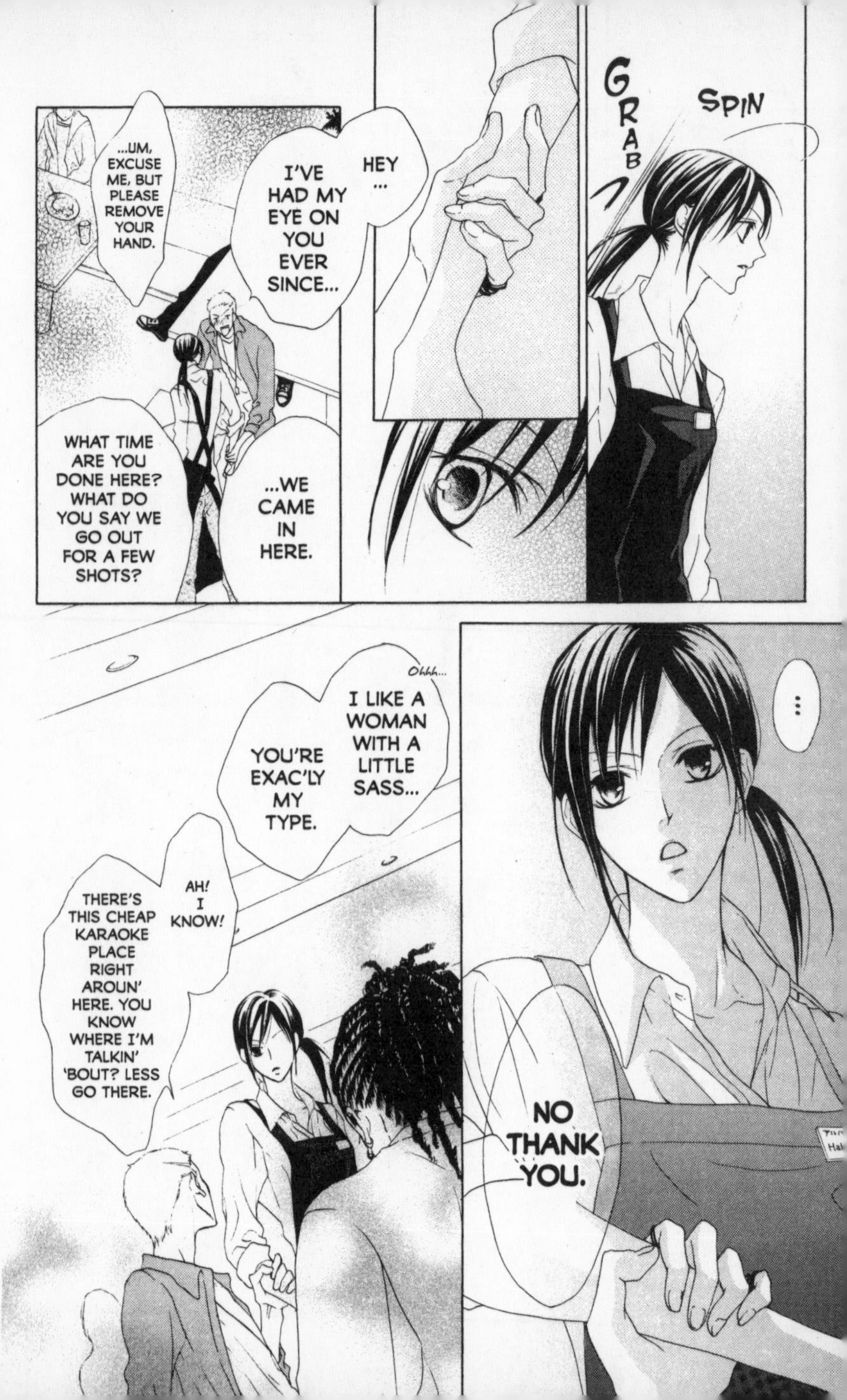
GRAB
SPIN
HEY ...
I'VE HAD MY EYE ON YOU EVER SINCE...
...UM, EXCUSE ME, BUT PLEASE REMOVE YOUR HAND.
...WE CAME IN HERE.
WHAT TIME ARE YOU DONE HERE? WHAT DO YOU SAY WE GO OUT FOR A FEW SHOTS?
...
NO THANK YOU.
Ohhh...
I LIKE A WOMAN WITH A LITTLE SASS...
YOU'RE EXAC'LY MY TYPE.
AH! I KNOW!
THERE'S THIS CHEAP KARAOKE PLACE RIGHT AROUN' HERE. YOU KNOW WHERE I'M TALKIN' 'BOUT? LESS GO THERE.

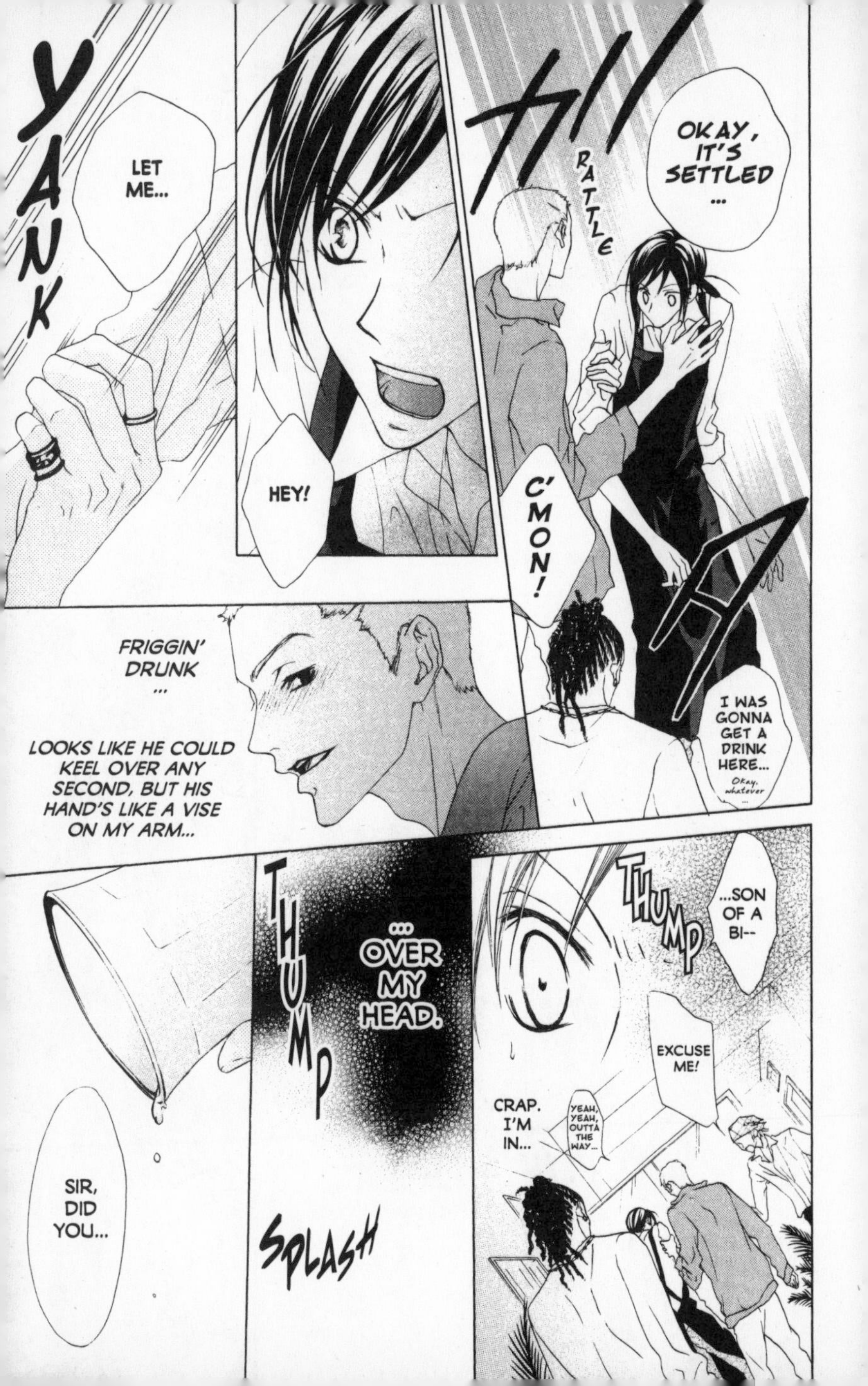
OKAY, IT'S SETTLED ...
RATTLE
C'MON!
I WAS GONNA GET A DRINK HERE...
Okay, whatever ...
HEY!
YANK
LET ME...
FRIGGIN' DRUNK ...
LOOKS LIKE HE COULD KEEL OVER ANY SECOND, BUT HIS HAND'S LIKE A VISE ON MY ARM...
THUMP
...SON OF A BI--
EXCUSE ME!
CRAP. I'M IN...
YEAH, YEAH, OUTTA THE WAY...
THUMP
... OVER MY HEAD.
SPLASH
SIR, DID YOU...

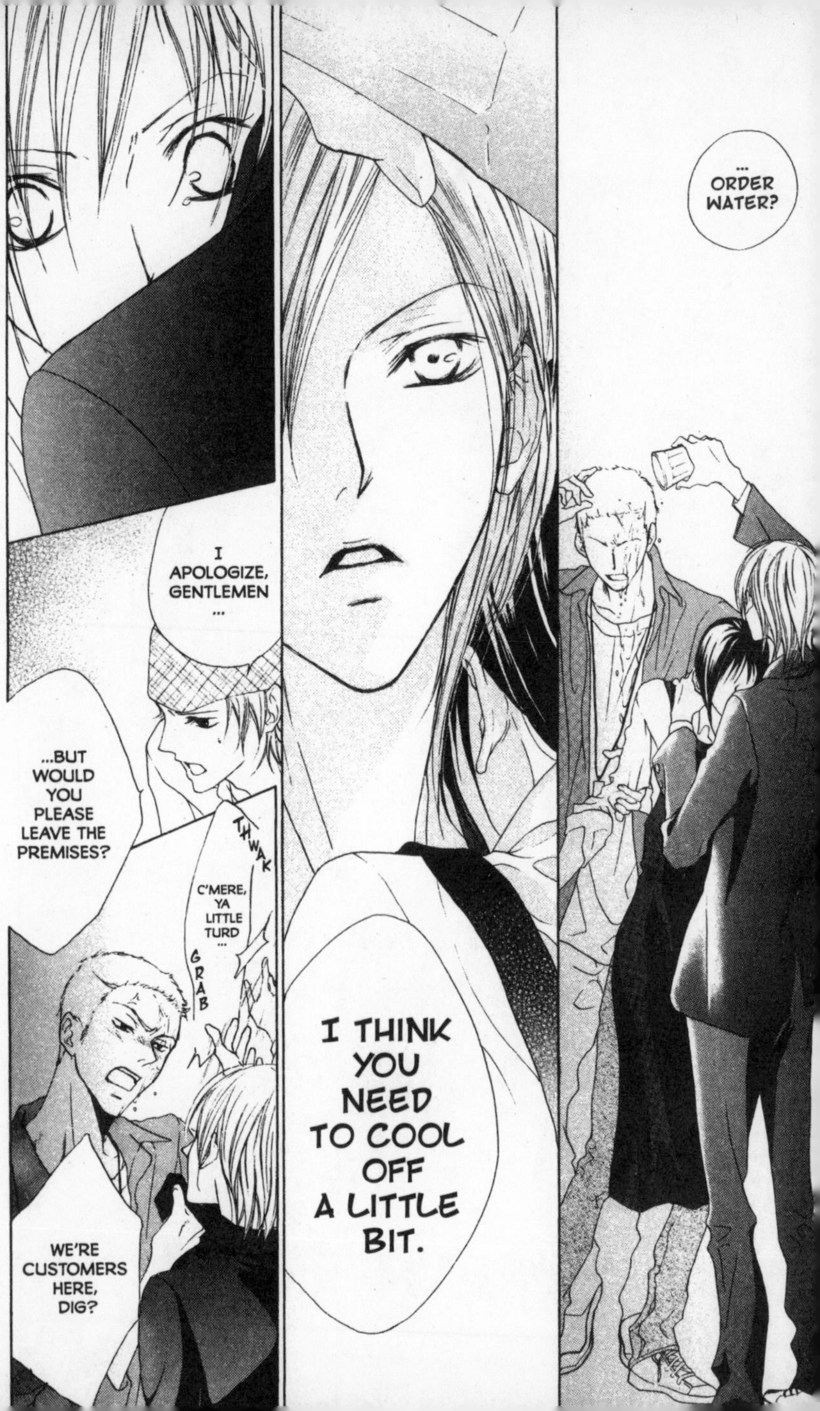
...ORDER WATER?
I THINK YOU NEED TO COOL OFF A LITTLE BIT.
I APOLOGIZE, GENTLEMEN...
...BUT WOULD YOU PLEASE LEAVE THE PREMISES?
THWAK
C'MERE, YA LITTLE TURD...
GRAB
WE'RE CUSTOMERS HERE, DIG?

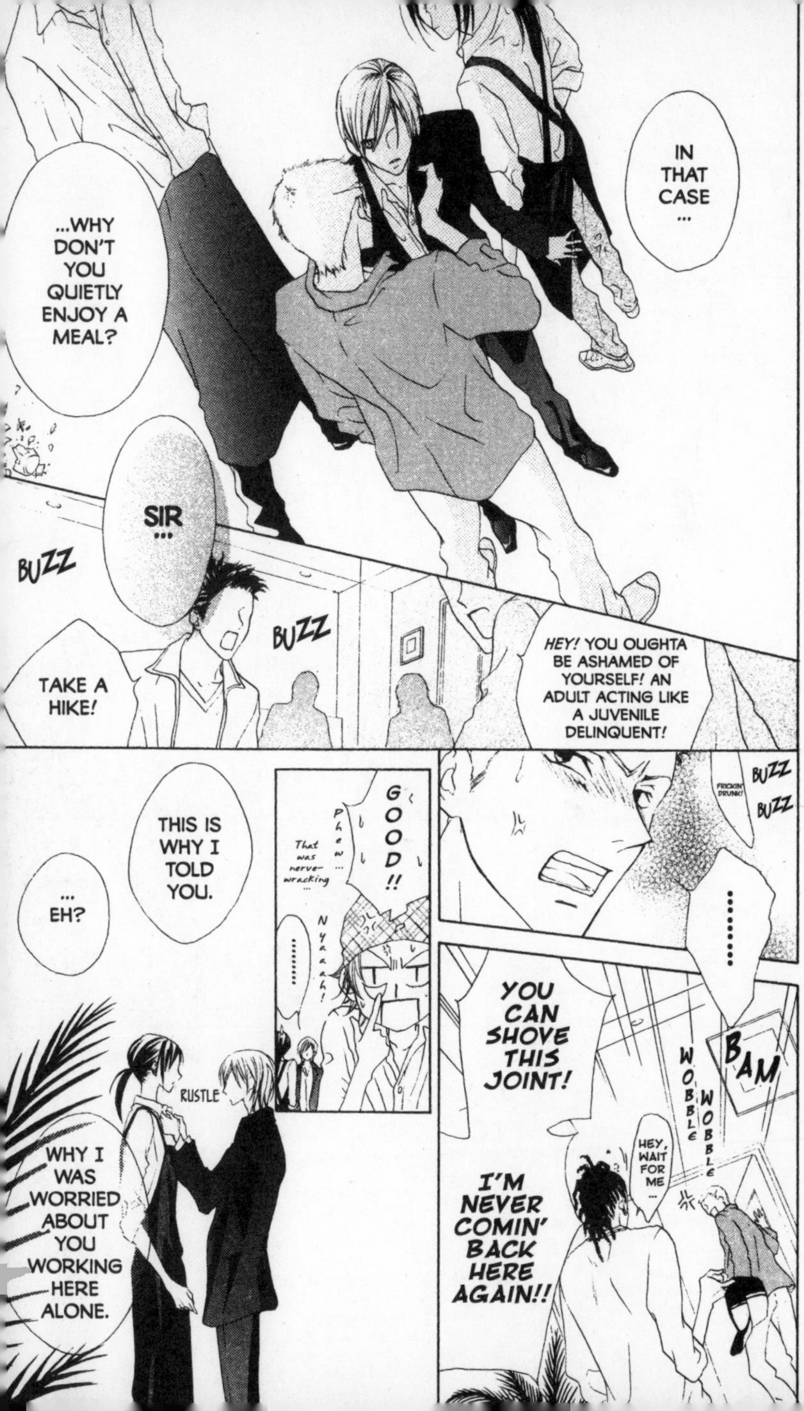
IN THAT CASE ...
...WHY DON'T YOU QUIETLY ENJOY A MEAL?
HEY! YOU OUGHTA BE ASHAMED OF YOURSELF! AN ADULT ACTING LIKE A JUVENILE DELINQUENT!
BUZZ
SIR ...
BUZZ
TAKE A HIKE!
BUZZ
BUZZ
FRICKIN' DRUNK!
....
YOU CAN SHOVE THIS JOINT!
BAM
WOBBLE
WOBBLE
HEY, WAIT FOR ME ...
I'M NEVER COMIN' BACK HERE AGAIN!!
GOOD!!
Phew ... That was nerve-wracking ...
Nyaaah!
....
THIS IS WHY I TOLD YOU.
... EH?
RUSTLE
WHY I WAS WORRIED ABOUT YOU WORKING HERE ALONE.

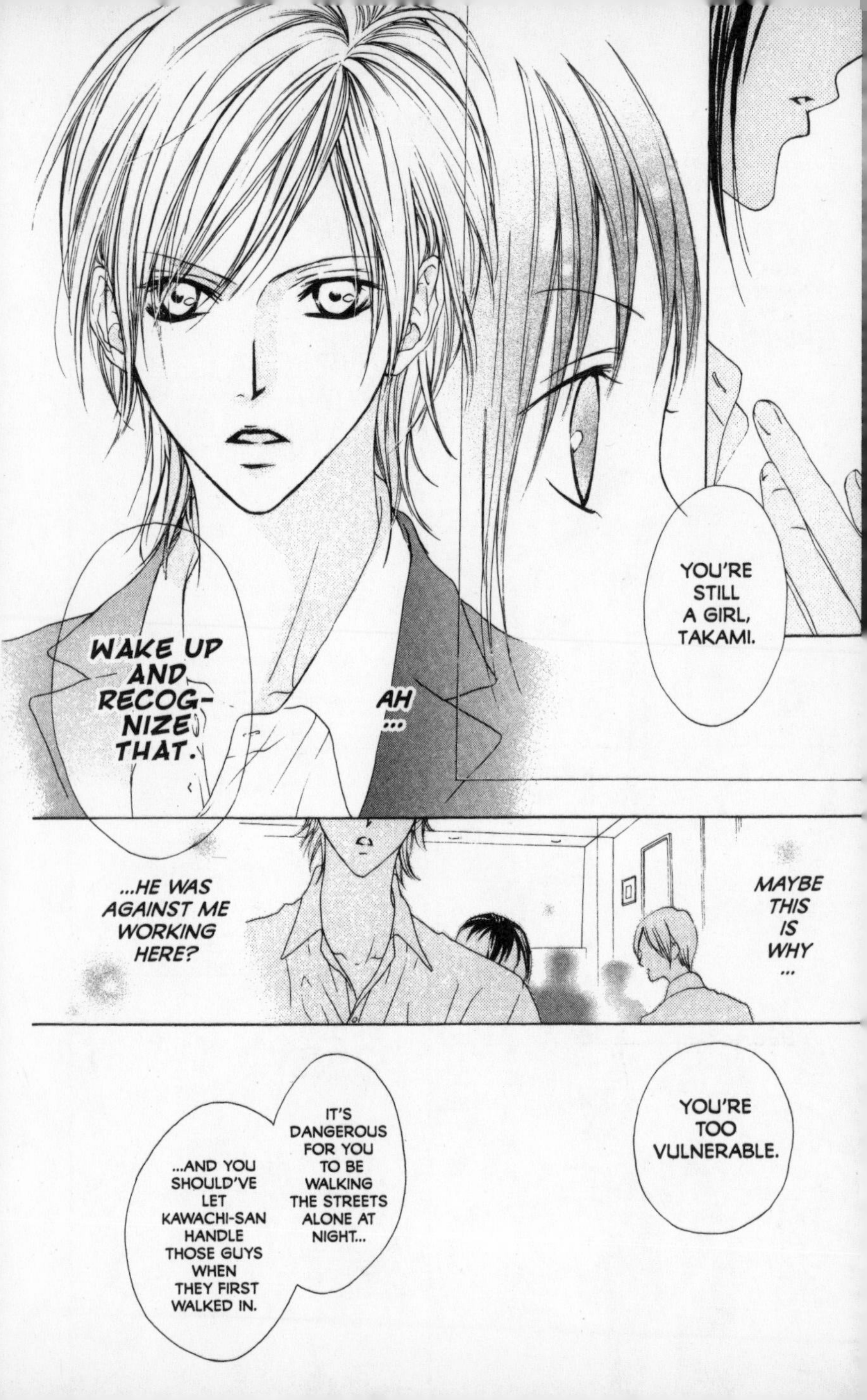
YOU'RE STILL A GIRL, TAKAMI.
AH...
WAKE UP AND RECOG-NIZE THAT.
MAYBE THIS IS WHY...
...HE WAS AGAINST ME WORKING HERE?
YOU'RE TOO VULNERABLE.
IT'S DANGEROUS FOR YOU TO BE WALKING THE STREETS ALONE AT NIGHT...
...AND YOU SHOULD'VE LET KAWACHI-SAN HANDLE THOSE GUYS WHEN THEY FIRST WALKED IN.

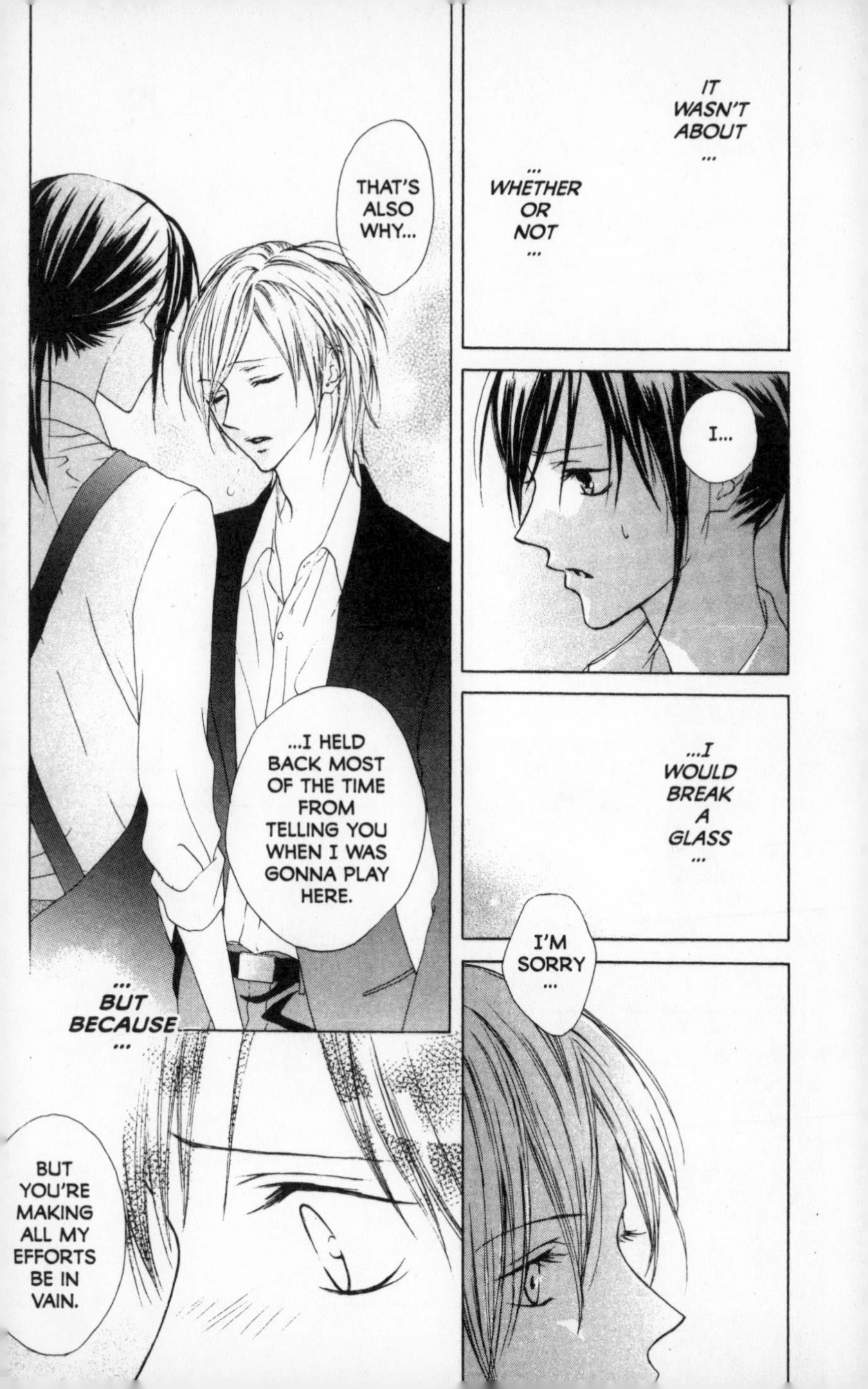
IT WASN'T ABOUT ...
... WHETHER OR NOT ...
I...
...I WOULD BREAK A GLASS ...
THAT'S ALSO WHY...
...I HELD BACK MOST OF THE TIME FROM TELLING YOU WHEN I WAS GONNA PLAY HERE.
... BUT BECAUSE ...
I'M SORRY ...
BUT YOU'RE MAKING ALL MY EFFORTS BE IN VAIN.

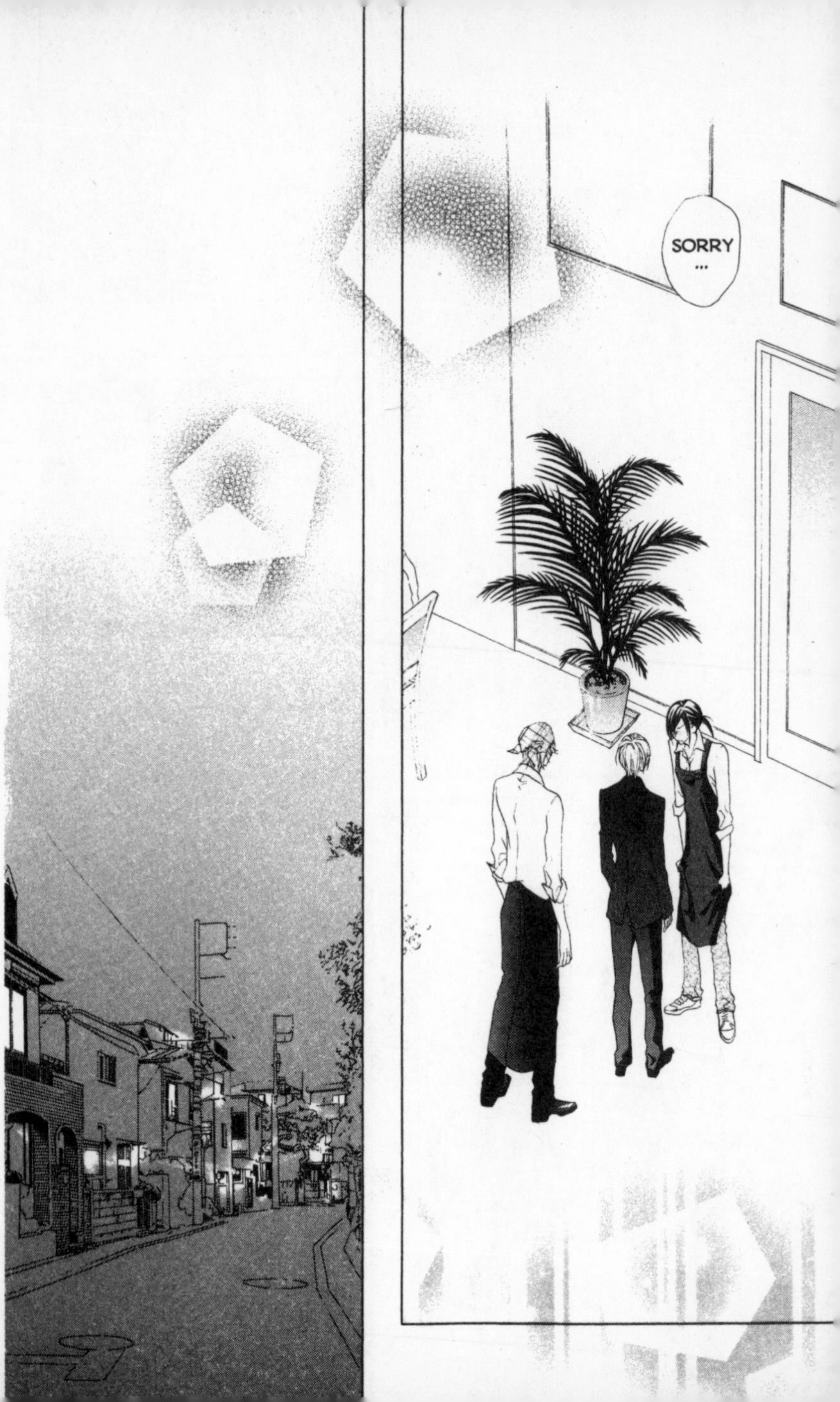
SORRY
...

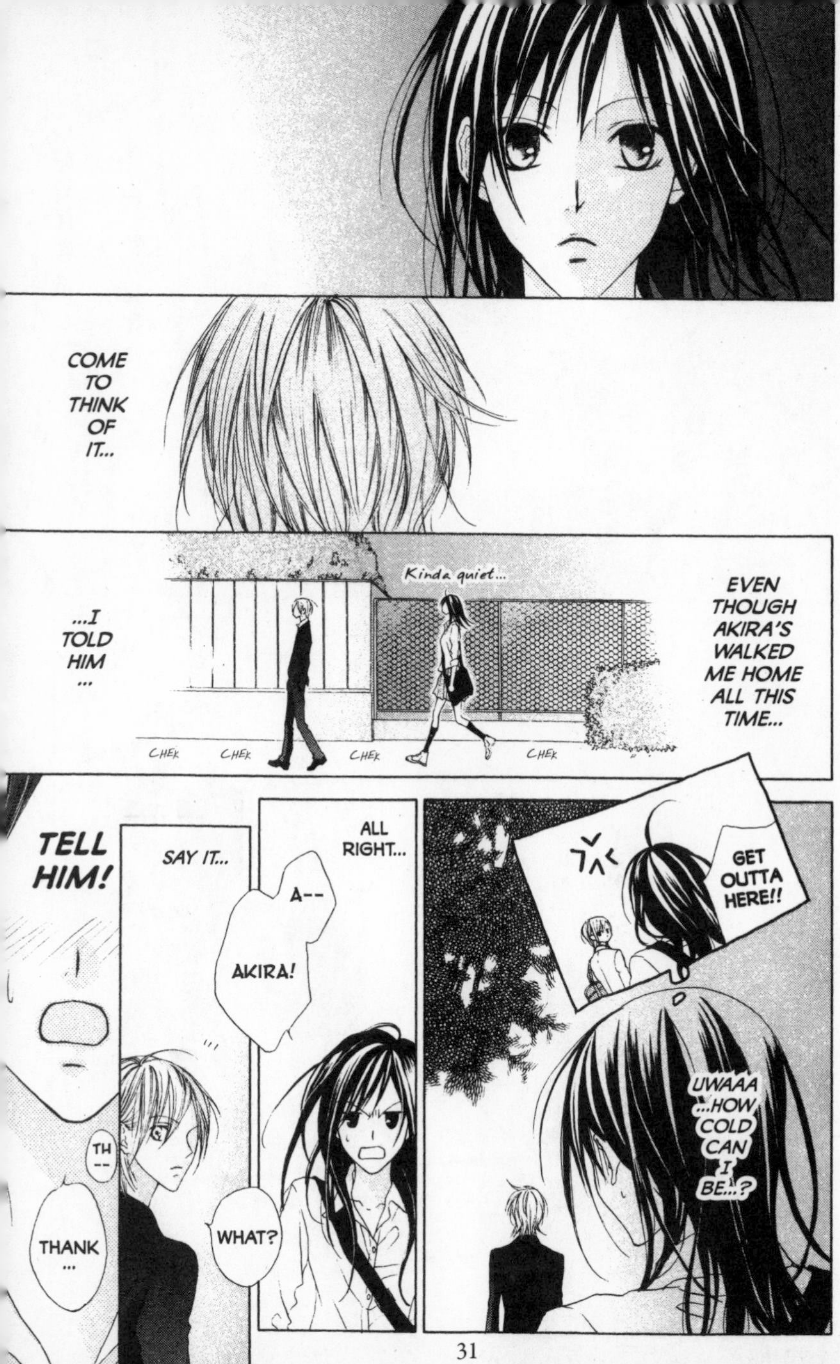
COME TO THINK OF IT...
EVEN THOUGH AKIRA'S WALKED ME HOME ALL THIS TIME...
Kinda quiet...
...I TOLD HIM ...
CHEK
CHEK
CHEK
CHEK
GET OUTTA HERE!!
UWAAA ...HOW COLD CAN I BE...?
ALL RIGHT...
A--
AKIRA!
WHAT?
SAY IT...
TELL HIM!
TH--
THANK ...

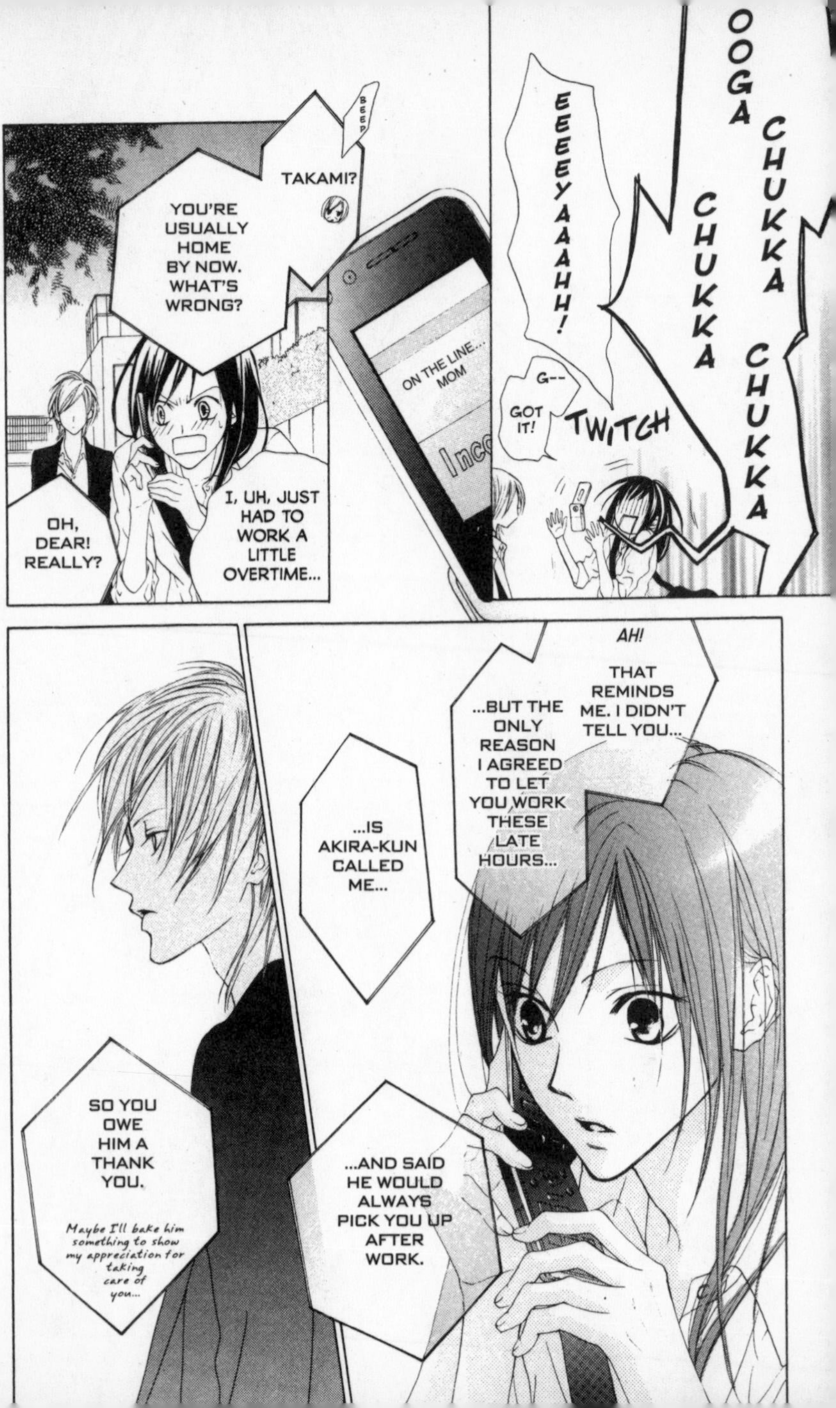
OOGA CHUKKA CHUKKA CHUKKA
EEEEYAAAAHH!
G-- GOT IT!
TWITCH
BEEP
TAKAMI?
YOU'RE USUALLY HOME BY NOW. WHAT'S WRONG?
ON THE LINE... MOM
I, UH, JUST HAD TO WORK A LITTLE OVERTIME...
OH, DEAR! REALLY?
AH!
THAT REMINDS ME. I DIDN'T TELL YOU...
...BUT THE ONLY REASON I AGREED TO LET YOU WORK THESE LATE HOURS...
...IS AKIRA-KUN CALLED ME...
...AND SAID HE WOULD ALWAYS PICK YOU UP AFTER WORK.
SO YOU OWE HIM A THANK YOU.
Maybe I'll bake him something to show my appreciation for taking care of you...

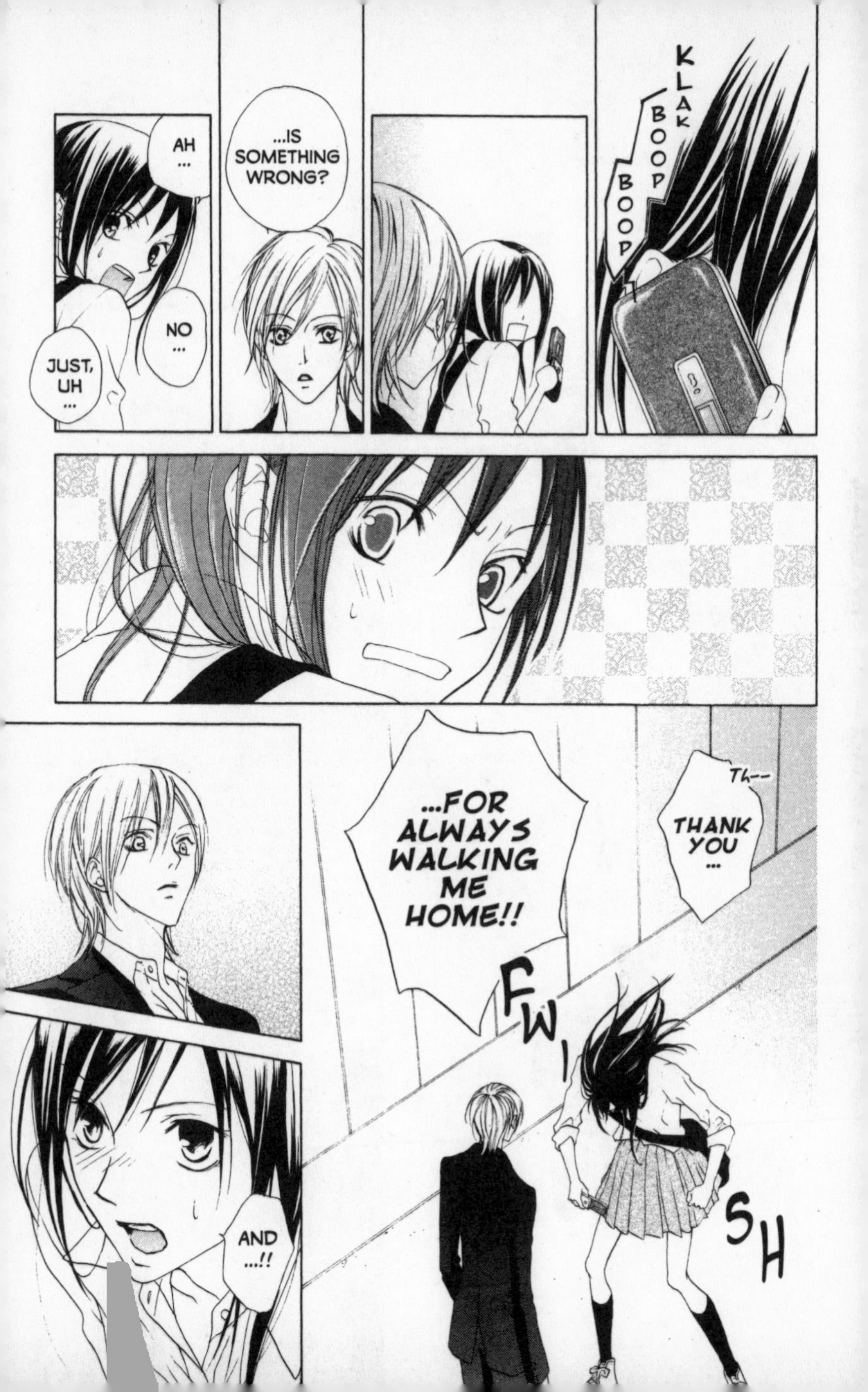
KLAK
BOOP
BOOP
...IS SOMETHING WRONG?
AH ...
NO ...
JUST, UH ...
Th--
THANK YOU ...
...FOR ALWAYS WALKING ME HOME!!
FWISH
AND ...!!

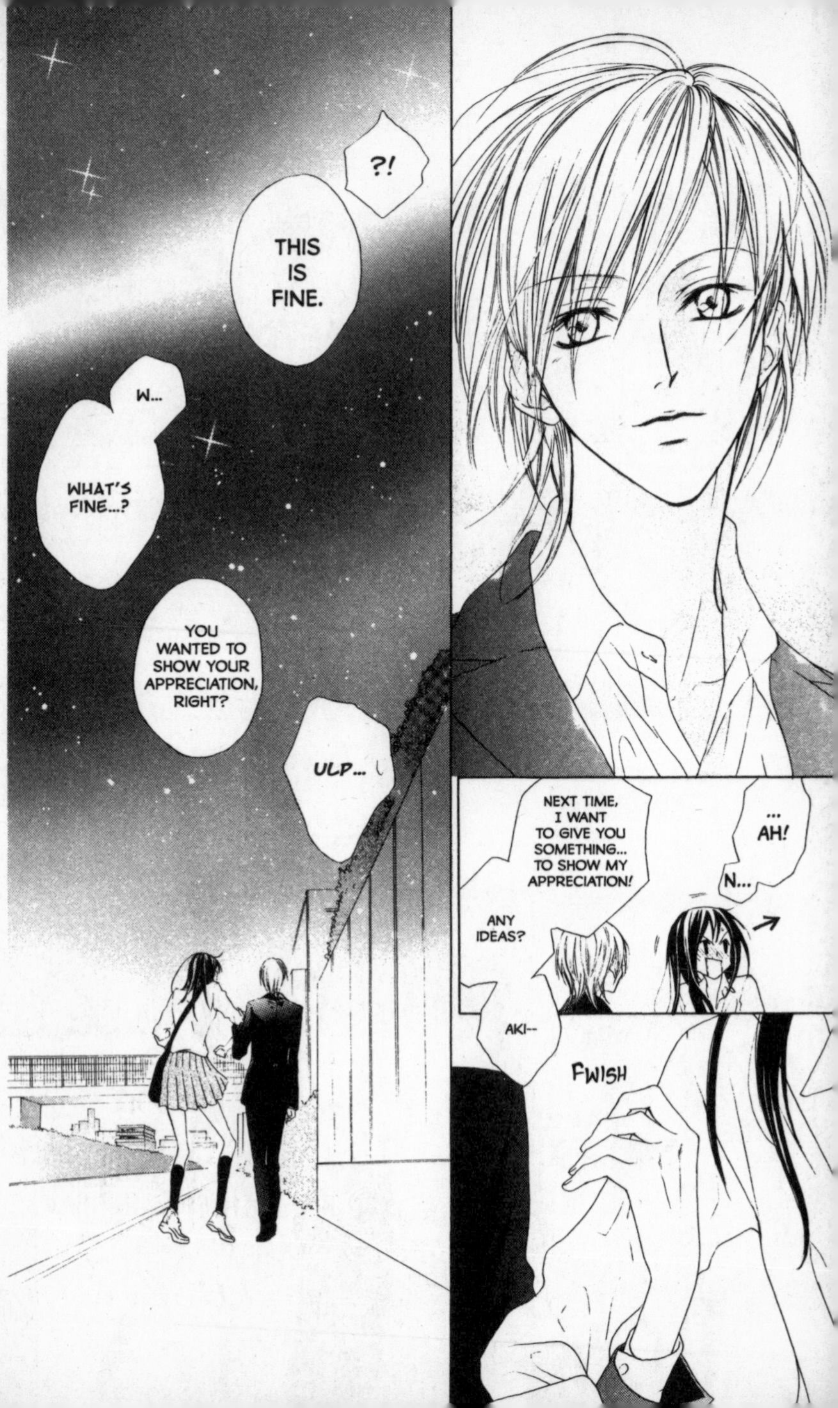
...AH!
N...
NEXT TIME, I WANT TO GIVE YOU SOMETHING... TO SHOW MY APPRECIATION!
ANY IDEAS?
AKI--
FWISH
?!
THIS IS FINE.
W...
WHAT'S FINE...?
YOU WANTED TO SHOW YOUR APPRECIATION, RIGHT?
ULP...

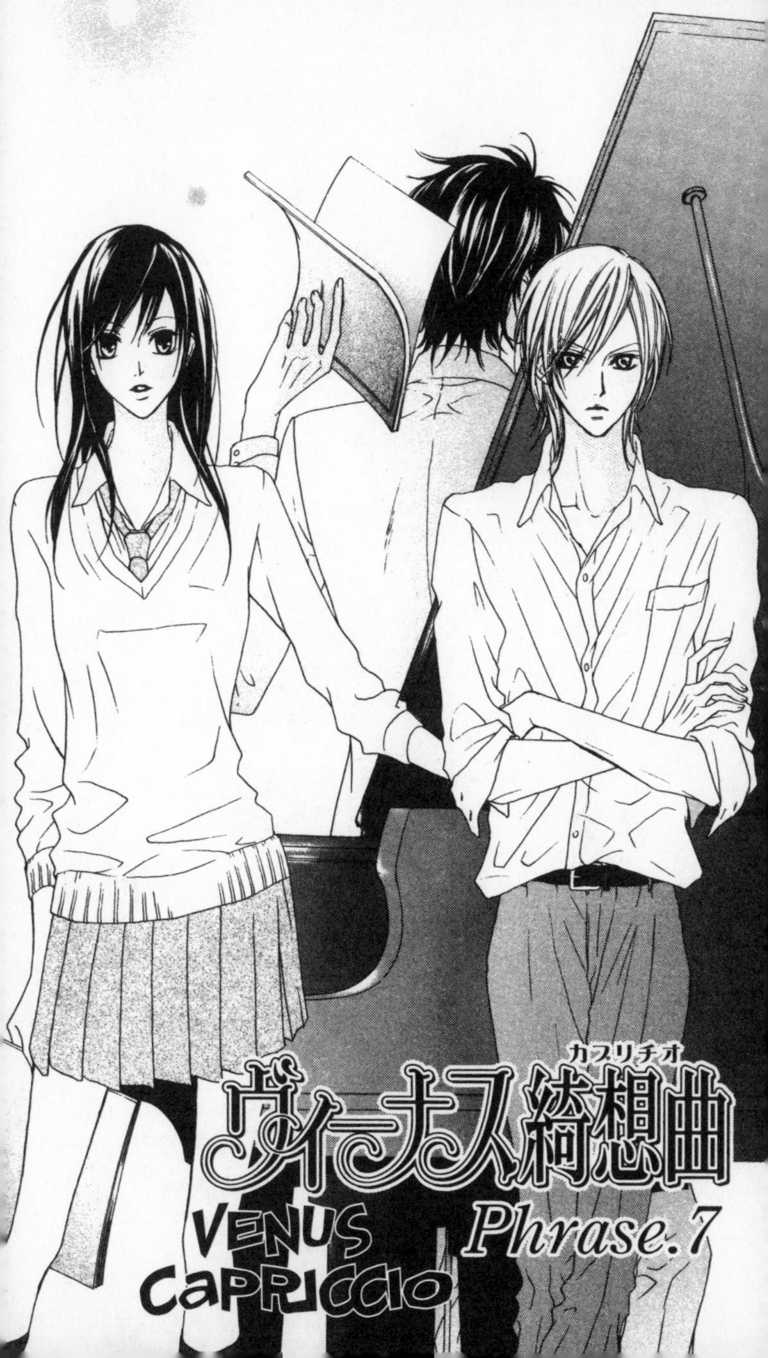
ヴィーナス綺想曲(カプリチオ)
Phrase.7
VENUS Capriccio

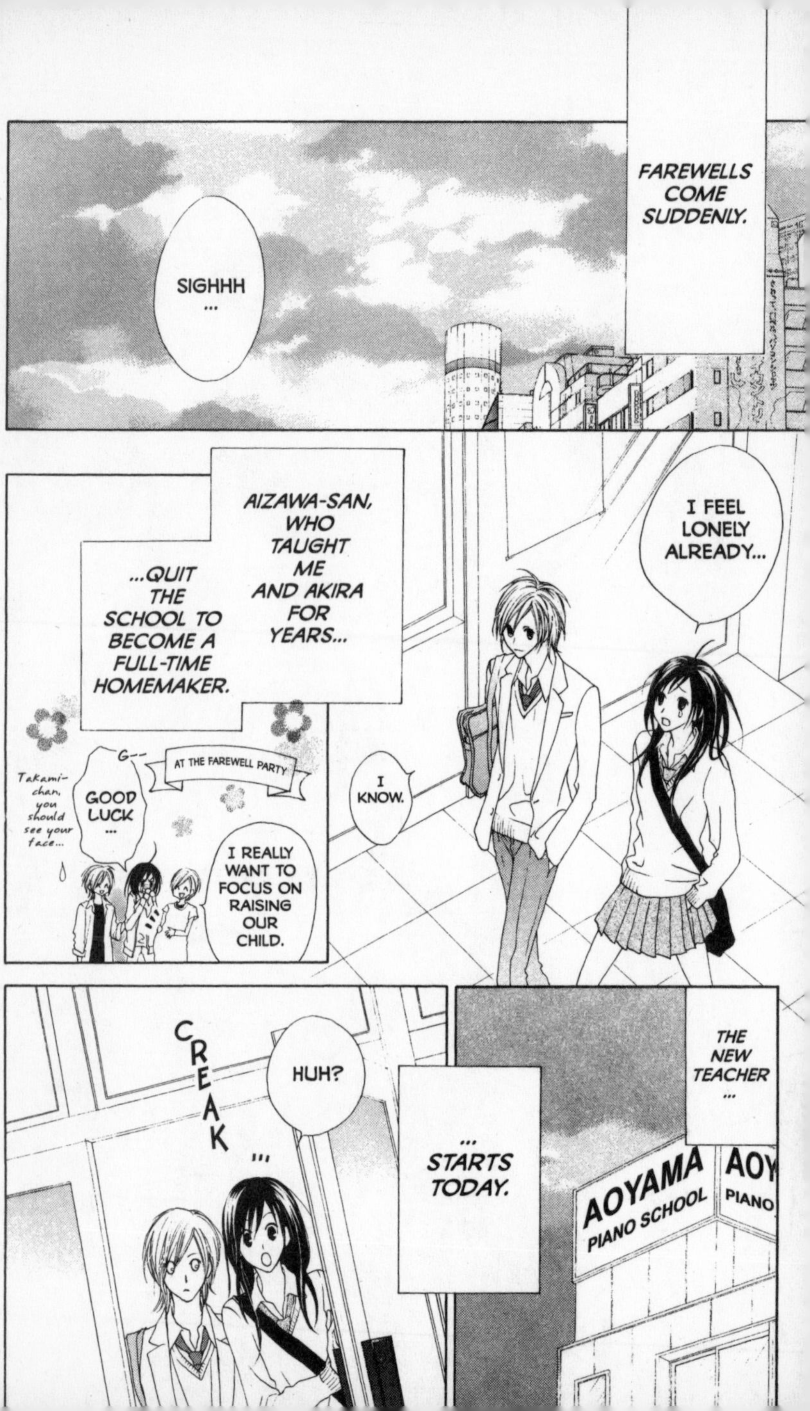
FAREWELLS COME SUDDENLY.
SIGHHH...
I FEEL LONELY ALREADY...
I KNOW.
AIZAWA-SAN, WHO TAUGHT ME AND AKIRA FOR YEARS...
...QUIT THE SCHOOL TO BECOME A FULL-TIME HOMEMAKER.
AT THE FAREWELL PARTY
I REALLY WANT TO FOCUS ON RAISING OUR CHILD.
G-- GOOD LUCK...
Takami-chan, you should see your face...
THE NEW TEACHER...
...STARTS TODAY.
AOYAMA PIANO SCHOOL
AOY PIANO
CREAK...
HUH?

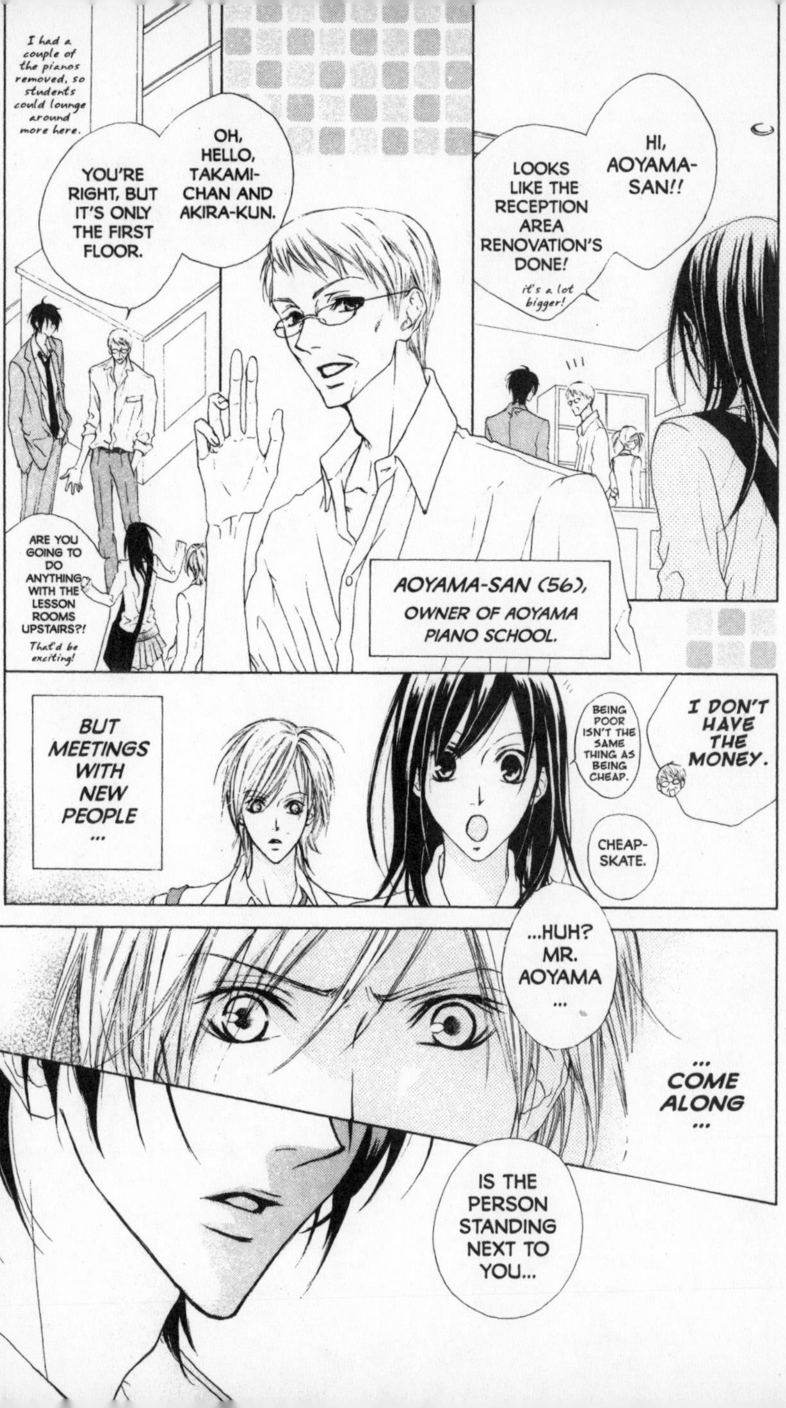
HI, AOYAMA-SAN!!
LOOKS LIKE THE RECEPTION AREA RENOVATION'S DONE!
it's a lot bigger!
OH, HELLO, TAKAMI-CHAN AND AKIRA-KUN.
YOU'RE RIGHT, BUT IT'S ONLY THE FIRST FLOOR.
I had a couple of the pianos removed, so students could lounge around more here.
ARE YOU GOING TO DO ANYTHING WITH THE LESSON ROOMS UPSTAIRS?!
That'd be exciting!
AOYAMA-SAN (56), OWNER OF AOYAMA PIANO SCHOOL.
I DON'T HAVE THE MONEY.
BEING POOR ISN'T THE SAME THING AS BEING CHEAP.
CHEAP-SKATE.
BUT MEETINGS WITH NEW PEOPLE ...
...HUH? MR. AOYAMA ...
... COME ALONG ...
IS THE PERSON STANDING NEXT TO YOU...

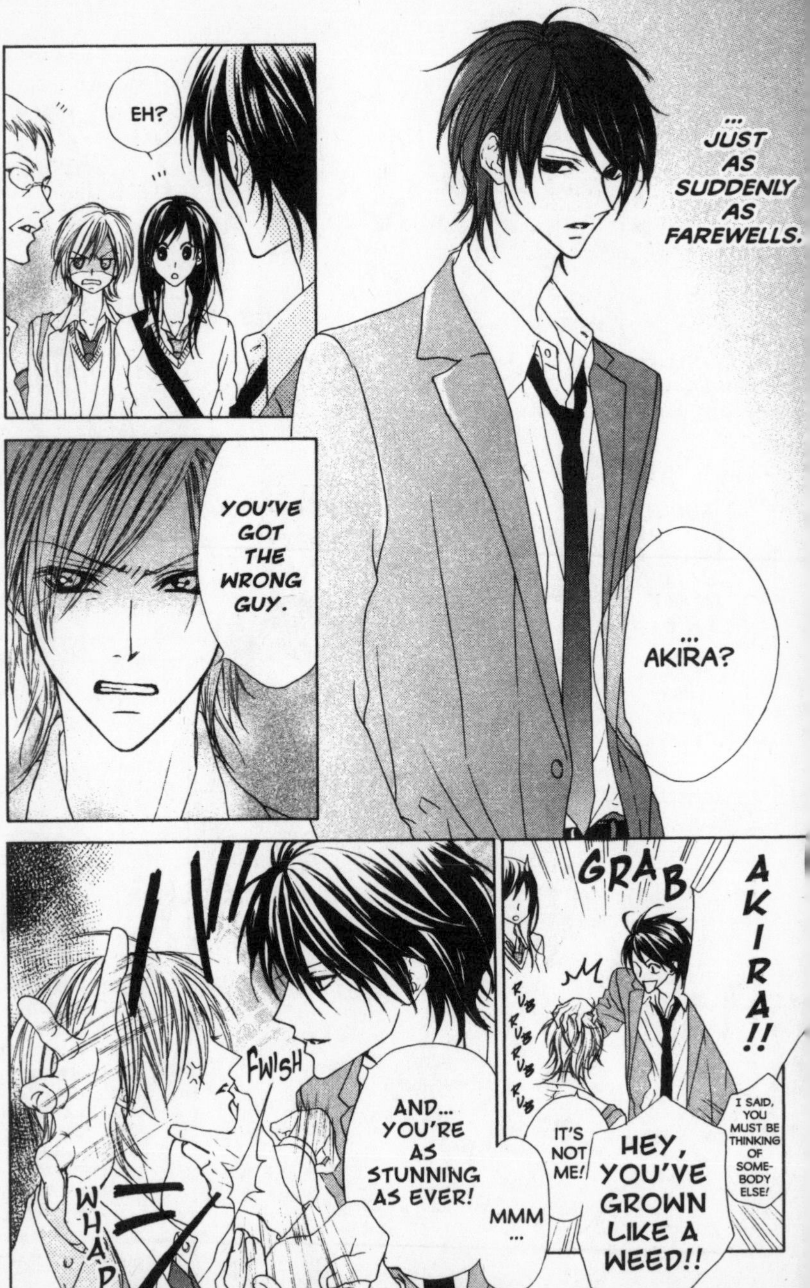
...JUST AS SUDDENLY AS FAREWELLS.
...AKIRA?
EH?
YOU'VE GOT THE WRONG GUY.
GRAB
AKIRA!!
RUB RUB RUB RUB RUB RUB
HEY, YOU'VE GROWN LIKE A WEED!!
I SAID, YOU MUST BE THINKING OF SOME-BODY ELSE!
IT'S NOT ME!
MMM...
FWISH
AND... YOU'RE AS STUNNING AS EVER!
WHAP

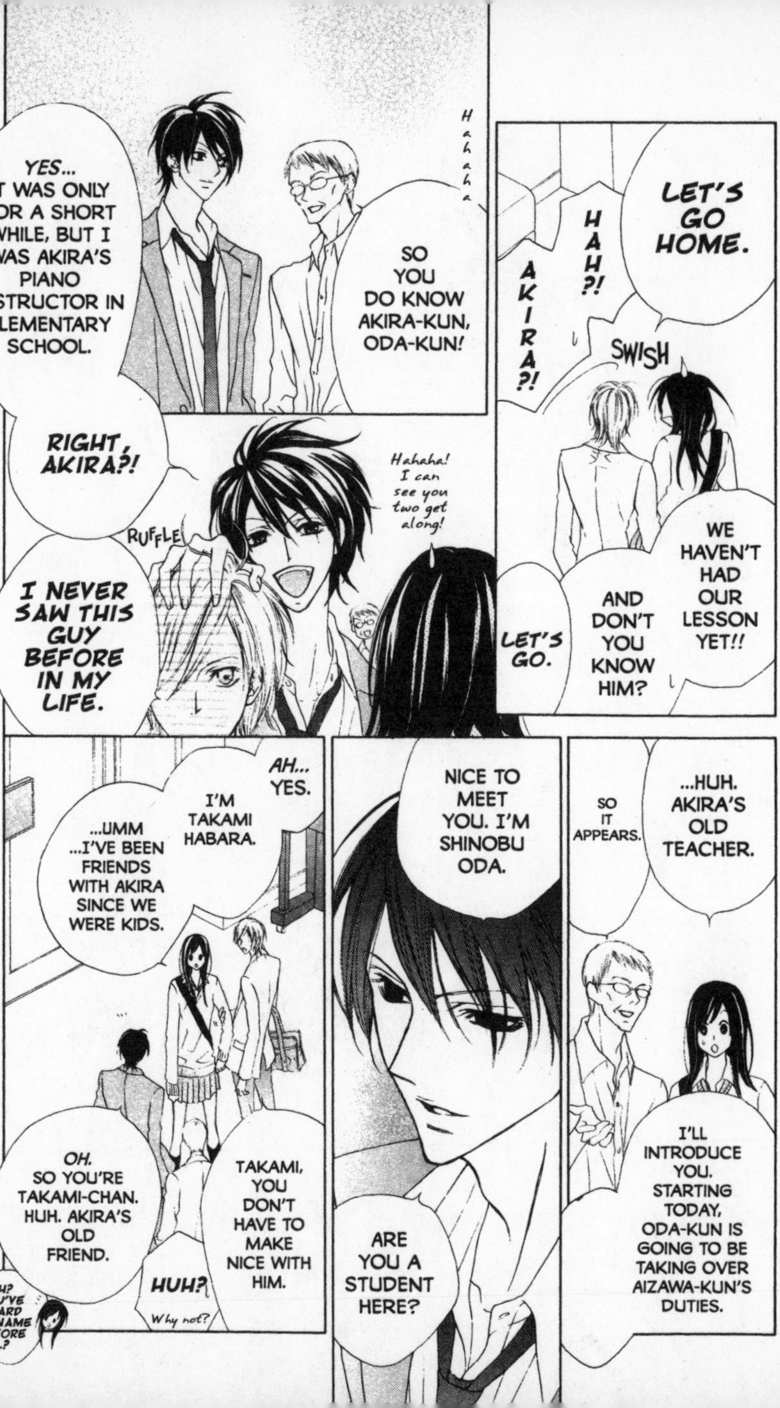
LET'S GO HOME.
HAH?!
AKIRA?!
SWISH
WE HAVEN'T HAD OUR LESSON YET!!
AND DON'T YOU KNOW HIM?
LET'S GO.
Hahaha
SO YOU DO KNOW AKIRA-KUN, ODA-KUN!
YES... IT WAS ONLY FOR A SHORT WHILE, BUT I WAS AKIRA'S PIANO INSTRUCTOR IN ELEMENTARY SCHOOL.
RIGHT, AKIRA?!
Hahaha! I can see you two get along!
RUFFLE
I NEVER SAW THIS GUY BEFORE IN MY LIFE.
...HUH. AKIRA'S OLD TEACHER.
SO IT APPEARS.
I'LL INTRODUCE YOU. STARTING TODAY, ODA-KUN IS GOING TO BE TAKING OVER AIZAWA-KUN'S DUTIES.
NICE TO MEET YOU. I'M SHINOBU ODA.
ARE YOU A STUDENT HERE?
AH... YES.
I'M TAKAMI HABARA.
...UMM ...I'VE BEEN FRIENDS WITH AKIRA SINCE WE WERE KIDS.
TAKAMI, YOU DON'T HAVE TO MAKE NICE WITH HIM.
Why not?
HUH?
OH. SO YOU'RE TAKAMI-CHAN. HUH. AKIRA'S OLD FRIEND.
EH? YOU'VE HEARD MY NAME BEFORE ...?

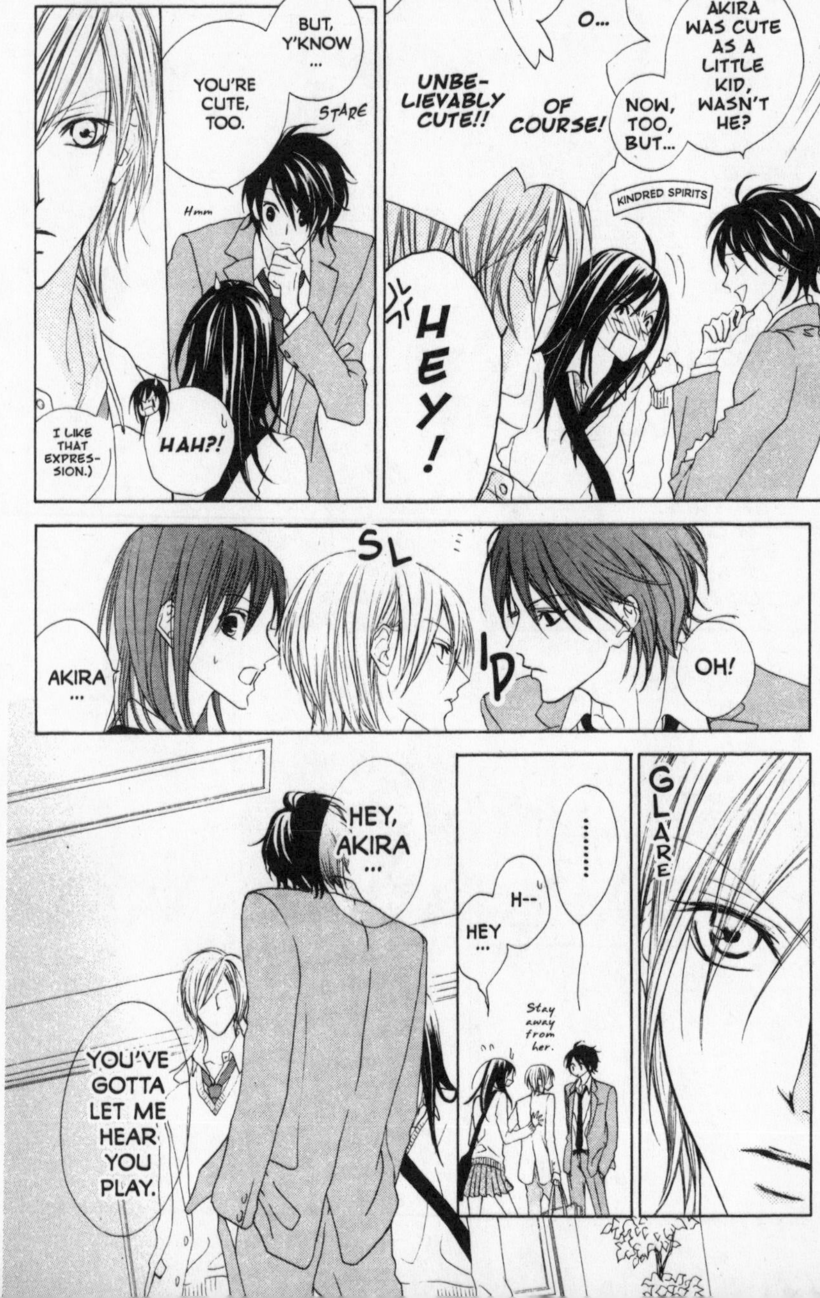
AKIRA WAS CUTE AS A LITTLE KID, WASN'T HE?
NOW, TOO, BUT...
O...
OF COURSE!
UNBE-LIEVABLY CUTE!!
KINDRED SPIRITS
HEY!
BUT, Y'KNOW ...
STARE
YOU'RE CUTE, TOO.
Hmm
HAH?!
I LIKE THAT EXPRES-SION.)
OH!
SLID
AKIRA ...
GLARE
....
H-- HEY ...
Stay away from her.
HEY, AKIRA ...
YOU'VE GOTTA LET ME HEAR YOU PLAY.

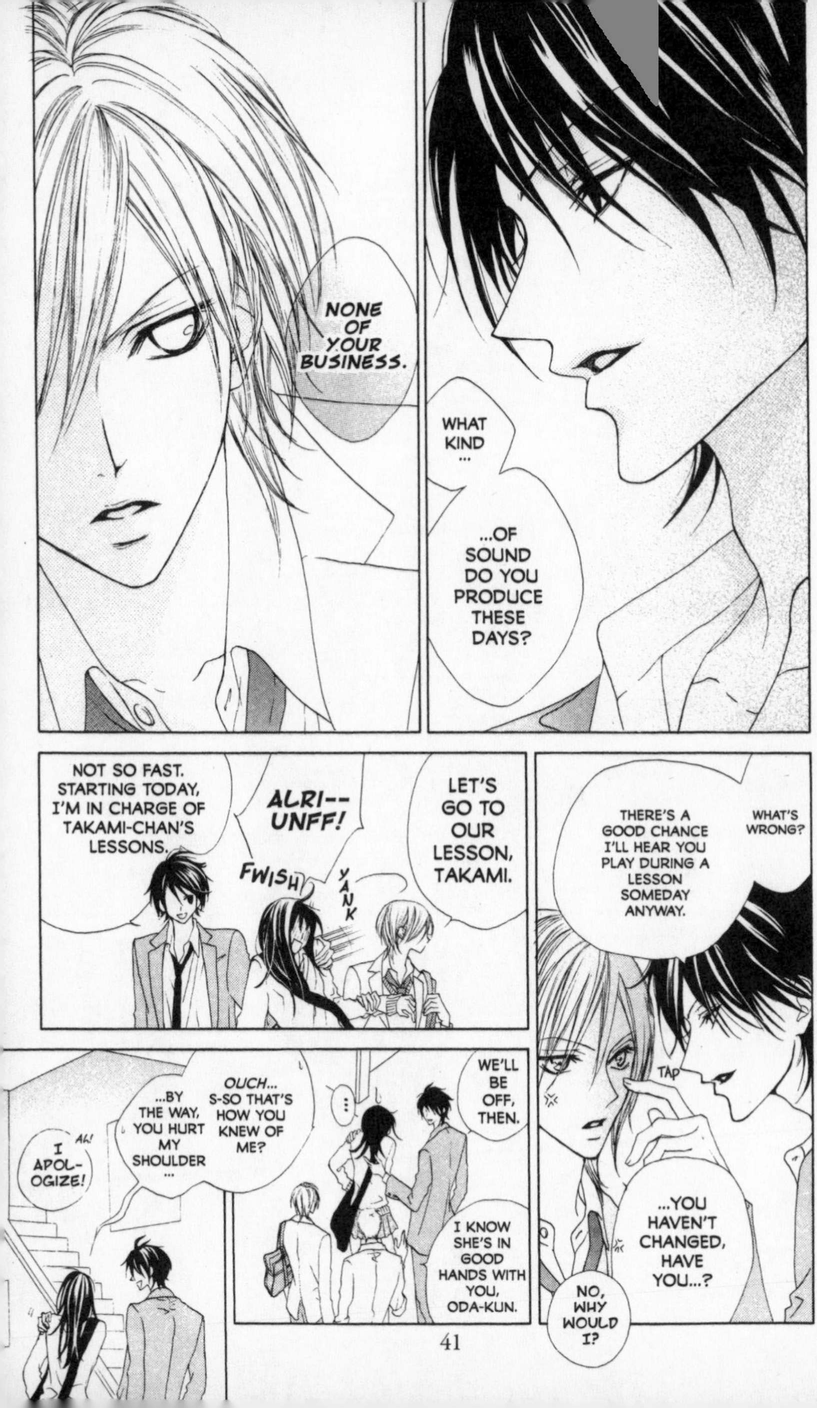
WHAT KIND ...
...OF SOUND DO YOU PRODUCE THESE DAYS?
NONE OF YOUR BUSINESS.
WHAT'S WRONG?
THERE'S A GOOD CHANCE I'LL HEAR YOU PLAY DURING A LESSON SOMEDAY ANYWAY.
TAP
...YOU HAVEN'T CHANGED, HAVE YOU...?
NO, WHY WOULD I?
LET'S GO TO OUR LESSON, TAKAMI.
ALRI-- UNFF!
YANK
FWISH
NOT SO FAST. STARTING TODAY, I'M IN CHARGE OF TAKAMI-CHAN'S LESSONS.
WE'LL BE OFF, THEN.
I KNOW SHE'S IN GOOD HANDS WITH YOU, ODA-KUN.
...
OUCH... S-SO THAT'S HOW YOU KNEW OF ME?
...BY THE WAY, YOU HURT MY SHOULDER ...
AH!
I APOLOGIZE!

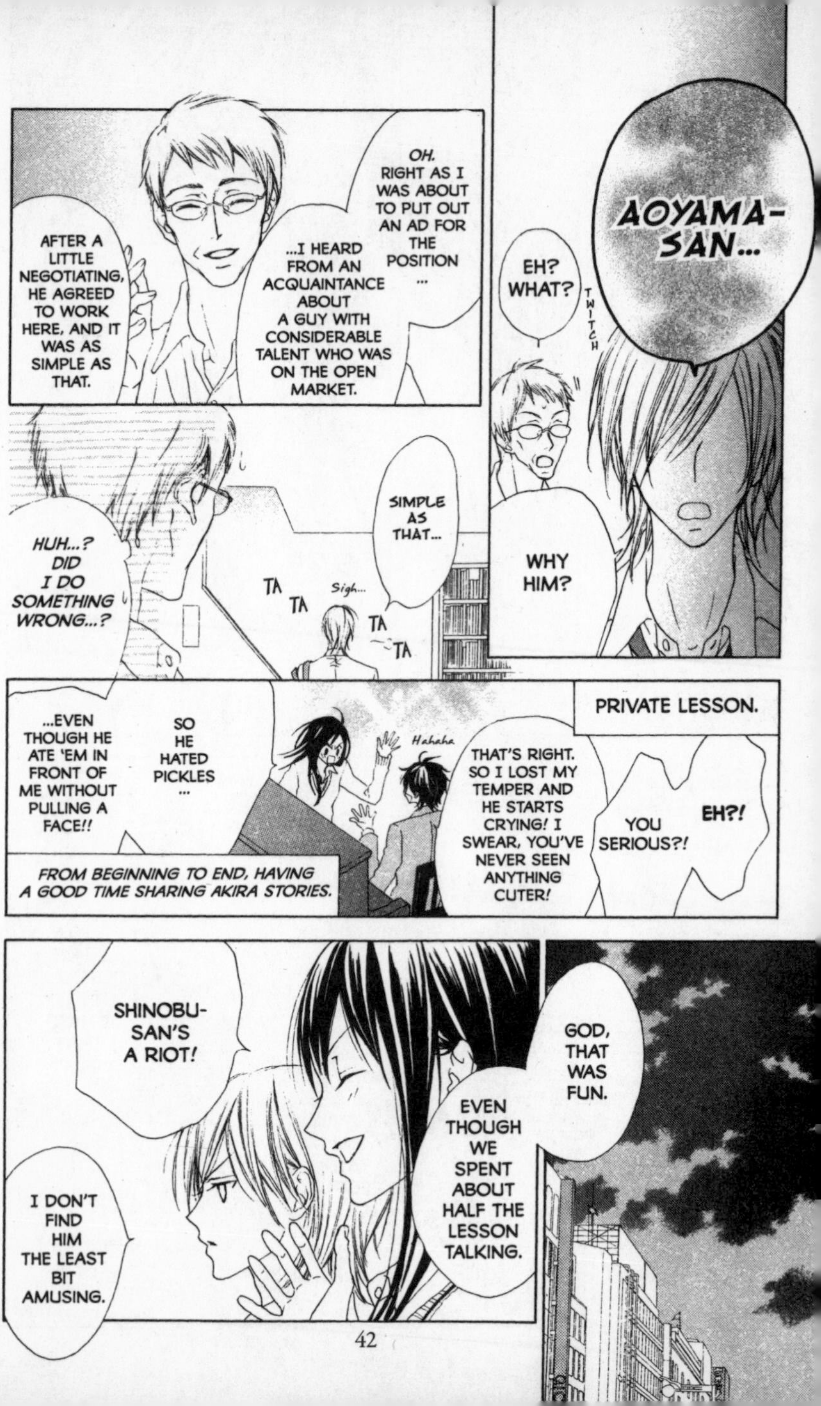
AOYAMA-SAN...
EH? WHAT?
TWITCH
WHY HIM?
OH. RIGHT AS I WAS ABOUT TO PUT OUT AN AD FOR THE POSITION ...
...I HEARD FROM AN ACQUAINTANCE ABOUT A GUY WITH CONSIDERABLE TALENT WHO WAS ON THE OPEN MARKET.
AFTER A LITTLE NEGOTIATING, HE AGREED TO WORK HERE, AND IT WAS AS SIMPLE AS THAT.
SIMPLE AS THAT...
TA TA
Sigh...
TA TA
HUH...? DID I DO SOMETHING WRONG...?
PRIVATE LESSON.
EH?!
YOU SERIOUS?!
THAT'S RIGHT. SO I LOST MY TEMPER AND HE STARTS CRYING! I SWEAR, YOU'VE NEVER SEEN ANYTHING CUTER!
Hahaha
SO HE HATED PICKLES ...
...EVEN THOUGH HE ATE 'EM IN FRONT OF ME WITHOUT PULLING A FACE!!
FROM BEGINNING TO END, HAVING A GOOD TIME SHARING AKIRA STORIES.
GOD, THAT WAS FUN.
EVEN THOUGH WE SPENT ABOUT HALF THE LESSON TALKING.
SHINOBU-SAN'S A RIOT!
I DON'T FIND HIM THE LEAST BIT AMUSING.

2

PHRASE.7

THIS IS THE FIRST EPISODE IN WHICH I HAD HELP FROM AN ASSISTANT.

UNTIL THEN, I'D MUDDLED THROUGH ON MY OWN, THINKING I WANTED TO DO IT ALL BY MYSELF, BUT FINALLY, MY EDITOR SAID, "ISN'T ABOUT TIME WE START SEARCHING FOR AN ASSISTANT FOR YOU?" I WAS SCARED, THOUGH... (ME BEING DUMB?)

BUT AFTER THE ASSISTANT CAME AND HELPED ME, I WAS FILLED WITH GRATITUDE.

I'M SO THANKFUL I GOT HELP.

THANK YOU!

SINCE I HADN'T HAD ANY EXPERIENCE WORKING WITH (OR AS AN) ASSISTANTS, I HAD NO IDEA HOW THE WHOLE DYNAMIC WORKED, SO I PEPPERED HER (AND STILL DO) WITH QUESTIONS AND RECEIVED (AND STILL RECEIVE) AN EDUCATION ABOUT WORKING WITH AN ASSISTANT.

MY ART'S GOTTEN A LOT BETTER FOR IT RECENTLY... I THINK.

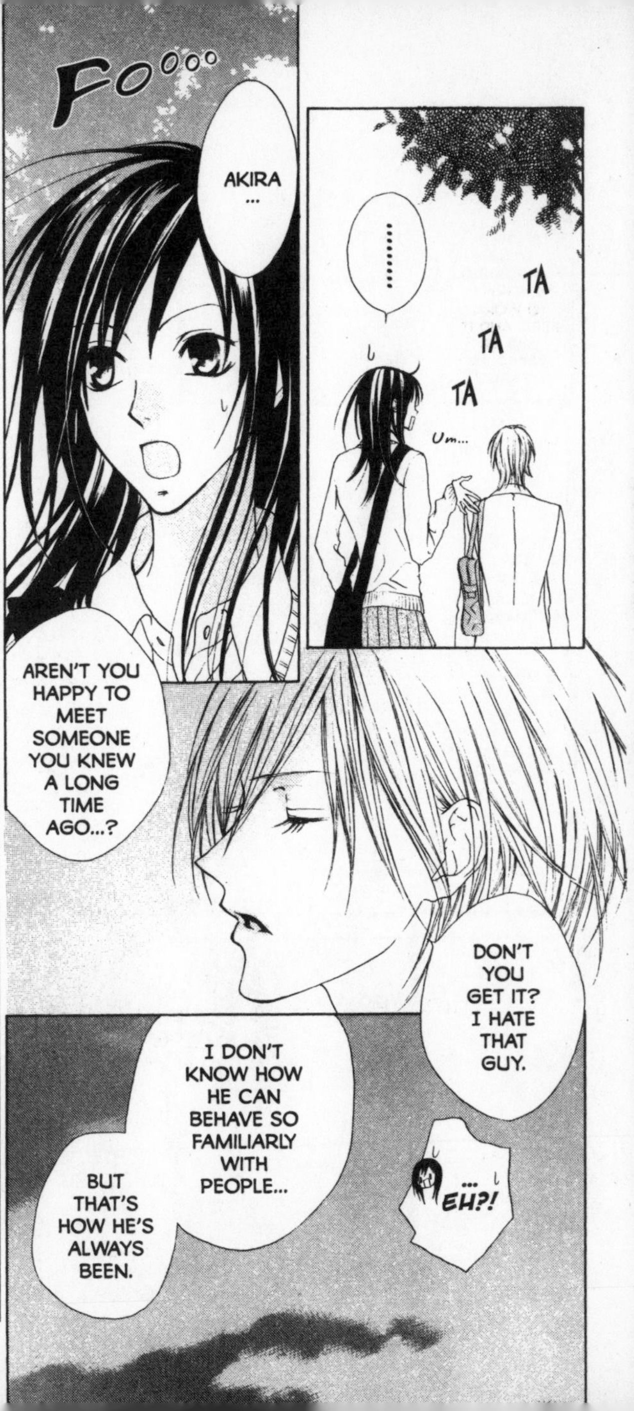

......
TA
TA
TA
Um...
FOooo
AKIRA ...
AREN'T YOU HAPPY TO MEET SOMEONE YOU KNEW A LONG TIME AGO...?
DON'T YOU GET IT? I HATE THAT GUY.
I DON'T KNOW HOW HE CAN BEHAVE SO FAMILIARLY WITH PEOPLE...
BUT THAT'S HOW HE'S ALWAYS BEEN.
...EH?!

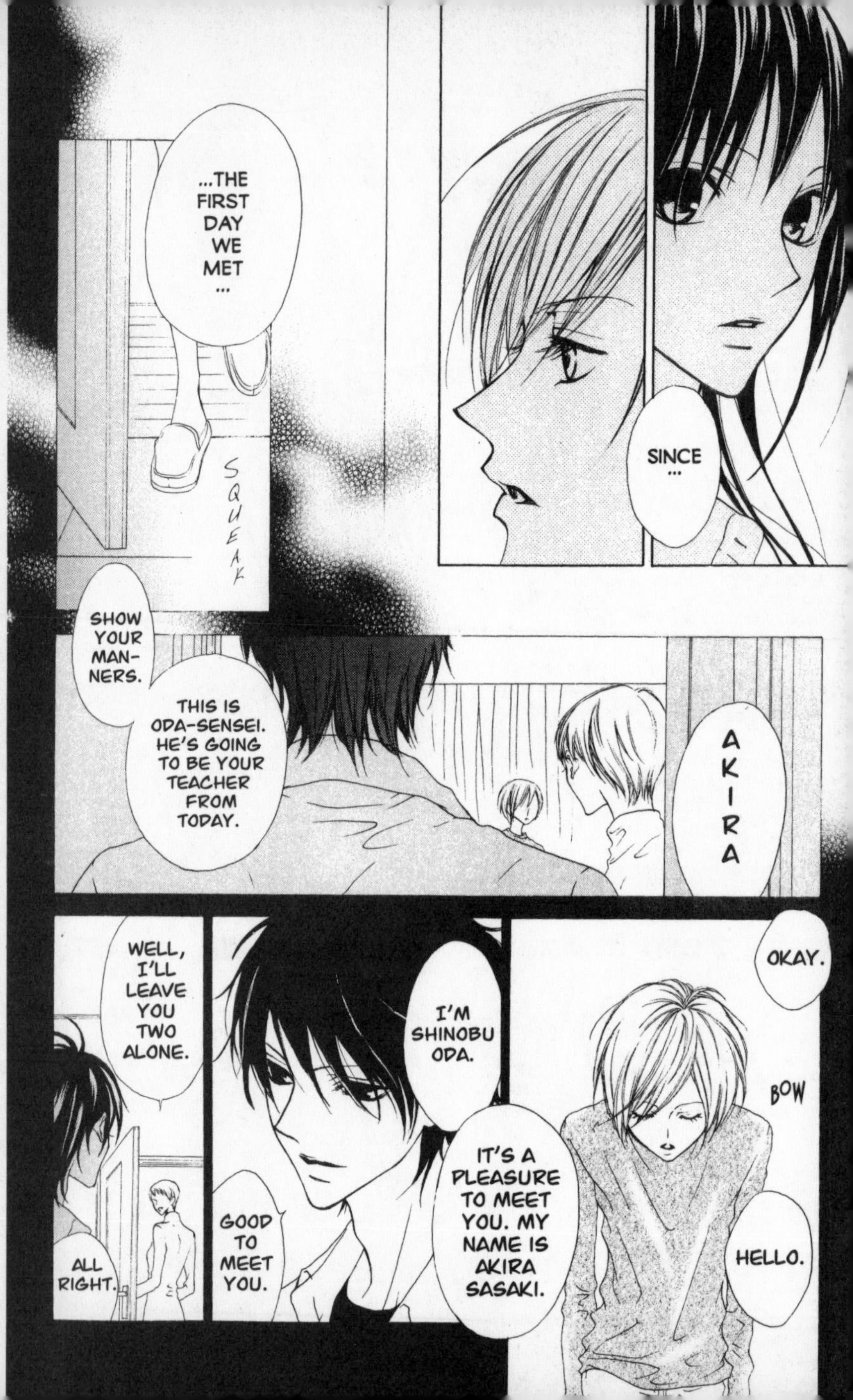
SINCE ...
...THE FIRST DAY WE MET ...
SQUEAK
AKIRA
SHOW YOUR MAN-NERS.
THIS IS ODA-SENSEI. HE'S GOING TO BE YOUR TEACHER FROM TODAY.
OKAY.
BOW
HELLO.
IT'S A PLEASURE TO MEET YOU. MY NAME IS AKIRA SASAKI.
I'M SHINOBU ODA.
GOOD TO MEET YOU.
WELL, I'LL LEAVE YOU TWO ALONE.
ALL RIGHT.

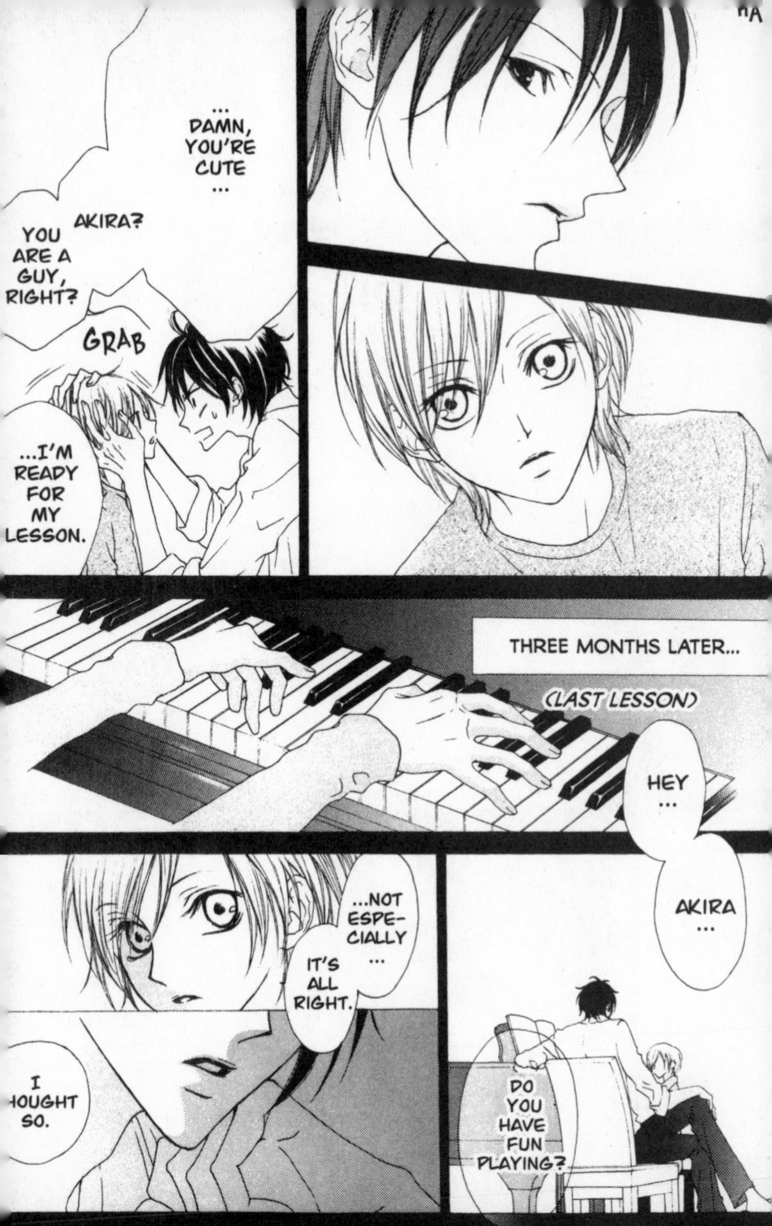
HA
... DAMN, YOU'RE CUTE ...
AKIRA?
YOU ARE A GUY, RIGHT?
GRAB
...I'M READY FOR MY LESSON.
THREE MONTHS LATER...
(LAST LESSON)
HEY ...
AKIRA ...
DO YOU HAVE FUN PLAYING?
...NOT ESPECIALLY ...
IT'S ALL RIGHT.
I HOUGHT SO.

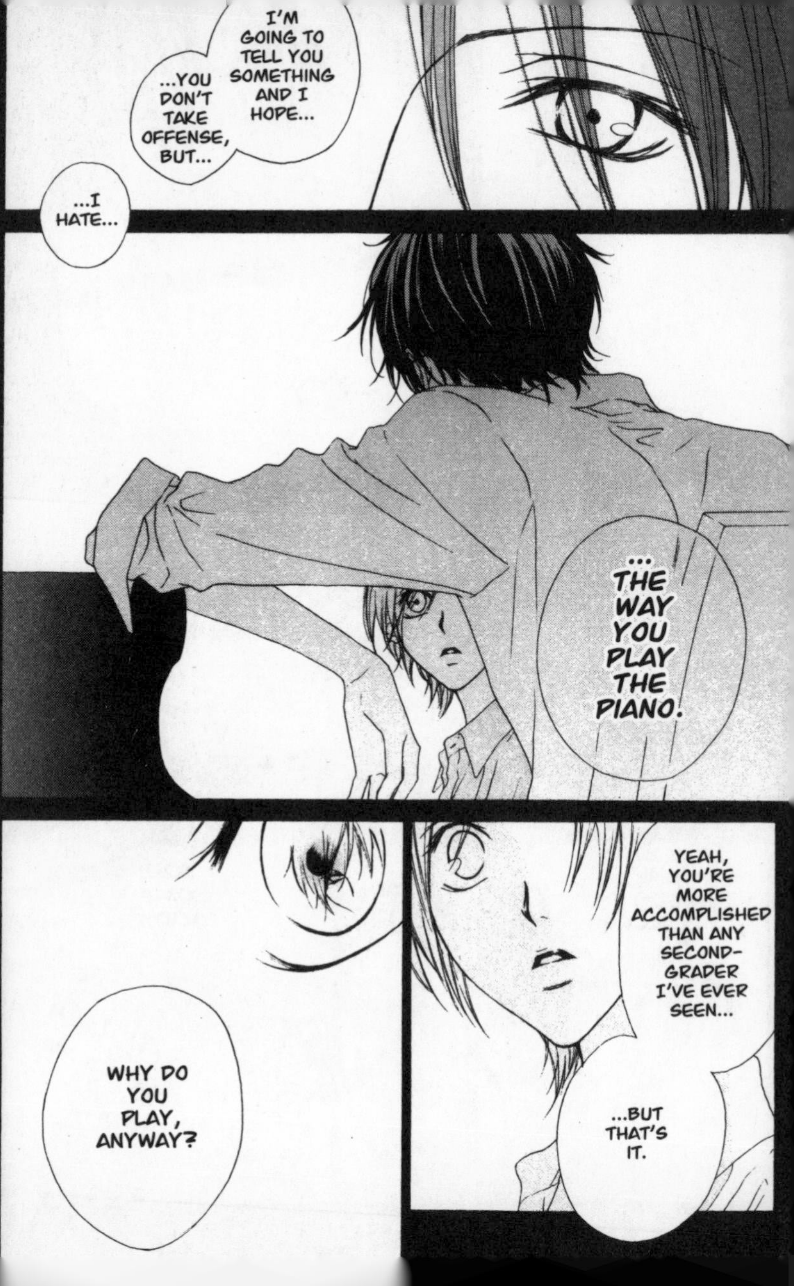
I'M GOING TO TELL YOU SOMETHING AND I HOPE...
...YOU DON'T TAKE OFFENSE, BUT...
...I HATE...
...THE WAY YOU PLAY THE PIANO.
YEAH, YOU'RE MORE ACCOMPLISHED THAN ANY SECOND-GRADER I'VE EVER SEEN...
...BUT THAT'S IT.
WHY DO YOU PLAY, ANYWAY?

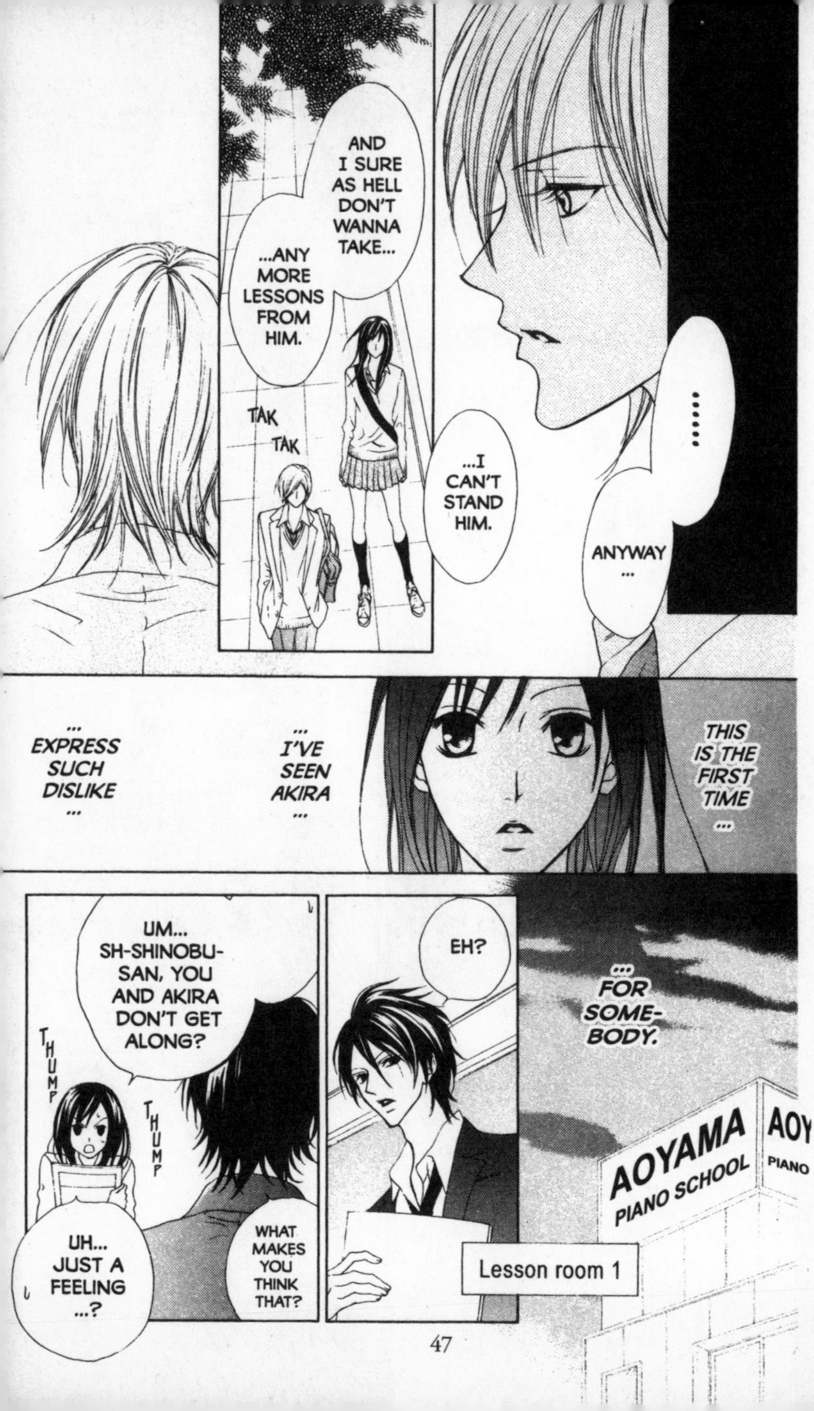

......
ANYWAY ...
...I CAN'T STAND HIM.
AND I SURE AS HELL DON'T WANNA TAKE...
...ANY MORE LESSONS FROM HIM.
TAK TAK
THIS IS THE FIRST TIME ...
... I'VE SEEN AKIRA ...
... EXPRESS SUCH DISLIKE ...
... FOR SOMEBODY.
AOYAMA PIANO SCHOOL
AOY PIANO
Lesson room 1
EH?
WHAT MAKES YOU THINK THAT?
UM... SH-SHINOBU-SAN, YOU AND AKIRA DON'T GET ALONG?
THUMP
THUMP
UH... JUST A FEELING ...?

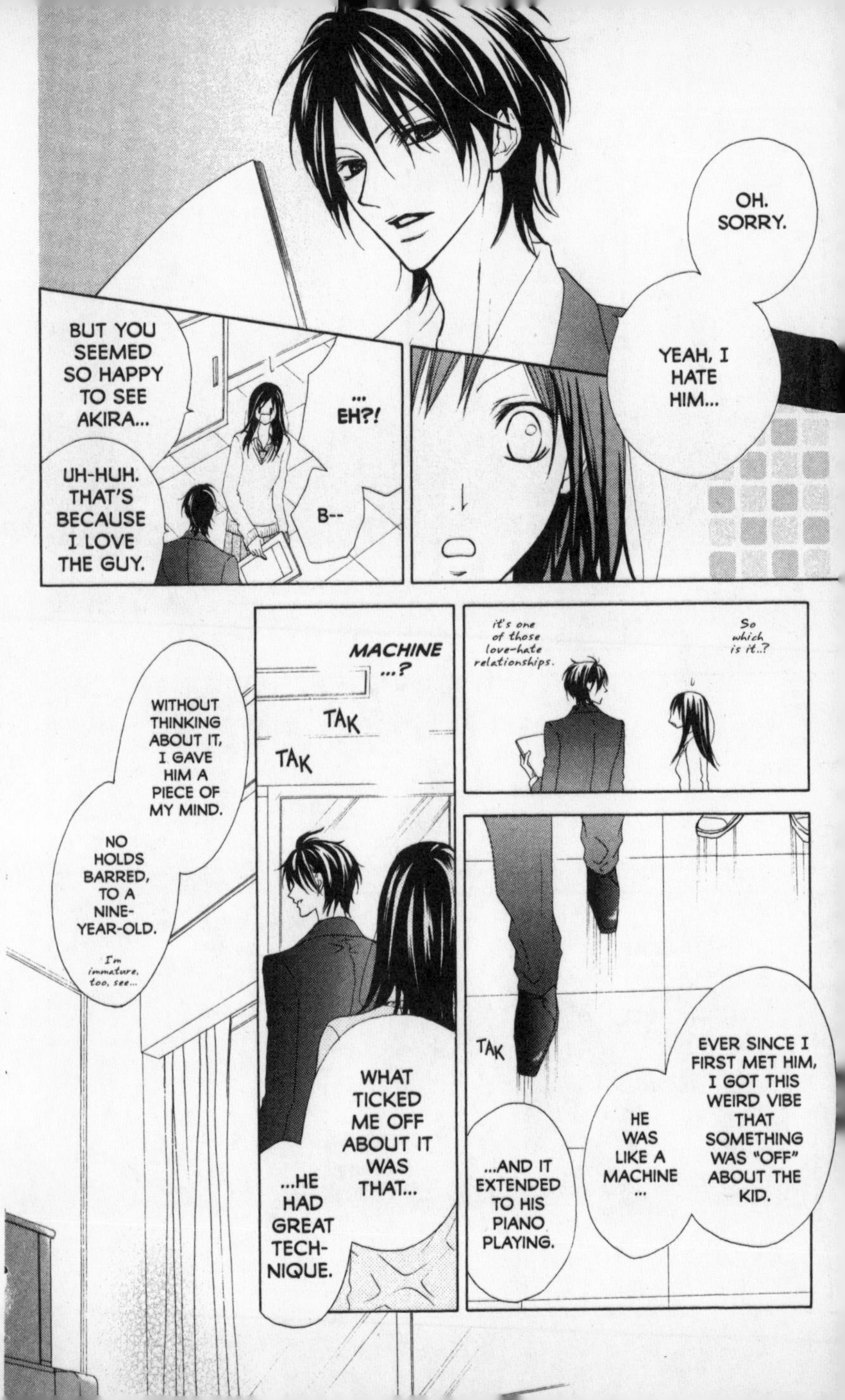

OH. SORRY.
YEAH, I HATE HIM...
... EH?!
B--
BUT YOU SEEMED SO HAPPY TO SEE AKIRA...
UH-HUH. THAT'S BECAUSE I LOVE THE GUY.
So which is it..?
it's one of those love-hate relationships.
EVER SINCE I FIRST MET HIM, I GOT THIS WEIRD VIBE THAT SOMETHING WAS "OFF" ABOUT THE KID.
HE WAS LIKE A MACHINE ...
...AND IT EXTENDED TO HIS PIANO PLAYING.
TAK
MACHINE ...?
TAK
TAK
WHAT TICKED ME OFF ABOUT IT WAS THAT...
...HE HAD GREAT TECHNIQUE.
WITHOUT THINKING ABOUT IT, I GAVE HIM A PIECE OF MY MIND.
NO HOLDS BARRED, TO A NINE-YEAR-OLD.
I'm immature, too, see...

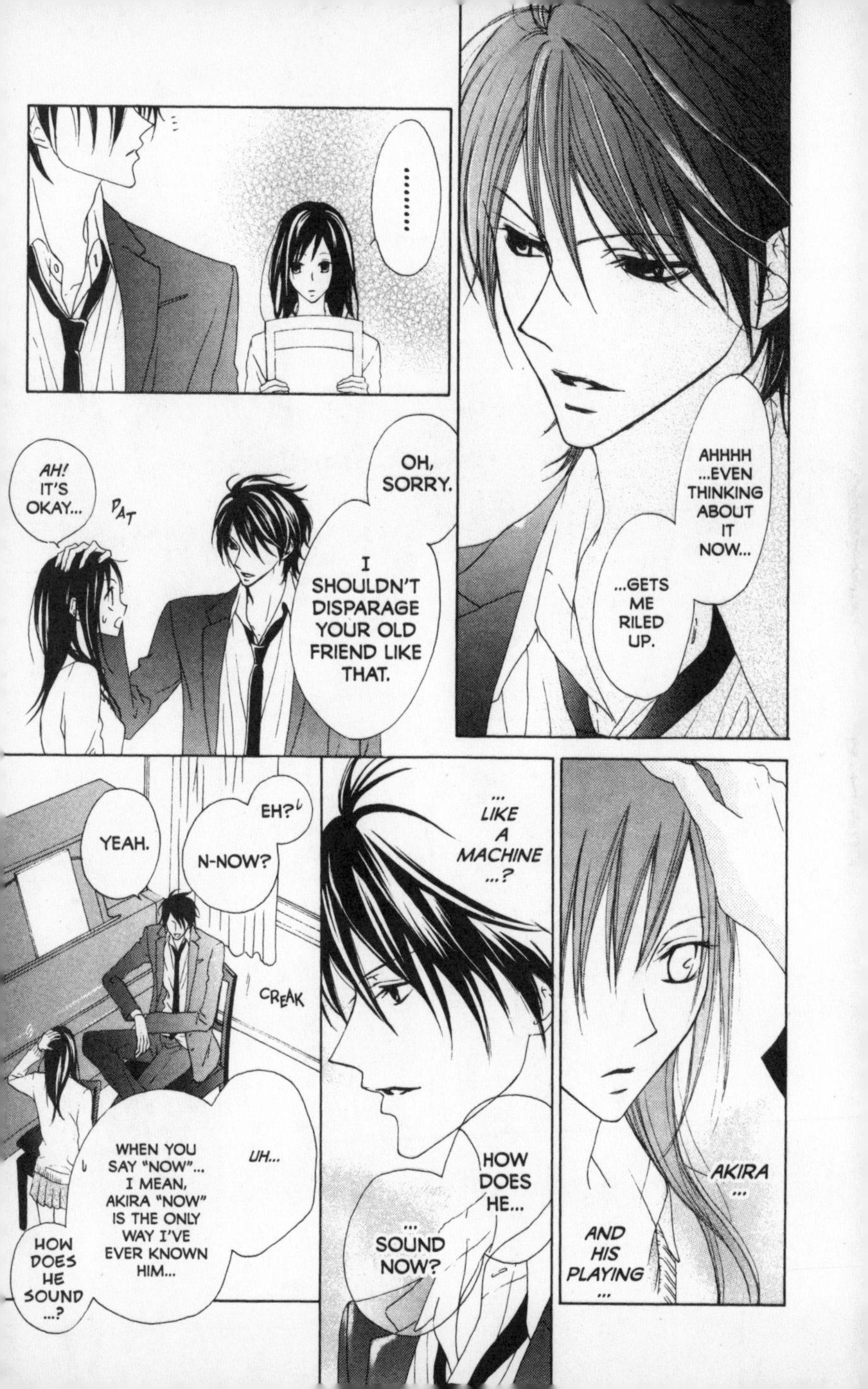
AHHHH ...EVEN THINKING ABOUT IT NOW...
...GETS ME RILED UP.
......
OH, SORRY.
I SHOULDN'T DISPARAGE YOUR OLD FRIEND LIKE THAT.
PAT
AH! IT'S OKAY...
AKIRA ...
AND HIS PLAYING ...
... LIKE A MACHINE ...?
HOW DOES HE...
... SOUND NOW?
EH?
N-NOW?
YEAH.
CREAK
UH...
WHEN YOU SAY "NOW"... I MEAN, AKIRA "NOW" IS THE ONLY WAY I'VE EVER KNOWN HIM...
HOW DOES HE SOUND ...?

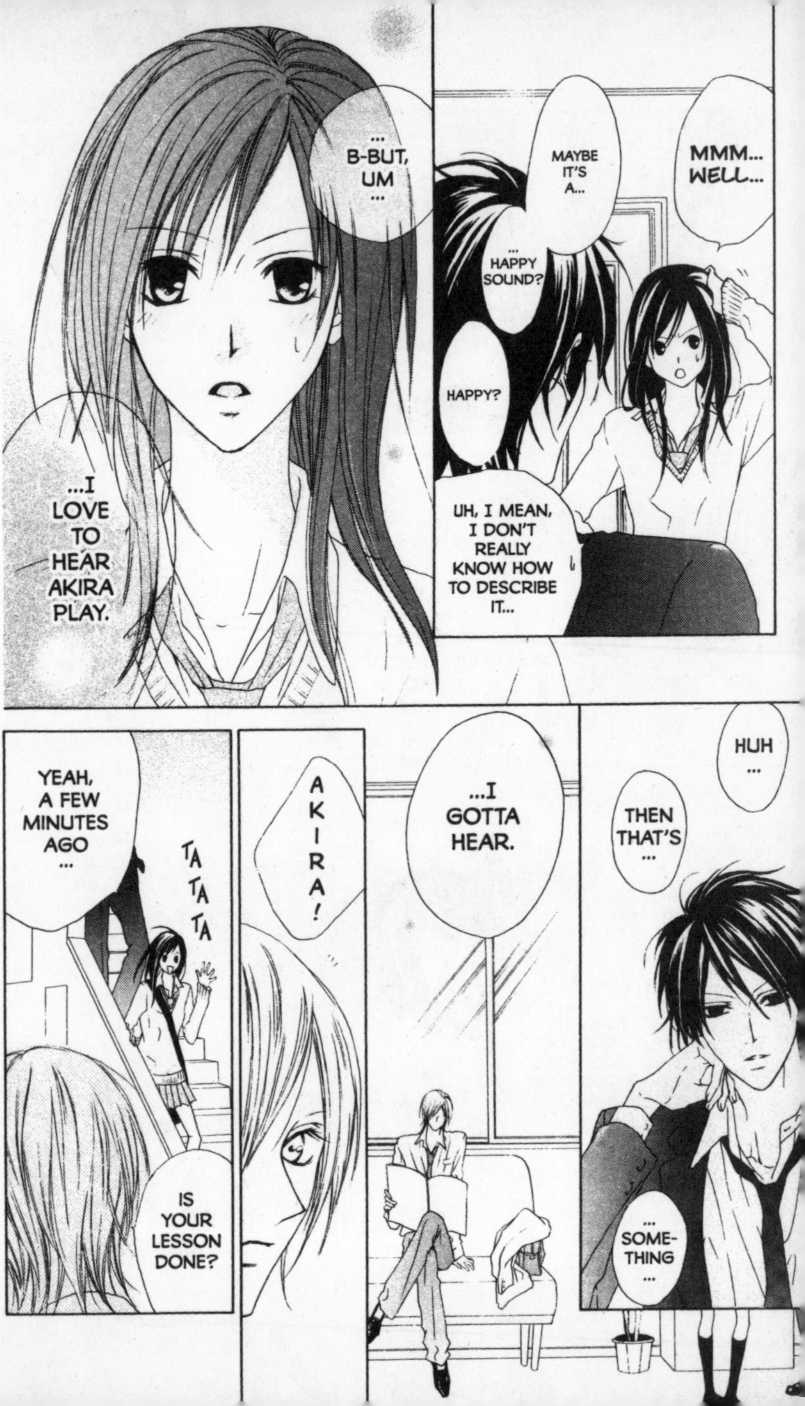

MMM... WELL...
MAYBE IT'S A...
...HAPPY SOUND?
HAPPY?
UH, I MEAN, I DON'T REALLY KNOW HOW TO DESCRIBE IT...
...B-BUT, UM ...
...I LOVE TO HEAR AKIRA PLAY.
HUH ...
THEN THAT'S ...
... SOME-THING ...
...I GOTTA HEAR.
AKIRA!
YEAH, A FEW MINUTES AGO ...
TA TA TA TA
IS YOUR LESSON DONE?

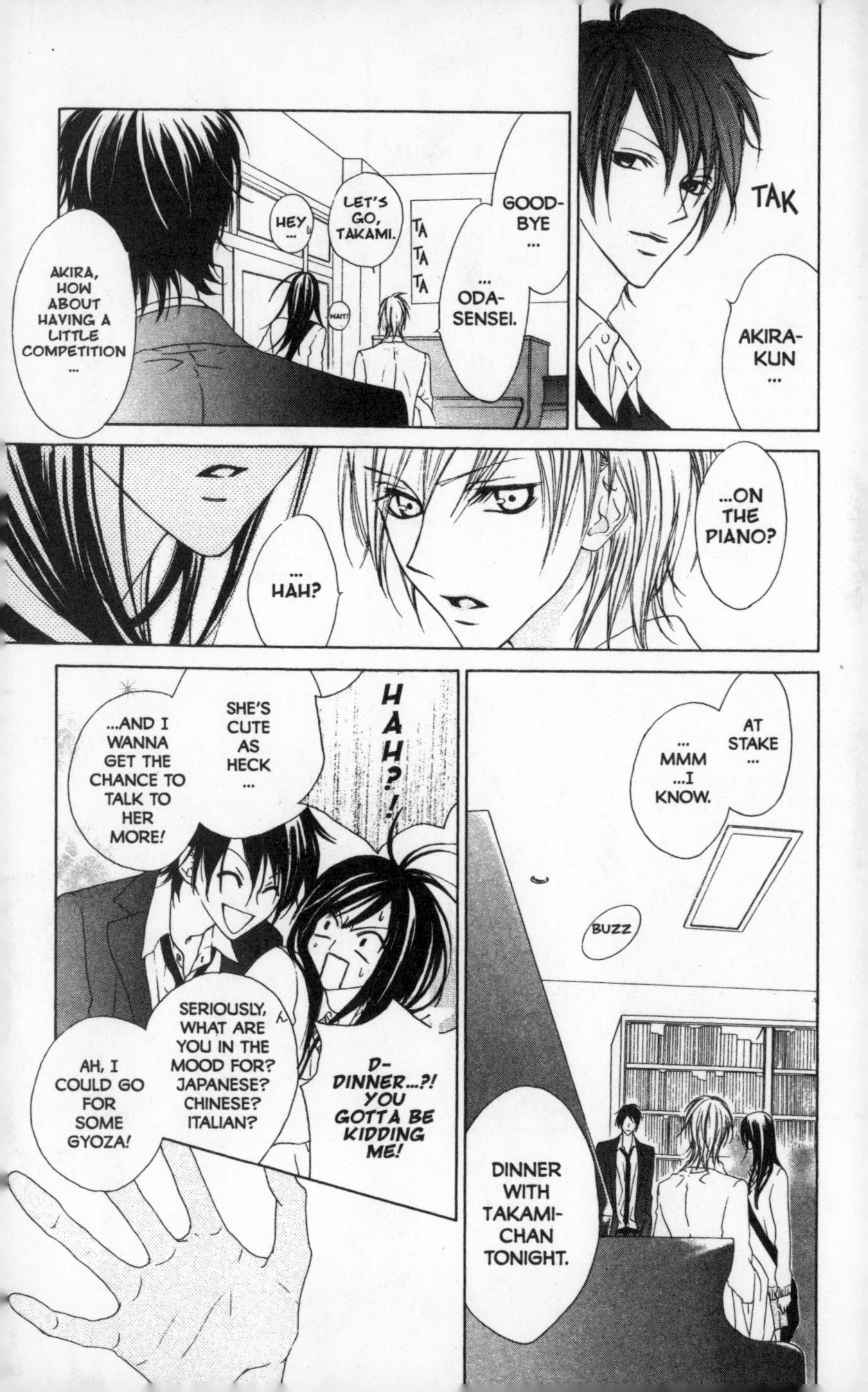
TAK
AKIRA-KUN ...
GOOD-BYE ...
... ODA-SENSEI.
TA TA TA
LET'S GO, TAKAMI.
HEY ...
WAIT!
AKIRA, HOW ABOUT HAVING A LITTLE COMPETITION ...
...ON THE PIANO?
... HAH?
AT STAKE ...
... MMM ...I KNOW.
BUZZ
DINNER WITH TAKAMI-CHAN TONIGHT.
HAH?!
SHE'S CUTE AS HECK ...
...AND I WANNA GET THE CHANCE TO TALK TO HER MORE!
D-DINNER...?! YOU GOTTA BE KIDDING ME!
SERIOUSLY, WHAT ARE YOU IN THE MOOD FOR? JAPANESE? CHINESE? ITALIAN?
AH, I COULD GO FOR SOME GYOZA!

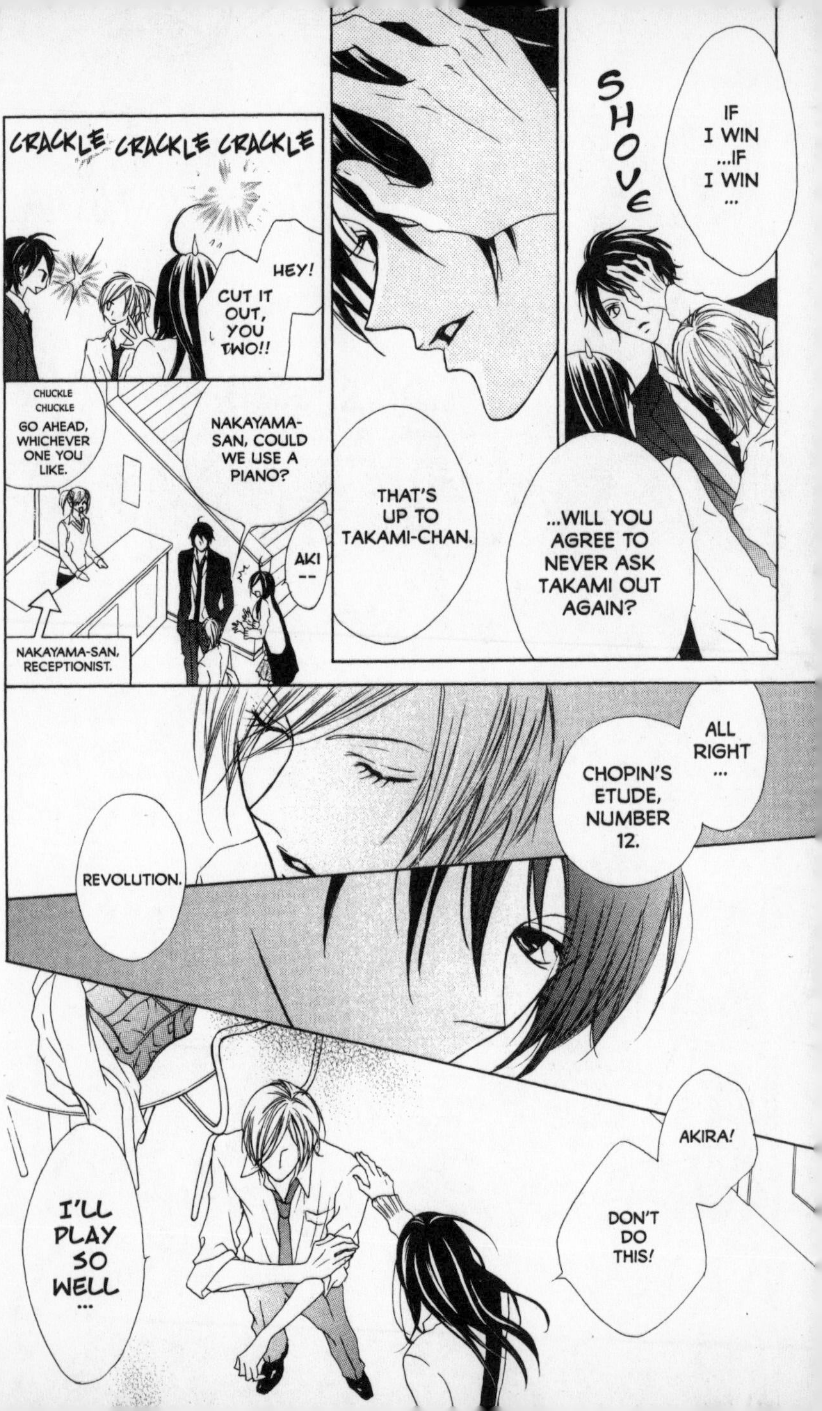
IF I WIN ...IF I WIN ...
SHOVE
...WILL YOU AGREE TO NEVER ASK TAKAMI OUT AGAIN?
THAT'S UP TO TAKAMI-CHAN.
CRACKLE CRACKLE CRACKLE
HEY!
CUT IT OUT, YOU TWO!!
NAKAYAMA-SAN, COULD WE USE A PIANO?
AKI --
CHUCKLE CHUCKLE
GO AHEAD, WHICHEVER ONE YOU LIKE.
NAKAYAMA-SAN, RECEPTIONIST.
ALL RIGHT ...
CHOPIN'S ETUDE, NUMBER 12.
REVOLUTION.
AKIRA!
DON'T DO THIS!
I'LL PLAY SO WELL ...

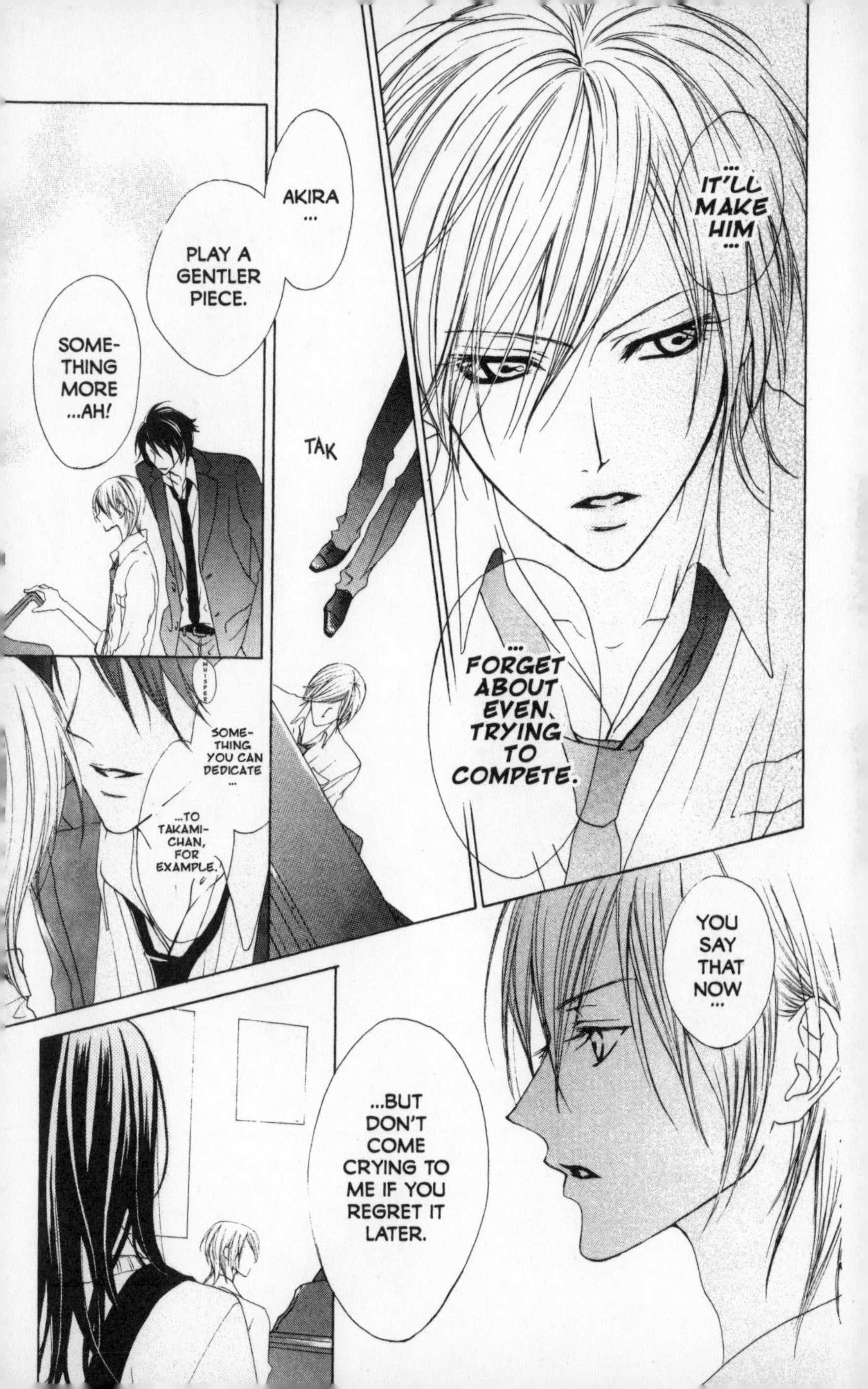

...IT'LL MAKE HIM...
...FORGET ABOUT EVEN TRYING TO COMPETE.
AKIRA...
PLAY A GENTLER PIECE.
SOMETHING MORE ...AH!
TAK
WHISPER
SOMETHING YOU CAN DEDICATE...
...TO TAKAMI-CHAN, FOR EXAMPLE.
YOU SAY THAT NOW...
...BUT DON'T COME CRYING TO ME IF YOU REGRET IT LATER.

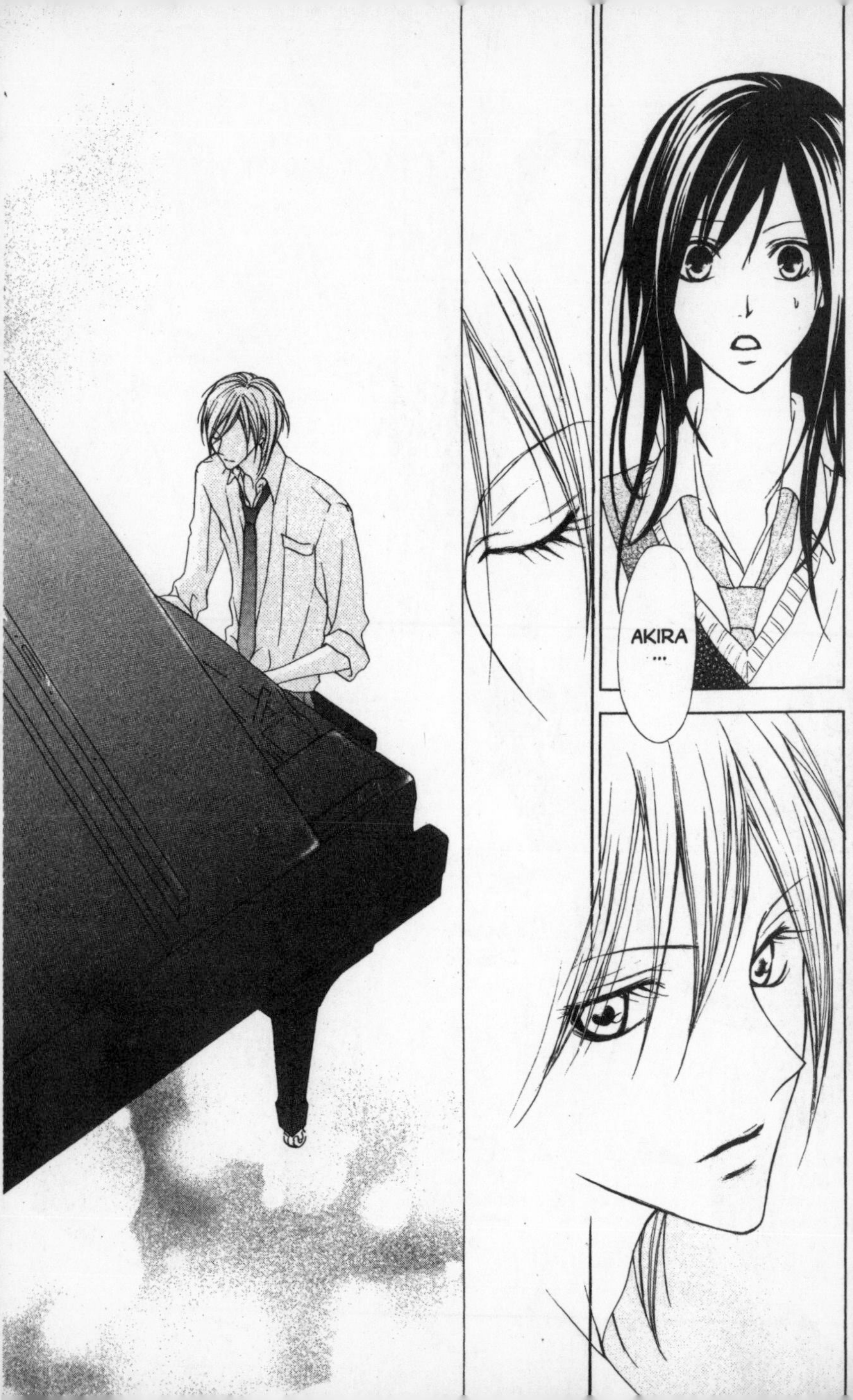
AKIRA
...

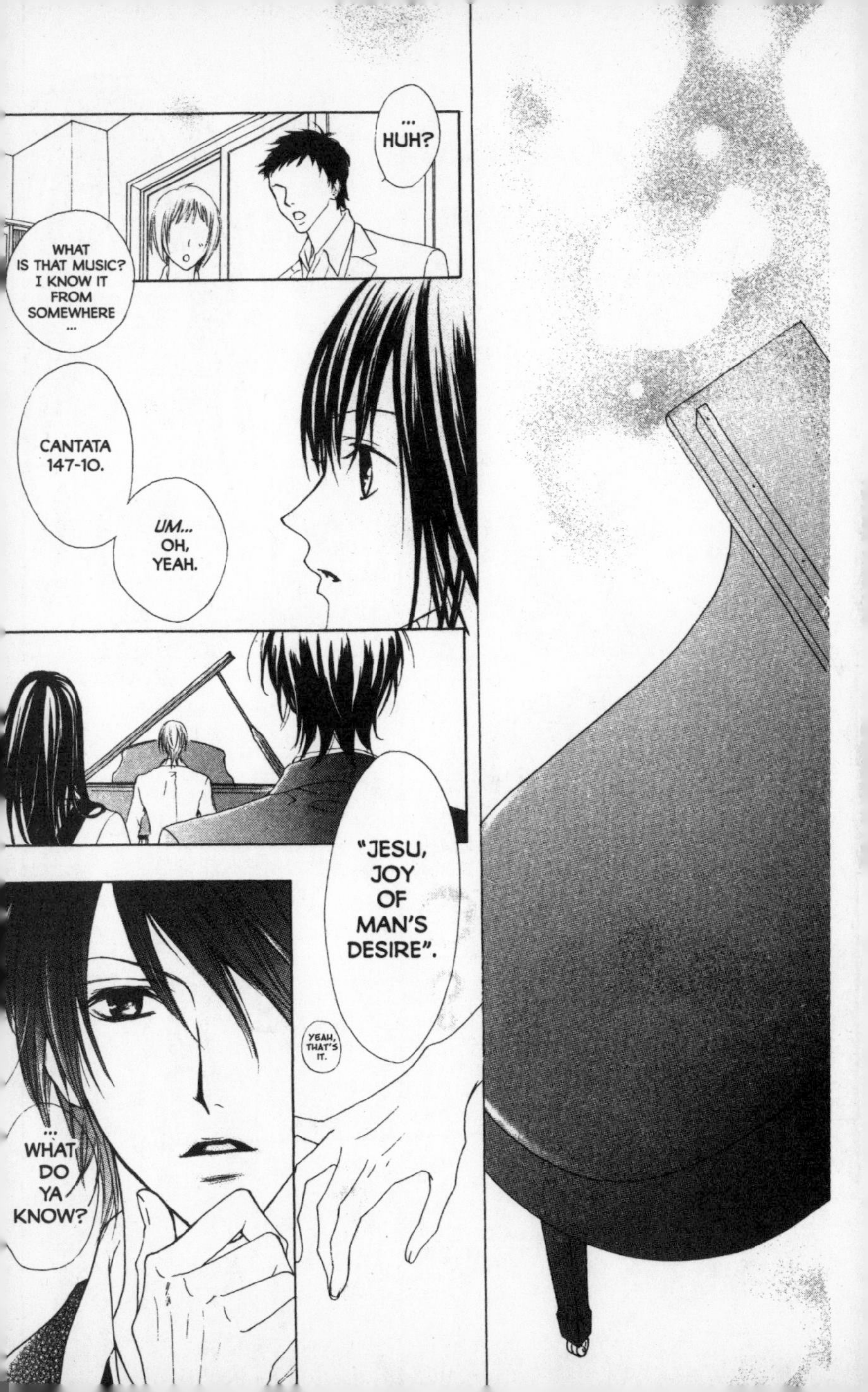
... HUH?
WHAT IS THAT MUSIC? I KNOW IT FROM SOMEWHERE ...
CANTATA 147-10.
UM... OH, YEAH.
"JESU, JOY OF MAN'S DESIRE".
YEAH, THAT'S IT.
... WHAT DO YA KNOW?

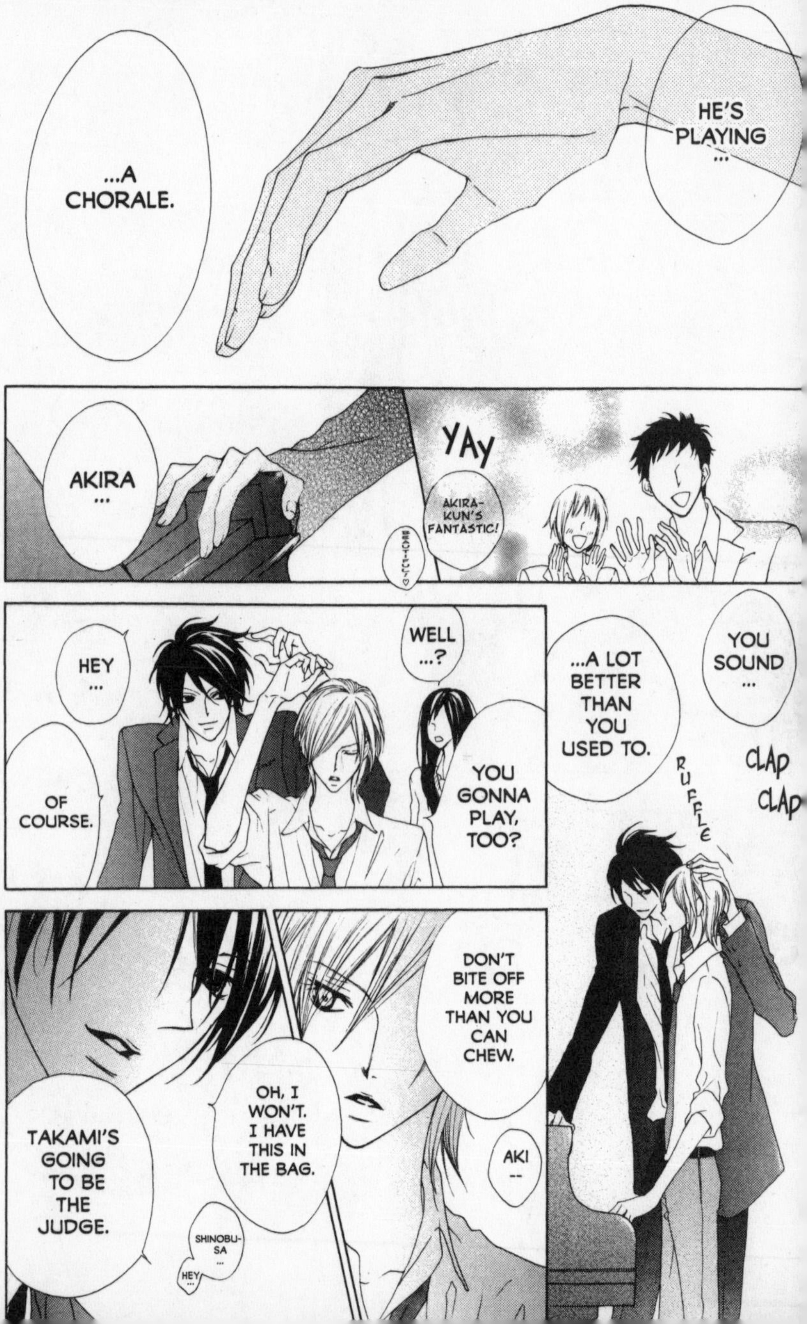
HE'S PLAYING ...
...A CHORALE.
YAY
AKIRA-KUN'S FANTASTIC!
AKIRA ...
YOU SOUND ...
...A LOT BETTER THAN YOU USED TO.
CLAP CLAP
RUFFLE
WELL ...?
YOU GONNA PLAY, TOO?
HEY ...
OF COURSE.
DON'T BITE OFF MORE THAN YOU CAN CHEW.
AKI --
OH, I WON'T. I HAVE THIS IN THE BAG.
SHINOBU-SA ...
HEY ...
TAKAMI'S GOING TO BE THE JUDGE.

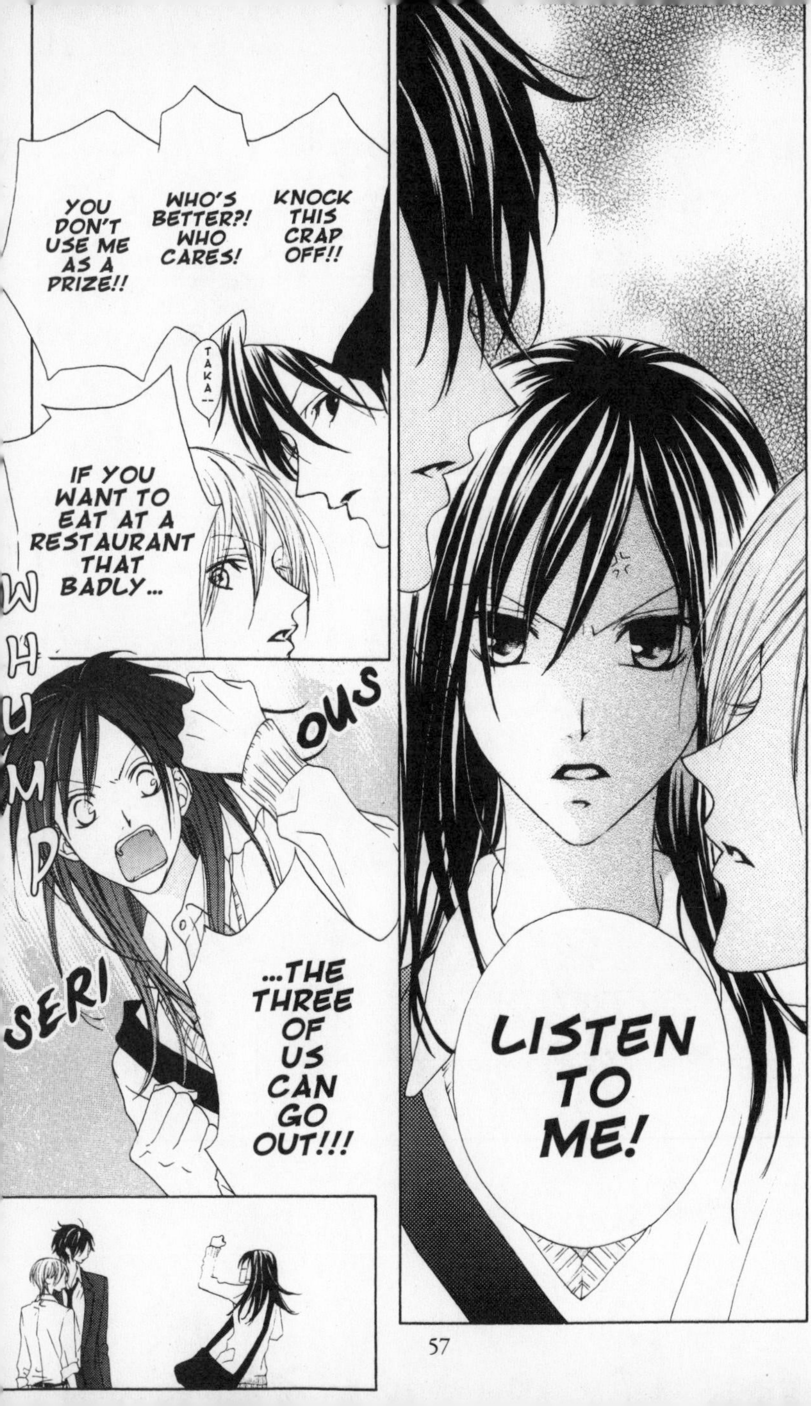
LISTEN TO ME!
KNOCK THIS CRAP OFF!!
WHO'S BETTER?! WHO CARES!
YOU DON'T USE ME AS A PRIZE!!
TAKA--
IF YOU WANT TO EAT AT A RESTAURANT THAT BADLY...
WHUMP
OUS
...THE THREE OF US CAN GO OUT!!!
SERI

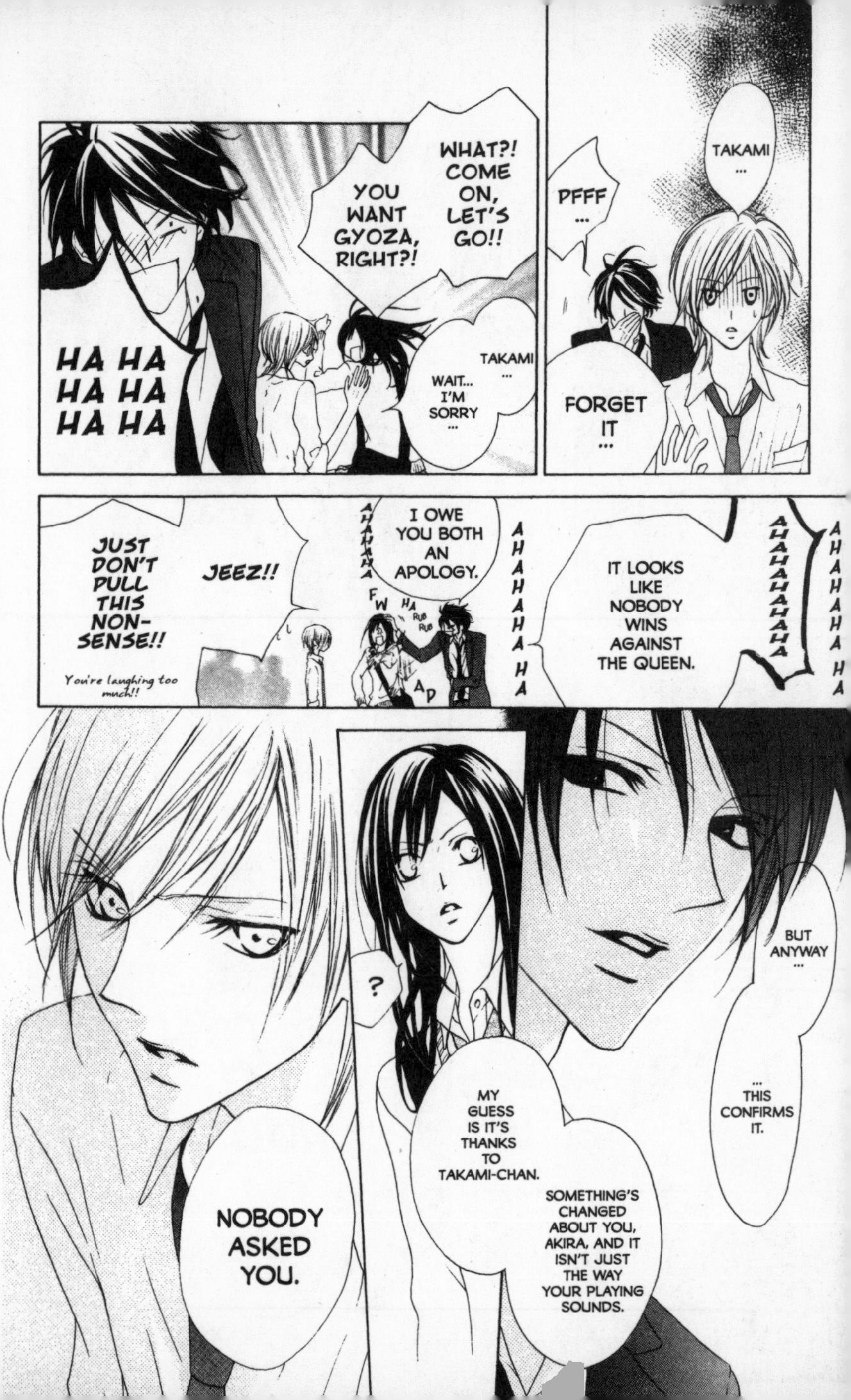
TAKAMI ...
PFFF ...
FORGET IT ...
WHAT?! COME ON, LET'S GO!!
YOU WANT GYOZA, RIGHT?!
TAKAMI ...
WAIT... I'M SORRY ...
HA HA HA HA HA HA
IT LOOKS LIKE NOBODY WINS AGAINST THE QUEEN.
I OWE YOU BOTH AN APOLOGY.
JEEZ!!
JUST DON'T PULL THIS NON-SENSE!!
You're laughing too much!!
BUT ANYWAY ...
... THIS CONFIRMS IT.
SOMETHING'S CHANGED ABOUT YOU, AKIRA, AND IT ISN'T JUST THE WAY YOUR PLAYING SOUNDS.
MY GUESS IS IT'S THANKS TO TAKAMI-CHAN.
?
NOBODY ASKED YOU.

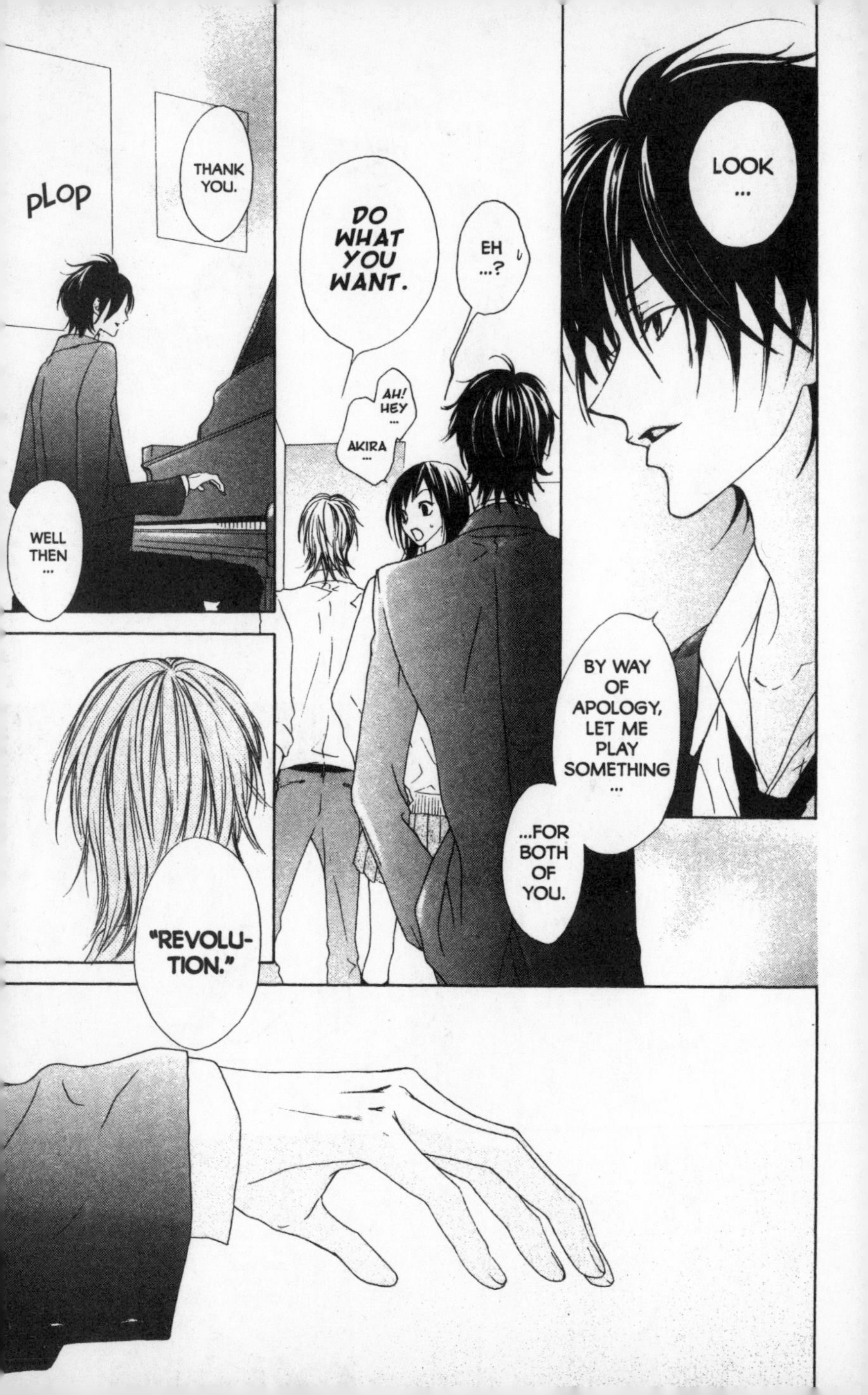
LOOK ...
BY WAY OF APOLOGY, LET ME PLAY SOMETHING ...
...FOR BOTH OF YOU.
EH ...?
DO WHAT YOU WANT.
AH! HEY ...
AKIRA ...
THANK YOU.
PLOP
WELL THEN ...
"REVOLUTION."

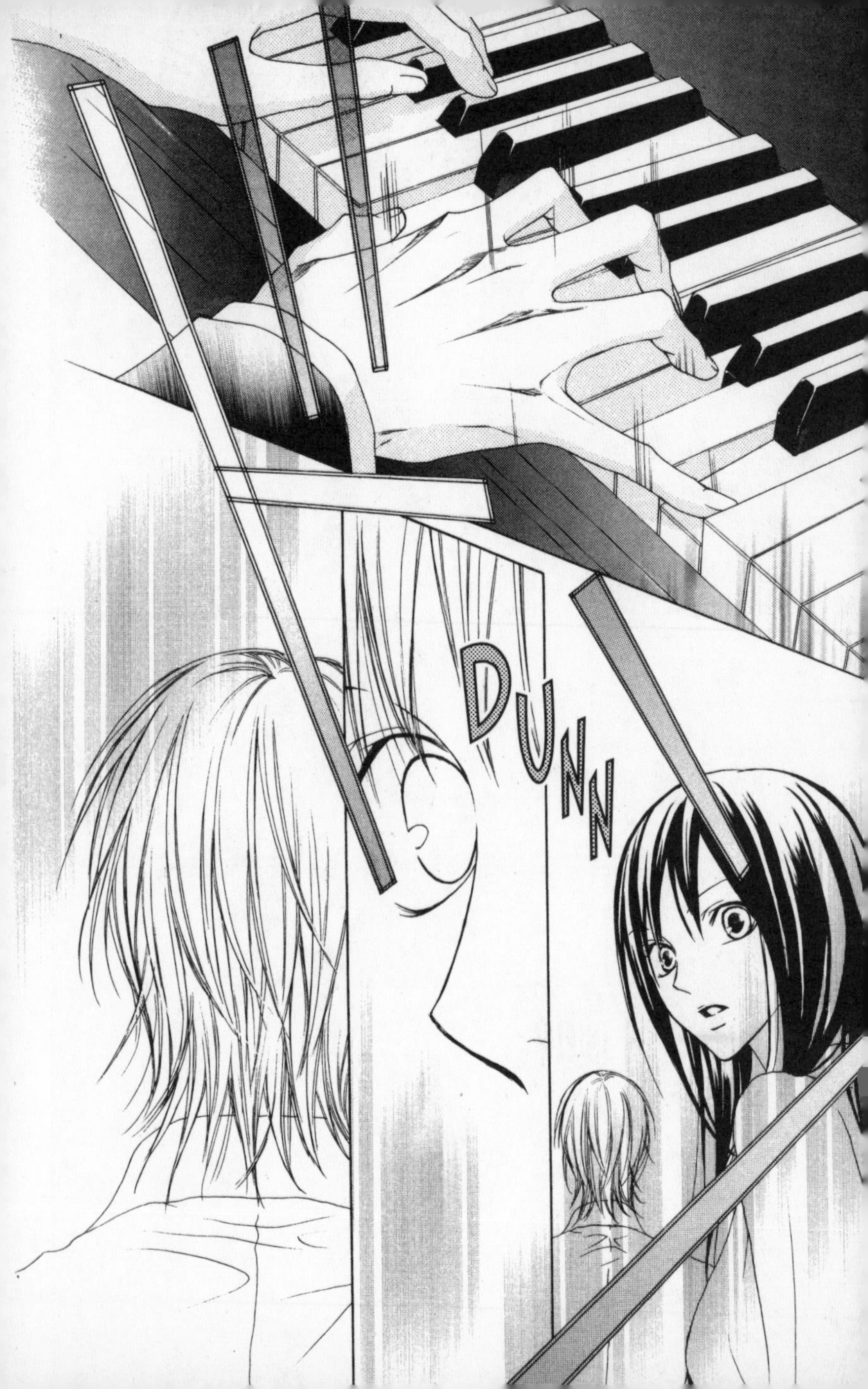
DUNN

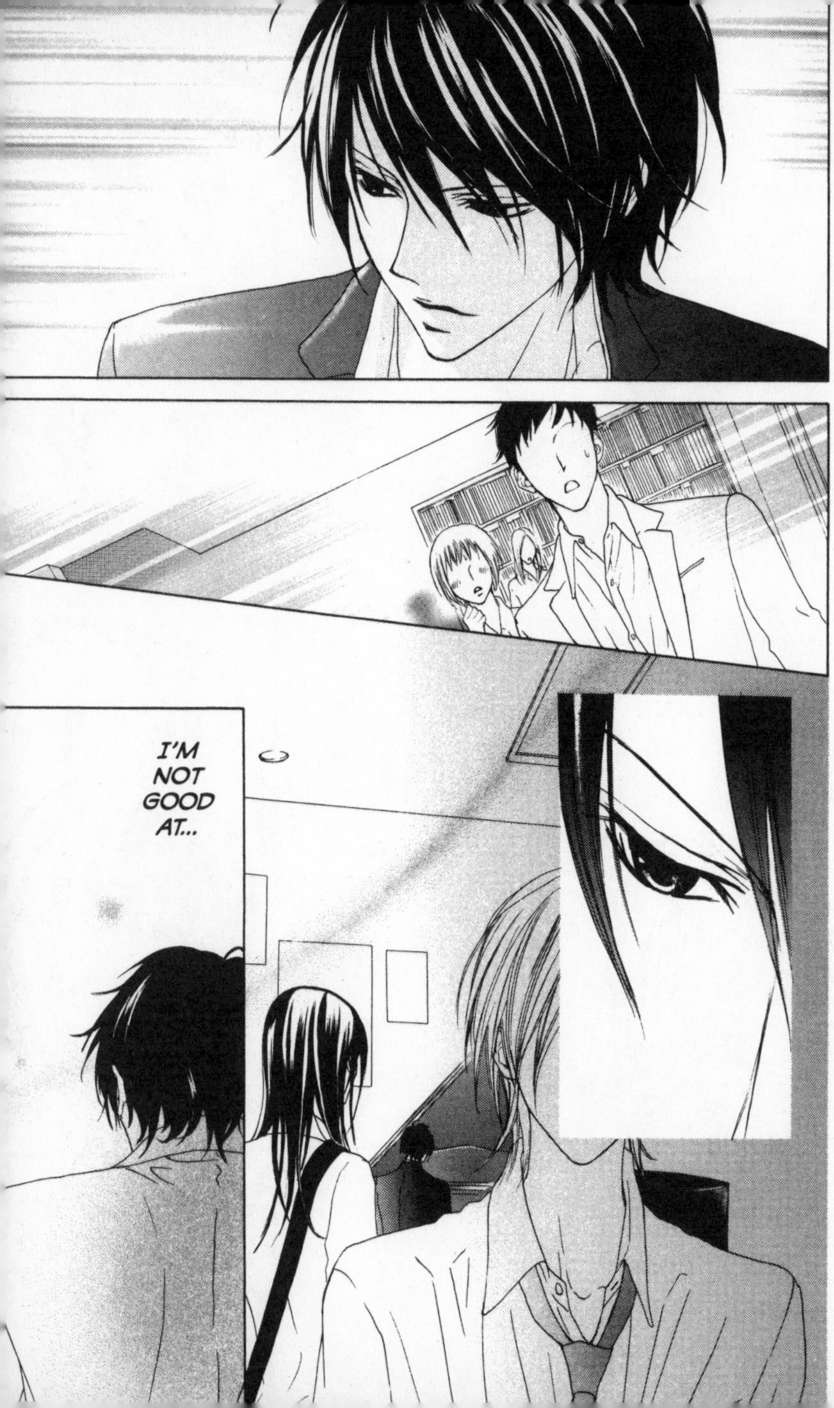
I'M NOT GOOD AT...

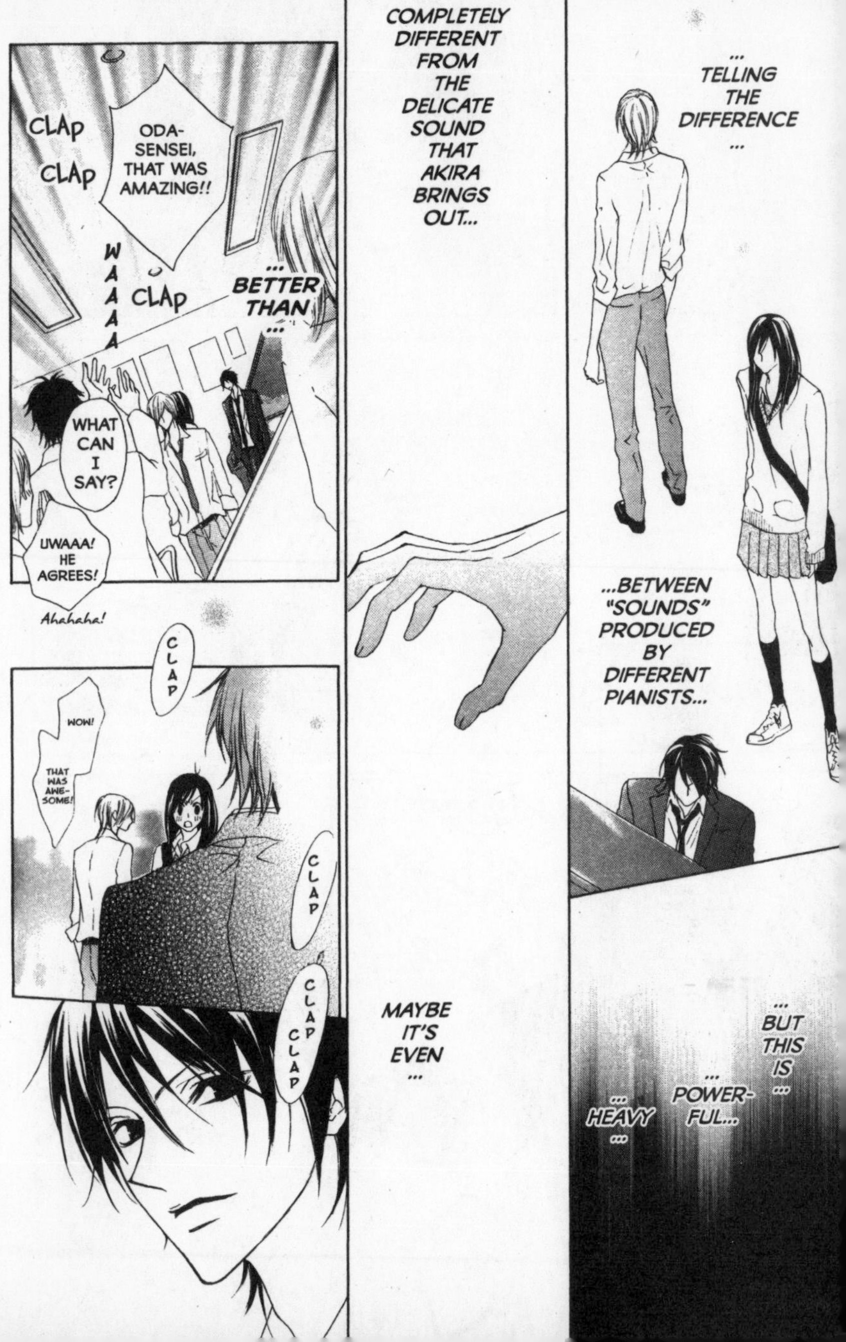
...TELLING THE DIFFERENCE...
...BETWEEN "SOUNDS" PRODUCED BY DIFFERENT PIANISTS...
...BUT THIS IS...
...POWERFUL...
...HEAVY...
COMPLETELY DIFFERENT FROM THE DELICATE SOUND THAT AKIRA BRINGS OUT...
MAYBE IT'S EVEN...
ODA-SENSEI, THAT WAS AMAZING!!
CLAp CLAp
...BETTER THAN...
CLAp
WAAAAA
WHAT CAN I SAY?
UWAAA! HE AGREES!
Ahahaha!
CLAP
WOW!
THAT WAS AWESOME!
CLAP
CLAP CLAP CLAP

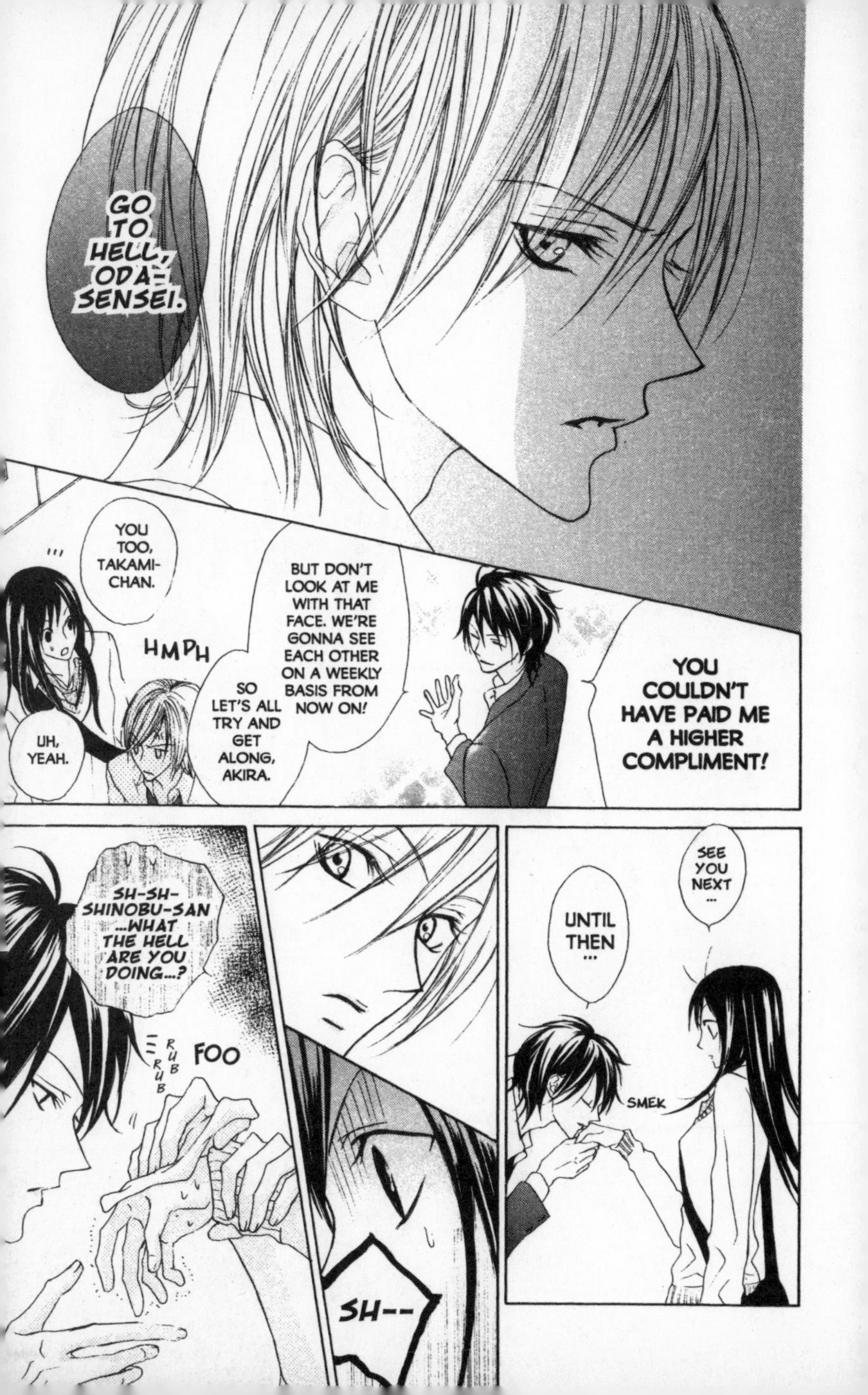
GO TO HELL, ODA-SENSEI.
YOU COULDN'T HAVE PAID ME A HIGHER COMPLIMENT!
BUT DON'T LOOK AT ME WITH THAT FACE. WE'RE GONNA SEE EACH OTHER ON A WEEKLY BASIS FROM NOW ON!
SO LET'S ALL TRY AND GET ALONG, AKIRA.
HMPH
YOU TOO, TAKAMI-CHAN.
UH, YEAH.
SEE YOU NEXT ...
UNTIL THEN ...
SMEK
SH--
SH-SH-SHINOBU-SAN ...WHAT THE HELL ARE YOU DOING...?
RUB RUB
FOO

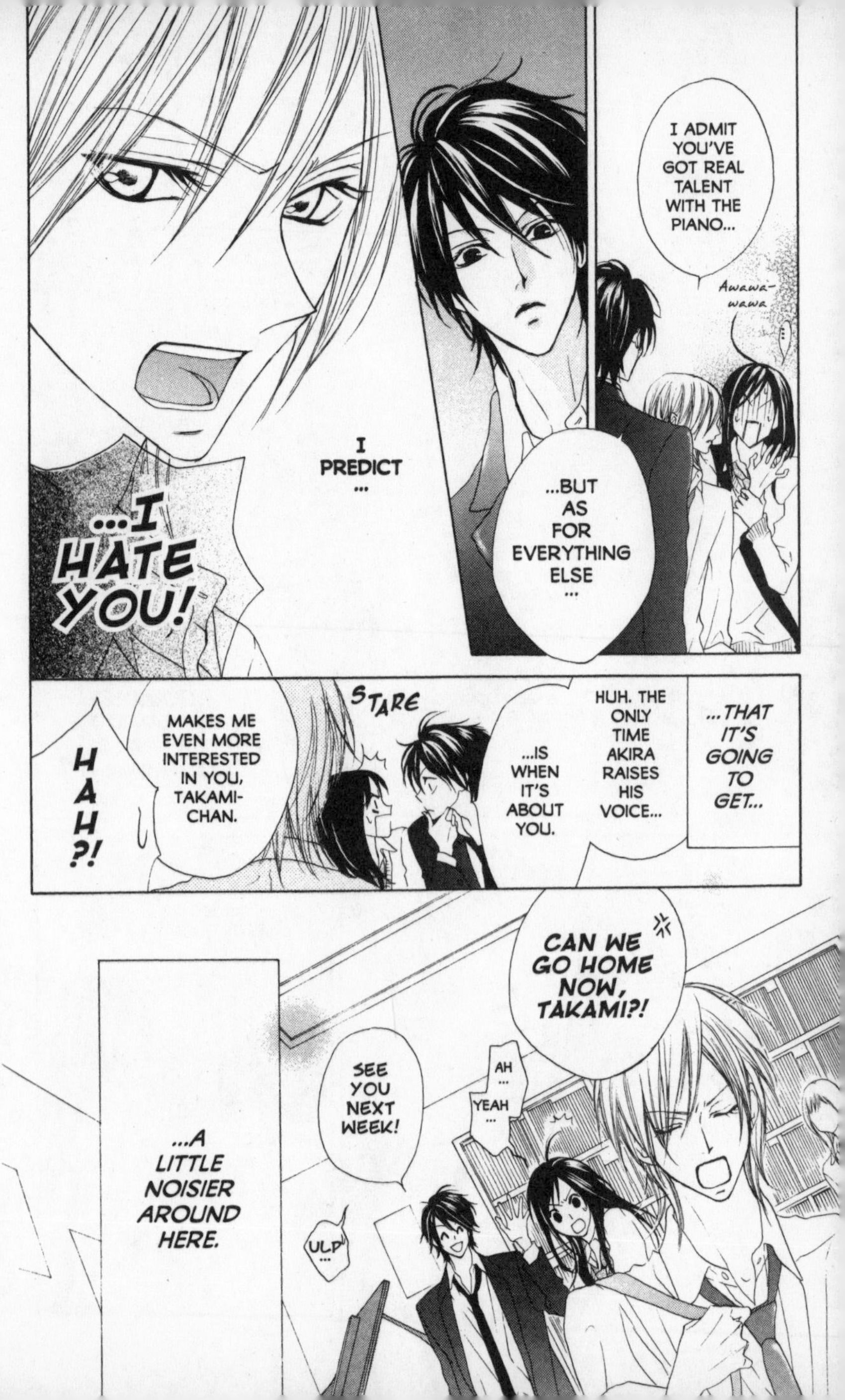
I ADMIT YOU'VE GOT REAL TALENT WITH THE PIANO...
Awawa-wawa
...BUT AS FOR EVERYTHING ELSE...
I PREDICT...
...I HATE YOU!
...THAT IT'S GOING TO GET...
HUH. THE ONLY TIME AKIRA RAISES HIS VOICE...
...IS WHEN IT'S ABOUT YOU.
STARE
MAKES ME EVEN MORE INTERESTED IN YOU, TAKAMI-CHAN.
HAH?!
CAN WE GO HOME NOW, TAKAMI?!
AH... YEAH...
SEE YOU NEXT WEEK!
ULP...
...A LITTLE NOISIER AROUND HERE.

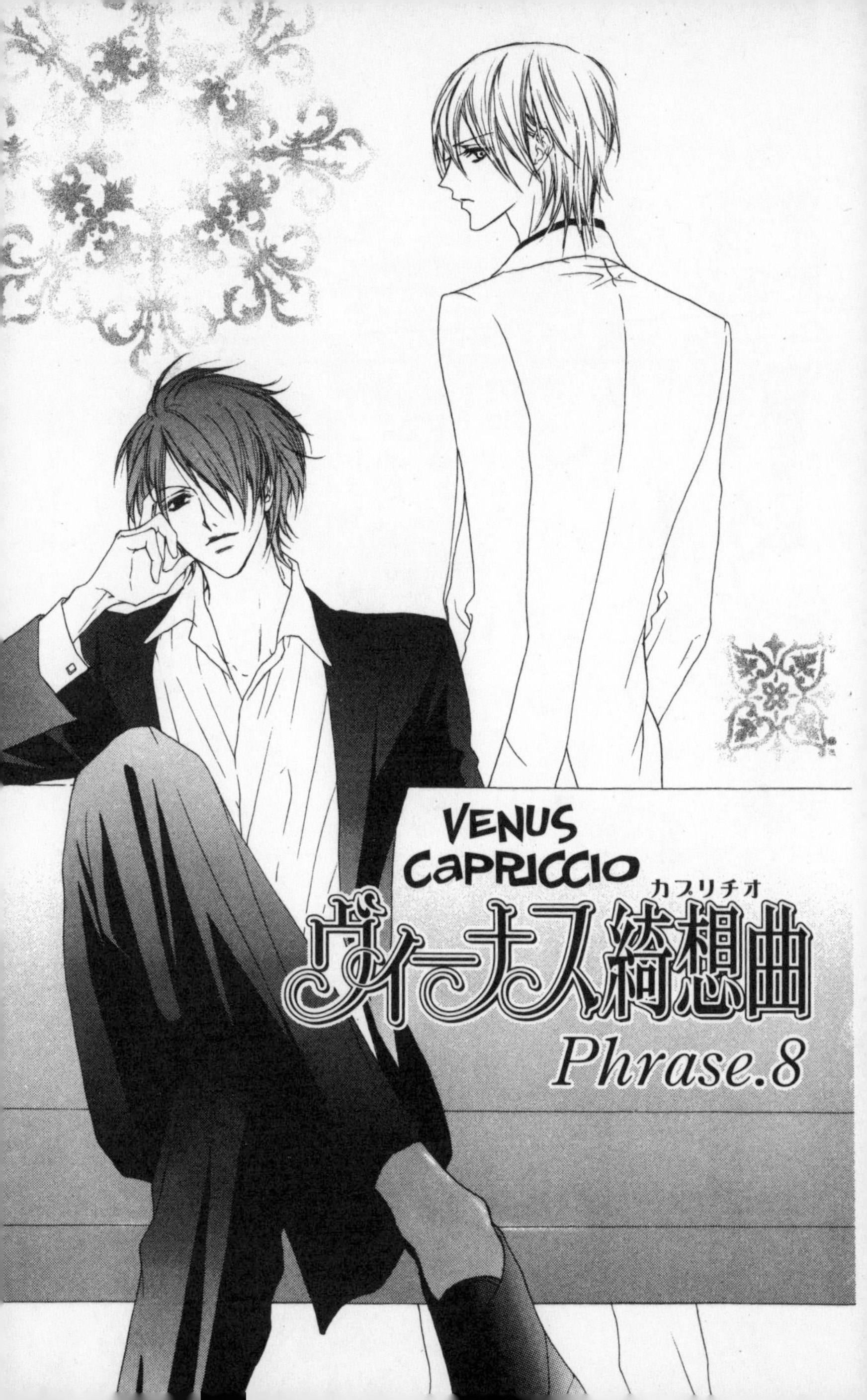
VENUS CAPRICCIO
カプリチオ
ヴィーナス綺想曲
Phrase.8

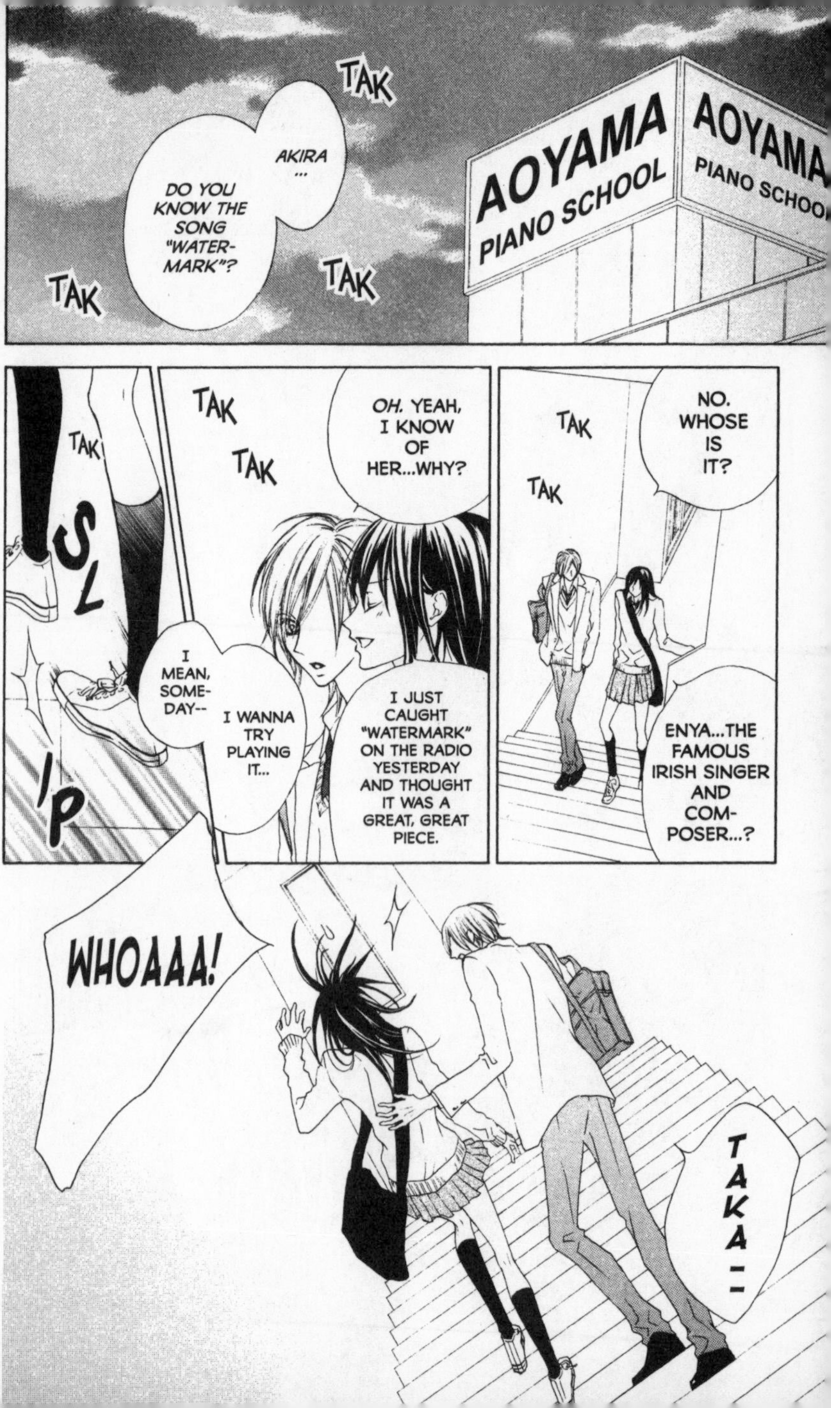
AOYAMA PIANO SCHOOL
AOYAMA PIANO SCHOOL
TAK
AKIRA ...
DO YOU KNOW THE SONG "WATER-MARK"?
TAK
TAK
NO. WHOSE IS IT?
TAK
TAK
ENYA...THE FAMOUS IRISH SINGER AND COM-POSER...?
OH. YEAH, I KNOW OF HER...WHY?
TAK
TAK
I JUST CAUGHT "WATERMARK" ON THE RADIO YESTERDAY AND THOUGHT IT WAS A GREAT, GREAT PIECE.
I WANNA TRY PLAYING IT...
I MEAN, SOME-DAY--
TAK
SLIP
TAKA--
WHOAAA!

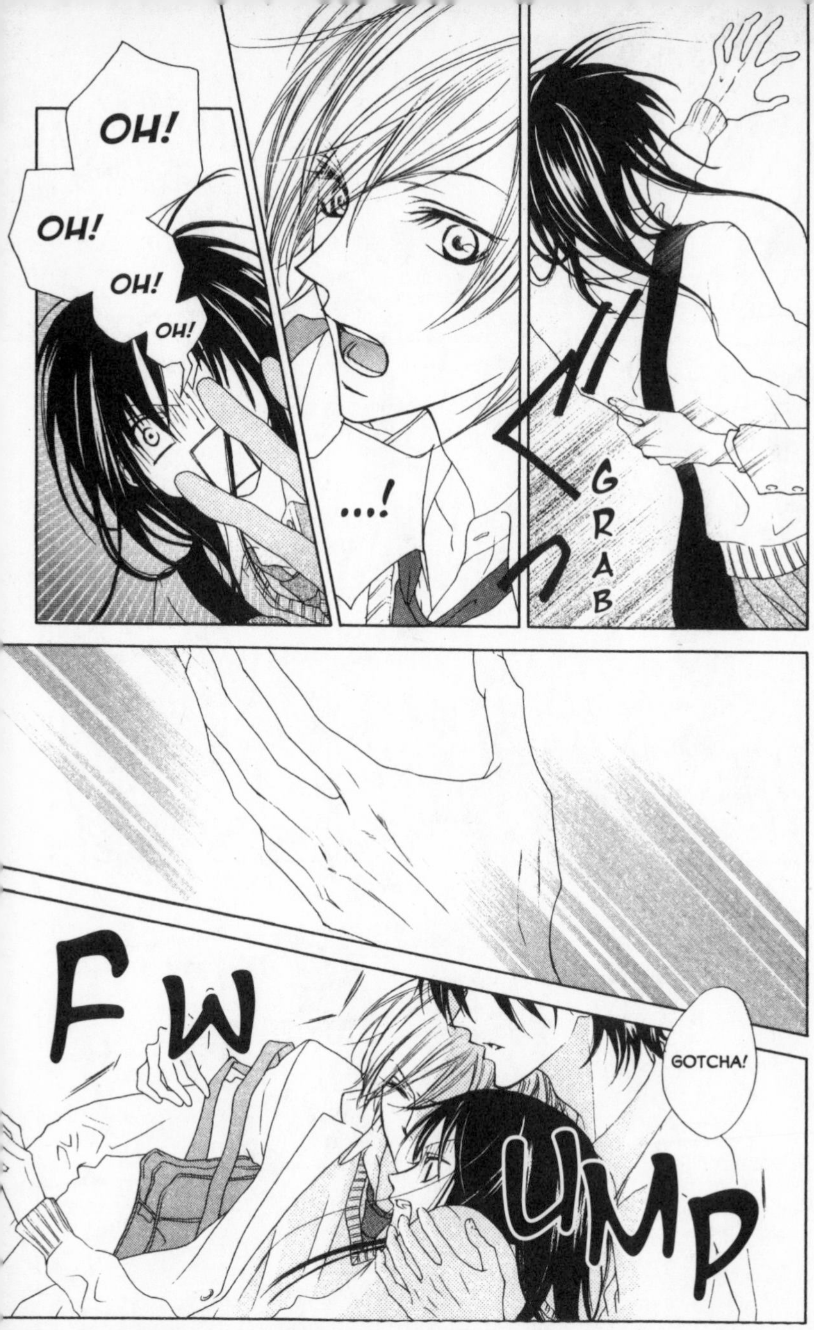
GRAB
...!
OH!
OH!
OH!
OH!
GOTCHA!
FW
UMP

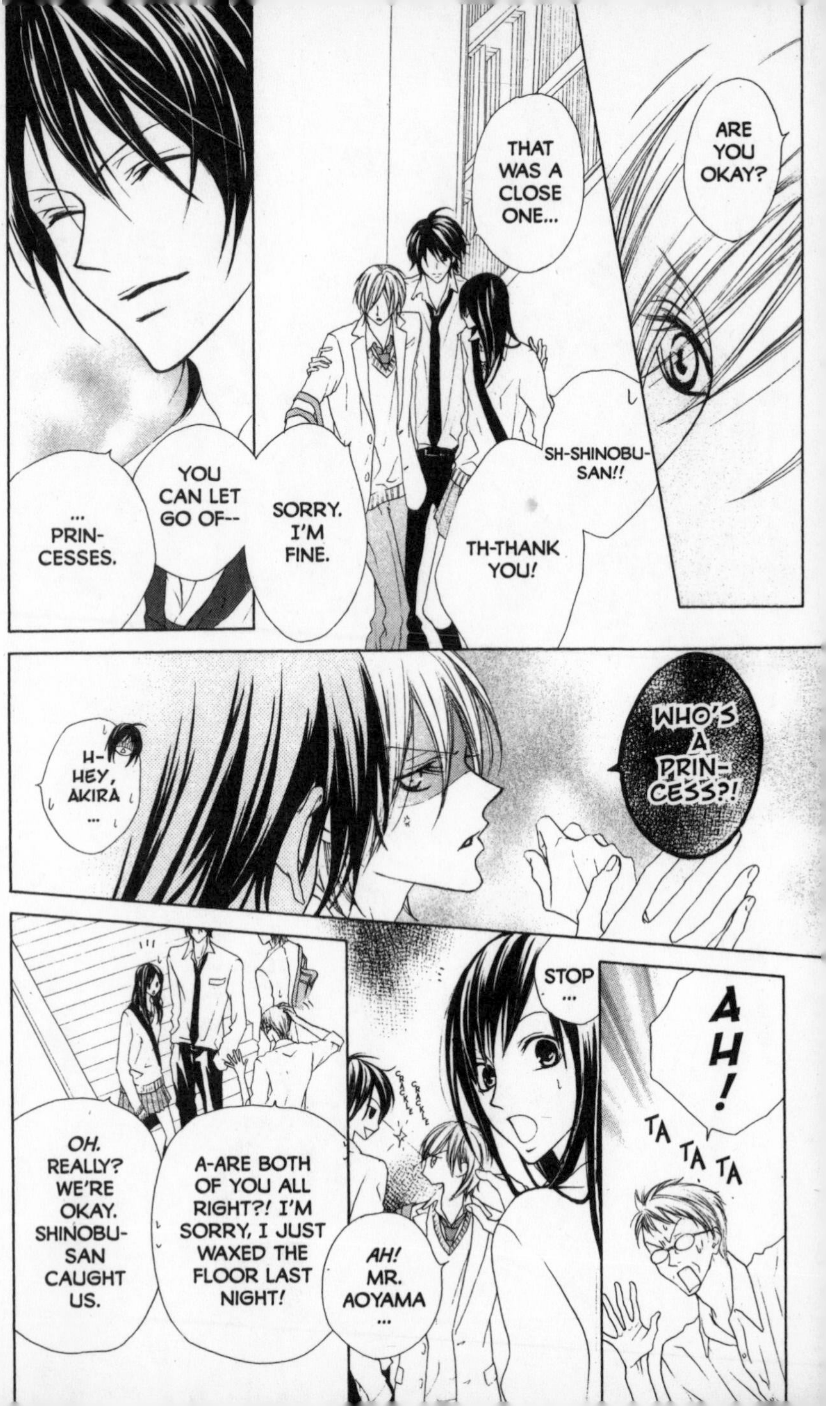
ARE YOU OKAY?
SH-SHINOBU-SAN!!
THAT WAS A CLOSE ONE...
TH-THANK YOU!
SORRY. I'M FINE.
YOU CAN LET GO OF--
... PRINCESSES.
WHO'S A PRINCESS?!
H-HEY, AKIRA ...
AH!
TA TA TA
STOP ...
AH! MR. AOYAMA ...
A-ARE BOTH OF YOU ALL RIGHT?! I'M SORRY, I JUST WAXED THE FLOOR LAST NIGHT!
OH. REALLY? WE'RE OKAY. SHINOBU-SAN CAUGHT US.

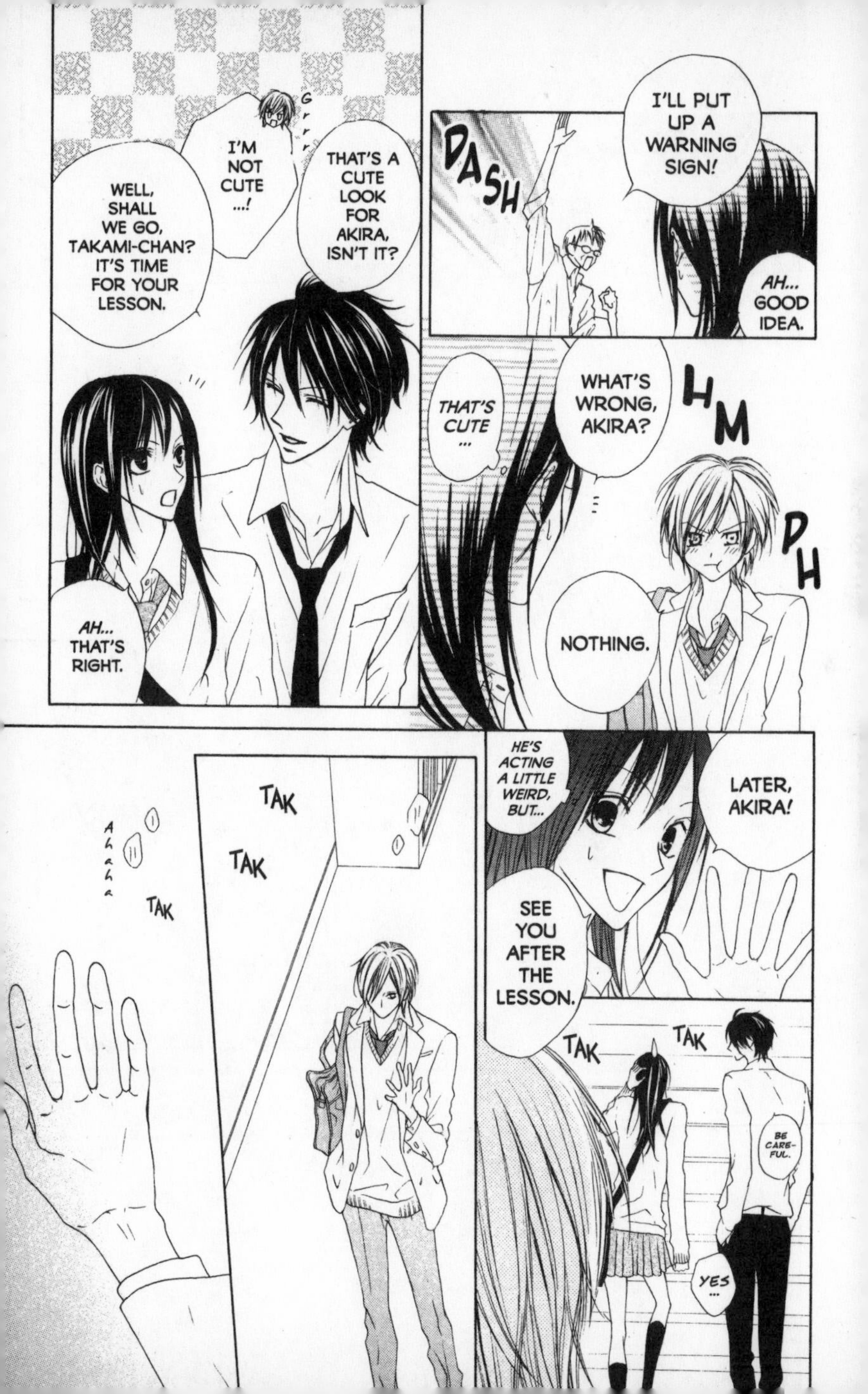
I'LL PUT UP A WARNING SIGN!
DASH
AH... GOOD IDEA.
WHAT'S WRONG, AKIRA?
THAT'S CUTE...
HMPH
NOTHING.
THAT'S A CUTE LOOK FOR AKIRA, ISN'T IT?
I'M NOT CUTE...!
Grrr
WELL, SHALL WE GO, TAKAMI-CHAN? IT'S TIME FOR YOUR LESSON.
AH... THAT'S RIGHT.
LATER, AKIRA!
HE'S ACTING A LITTLE WEIRD, BUT...
SEE YOU AFTER THE LESSON.
TAK
TAK
BE CAREFUL.
YES...
TAK
TAK
TAK
Ahaha

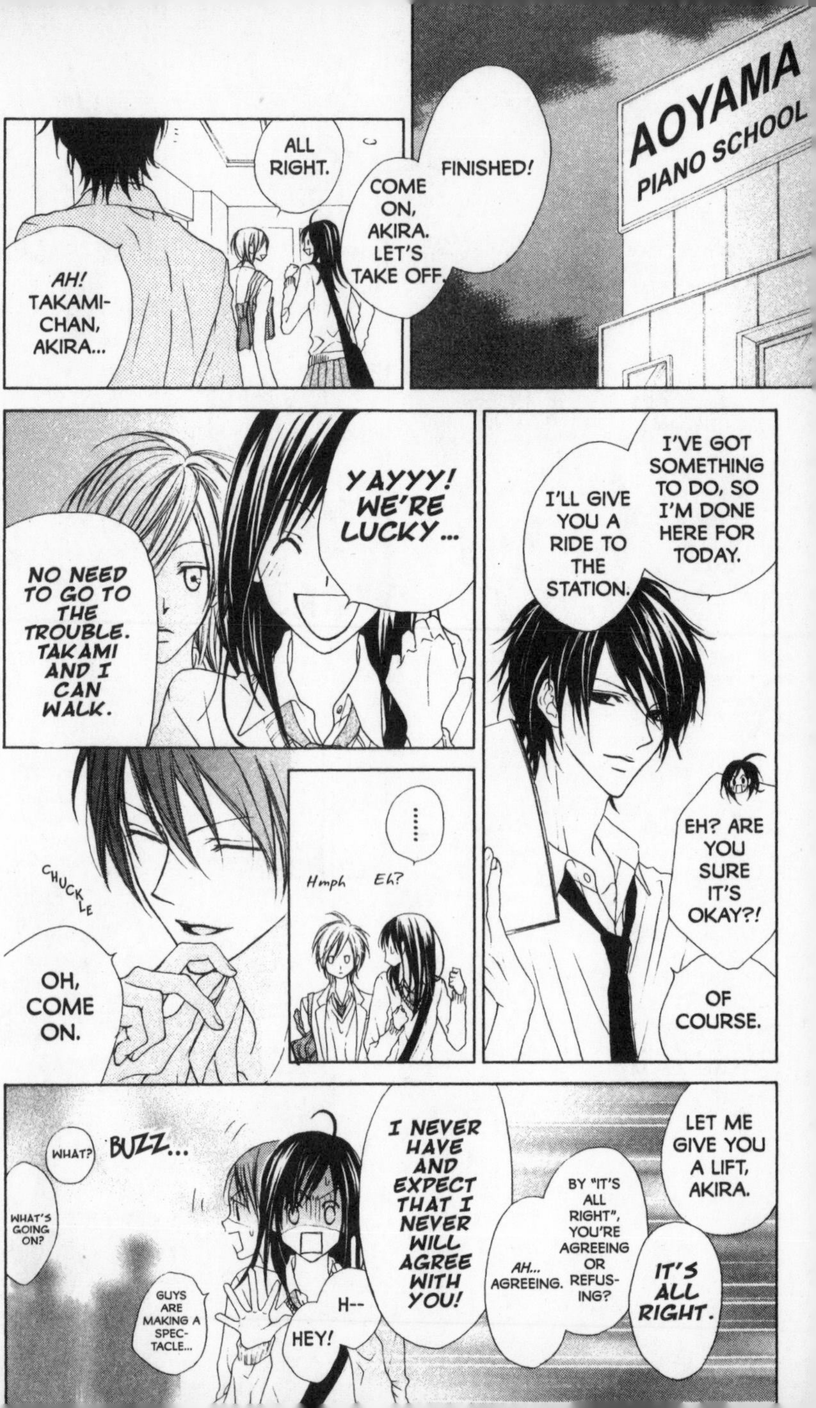
AOYAMA PIANO SCHOOL
FINISHED!
COME ON, AKIRA. LET'S TAKE OFF.
ALL RIGHT.
AH! TAKAMI-CHAN, AKIRA...
I'VE GOT SOMETHING TO DO, SO I'M DONE HERE FOR TODAY.
I'LL GIVE YOU A RIDE TO THE STATION.
EH? ARE YOU SURE IT'S OKAY?!
OF COURSE.
YAYYY! WE'RE LUCKY...
NO NEED TO GO TO THE TROUBLE. TAKAMI AND I CAN WALK.
......
Eh?
Hmph
CHUCKLE
OH, COME ON.
LET ME GIVE YOU A LIFT, AKIRA.
IT'S ALL RIGHT.
BY "IT'S ALL RIGHT", YOU'RE AGREEING OR REFUSING?
AH... AGREEING.
I NEVER HAVE AND EXPECT THAT I NEVER WILL AGREE WITH YOU!
H--
HEY!
BUZZ...
WHAT?
WHAT'S GOING ON?
GUYS ARE MAKING A SPECTACLE...

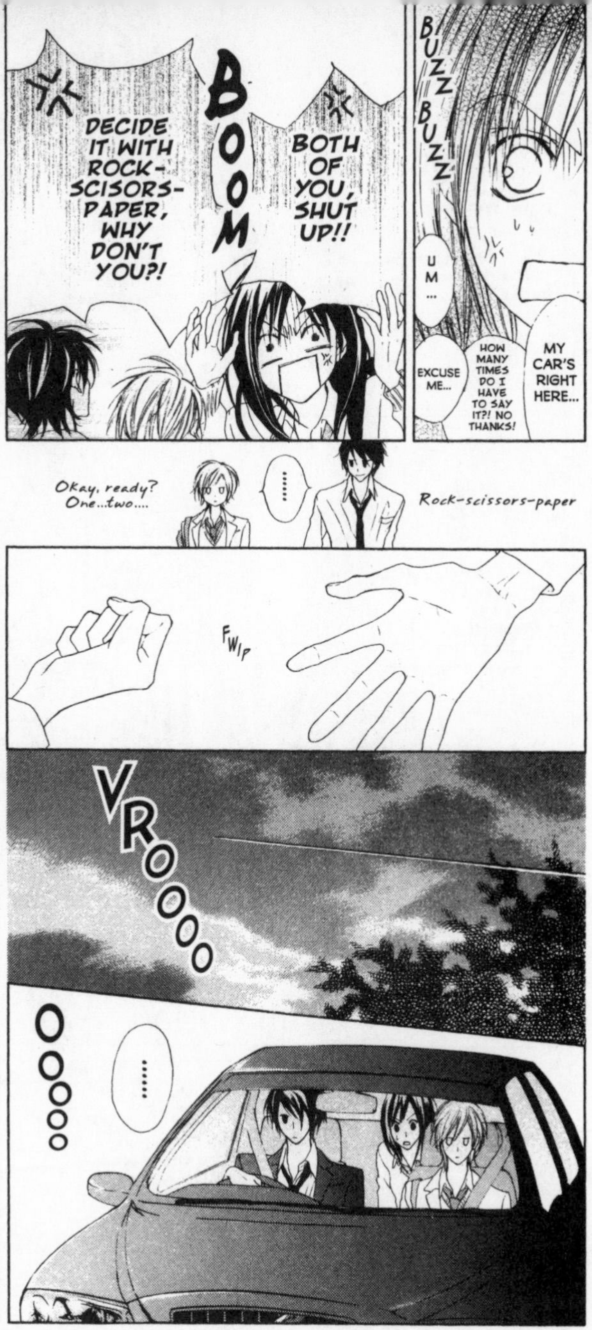
BUZZ BUZZ
UM...
MY CAR'S RIGHT HERE...
HOW MANY TIMES DO I HAVE TO SAY IT?! NO THANKS!
EXCUSE ME...
BOTH OF YOU, SHUT UP!!
BOOM
DECIDE IT WITH ROCK-SCISORS-PAPER, WHY DON'T YOU?!
Rock-scissors-paper
......
Okay, ready? One...two....
FWIP
VROOOOOOOOOO
......

3

RECENTLY, IT'S FINALLY GOTTEN EASY TO DRAW AKIRA.

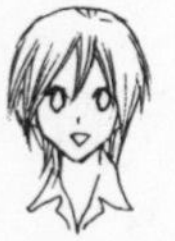

IT'S GOTTEN EASIER COLORING HIS HAIR BLACK FOR THE COLORED ART, TOO.

ON THE OTHER HAND, IT'S GOTTEN HARDER FOR ME TO DRAW TAKAMI.

I DON'T KNOW WHY.

I WANNA GO BACK TO THE BASICS AND STUDY ROUGH SKETCHING. PERSPECTIVE, TOO.

THERE ARE A LOT OF THINGS I WANT TO TRY, BUT WITH MY CURRENT TIME-MANAGEMENT ABILITY, I'D SAY THE CHANCES OF MY ENGAGING IN ANY OF THEM ARE SLIM TO NONE.

SO THAT'S WHAT I HAVE TO WORK ON FIRST, MY TIME-MANAGEMENT SKILLS...

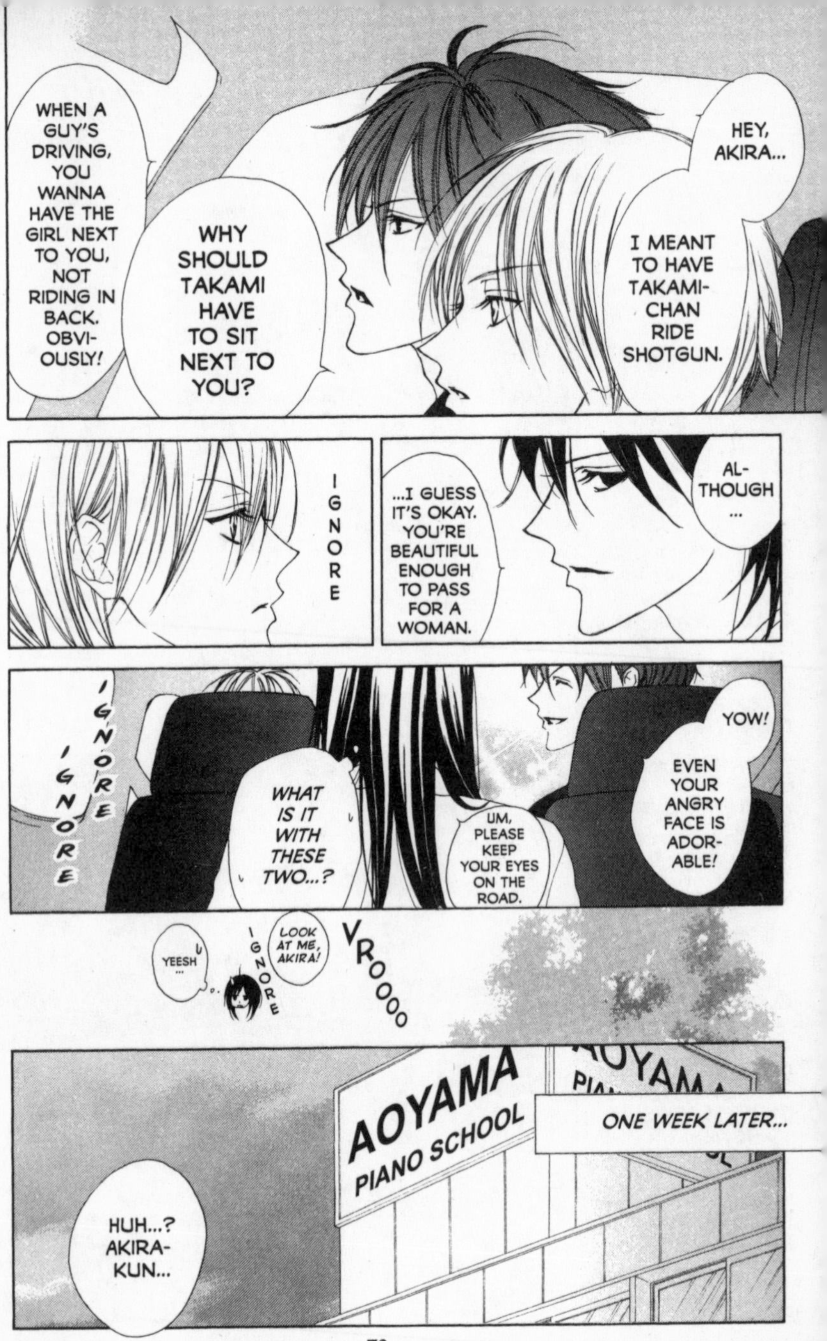
HEY, AKIRA...
I MEANT TO HAVE TAKAMI-CHAN RIDE SHOTGUN.
WHY SHOULD TAKAMI HAVE TO SIT NEXT TO YOU?
WHEN A GUY'S DRIVING, YOU WANNA HAVE THE GIRL NEXT TO YOU, NOT RIDING IN BACK. OBVI-OUSLY!
AL-THOUGH ...
...I GUESS IT'S OKAY. YOU'RE BEAUTIFUL ENOUGH TO PASS FOR A WOMAN.
IGNORE
YOW!
EVEN YOUR ANGRY FACE IS ADOR-ABLE!
UM, PLEASE KEEP YOUR EYES ON THE ROAD.
WHAT IS IT WITH THESE TWO...?
IGNORE
IGNORE
VROOOOO
LOOK AT ME, AKIRA!
IGNORE
YEESH ...
AOYAMA PIANO SCHOOL
AOYAMA
ONE WEEK LATER...
HUH...? AKIRA-KUN...

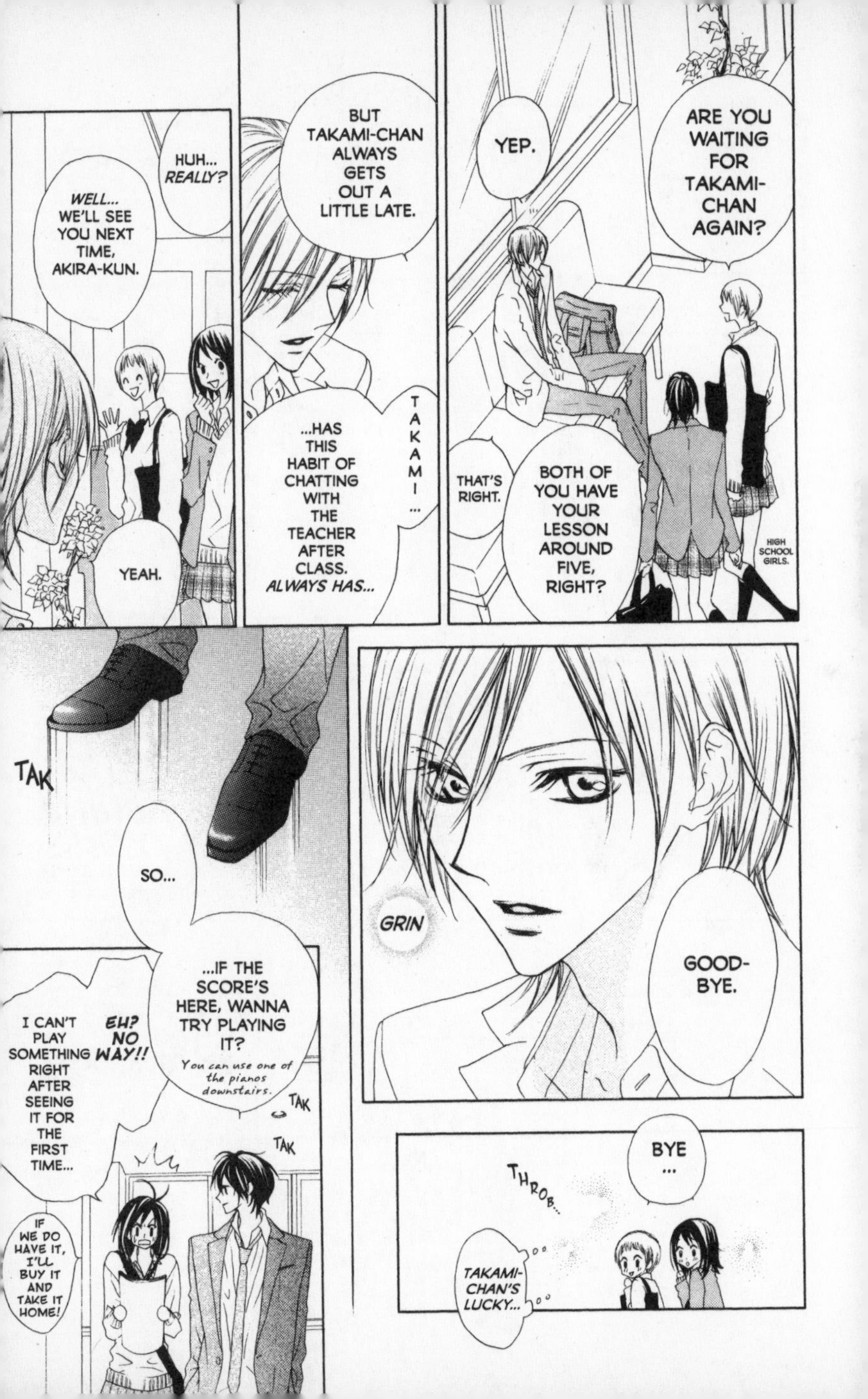
ARE YOU WAITING FOR TAKAMI-CHAN AGAIN?
YEP.
BOTH OF YOU HAVE YOUR LESSON AROUND FIVE, RIGHT?
THAT'S RIGHT.
HIGH SCHOOL GIRLS.
BUT TAKAMI-CHAN ALWAYS GETS OUT A LITTLE LATE.
TAKAMI...
...HAS THIS HABIT OF CHATTING WITH THE TEACHER AFTER CLASS. *ALWAYS HAS...*
HUH... *REALLY?*
WELL... WE'LL SEE YOU NEXT TIME, AKIRA-KUN.
YEAH.
GRIN
GOOD-BYE.
BYE ...
THROB...
TAKAMI-CHAN'S LUCKY...
TAK
SO...
...IF THE SCORE'S HERE, WANNA TRY PLAYING IT?
You can use one of the pianos downstairs.
TAK
TAK
EH? NO WAY!!
I CAN'T PLAY SOMETHING RIGHT AFTER SEEING IT FOR THE FIRST TIME...
IF WE DO HAVE IT, I'LL BUY IT AND TAKE IT HOME!

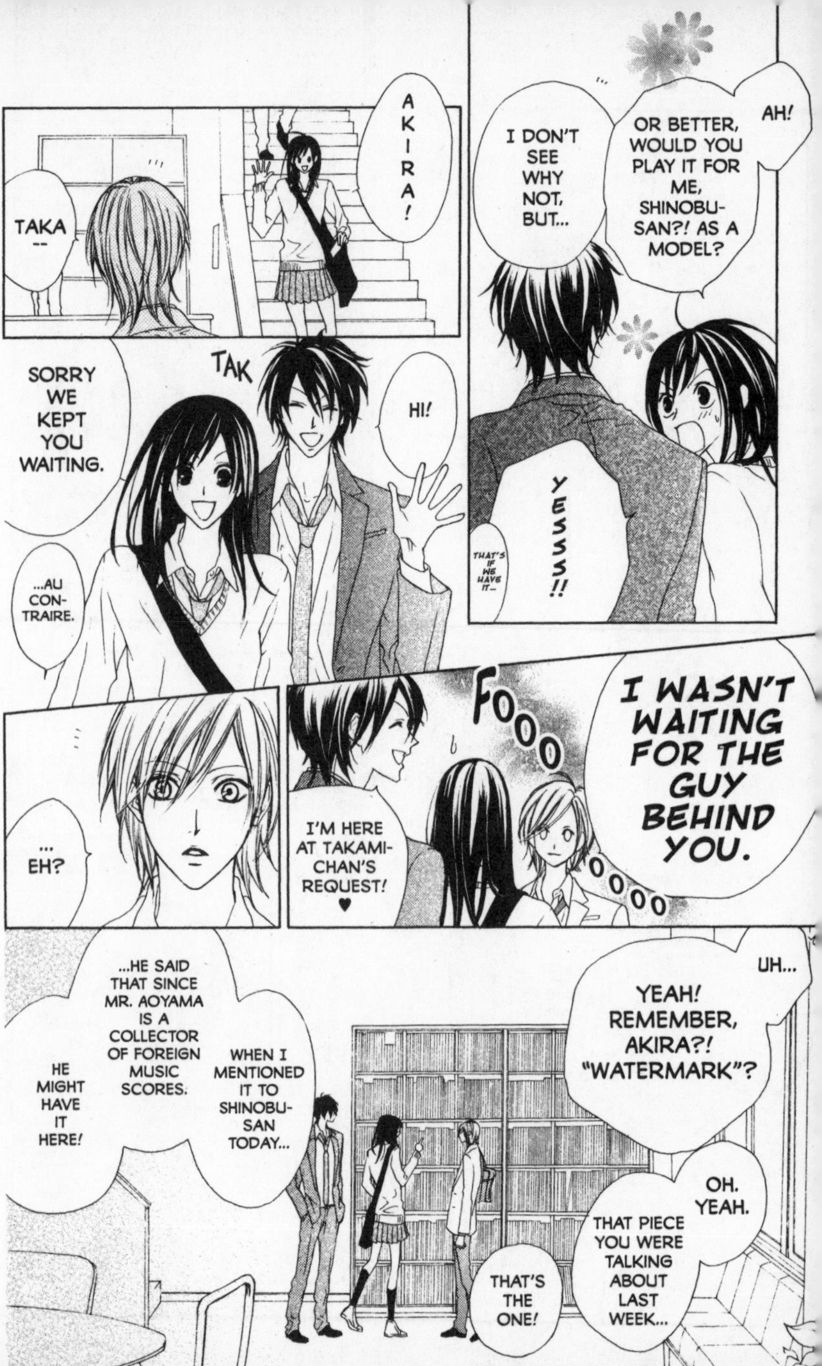
AH!
OR BETTER, WOULD YOU PLAY IT FOR ME, SHINOBU-SAN?! AS A MODEL?
I DON'T SEE WHY NOT, BUT...
YESSS!!
THAT'S IF WE HAVE IT...
AKIRA!
TAKA--
HI!
TAK
SORRY WE KEPT YOU WAITING.
...AU CONTRAIRE.
I WASN'T WAITING FOR THE GUY BEHIND YOU.
FOOOOOOO
I'M HERE AT TAKAMI-CHAN'S REQUEST! ♥
... EH?
UH...
YEAH! REMEMBER, AKIRA?! "WATERMARK"?
OH. YEAH.
THAT PIECE YOU WERE TALKING ABOUT LAST WEEK...
THAT'S THE ONE!
WHEN I MENTIONED IT TO SHINOBU-SAN TODAY...
...HE SAID THAT SINCE MR. AOYAMA IS A COLLECTOR OF FOREIGN MUSIC SCORES.
HE MIGHT HAVE IT HERE!

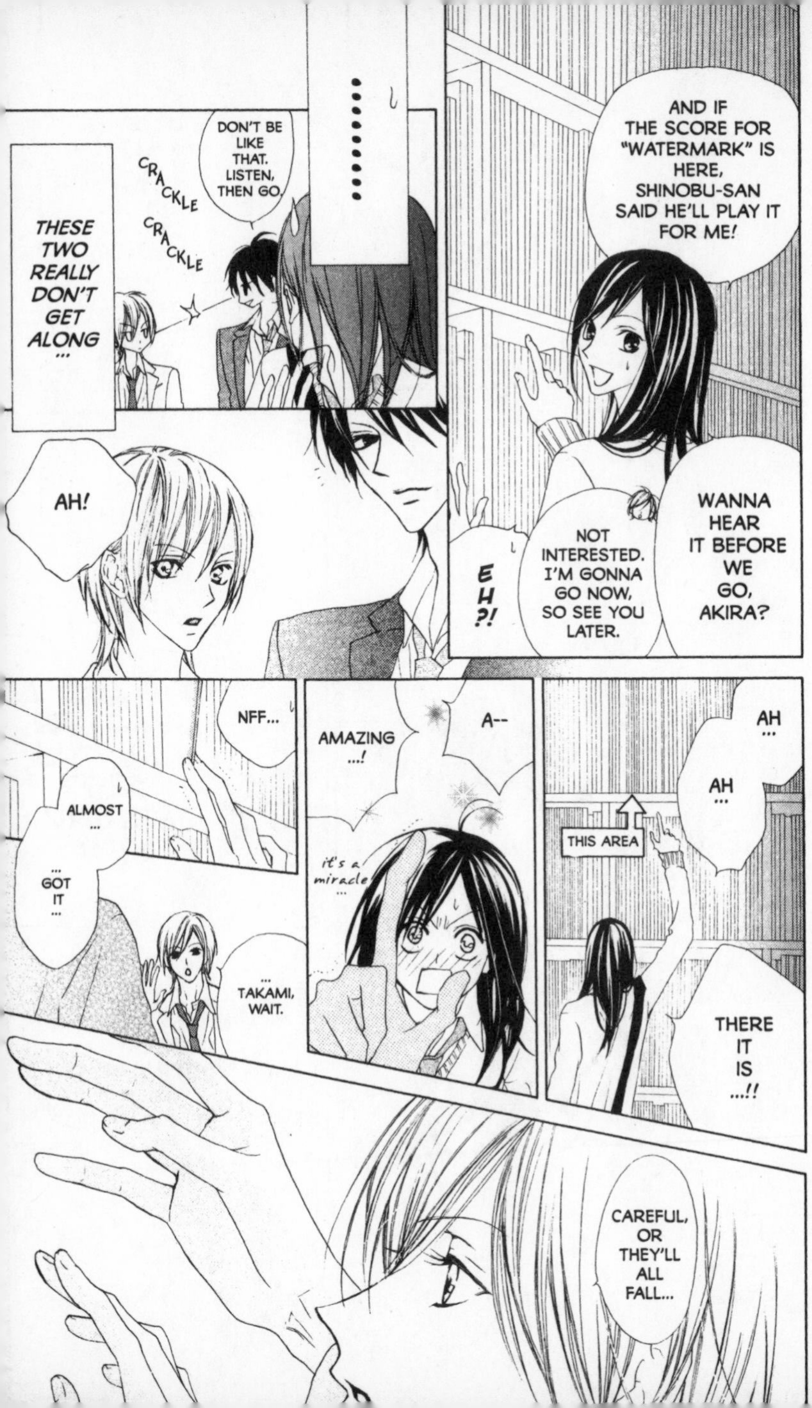
AND IF THE SCORE FOR "WATERMARK" IS HERE, SHINOBU-SAN SAID HE'LL PLAY IT FOR ME!
WANNA HEAR IT BEFORE WE GO, AKIRA?
NOT INTERESTED. I'M GONNA GO NOW, SO SEE YOU LATER.
EH?!
....
DON'T BE LIKE THAT. LISTEN, THEN GO.
CRACKLE
CRACKLE
THESE TWO REALLY DON'T GET ALONG...
AH!
AH...
AH...
THIS AREA
THERE IT IS...!!
A--
AMAZING...!
it's a miracle...
NFF...
ALMOST...
...GOT IT...
...TAKAMI, WAIT.
CAREFUL, OR THEY'LL ALL FALL...

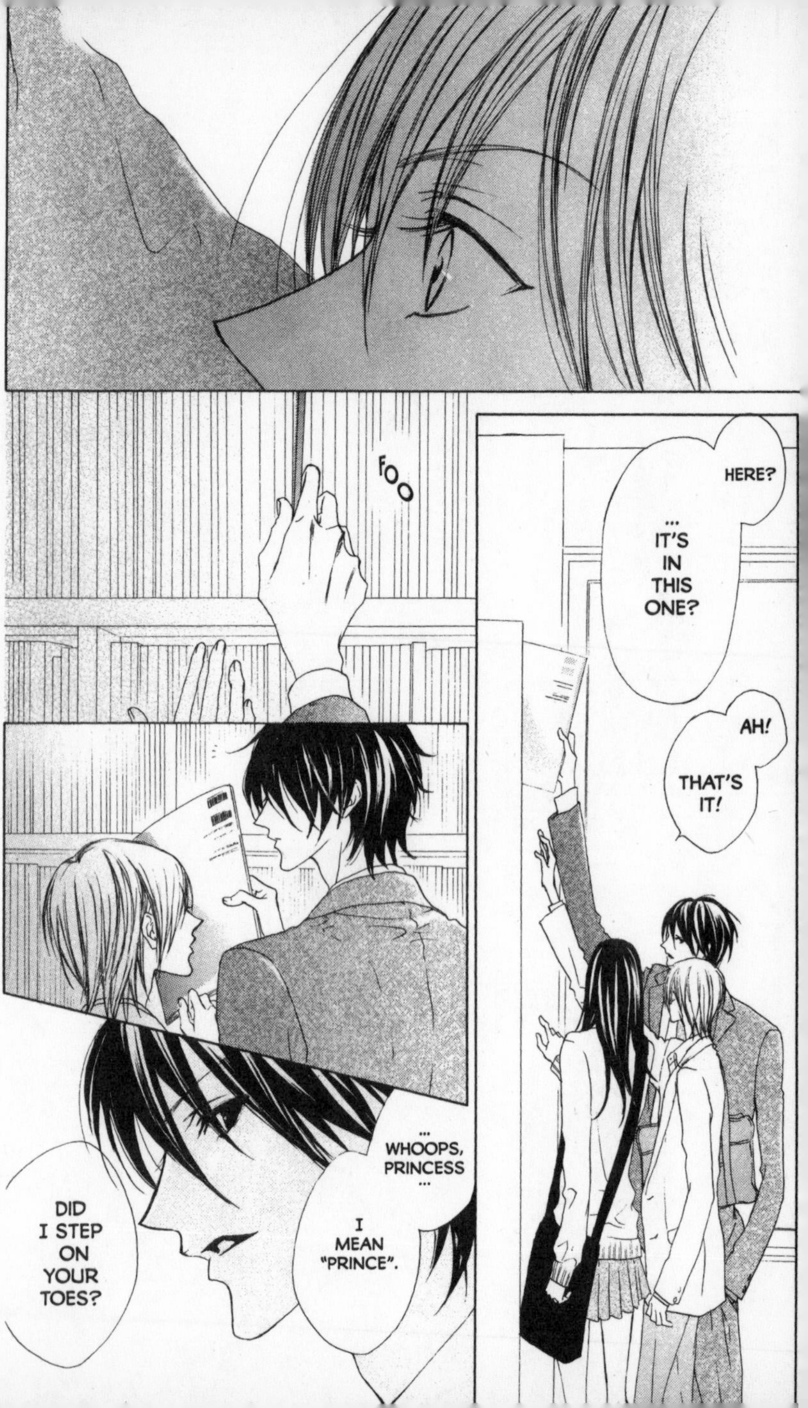
HERE?
... IT'S IN THIS ONE?
AH!
THAT'S IT!
FOO
... WHOOPS, PRINCESS ...
I MEAN "PRINCE".
DID I STEP ON YOUR TOES?

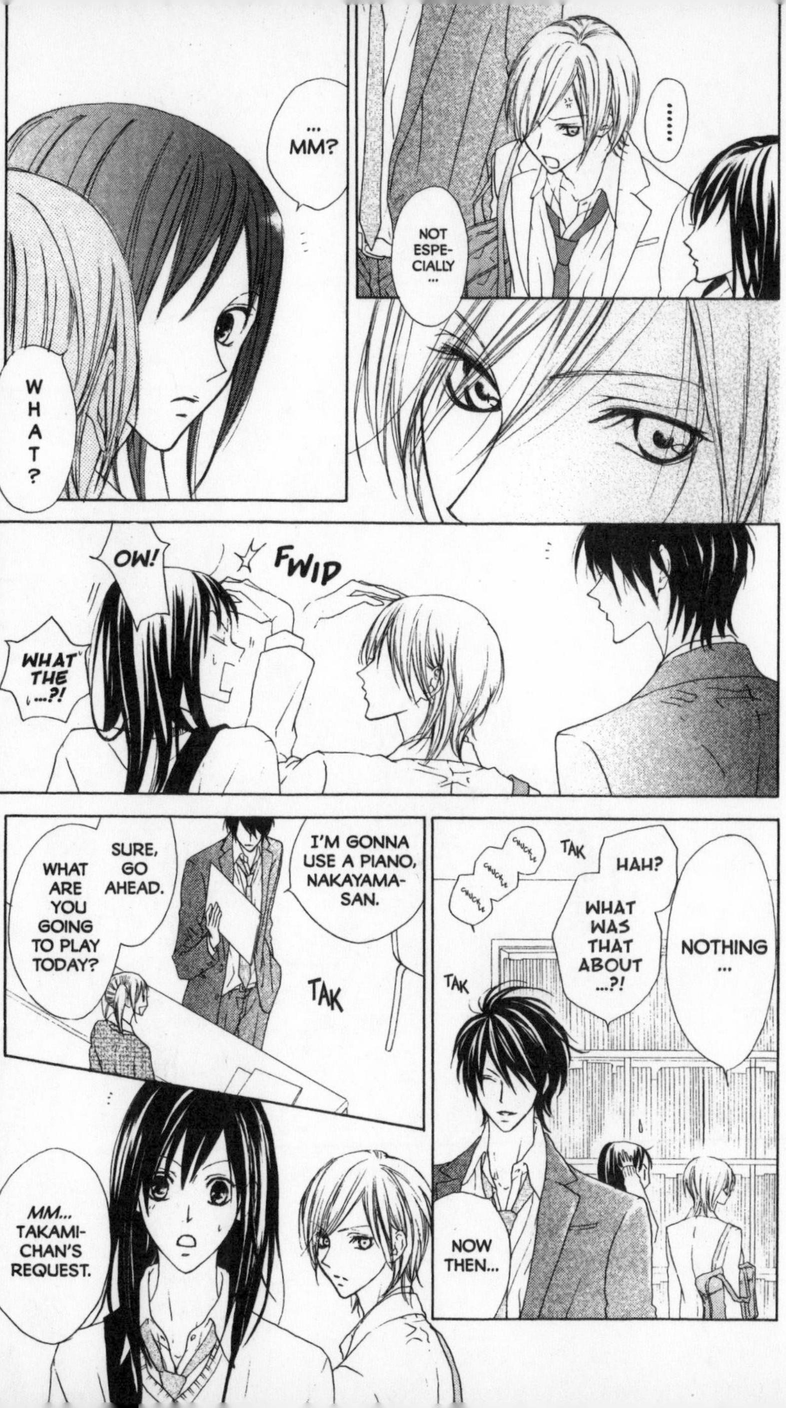
......
NOT ESPE-CIALLY ...
... MM?
WHAT?
FWIP
OW!
WHAT THE ...?!
NOTHING ...
TAK
HAH?
WHAT WAS THAT ABOUT ...?!
CHUCKLE
CHUCKLE
CHUCKLE
TAK
NOW THEN...
I'M GONNA USE A PIANO, NAKAYAMA-SAN.
SURE, GO AHEAD.
WHAT ARE YOU GOING TO PLAY TODAY?
TAK
MM... TAKAMI-CHAN'S REQUEST.

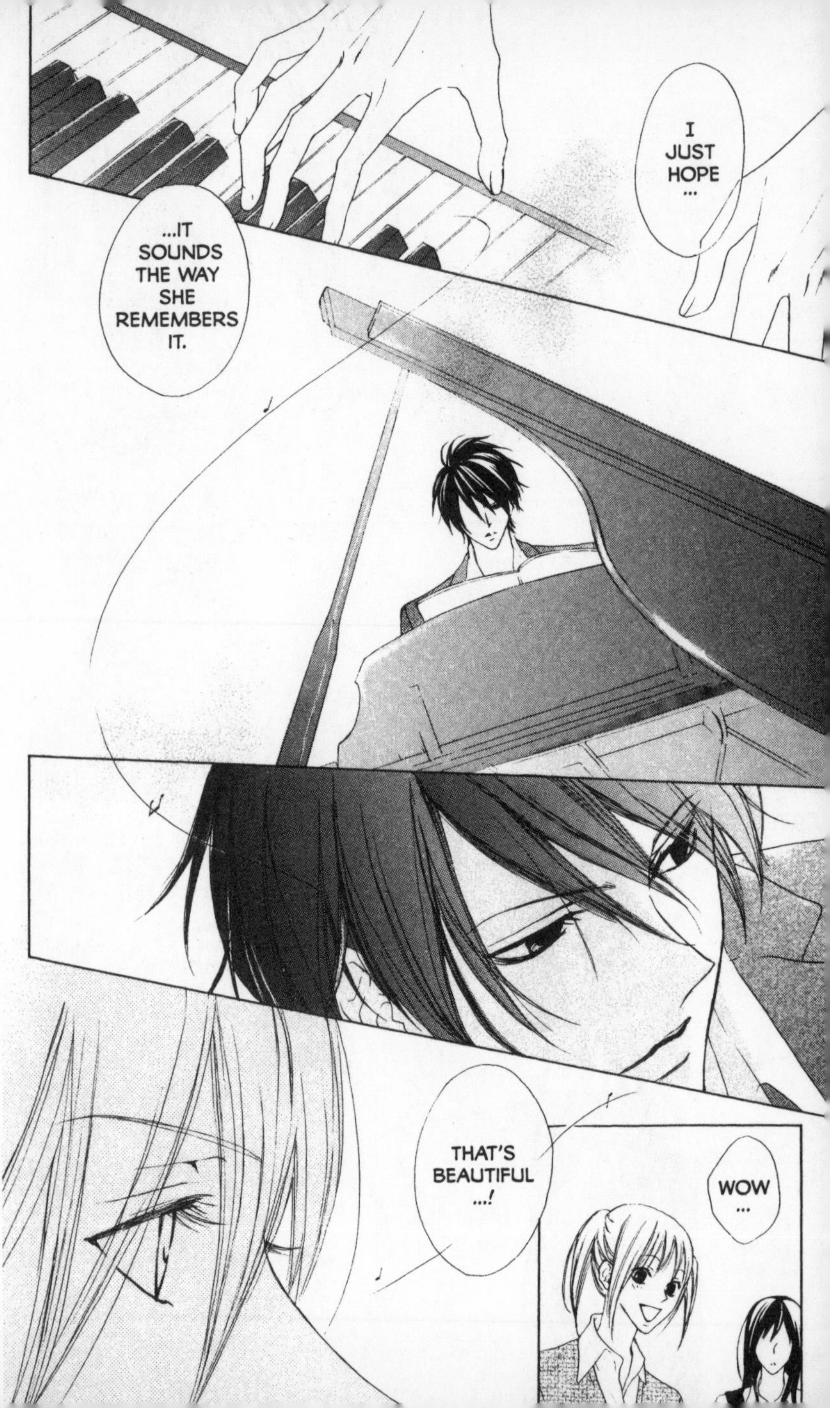
I JUST HOPE ...
...IT SOUNDS THE WAY SHE REMEMBERS IT.
WOW ...
THAT'S BEAUTIFUL ...!

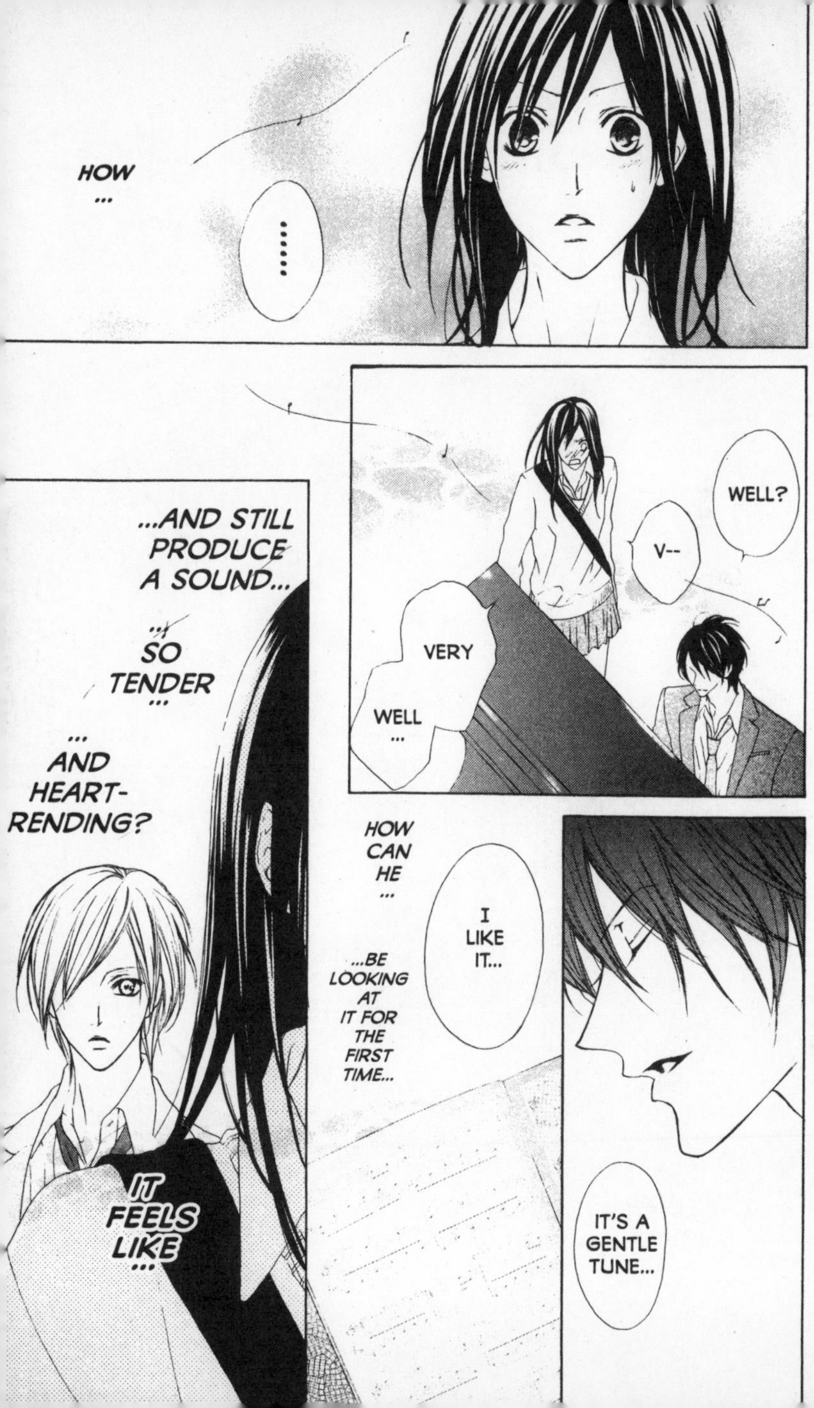

......
HOW ...
WELL?
V--
VERY WELL ...
I LIKE IT...
IT'S A GENTLE TUNE...
HOW CAN HE ...
...BE LOOKING AT IT FOR THE FIRST TIME...
...AND STILL PRODUCE A SOUND...
...SO TENDER ...
... AND HEART-RENDING?
IT FEELS LIKE ...

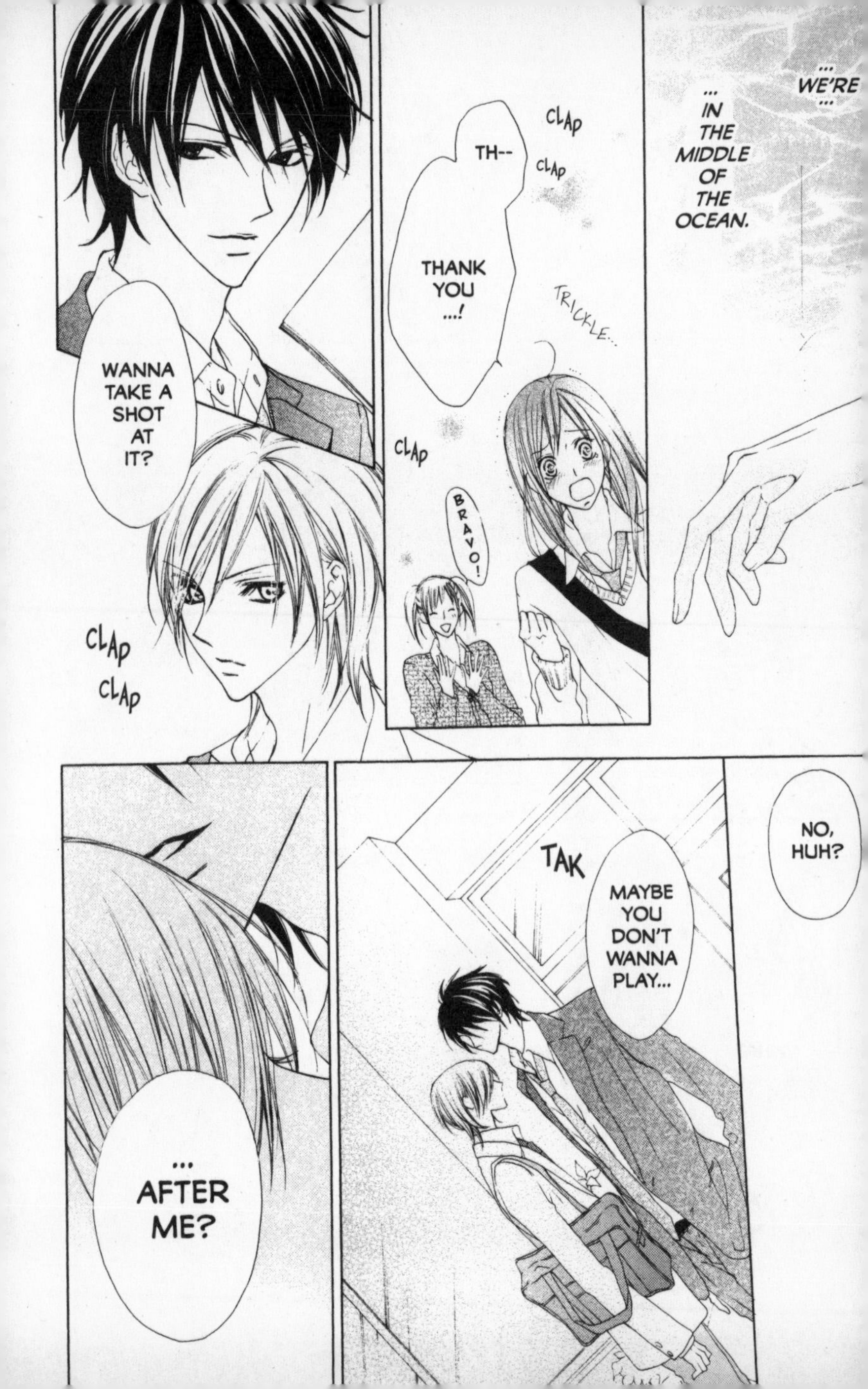
... WE'RE ...
... IN THE MIDDLE OF THE OCEAN.
CLAP
CLAP
TH--
THANK YOU ...!
TRICKLE...
CLAP
BRAVO!
WANNA TAKE A SHOT AT IT?
CLAP
CLAP
NO, HUH?
TAK
MAYBE YOU DON'T WANNA PLAY...
... AFTER ME?

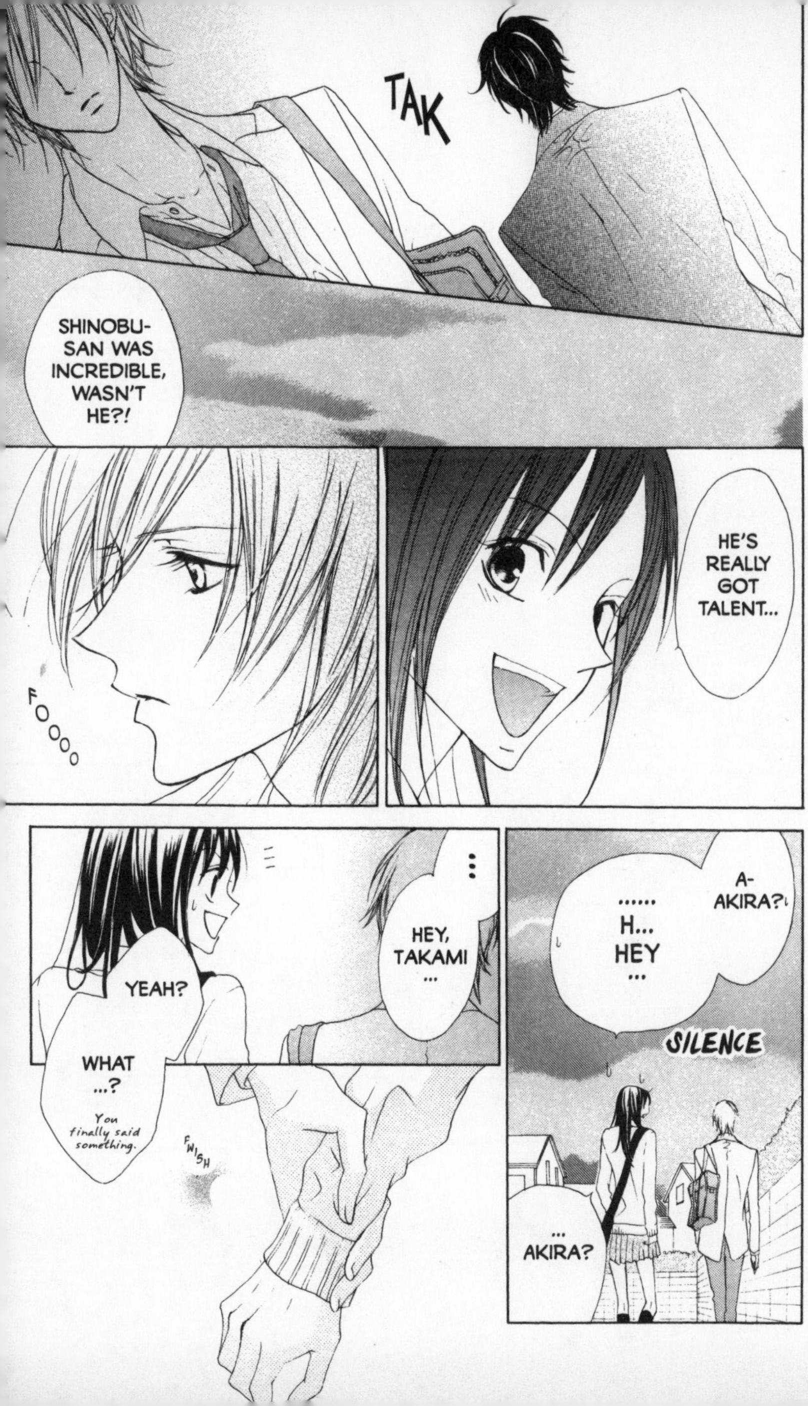
TAK
SHINOBU-SAN WAS INCREDIBLE, WASN'T HE?!
HE'S REALLY GOT TALENT...
FOOOO
A-AKIRA?
......H... HEY ...
SILENCE
... AKIRA?
...
HEY, TAKAMI ...
YEAH?
WHAT ...?
You finally said something.
FWISH

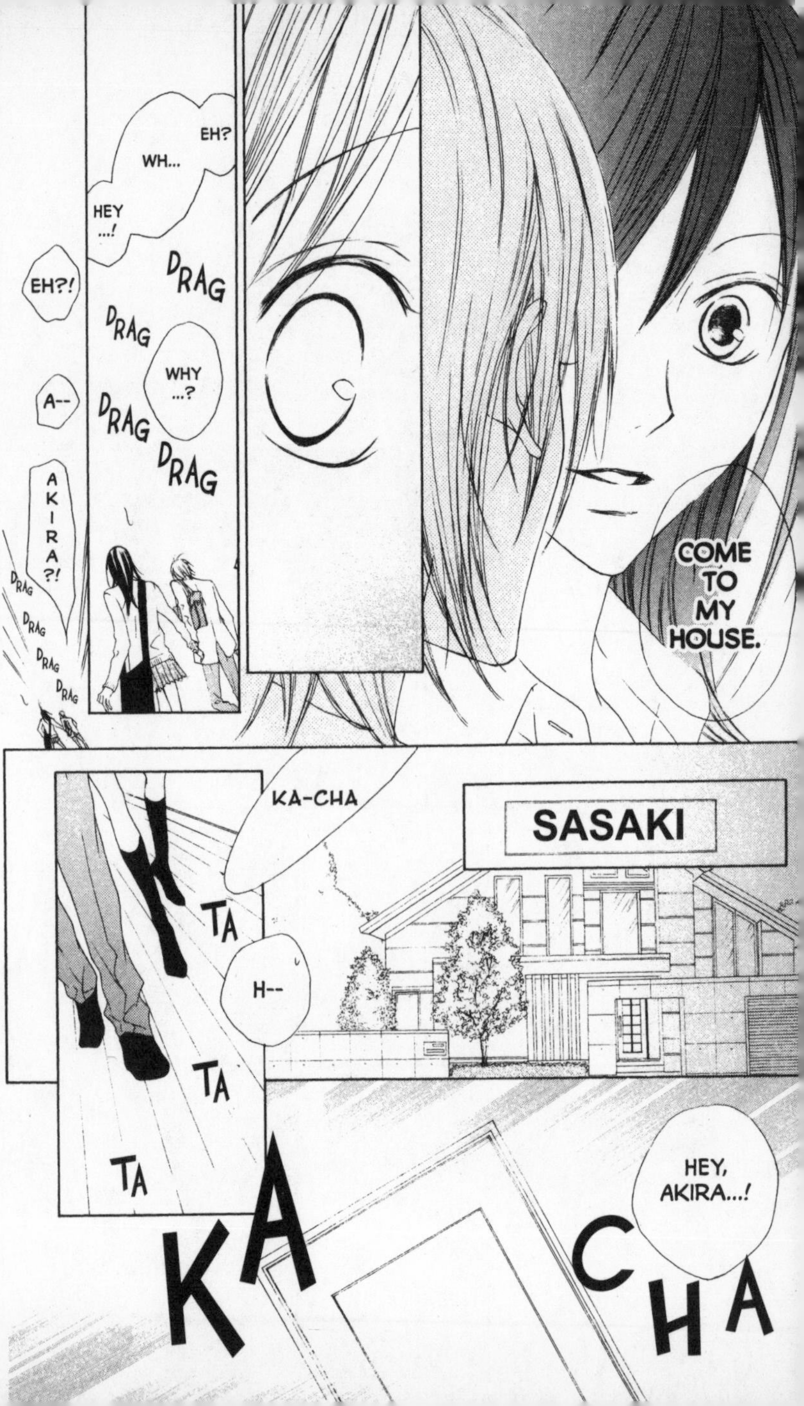
COME TO MY HOUSE.
EH?
WH...
HEY ...!
DRAG
DRAG
WHY ...?
DRAG
DRAG
EH?!
A--
AKIRA?!
DRAG
DRAG
DRAG
DRAG
KA-CHA
SASAKI
TA
H--
TA
TA
HEY, AKIRA...!
KACHA

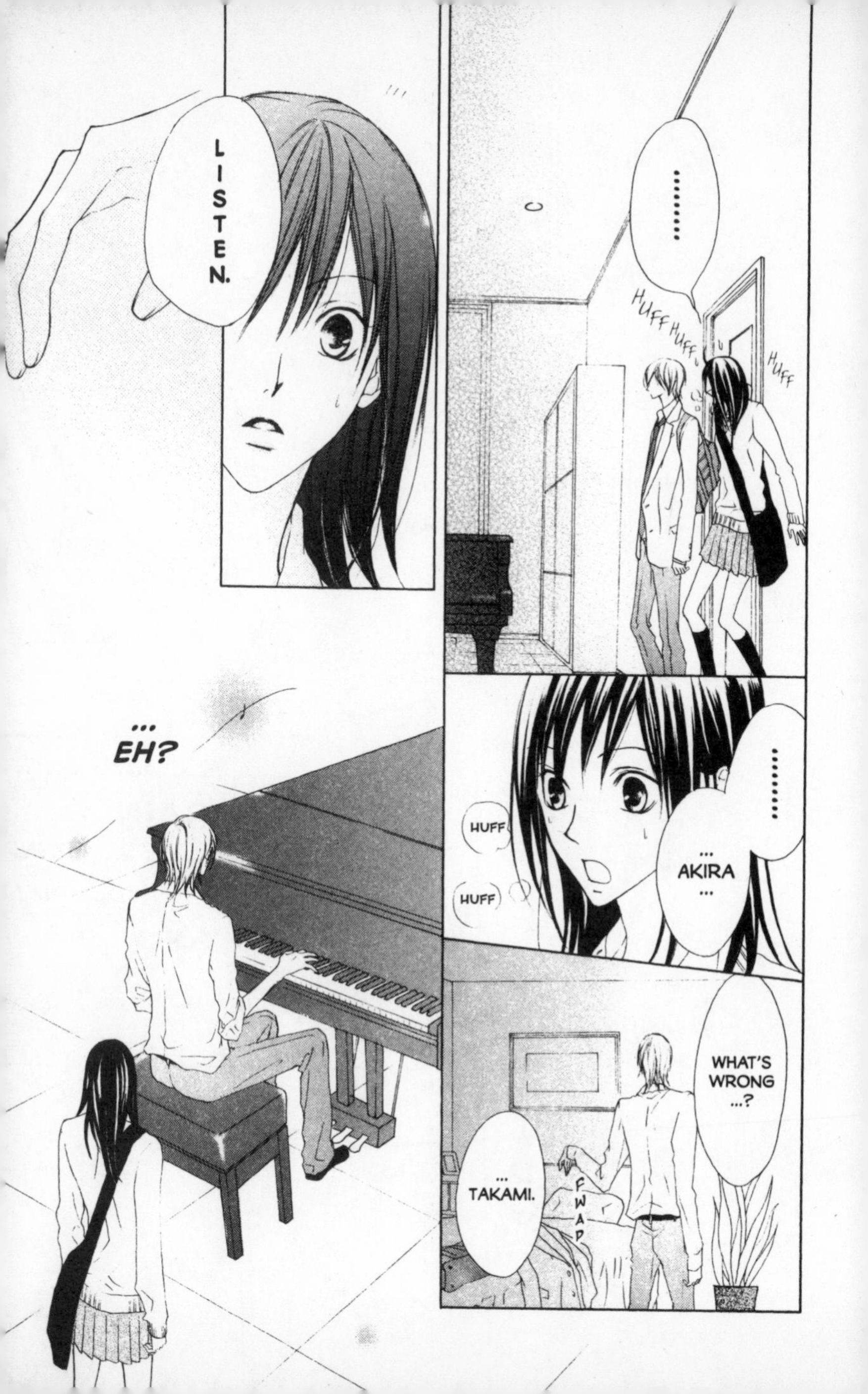
......
HUFF HUFF HUFF
HUFF
LISTEN.
......
... AKIRA ...
HUFF
HUFF
WHAT'S WRONG ...?
... TAKAMI.
FWAP
... EH?

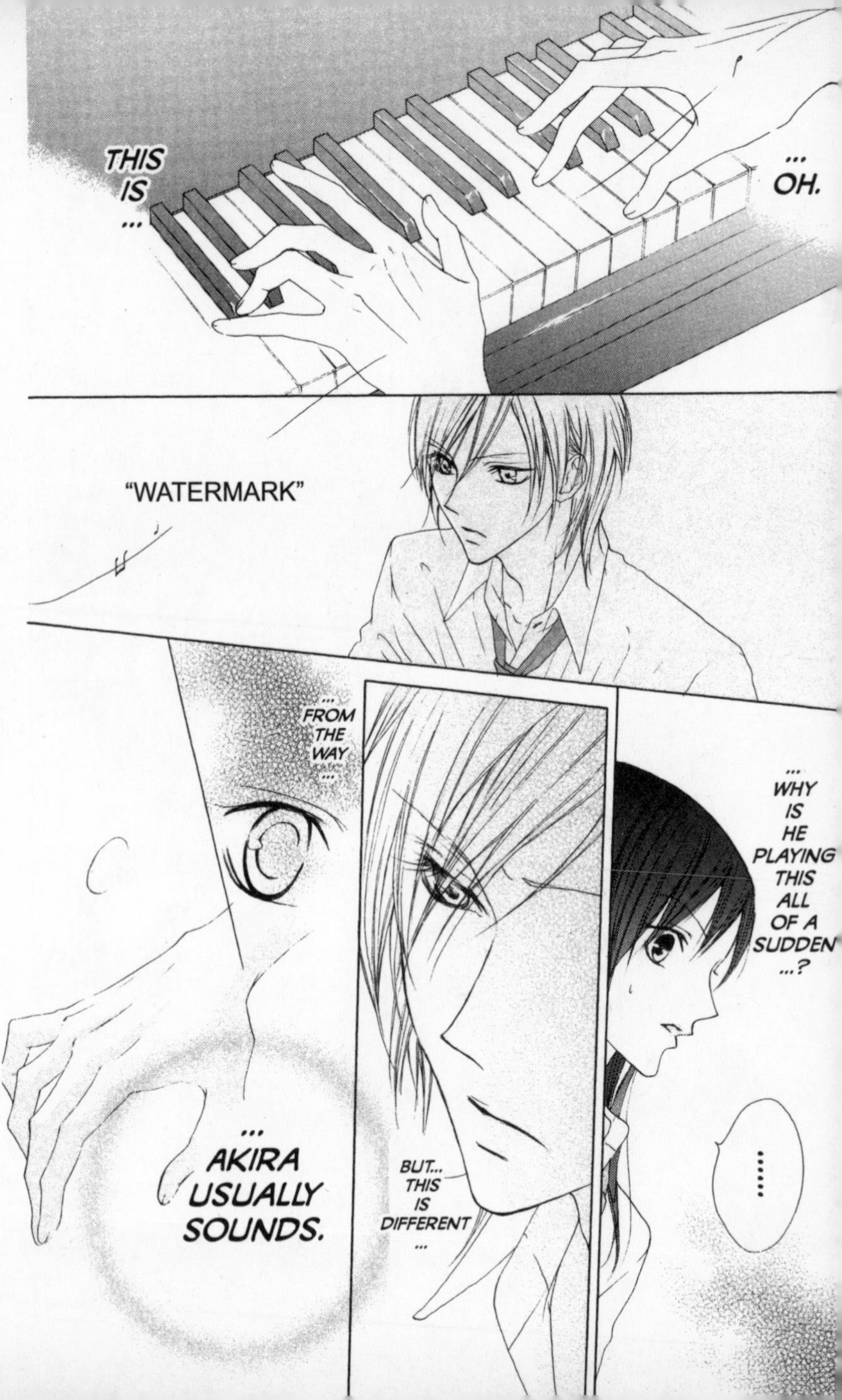
...OH.
THIS IS ...
"WATERMARK"
...WHY IS HE PLAYING THIS ALL OF A SUDDEN ...?
......
BUT... THIS IS DIFFERENT ...
...FROM THE WAY ...
...AKIRA USUALLY SOUNDS.

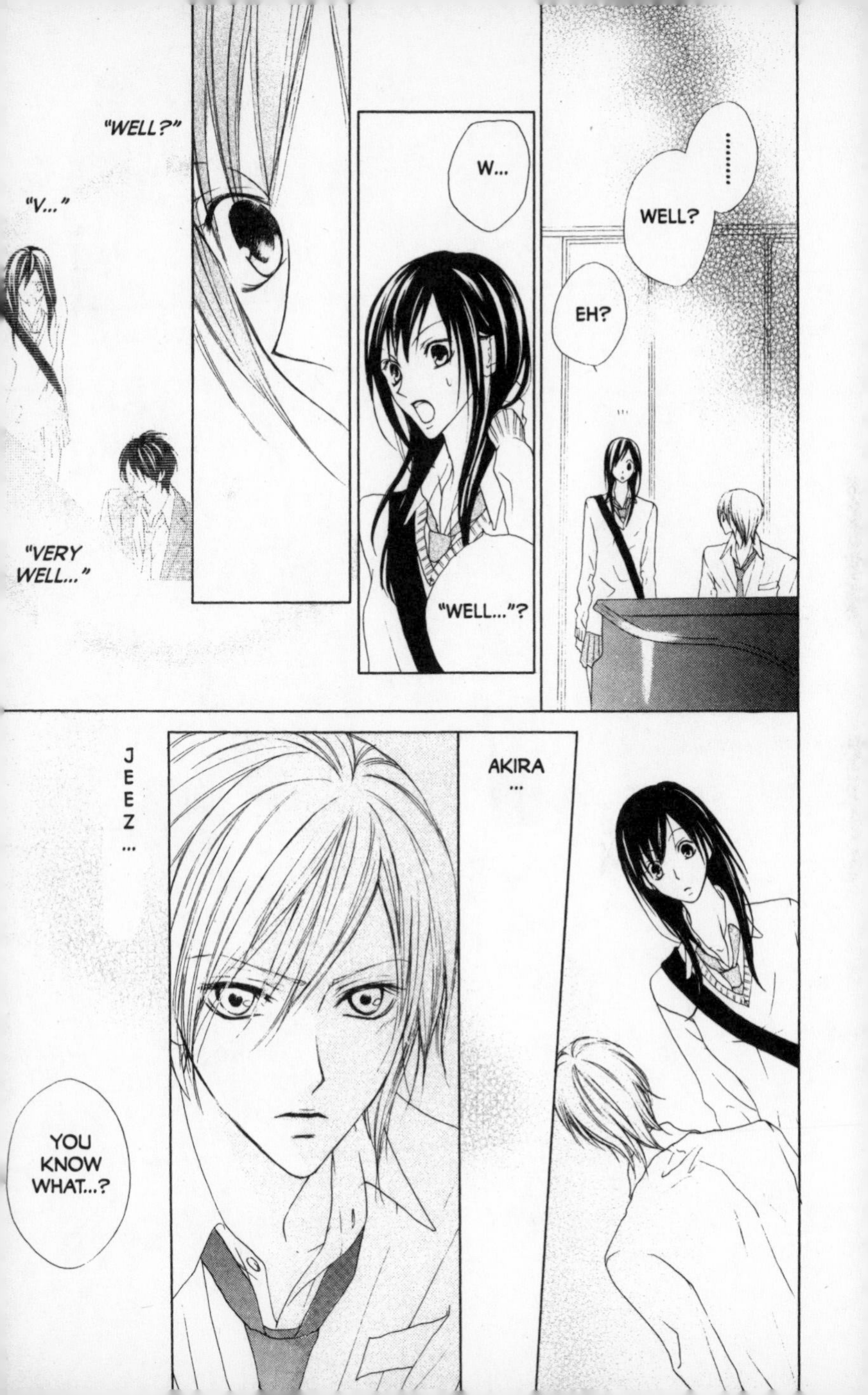
......
WELL?
EH?
W...
"WELL..."?
"WELL?"
"V..."
"VERY WELL..."
AKIRA ...
JEEZ ...
YOU KNOW WHAT...?

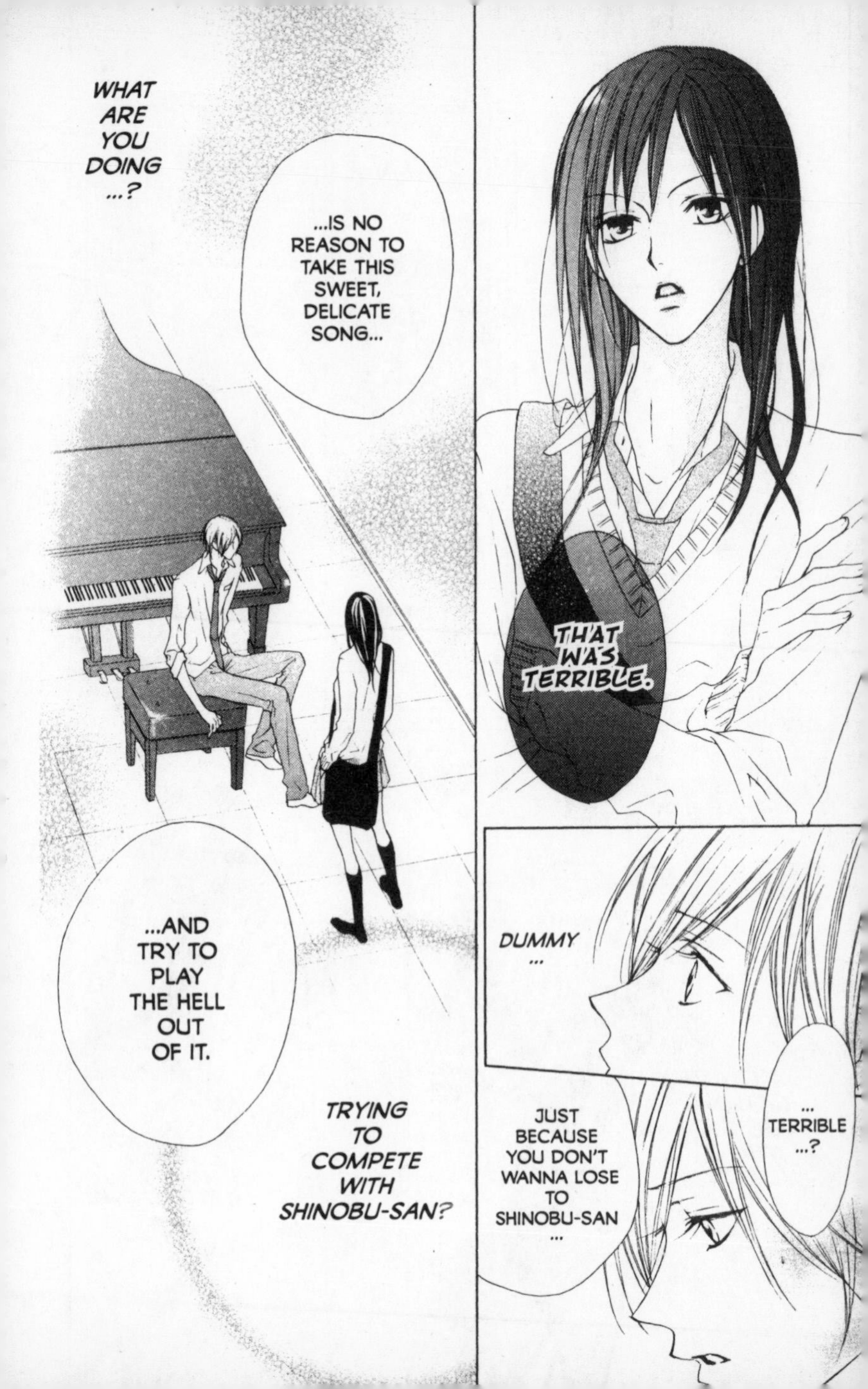
THAT WAS TERRIBLE.
...TERRIBLE...?
DUMMY...
JUST BECAUSE YOU DON'T WANNA LOSE TO SHINOBU-SAN...
WHAT ARE YOU DOING...?
...IS NO REASON TO TAKE THIS SWEET, DELICATE SONG...
...AND TRY TO PLAY THE HELL OUT OF IT.
TRYING TO COMPETE WITH SHINOBU-SAN?

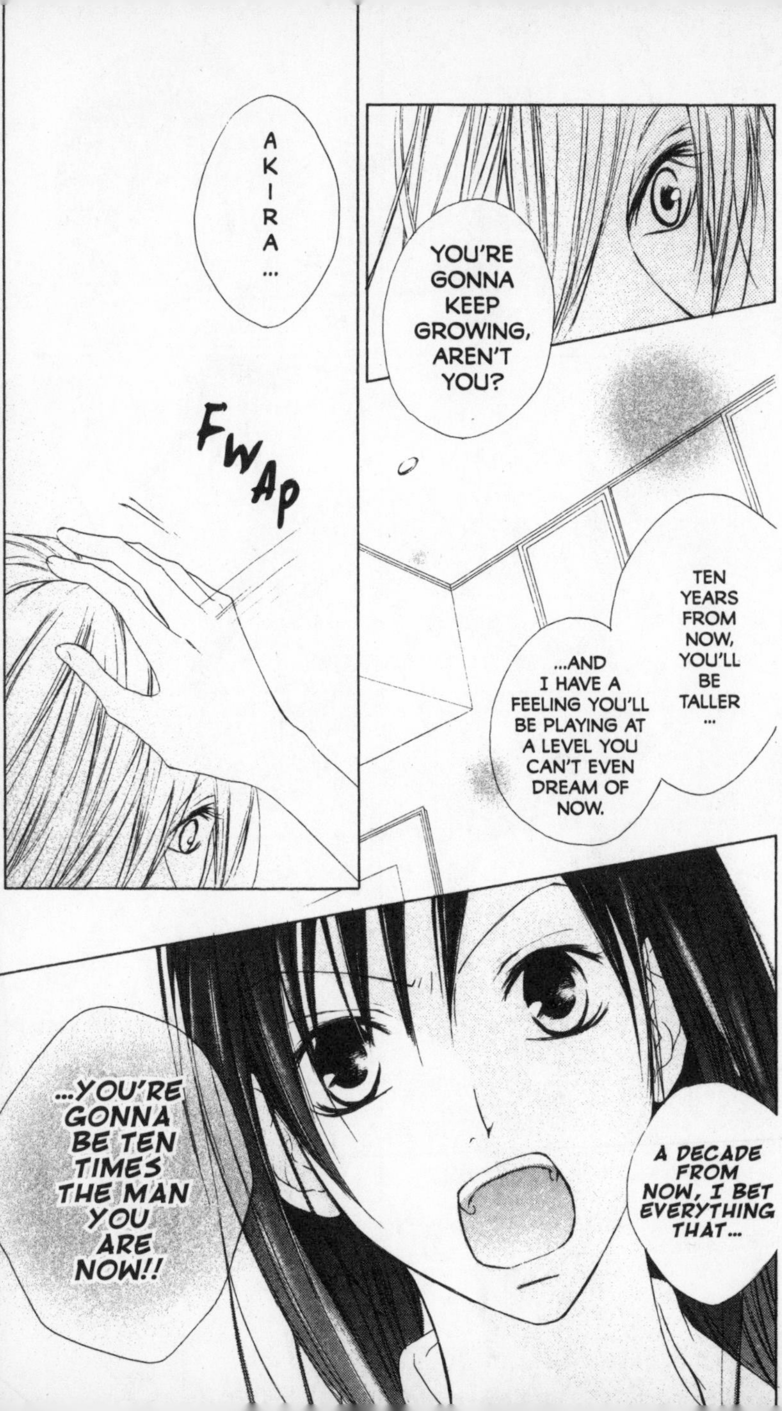
YOU'RE GONNA KEEP GROWING, AREN'T YOU?
TEN YEARS FROM NOW, YOU'LL BE TALLER ...
...AND I HAVE A FEELING YOU'LL BE PLAYING AT A LEVEL YOU CAN'T EVEN DREAM OF NOW.
AKIRA ...
FWAP
A DECADE FROM NOW, I BET EVERYTHING THAT...
...YOU'RE GONNA BE TEN TIMES THE MAN YOU ARE NOW!!

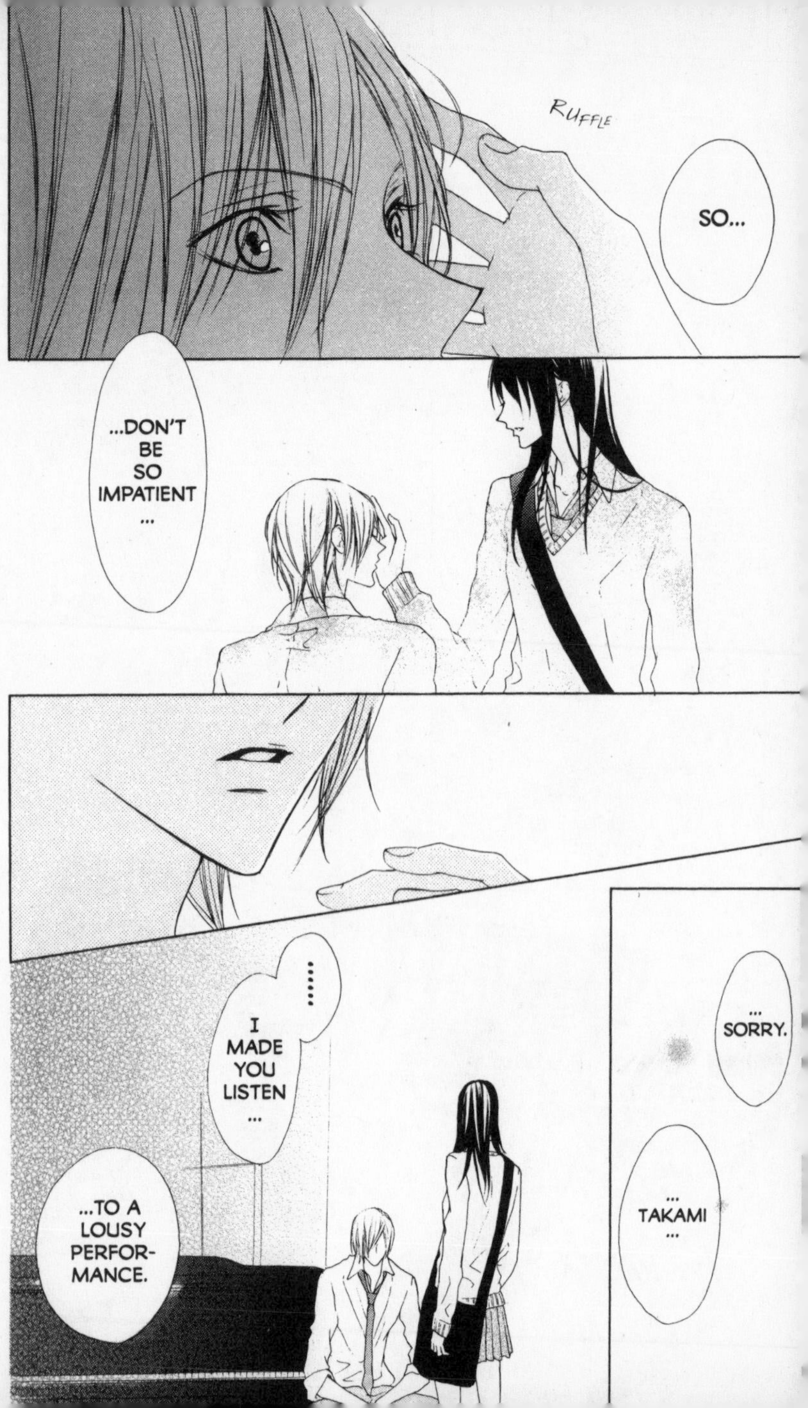
RUFFLE
SO...
...DON'T BE SO IMPATIENT...
... SORRY.
... TAKAMI ...
......
I MADE YOU LISTEN...
...TO A LOUSY PERFOR-MANCE.

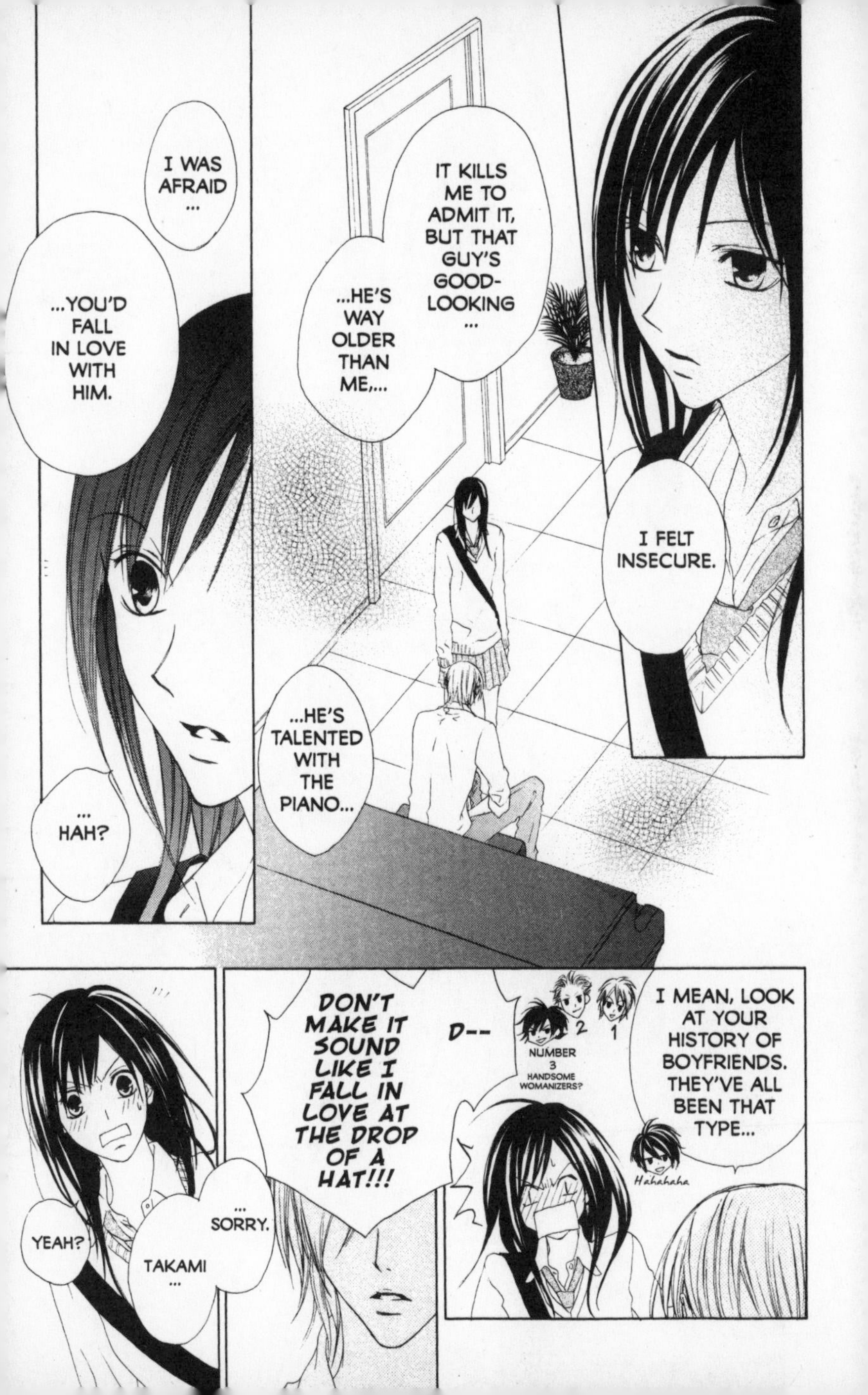
I FELT INSECURE.
IT KILLS ME TO ADMIT IT, BUT THAT GUY'S GOOD-LOOKING...
...HE'S WAY OLDER THAN ME,...
...HE'S TALENTED WITH THE PIANO...
I WAS AFRAID...
...YOU'D FALL IN LOVE WITH HIM.
...HAH?
I MEAN, LOOK AT YOUR HISTORY OF BOYFRIENDS. THEY'VE ALL BEEN THAT TYPE...
1
2
NUMBER 3
HANDSOME WOMANIZERS?
Hahahaha
D--
DON'T MAKE IT SOUND LIKE I FALL IN LOVE AT THE DROP OF A HAT!!!
...SORRY.
TAKAMI...
YEAH?

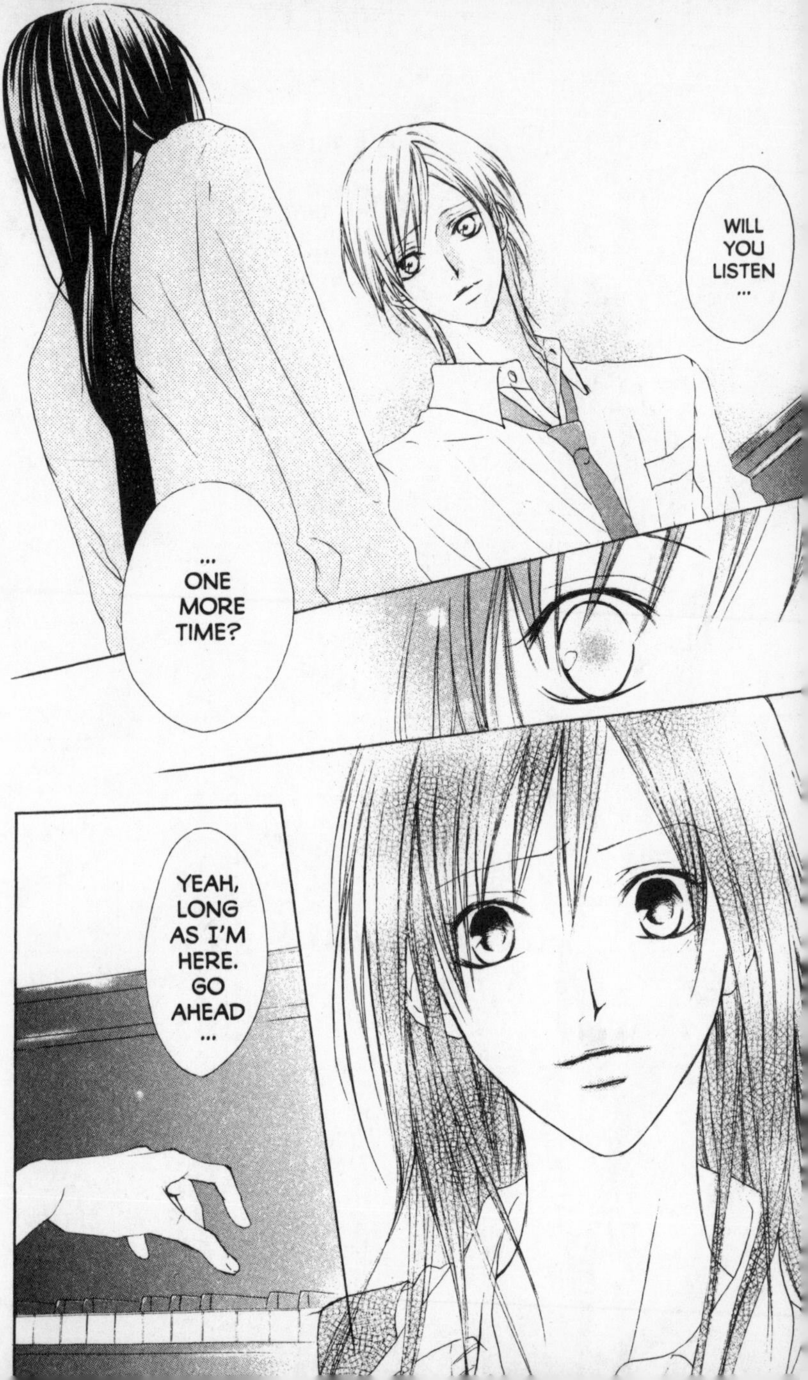
WILL YOU LISTEN ...
... ONE MORE TIME?
YEAH, LONG AS I'M HERE. GO AHEAD ...

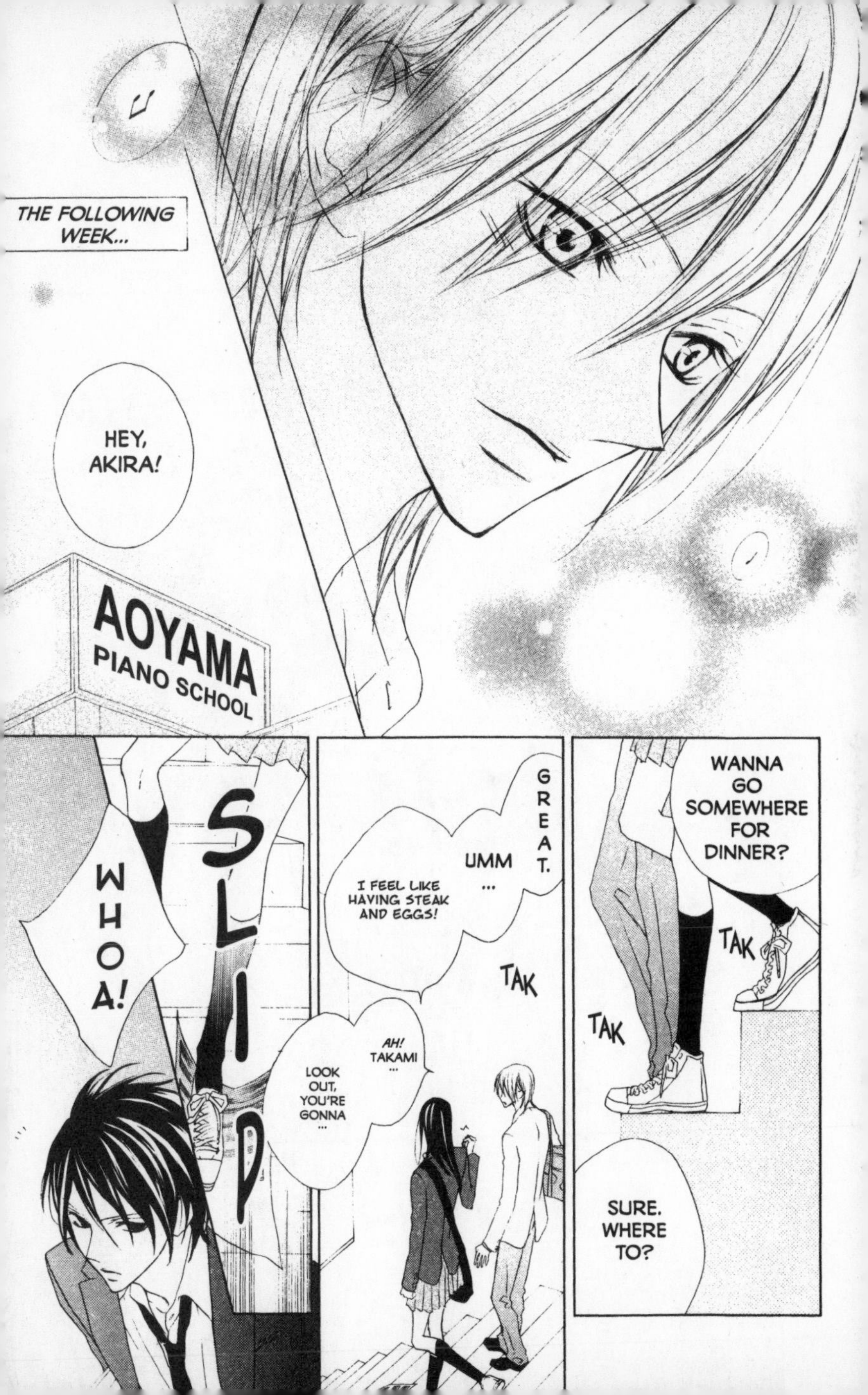
THE FOLLOWING WEEK...
HEY, AKIRA!
AOYAMA PIANO SCHOOL
WANNA GO SOMEWHERE FOR DINNER?
TAK
TAK
SURE. WHERE TO?
GREAT.
UMM...
I FEEL LIKE HAVING STEAK AND EGGS!
TAK
AH! TAKAMI...
LOOK OUT, YOU'RE GONNA...
SLID
WHOA!

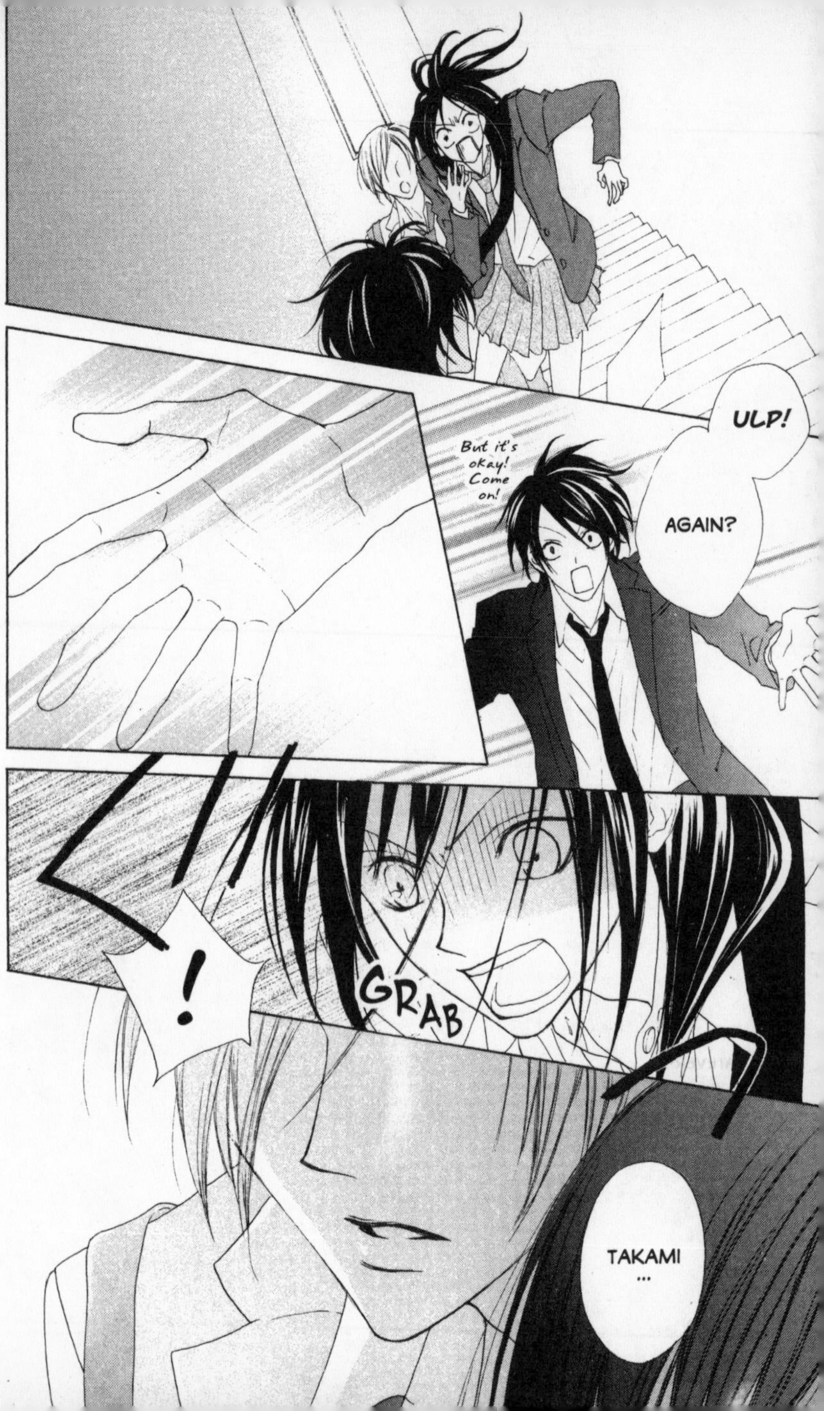
ULP!
AGAIN?
But it's okay! Come on!
!
GRAB
TAKAMI ...

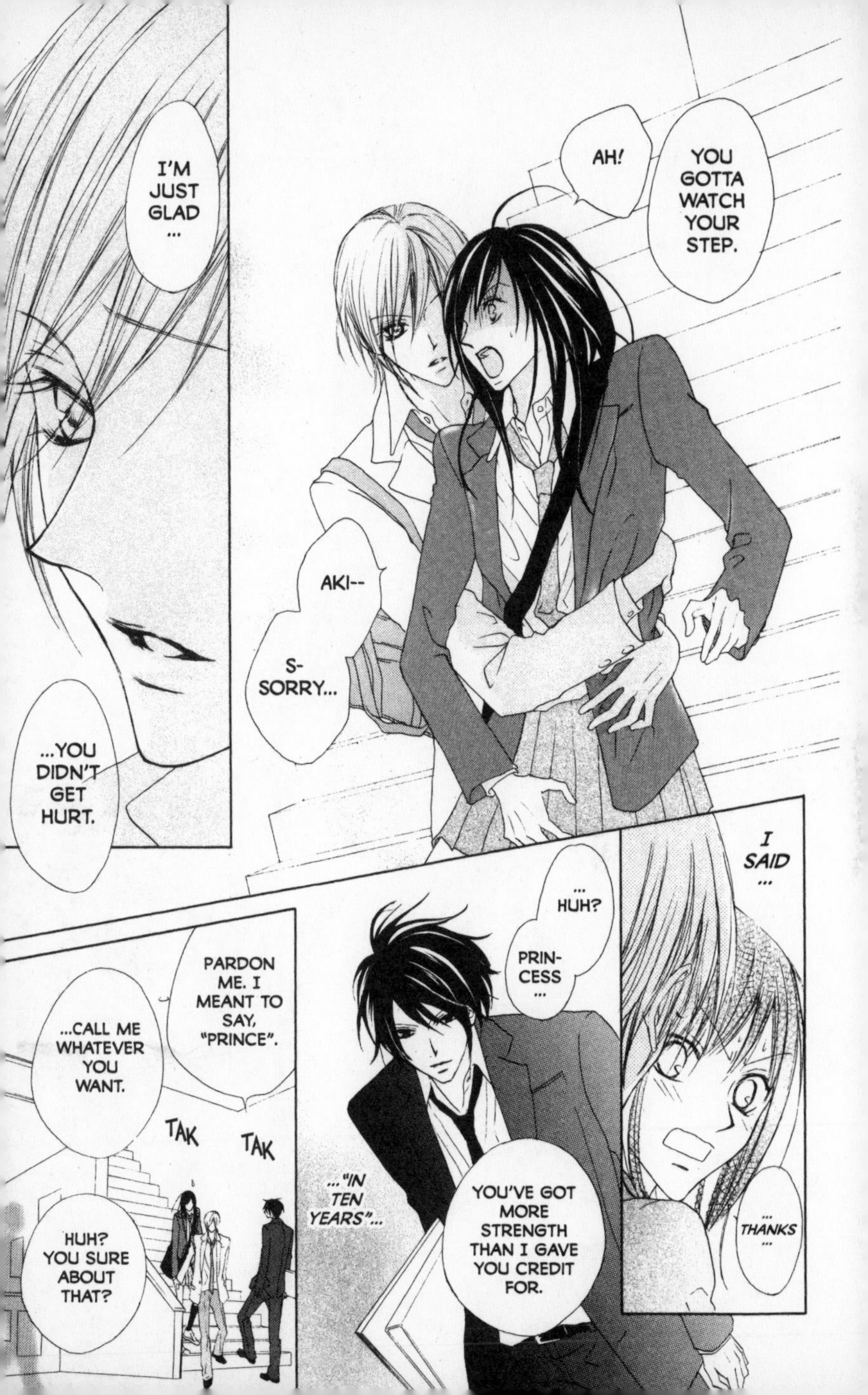
YOU GOTTA WATCH YOUR STEP.
AH!
AKI--
S-SORRY...
I'M JUST GLAD...
...YOU DIDN'T GET HURT.
I SAID...
...THANKS...
...HUH?
PRIN-CESS...
YOU'VE GOT MORE STRENGTH THAN I GAVE YOU CREDIT FOR.
..."IN TEN YEARS"...
PARDON ME. I MEANT TO SAY, "PRINCE".
...CALL ME WHATEVER YOU WANT.
TAK
TAK
HUH? YOU SURE ABOUT THAT?

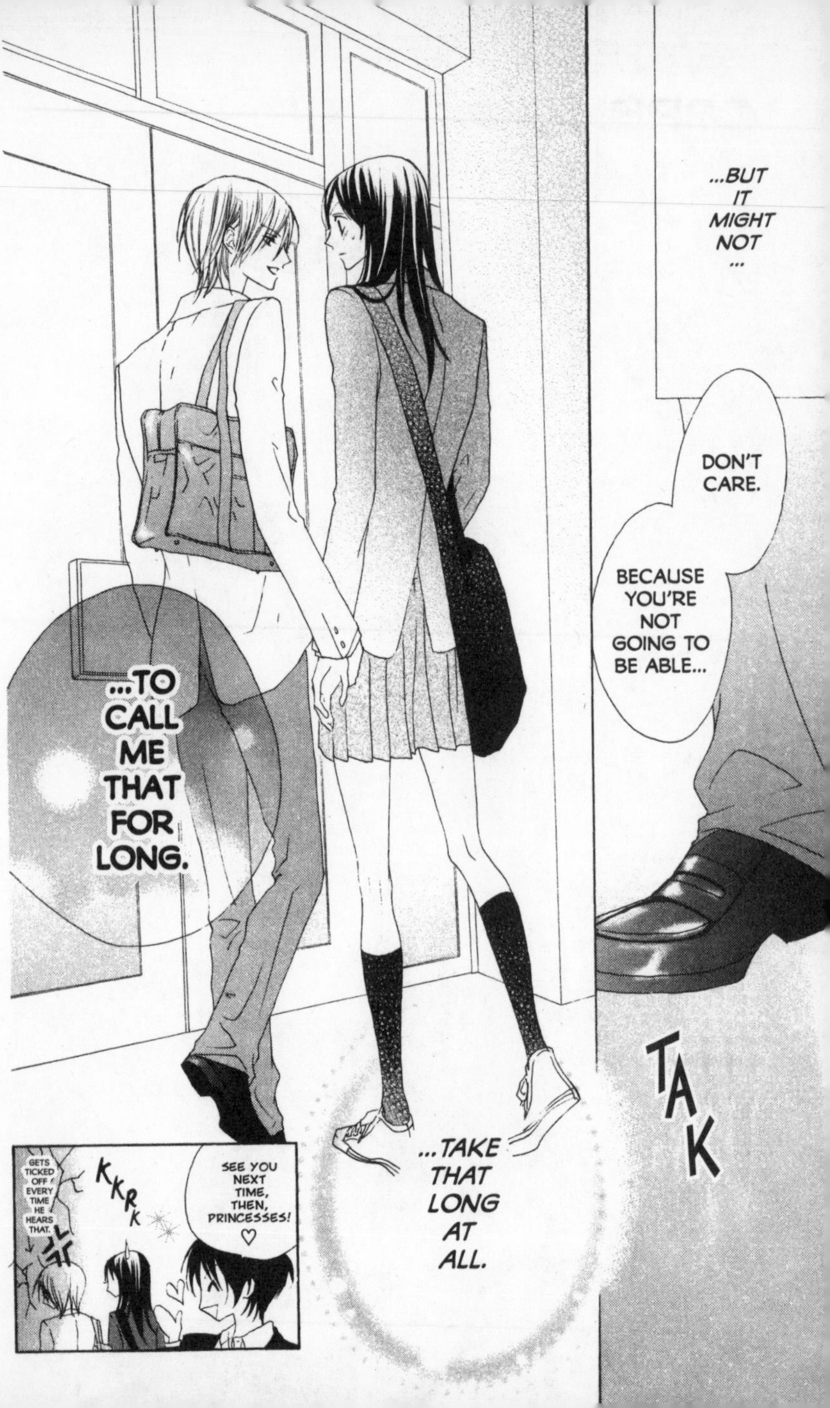
...BUT IT MIGHT NOT...
DON'T CARE.
BECAUSE YOU'RE NOT GOING TO BE ABLE...
TAK
...TO CALL ME THAT FOR LONG.
...TAKE THAT LONG AT ALL.
SEE YOU NEXT TIME, THEN, PRINCESSES! ♡
KKRK
GETS TICKED OFF EVERY TIME HE HEARS THAT.

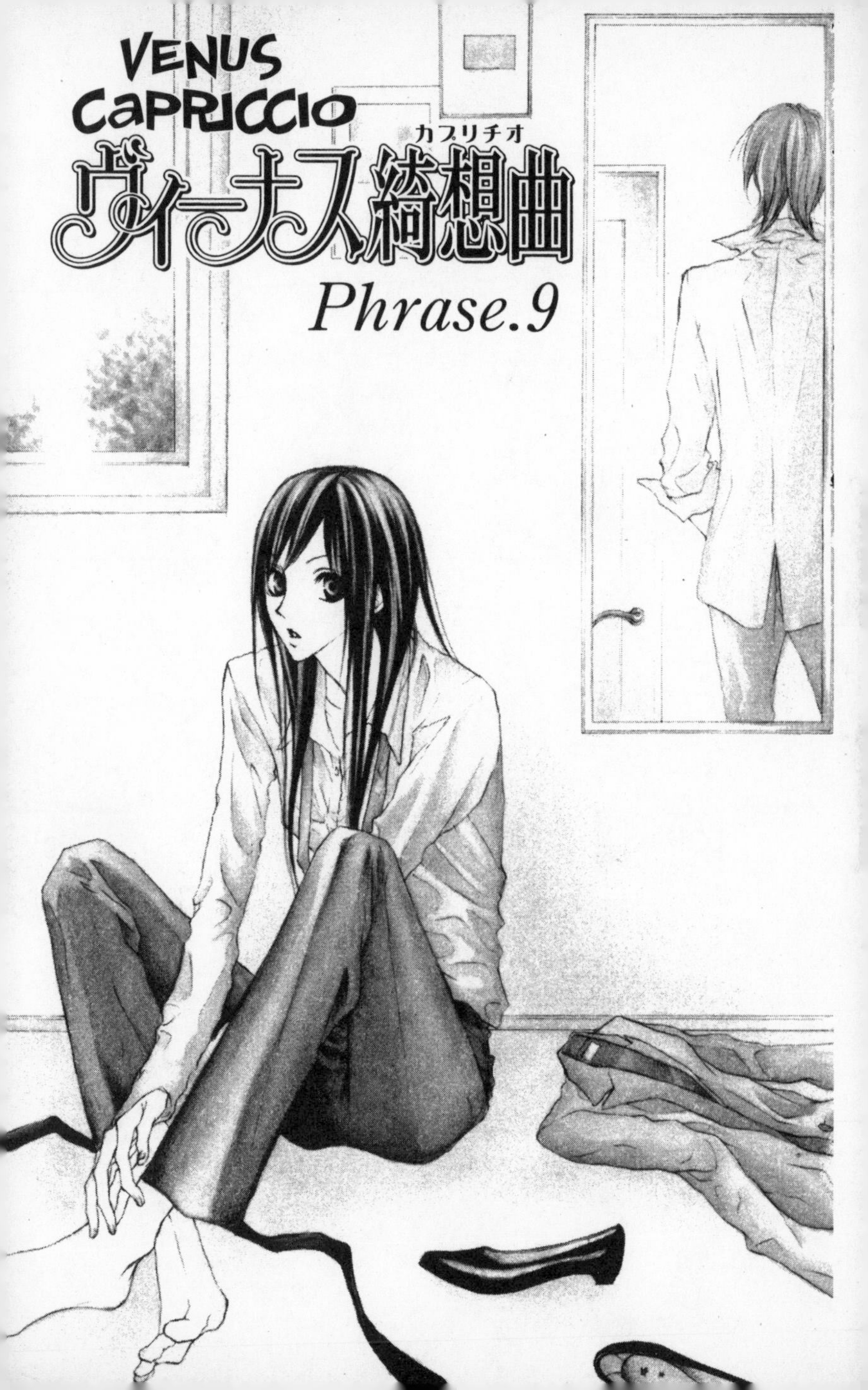
VENUS Capriccio
ヴィーナス綺想曲
カプリチオ
Phrase.9

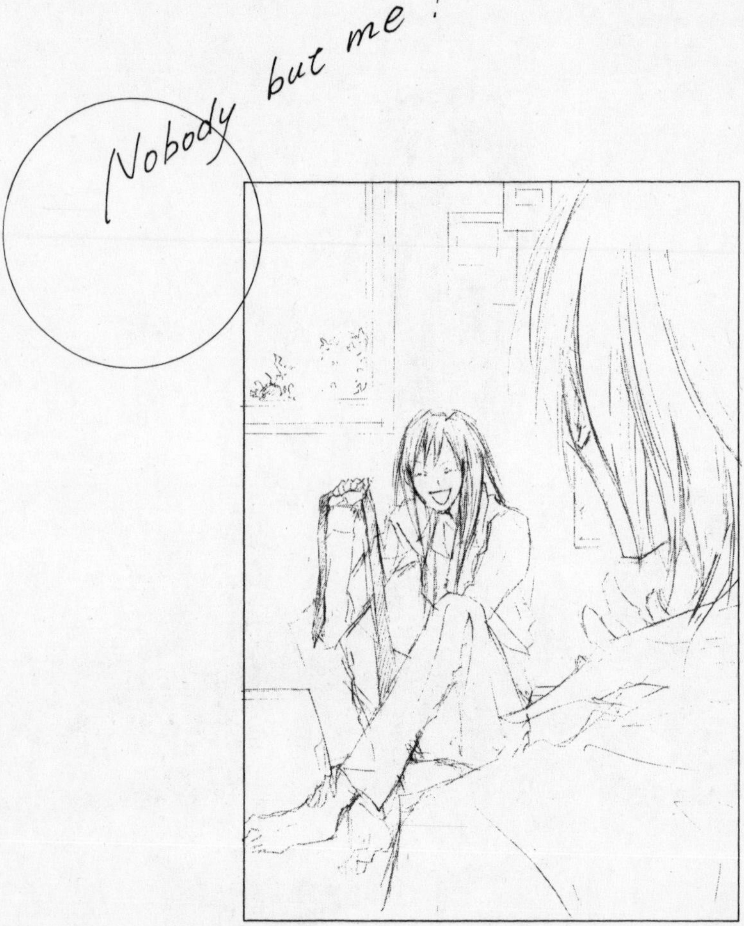
Nobody but me!

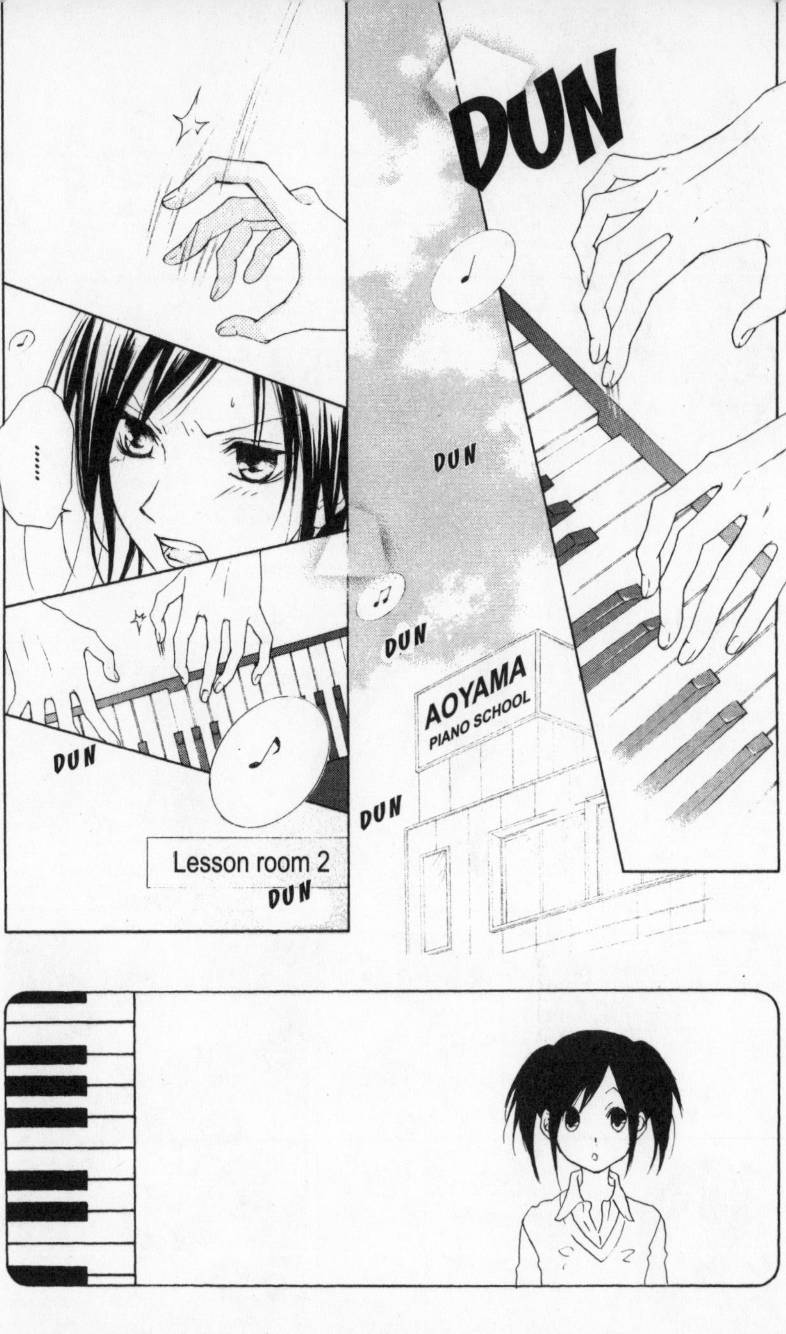
DUN
DUN
DUN
AOYAMA
PIANO SCHOOL
DUN
......
DUN
Lesson room 2
DUN

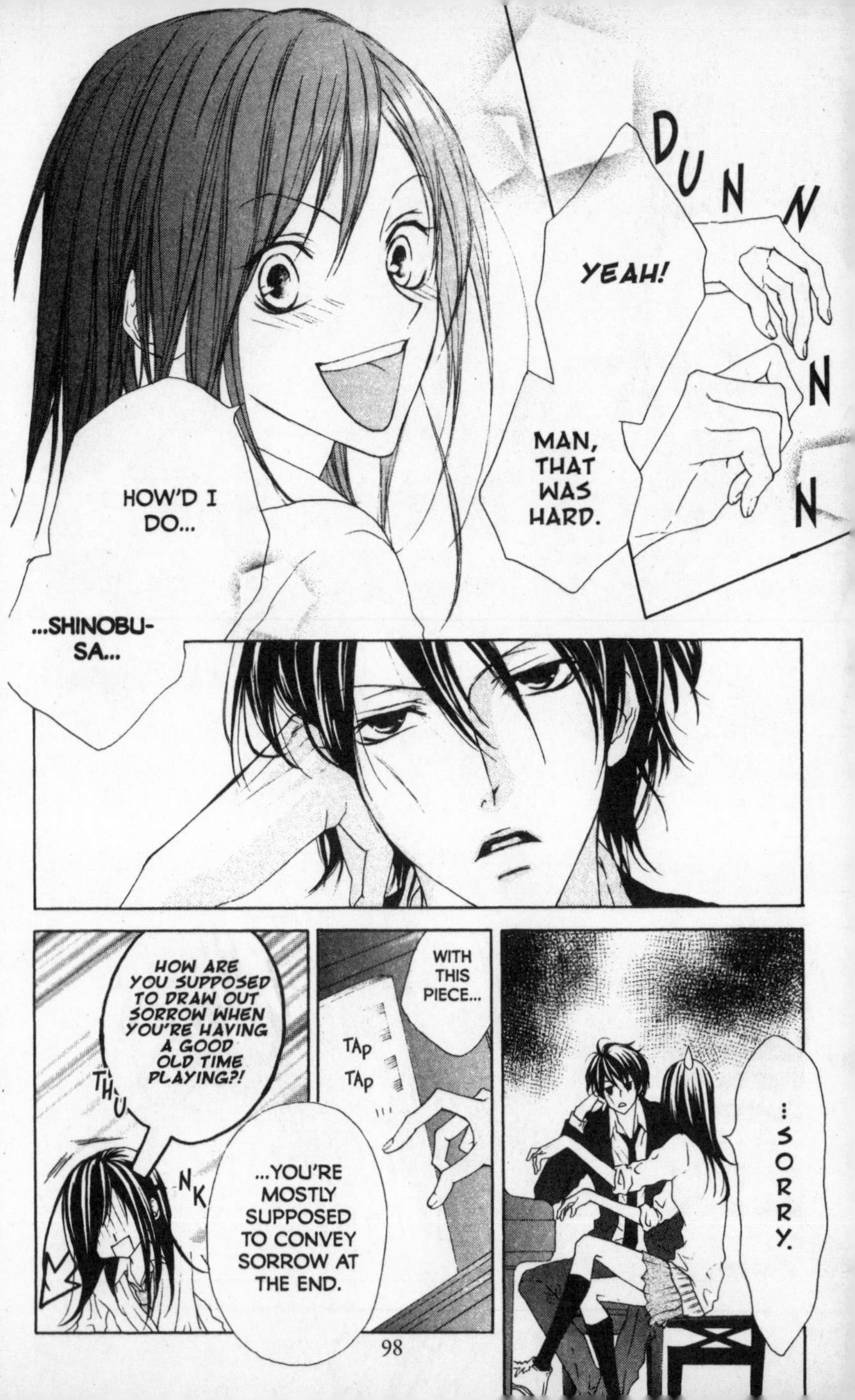
DUNNNNN
YEAH!
MAN, THAT WAS HARD.
HOW'D I DO...
...SHINOBU-SA...
...SORRY.
WITH THIS PIECE...
TAP TAP
...YOU'RE MOSTLY SUPPOSED TO CONVEY SORROW AT THE END.
HOW ARE YOU SUPPOSED TO DRAW OUT SORROW WHEN YOU'RE HAVING A GOOD OLD TIME PLAYING?!
THUNK

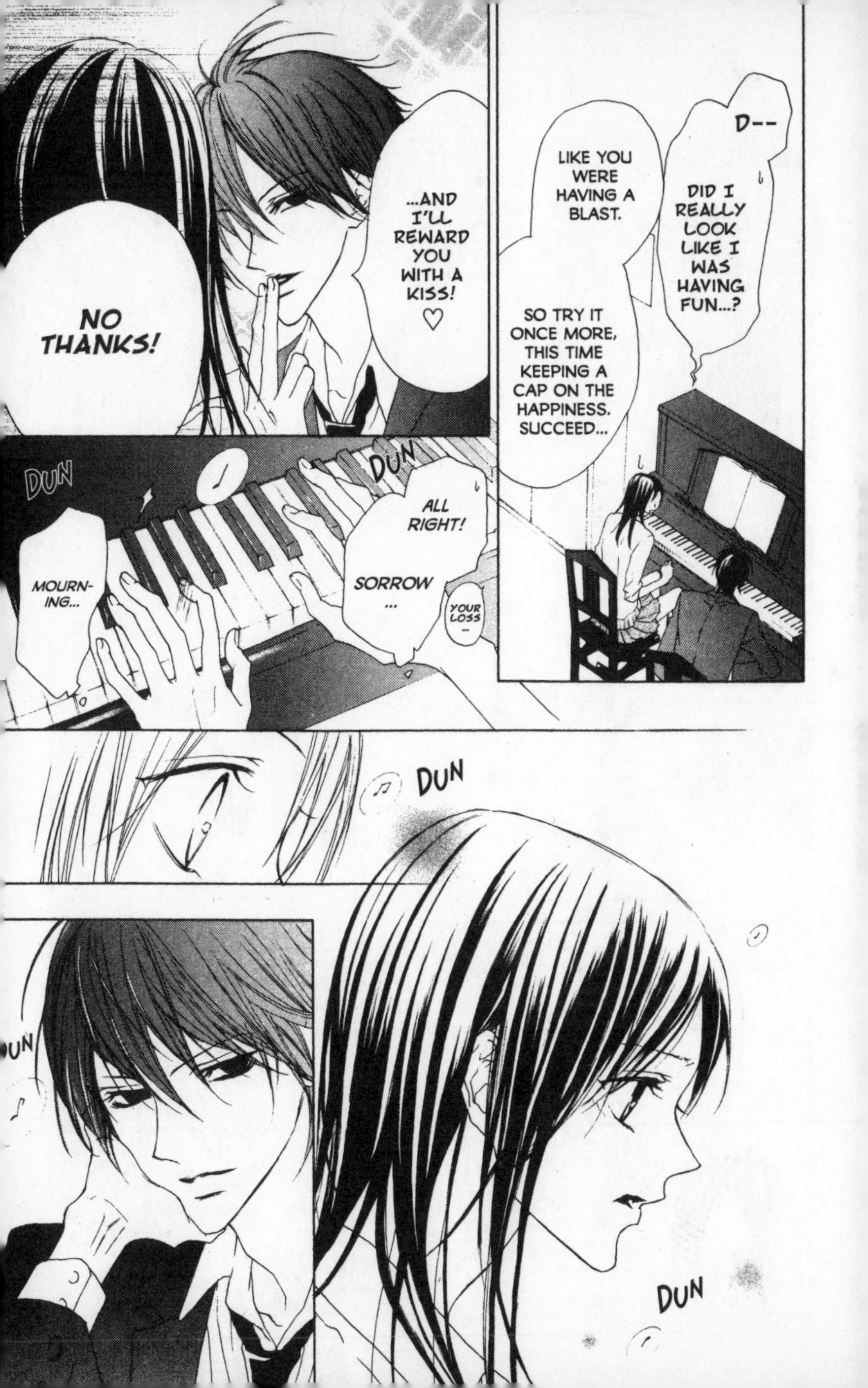
D--
DID I REALLY LOOK LIKE I WAS HAVING FUN...?
LIKE YOU WERE HAVING A BLAST.
SO TRY IT ONCE MORE, THIS TIME KEEPING A CAP ON THE HAPPINESS. SUCCEED...
...AND I'LL REWARD YOU WITH A KISS! ♡
NO THANKS!
DUN
ALL RIGHT!
DUN
SORROW ...
YOUR LOSS ...
MOURNING...
DUN
DUN
DUN

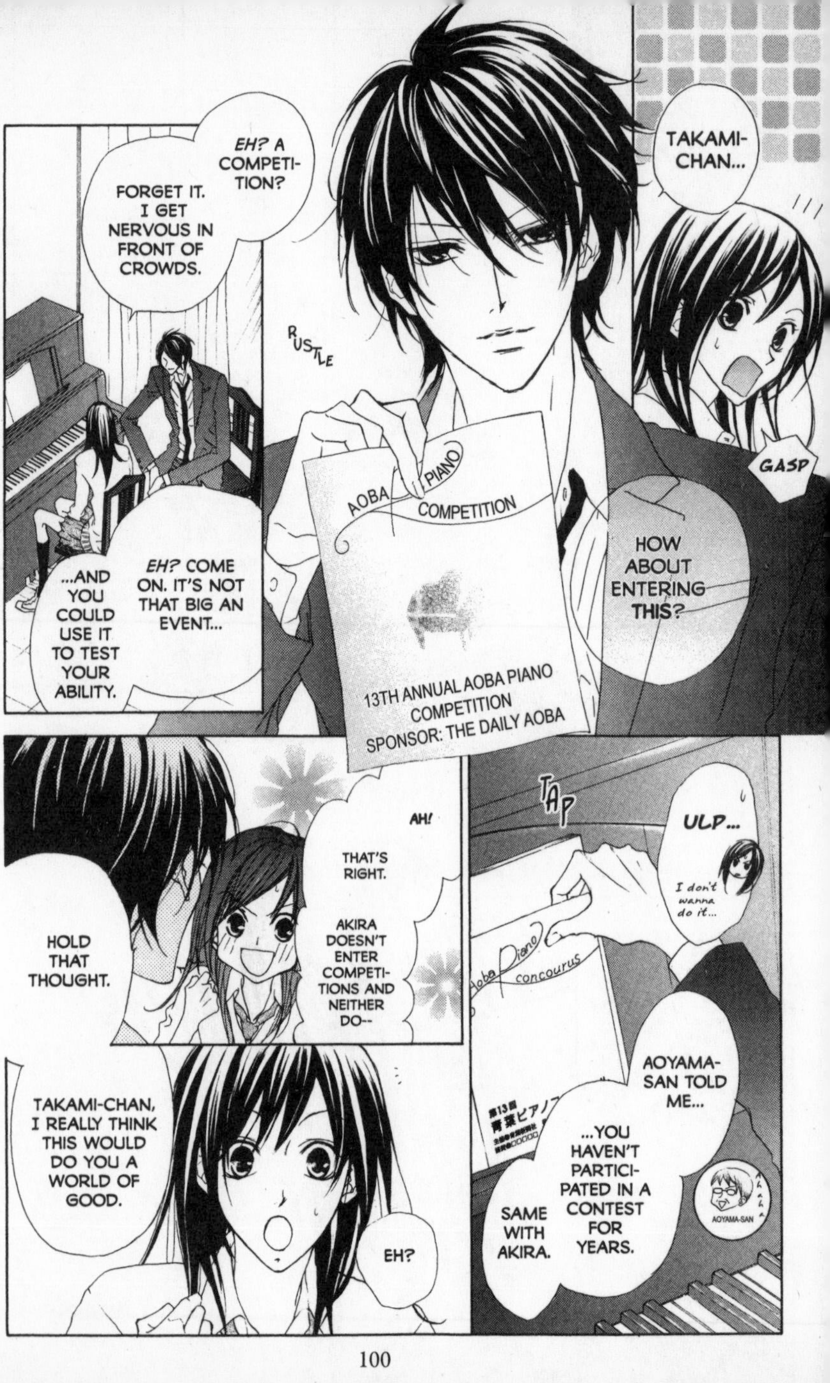
TAKAMI-CHAN...
GASP
HOW ABOUT ENTERING THIS?
AOBA PIANO COMPETITION
13TH ANNUAL AOBA PIANO COMPETITION
SPONSOR: THE DAILY AOBA
RUSTLE
EH? A COMPETITION?
FORGET IT. I GET NERVOUS IN FRONT OF CROWDS.
EH? COME ON. IT'S NOT THAT BIG AN EVENT...
...AND YOU COULD USE IT TO TEST YOUR ABILITY.
TAP
ULP...
I don't wanna do it...
Aoba Piano concourus
AOYAMA-SAN TOLD ME...
...YOU HAVEN'T PARTICIPATED IN A CONTEST FOR YEARS.
SAME WITH AKIRA.
Ahaha
AOYAMA-SAN
AH!
THAT'S RIGHT.
AKIRA DOESN'T ENTER COMPETITIONS AND NEITHER DO--
HOLD THAT THOUGHT.
EH?
TAKAMI-CHAN, I REALLY THINK THIS WOULD DO YOU A WORLD OF GOOD.

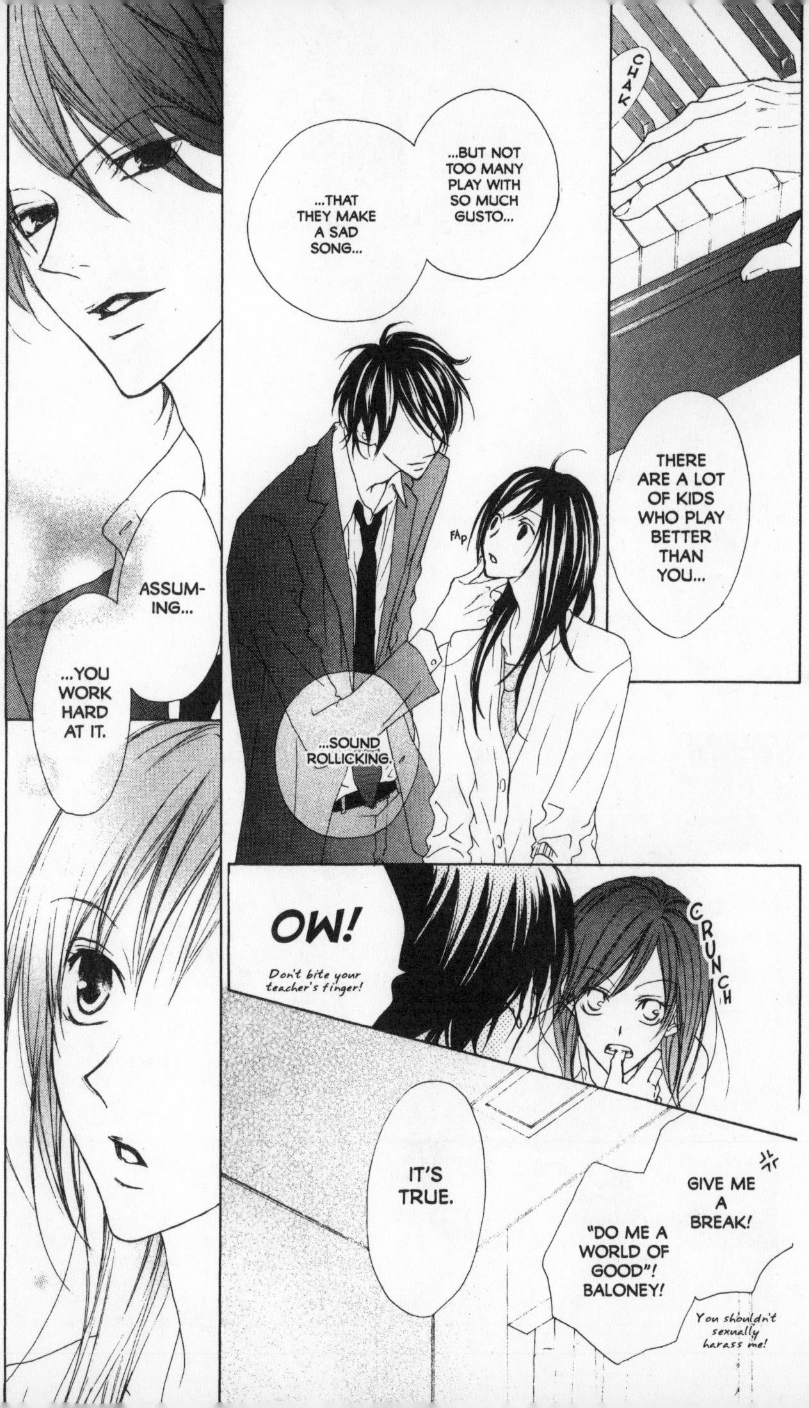
CHAK
THERE ARE A LOT OF KIDS WHO PLAY BETTER THAN YOU...
...BUT NOT TOO MANY PLAY WITH SO MUCH GUSTO...
...THAT THEY MAKE A SAD SONG...
FAP
...SOUND ROLLICKING.
ASSUM-ING...
...YOU WORK HARD AT IT.
CRUNCH
OW!
Don't bite your teacher's finger!
GIVE ME A BREAK!
"DO ME A WORLD OF GOOD"! BALONEY!
You shouldn't sexually harass me!
IT'S TRUE.

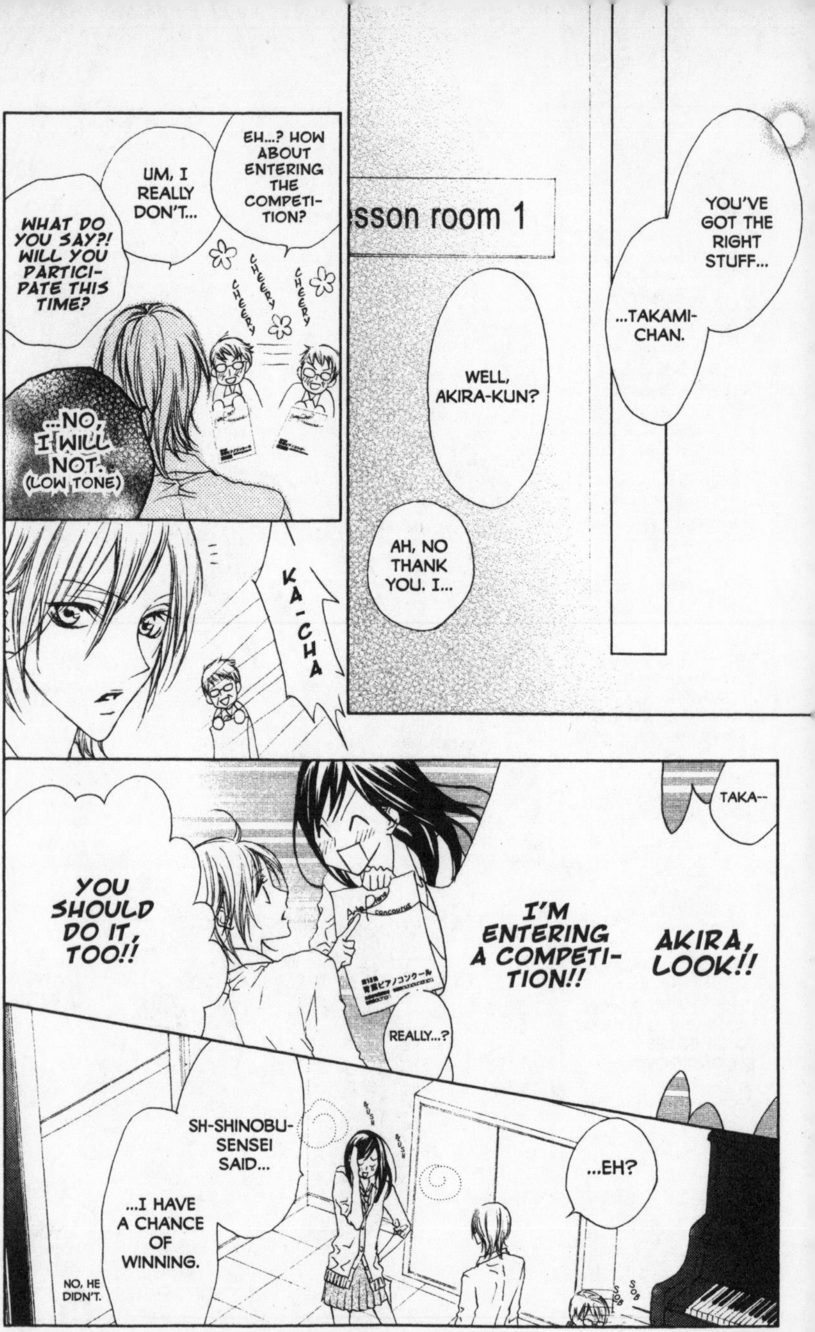
esson room 1
YOU'VE GOT THE RIGHT STUFF...
...TAKAMI-CHAN.
WELL, AKIRA-KUN?
AH, NO THANK YOU. I...
EH...? HOW ABOUT ENTERING THE COMPETITION?
UM, I REALLY DON'T...
WHAT DO YOU SAY?! WILL YOU PARTICIPATE THIS TIME?
CHEERY CHEERY CHEERY
...NO, I WILL NOT. (LOW TONE)
KA-CHA
TAKA--
AKIRA, LOOK!!
I'M ENTERING A COMPETITION!!
YOU SHOULD DO IT, TOO!!
REALLY...?
...EH?
SOB SOB
SH-SHINOBU-SENSEI SAID...
...I HAVE A CHANCE OF WINNING.
NO, HE DIDN'T.

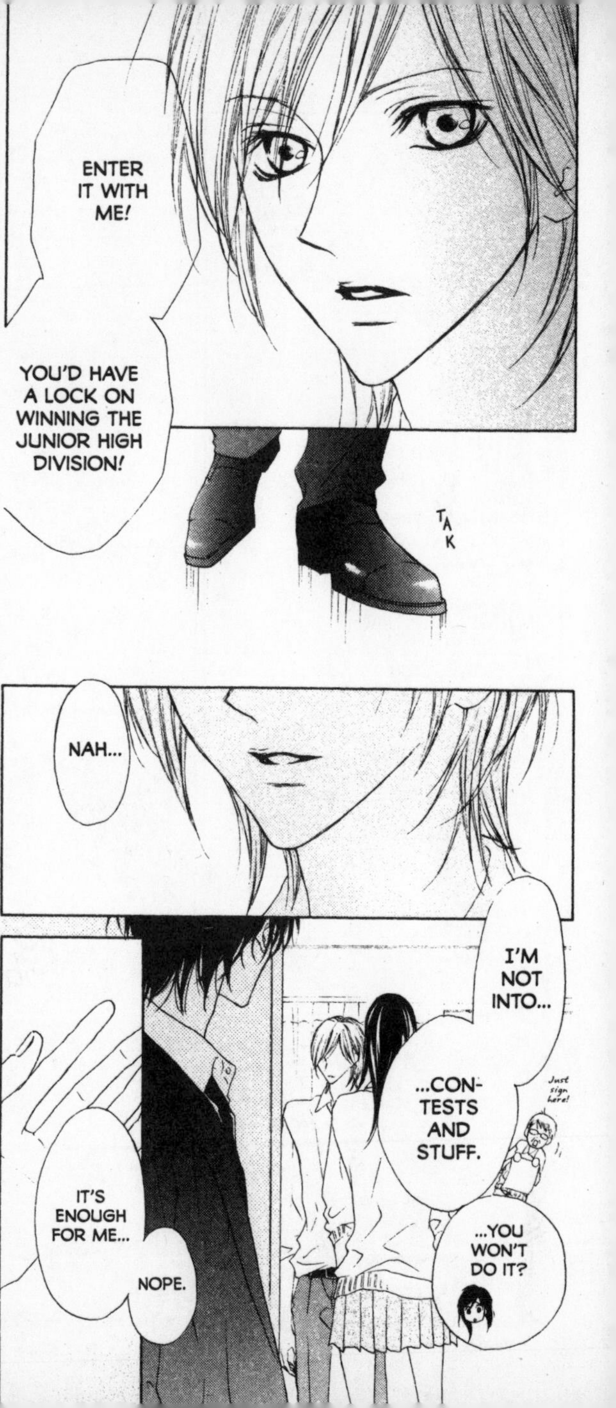
ENTER IT WITH ME!
YOU'D HAVE A LOCK ON WINNING THE JUNIOR HIGH DIVISION!
TAK
NAH...
I'M NOT INTO...
...CON-TESTS AND STUFF.
Just sign here!
...YOU WON'T DO IT?
IT'S ENOUGH FOR ME...
NOPE.

4

RECENTLY, I'VE BEEN REALLY HAPPY!

I LOVE THE SINGER-SONGWRITER JYONGRI AND AM LISTENING TO HER ALBUM EVEN AS I WRITE THIS.

LATELY, THOUGH, I WON TICKETS TO ONE OF HER SHOWS! I DANCED WITH JOY WHEN I FOUND OUT.

IT WAS MY FIRST TIME SEEING HER LIVE, SO I WAS SOOO LOOKING FORWARD TO IT...

AND IT WAS EXCELLENT.

JYONGRIL ENCHANTED FROM BEGINNING TO END IN A CAPELLA.
SHE MOVED ME WITH THE SAME VOICE I'VE HEARD COUNTLESS TIMES ON CD.
I REALLY LOVE HER VOICE. SHE DID A GREAT JOB PLAYING THE PIANO, TOO.

I WENT WITH MY LITTLE SISTER AND MAYBE IT WAS BECAUSE WE WERE THE FIRST TO ARRIVE OUT OF THE 100 PEOPLE WHO'D WON TICKETS, BUT WE GOT TO SIT IN THE SECOND ROW.

I'M REALLY LOOKING FORWARD TO WHATEVER SHE DOES NEXT.

THIS IS MEANT TO BE HER.

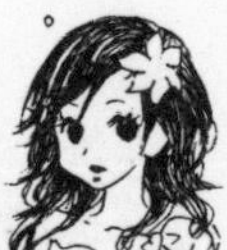

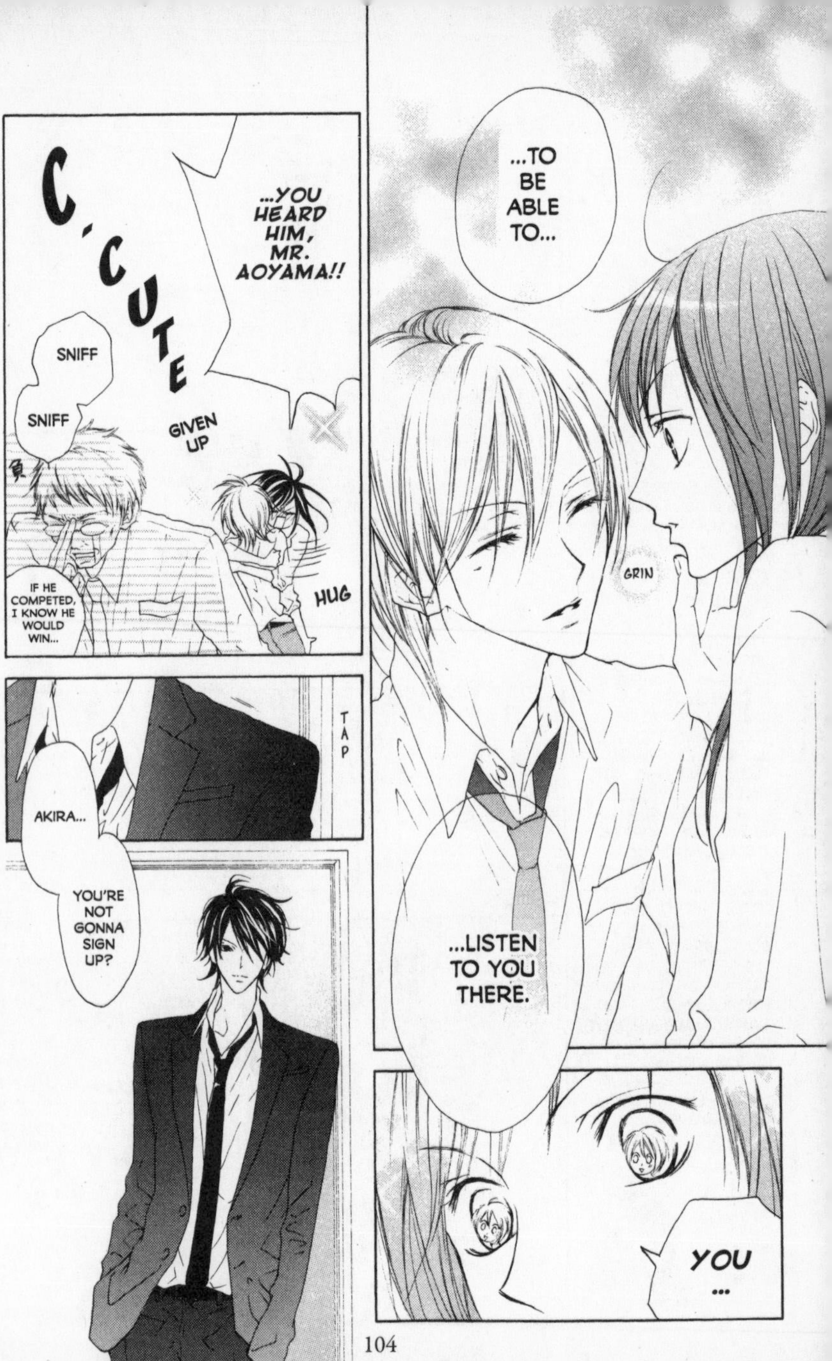

...TO BE ABLE TO...
GRIN
...LISTEN TO YOU THERE.
YOU ...
...YOU HEARD HIM, MR. AOYAMA!!
C-CUTE
SNIFF
SNIFF
GIVEN UP
IF HE COMPETED, I KNOW HE WOULD WIN...
HUG
TAP
AKIRA...
YOU'RE NOT GONNA SIGN UP?

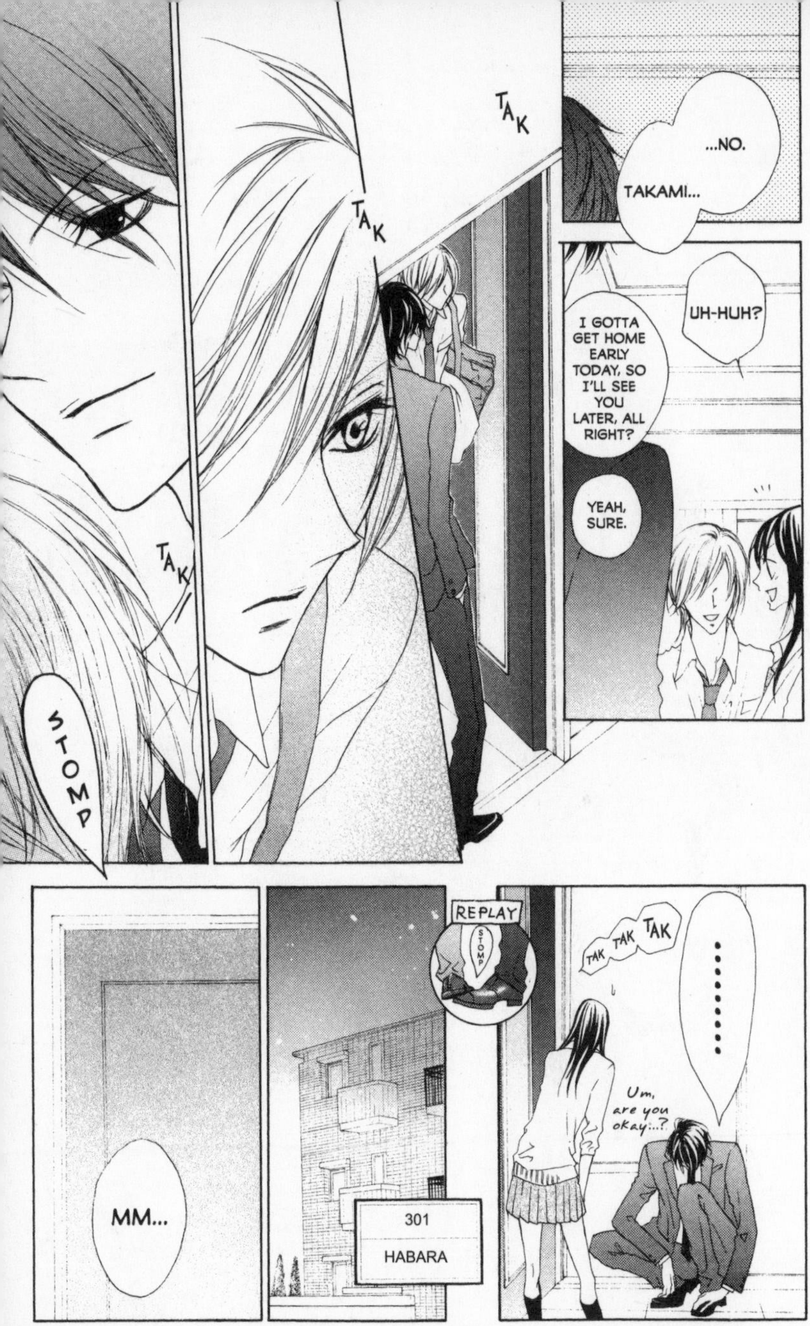
...NO.
TAKAMI...
UH-HUH?
I GOTTA GET HOME EARLY TODAY, SO I'LL SEE YOU LATER, ALL RIGHT?
YEAH, SURE.
TAK
TAK
TAK
STOMP
TAK TAK TAK
......
Um, are you okay...?
REPLAY
STOMP
301
HABARA
MM...

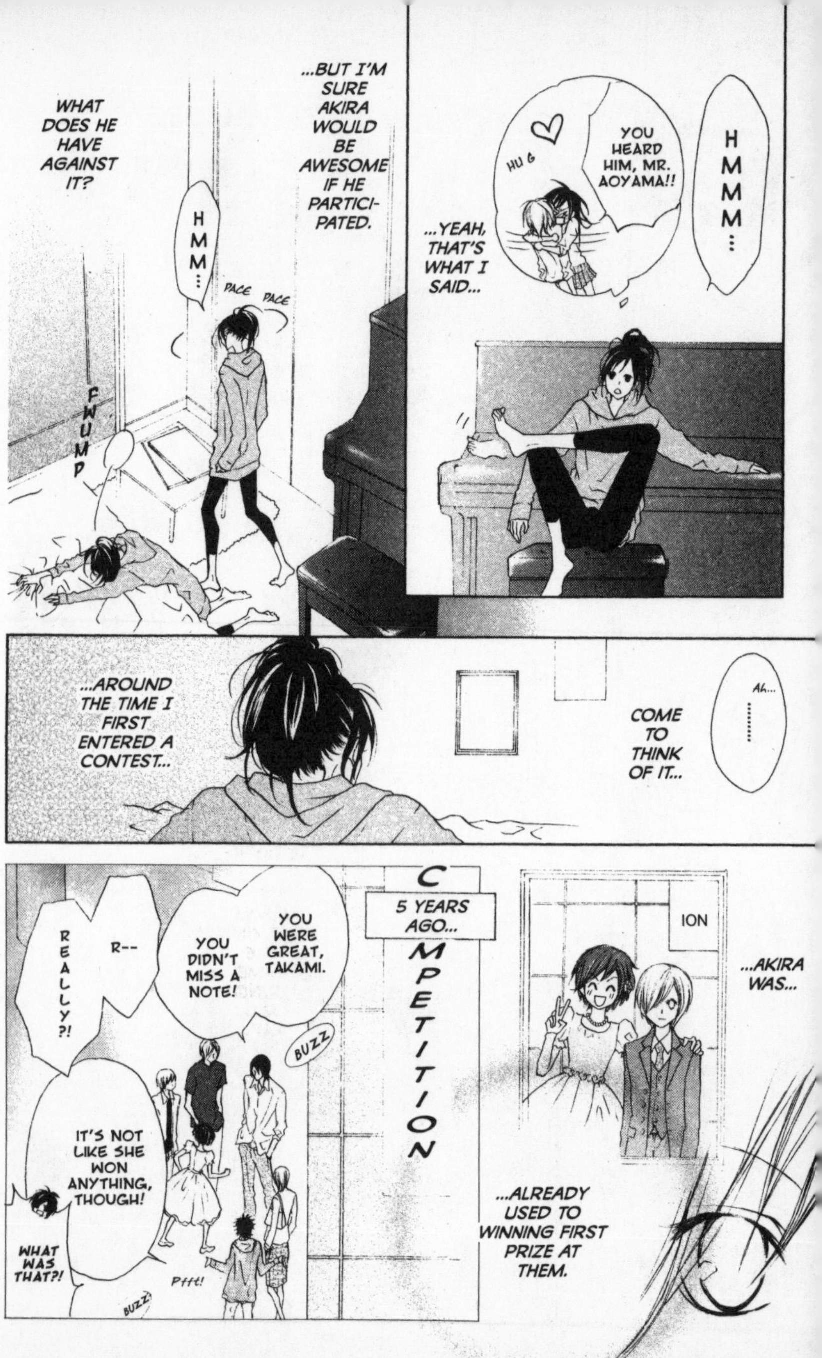
HMMM...
YOU HEARD HIM, MR. AOYAMA!!
HUG
...YEAH, THAT'S WHAT I SAID...
...BUT I'M SURE AKIRA WOULD BE AWESOME IF HE PARTICIPATED.
HMM...
PACE PACE
WHAT DOES HE HAVE AGAINST IT?
FWUMP
Ah... ....
COME TO THINK OF IT...
...AROUND THE TIME I FIRST ENTERED A CONTEST...
ION
...AKIRA WAS...
...ALREADY USED TO WINNING FIRST PRIZE AT THEM.
COMPETITION
5 YEARS AGO...
YOU WERE GREAT, TAKAMI.
YOU DIDN'T MISS A NOTE!
R--
REALLY?!
BUZZ
IT'S NOT LIKE SHE WON ANYTHING, THOUGH!
WHAT WAS THAT?!
Pfft!
BUZZ

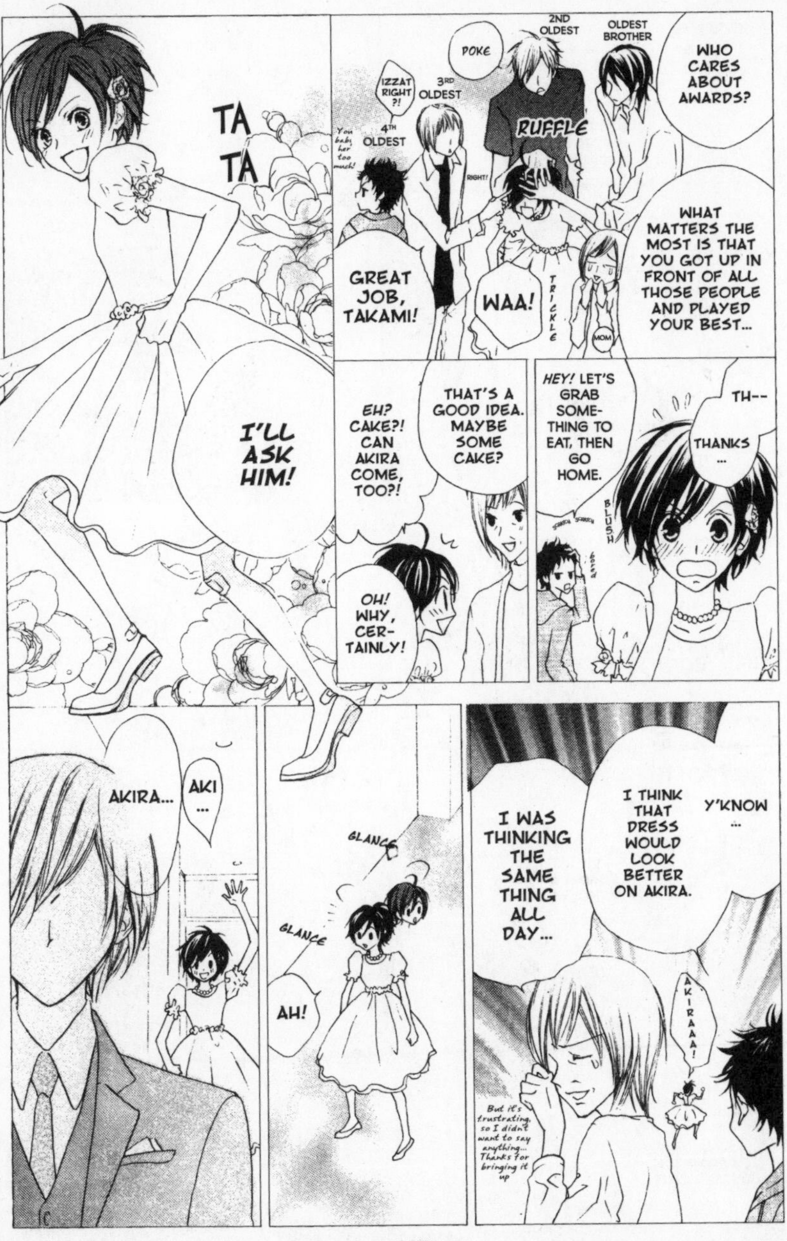
WHO CARES ABOUT AWARDS?
OLDEST BROTHER
2ND OLDEST
POKE
RUFFLE
3RD OLDEST
IZZAT RIGHT ?!
4TH OLDEST
You baby her too much!
RIGHT!
WHAT MATTERS THE MOST IS THAT YOU GOT UP IN FRONT OF ALL THOSE PEOPLE AND PLAYED YOUR BEST...
MOM
TRICKLE
WAA!
GREAT JOB, TAKAMI!
TH-- THANKS...
HEY! LET'S GRAB SOME-THING TO EAT, THEN GO HOME.
BLUSH
SCRATCH SCRATCH
THAT'S A GOOD IDEA. MAYBE SOME CAKE?
EH? CAKE?! CAN AKIRA COME, TOO?!
OH! WHY, CER-TAINLY!
TA TA
I'LL ASK HIM!
Y'KNOW...
I THINK THAT DRESS WOULD LOOK BETTER ON AKIRA.
I WAS THINKING THE SAME THING ALL DAY...
AKIRAAA!
But it's frustrating, so I didn't want to say anything... Thanks for bringing it up
GLANCE
GLANCE
AH!
AKI...
AKIRA...

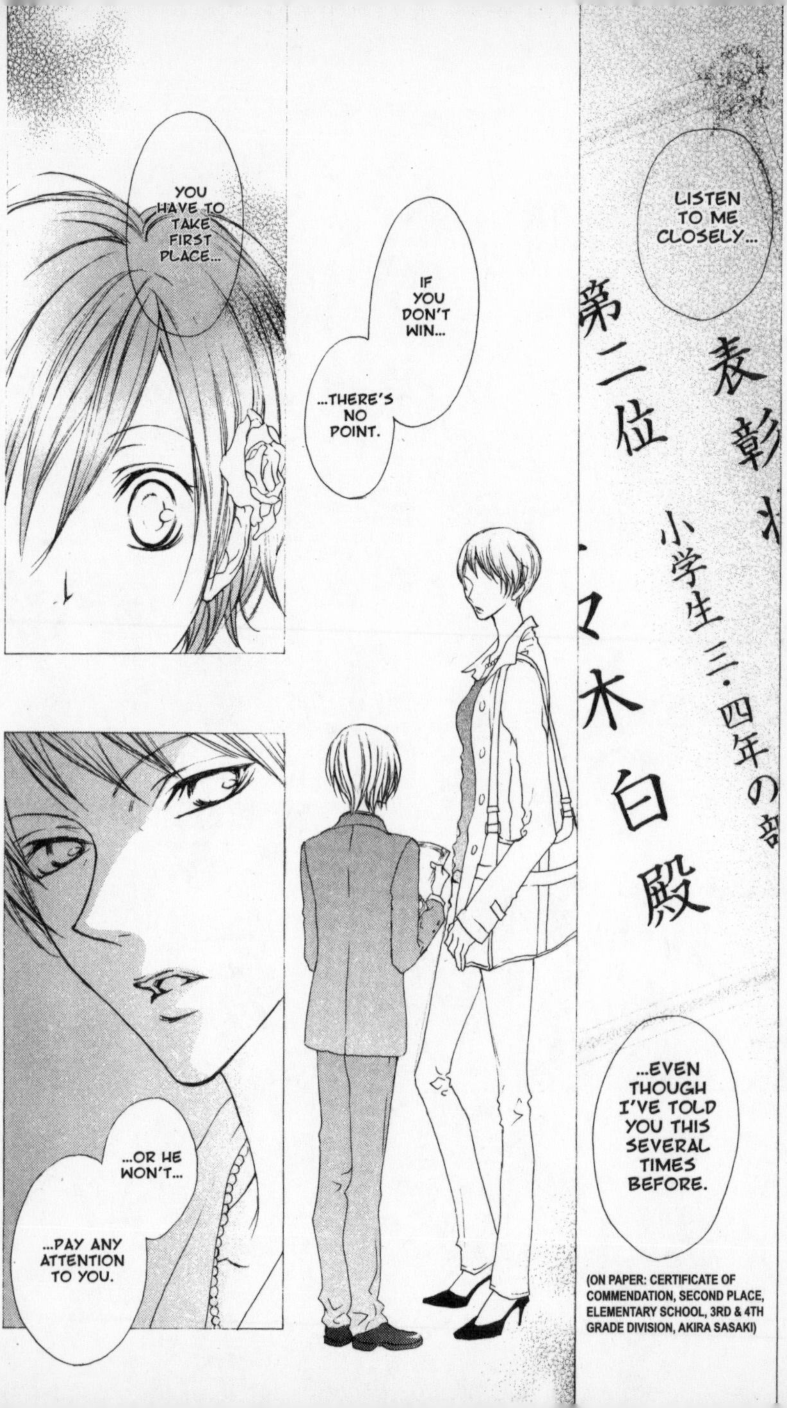
LISTEN TO ME CLOSELY...
表彰
第二位
小学生三・四年の
木白殿
...EVEN THOUGH I'VE TOLD YOU THIS SEVERAL TIMES BEFORE.
IF YOU DON'T WIN...
...THERE'S NO POINT.
YOU HAVE TO TAKE FIRST PLACE...
...OR HE WON'T...
...PAY ANY ATTENTION TO YOU.
(ON PAPER: CERTIFICATE OF COMMENDATION, SECOND PLACE, ELEMENTARY SCHOOL, 3RD & 4TH GRADE DIVISION, AKIRA SASAKI)

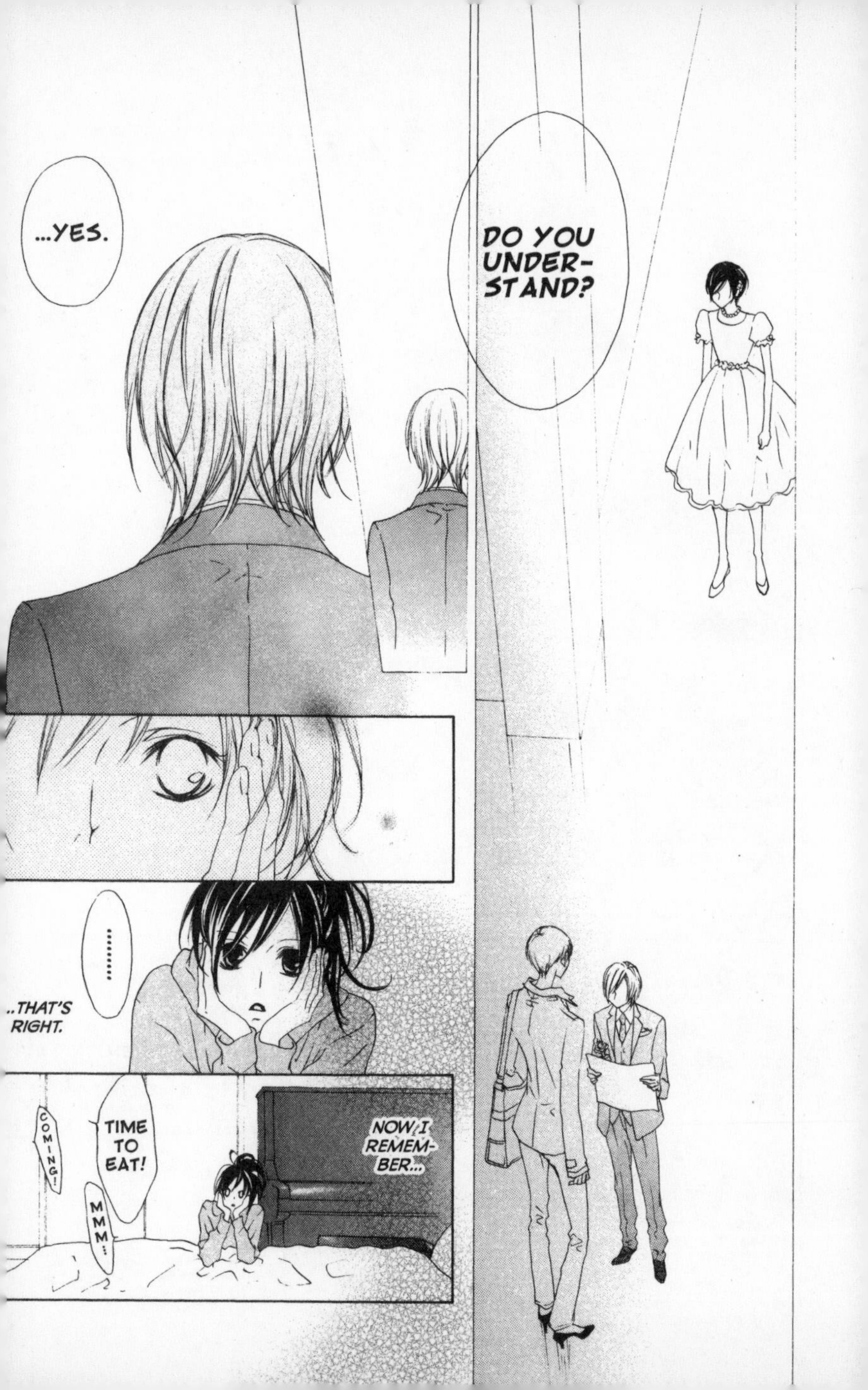
DO YOU UNDER-STAND?
...YES.
....
..THAT'S RIGHT.
NOW I REMEM-BER...
TIME TO EAT!
COMING!
MMM...

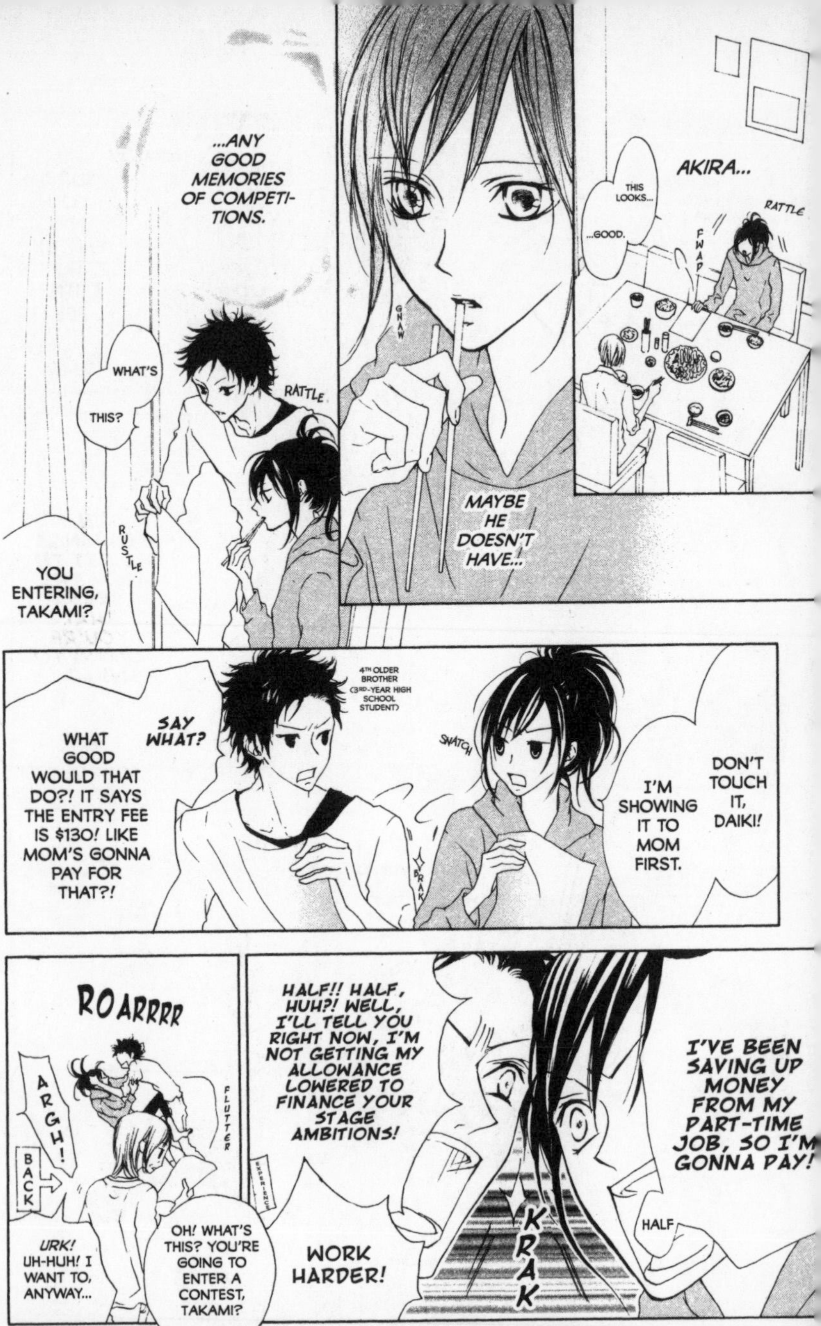
AKIRA...
THIS LOOKS...
...GOOD.
RATTLE
FWAP
GNAW
MAYBE HE DOESN'T HAVE...
...ANY GOOD MEMORIES OF COMPETITIONS.
WHAT'S
THIS?
RATTLE
RUSTLE
YOU ENTERING, TAKAMI?
DON'T TOUCH IT, DAIKI!
I'M SHOWING IT TO MOM FIRST.
SNATCH
BRAK
4TH OLDER BROTHER (3RD-YEAR HIGH SCHOOL STUDENT)
SAY WHAT?
WHAT GOOD WOULD THAT DO?! IT SAYS THE ENTRY FEE IS $130! LIKE MOM'S GONNA PAY FOR THAT?!
I'VE BEEN SAVING UP MONEY FROM MY PART-TIME JOB, SO I'M GONNA PAY!
HALF
KRAK
HALF!! HALF, HUH?! WELL, I'LL TELL YOU RIGHT NOW, I'M NOT GETTING MY ALLOWANCE LOWERED TO FINANCE YOUR STAGE AMBITIONS!
WORK HARDER!
EXPERIENCE
ROARRRR
FLUTTER
ARGH!
BACK
OH! WHAT'S THIS? YOU'RE GOING TO ENTER A CONTEST, TAKAMI?
URK! UH-HUH! I WANT TO, ANYWAY...

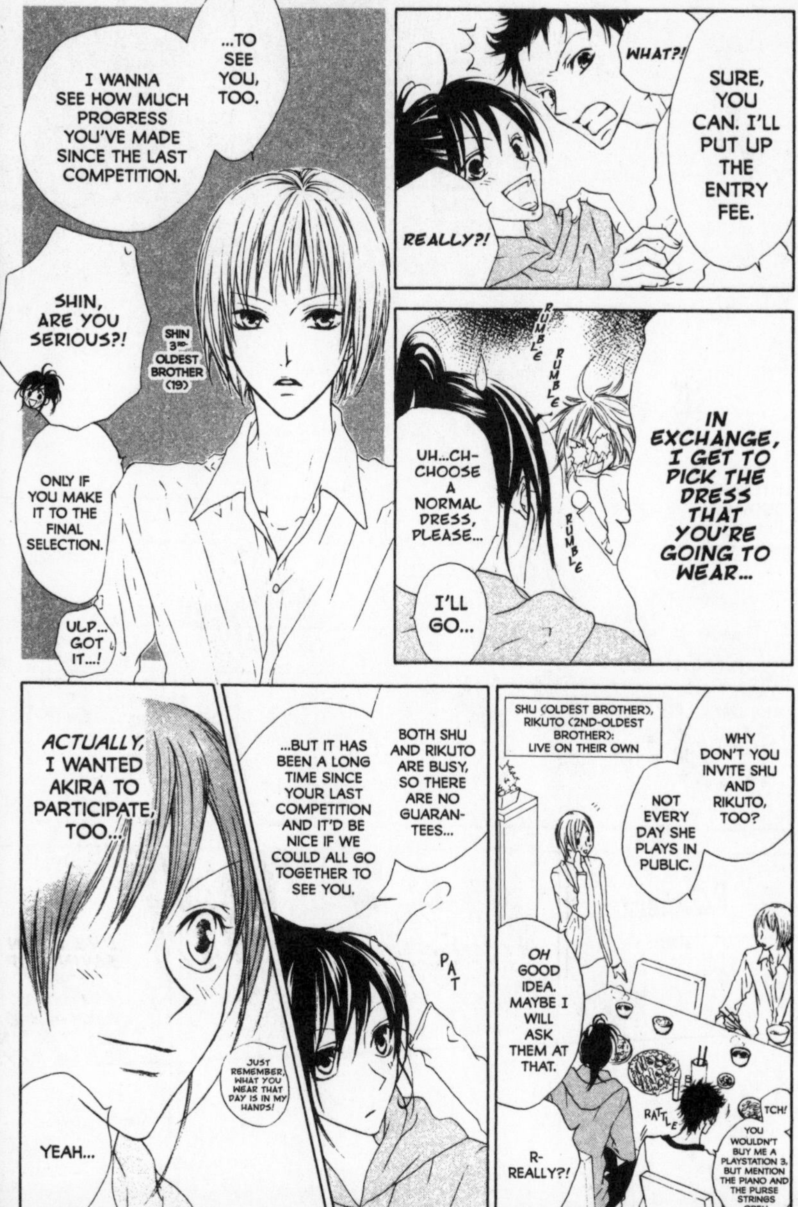
SURE, YOU CAN. I'LL PUT UP THE ENTRY FEE.
WHAT?!
REALLY?!
IN EXCHANGE, I GET TO PICK THE DRESS THAT YOU'RE GOING TO WEAR...
RUMBLE
RUMBLE
RUMBLE
UH...CH-CHOOSE A NORMAL DRESS, PLEASE...
I'LL GO...
...TO SEE YOU, TOO.
I WANNA SEE HOW MUCH PROGRESS YOU'VE MADE SINCE THE LAST COMPETITION.
SHIN 3RD-OLDEST BROTHER (19)
SHIN, ARE YOU SERIOUS?!
ONLY IF YOU MAKE IT TO THE FINAL SELECTION.
ULP... GOT IT...!
SHU (OLDEST BROTHER), RIKUTO (2ND-OLDEST BROTHER): LIVE ON THEIR OWN
WHY DON'T YOU INVITE SHU AND RIKUTO, TOO?
NOT EVERY DAY SHE PLAYS IN PUBLIC.
OH GOOD IDEA. MAYBE I WILL ASK THEM AT THAT.
TCH!
YOU WOULDN'T BUY ME A PLAYSTATION 3, BUT MENTION THE PIANO AND THE PURSE STRINGS OPEN...
RATTLE
R-REALLY?!
BOTH SHU AND RIKUTO ARE BUSY, SO THERE ARE NO GUARANTEES...
...BUT IT HAS BEEN A LONG TIME SINCE YOUR LAST COMPETITION AND IT'D BE NICE IF WE COULD ALL GO TOGETHER TO SEE YOU.
PAT
JUST REMEMBER, WHAT YOU WEAR THAT DAY IS IN MY HANDS!
ACTUALLY, I WANTED AKIRA TO PARTICIPATE, TOO...
YEAH...

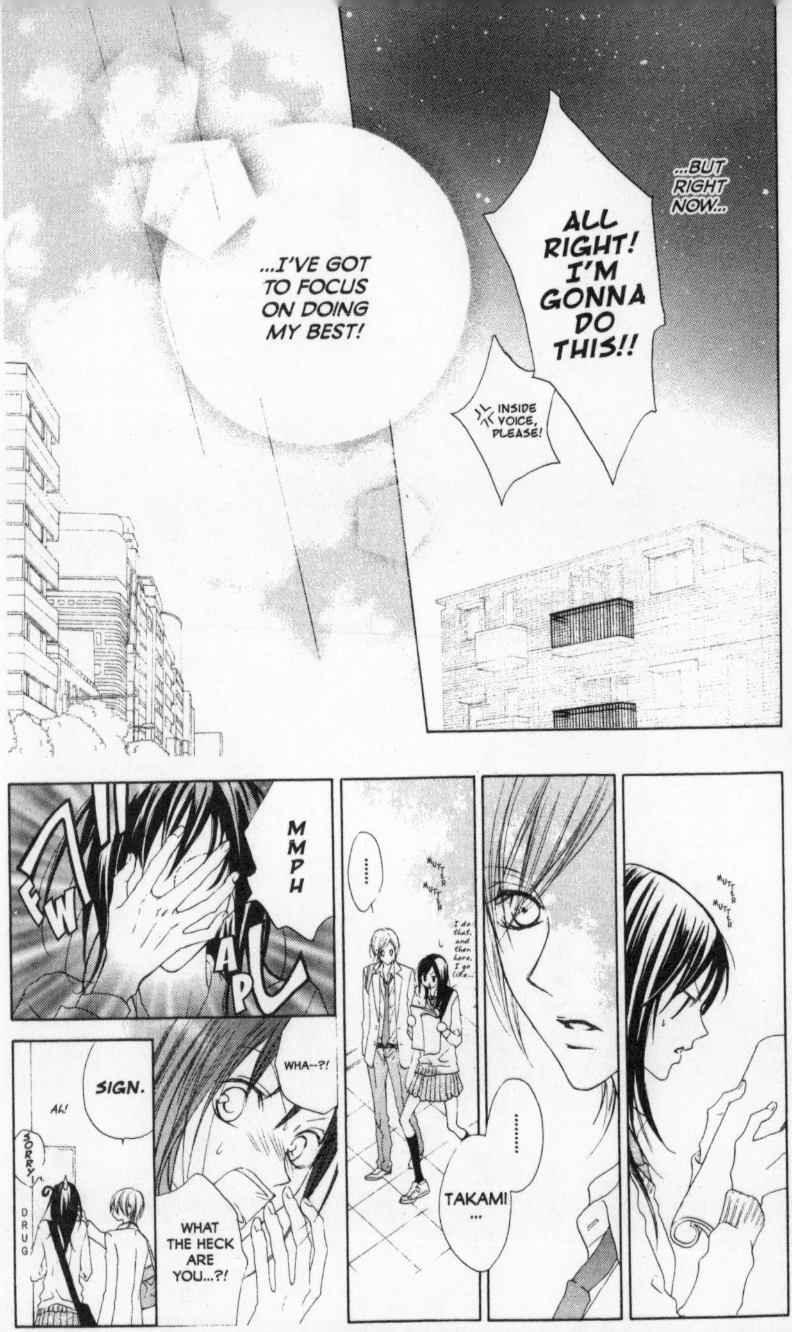
...BUT RIGHT NOW...
...I'VE GOT TO FOCUS ON DOING MY BEST!
ALL RIGHT! I'M GONNA DO THIS!!
INSIDE VOICE, PLEASE!
MUTTER MUTTER
......
TAKAMI ...
......
MUTTER MUTTER
I do that, and then here, I go like...
MMPH
FWAP
WHA--?!
SIGN.
Ah!
WHAT THE HECK ARE YOU...?!
SORRY!
DRUG

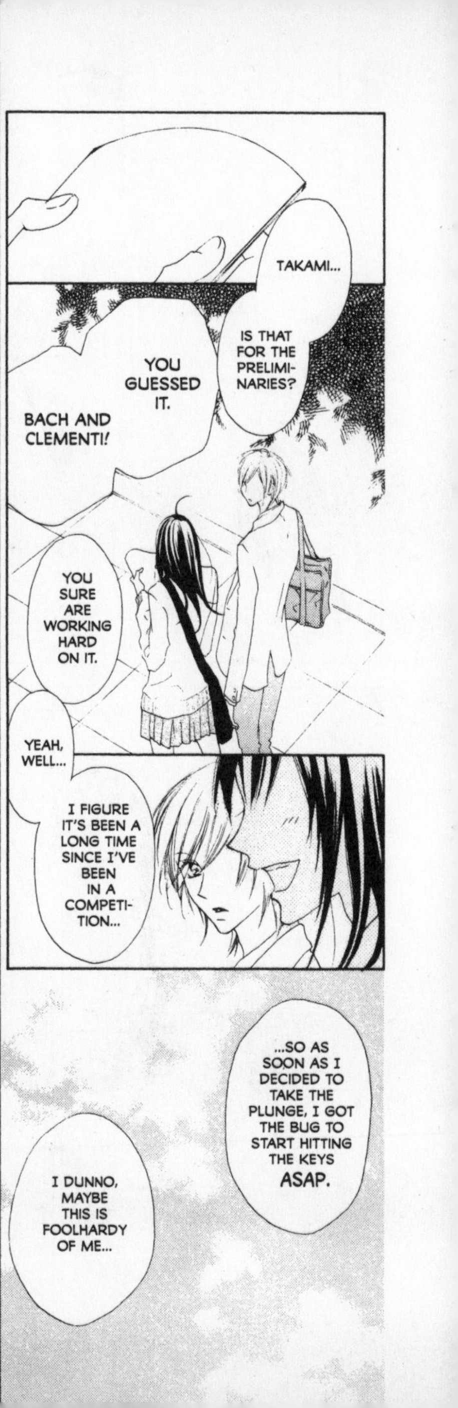
TAKAMI...
IS THAT FOR THE PRELIMINARIES?
YOU GUESSED IT.
BACH AND CLEMENTI!
YOU SURE ARE WORKING HARD ON IT.
YEAH, WELL...
I FIGURE IT'S BEEN A LONG TIME SINCE I'VE BEEN IN A COMPETITION...
...SO AS SOON AS I DECIDED TO TAKE THE PLUNGE, I GOT THE BUG TO START HITTING THE KEYS ASAP.
I DUNNO, MAYBE THIS IS FOOLHARDY OF ME...
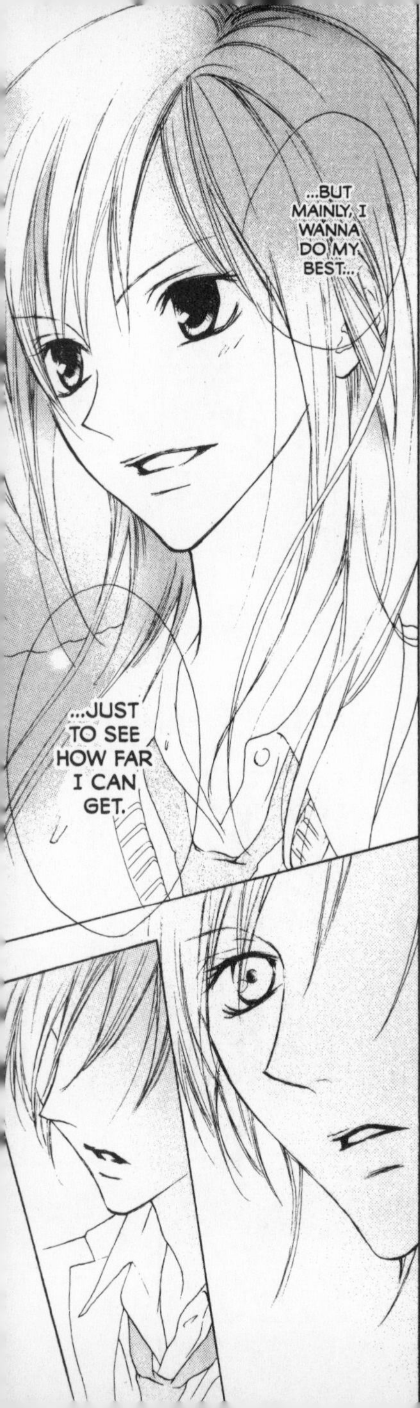
...BUT MAINLY, I WANNA DO MY BEST...
...JUST TO SEE HOW FAR I CAN GET.

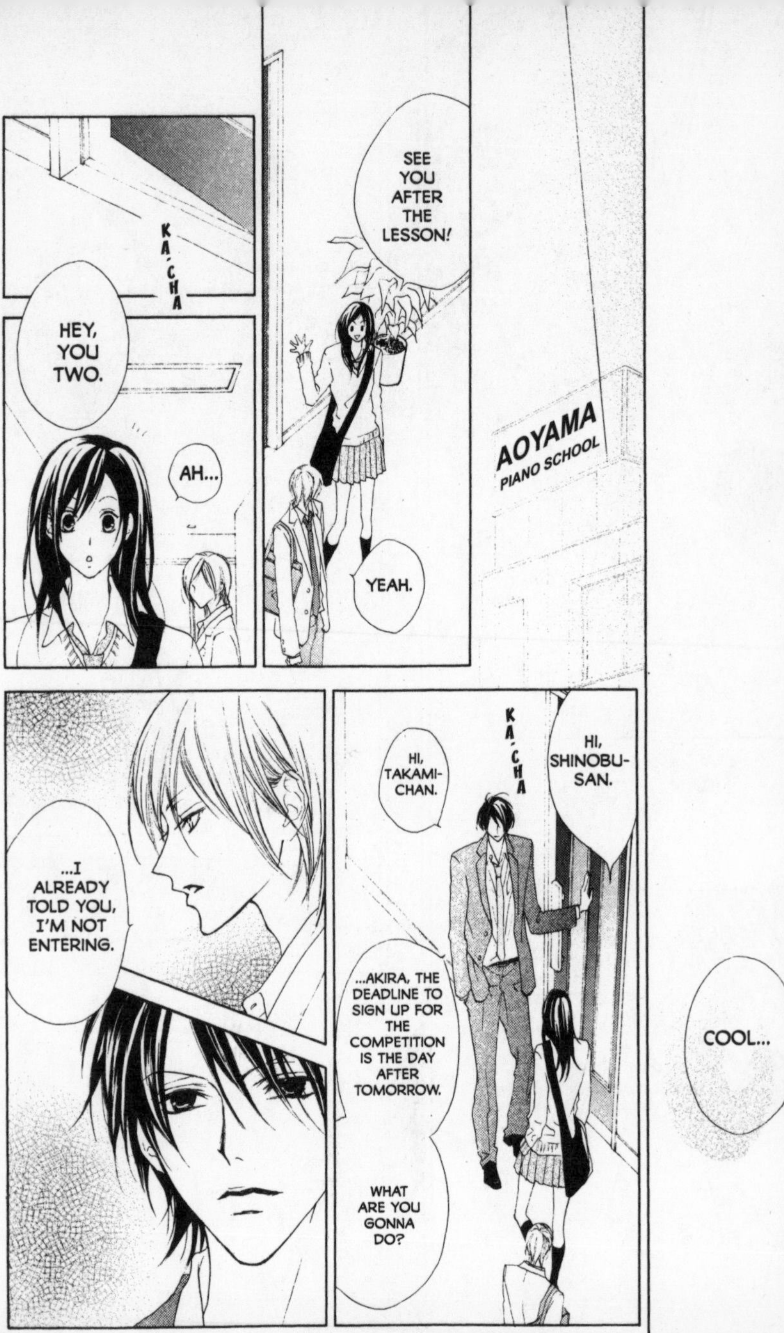
AOYAMA
PIANO SCHOOL
SEE YOU AFTER THE LESSON!
YEAH.
KA-CHA
HEY, YOU TWO.
AH...
COOL...
HI, SHINOBU-SAN.
KA-CHA
HI, TAKAMI-CHAN.
...AKIRA, THE DEADLINE TO SIGN UP FOR THE COMPETITION IS THE DAY AFTER TOMORROW.
WHAT ARE YOU GONNA DO?
...I ALREADY TOLD YOU, I'M NOT ENTERING.

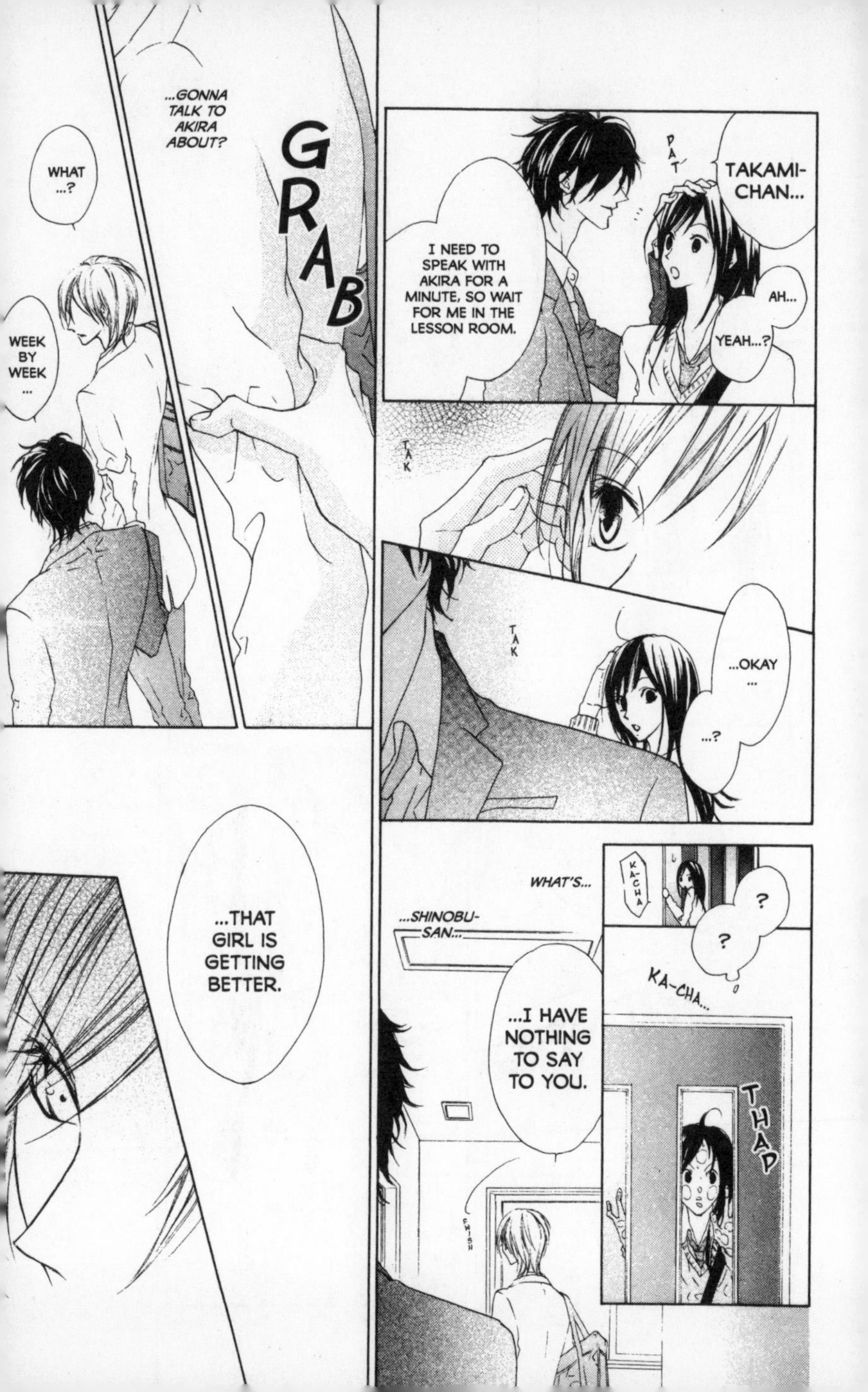
PAT
TAKAMI-CHAN...
I NEED TO SPEAK WITH AKIRA FOR A MINUTE, SO WAIT FOR ME IN THE LESSON ROOM.
AH...
YEAH...?
TAK
TAK
...OKAY ...
...?
KA-CHA
?
?
WHAT'S...
...SHINOBU-SAN...
KA-CHA...
...I HAVE NOTHING TO SAY TO YOU.
THAP
FWISH
...GONNA TALK TO AKIRA ABOUT?
GRAB
WHAT ...?
WEEK BY WEEK ...
...THAT GIRL IS GETTING BETTER.

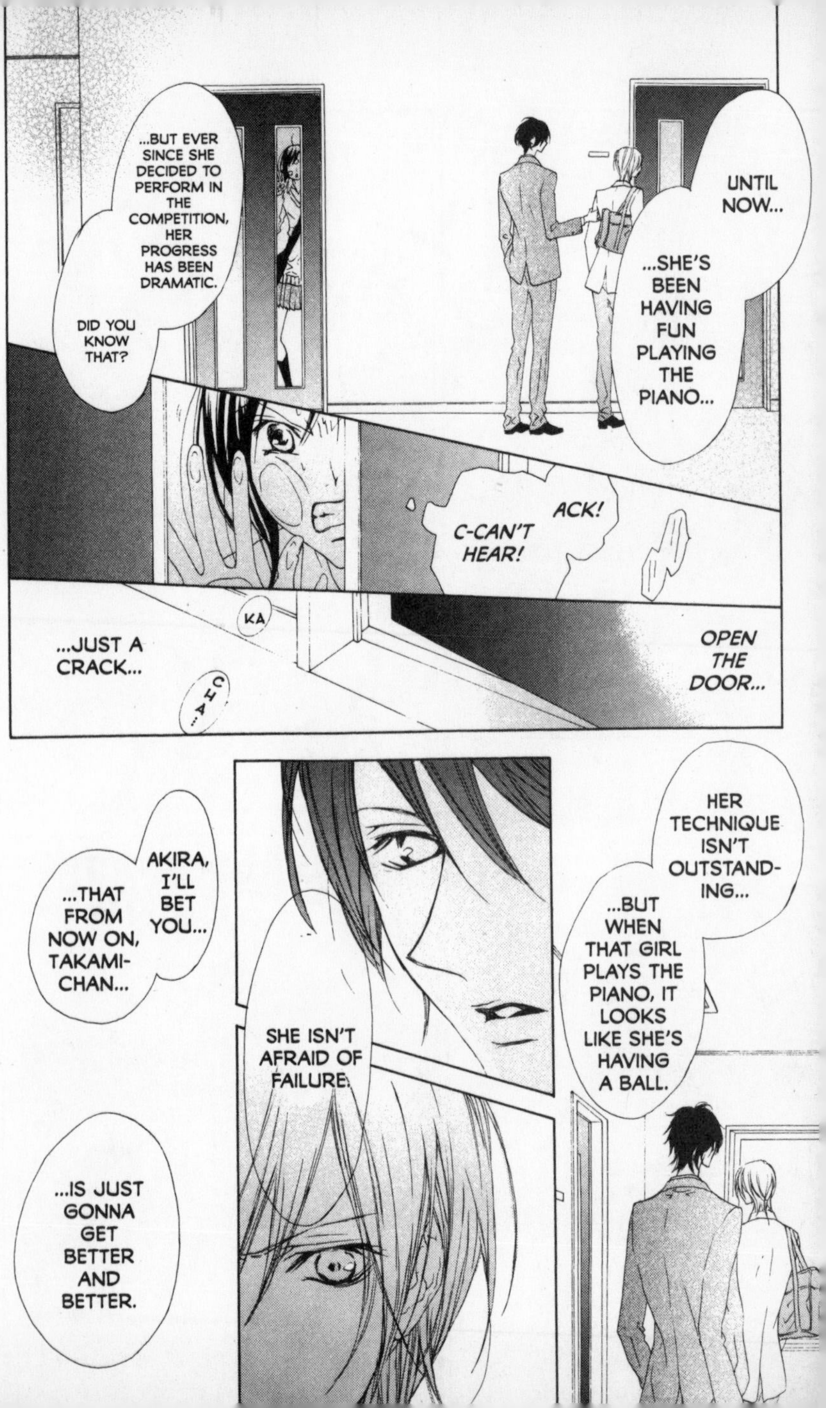
UNTIL NOW...
...SHE'S BEEN HAVING FUN PLAYING THE PIANO...
...BUT EVER SINCE SHE DECIDED TO PERFORM IN THE COMPETITION, HER PROGRESS HAS BEEN DRAMATIC.
DID YOU KNOW THAT?
ACK! C-CAN'T HEAR!
OPEN THE DOOR...
KA
CHA...
...JUST A CRACK...
HER TECHNIQUE ISN'T OUTSTAND-ING...
...BUT WHEN THAT GIRL PLAYS THE PIANO, IT LOOKS LIKE SHE'S HAVING A BALL.
SHE ISN'T AFRAID OF FAILURE.
AKIRA, I'LL BET YOU...
...THAT FROM NOW ON, TAKAMI-CHAN...
...IS JUST GONNA GET BETTER AND BETTER.

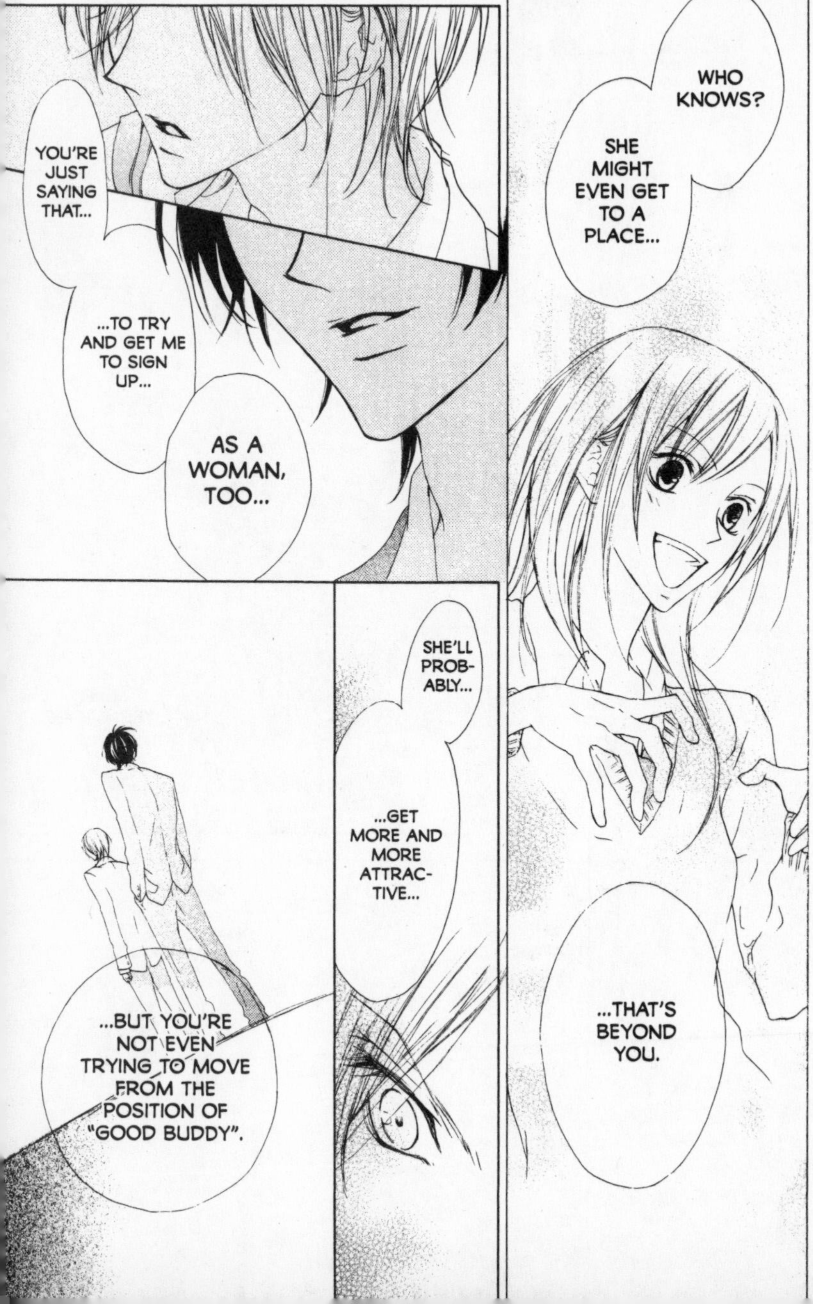
WHO KNOWS?
SHE MIGHT EVEN GET TO A PLACE...
...THAT'S BEYOND YOU.
YOU'RE JUST SAYING THAT...
...TO TRY AND GET ME TO SIGN UP...
AS A WOMAN, TOO...
SHE'LL PROBABLY...
...GET MORE AND MORE ATTRACTIVE...
...BUT YOU'RE NOT EVEN TRYING TO MOVE FROM THE POSITION OF "GOOD BUDDY".

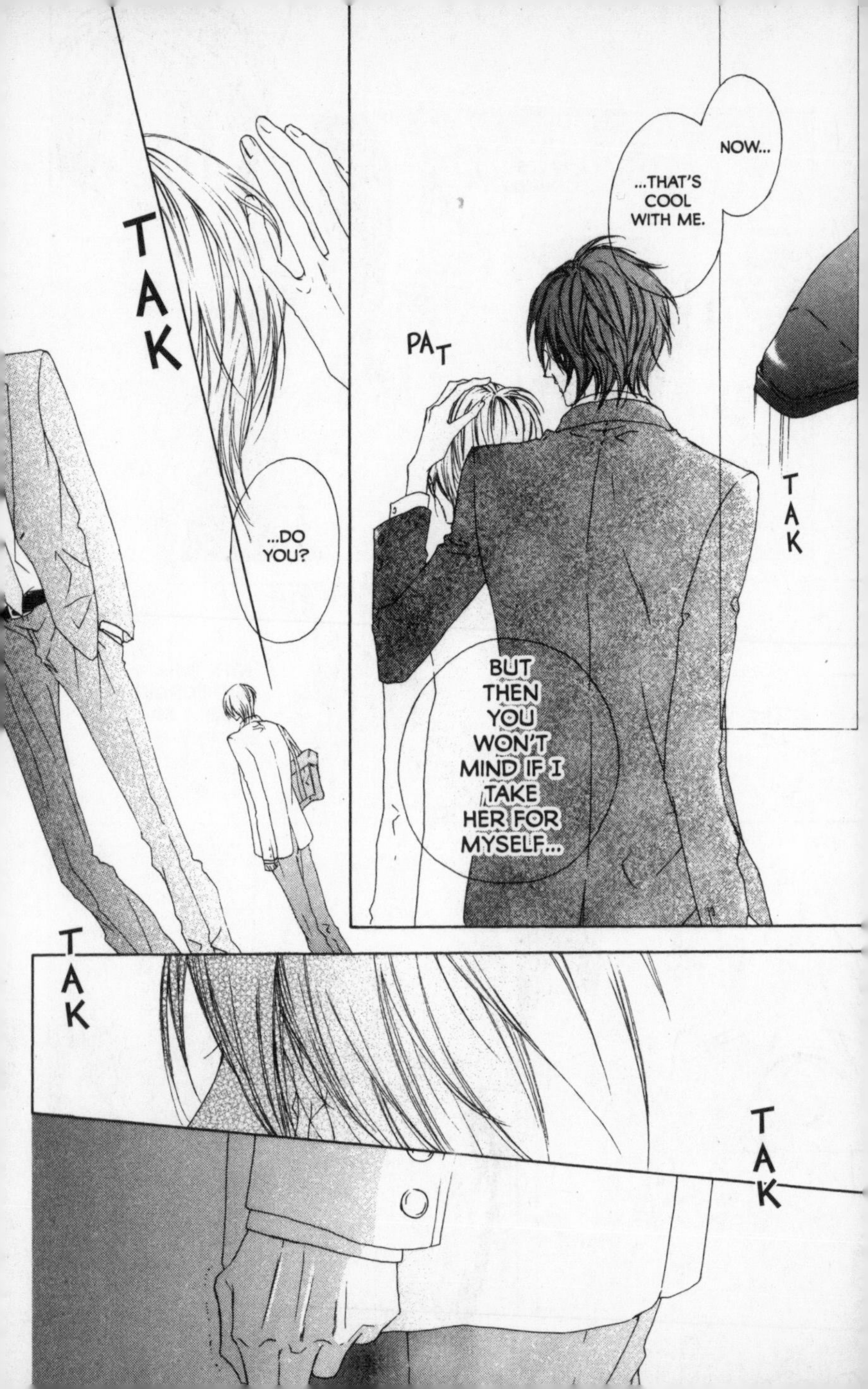
NOW... ...THAT'S COOL WITH ME.
TAK
PAT
BUT THEN YOU WON'T MIND IF I TAKE HER FOR MYSELF...
TAK
...DO YOU?
TAK
TAK

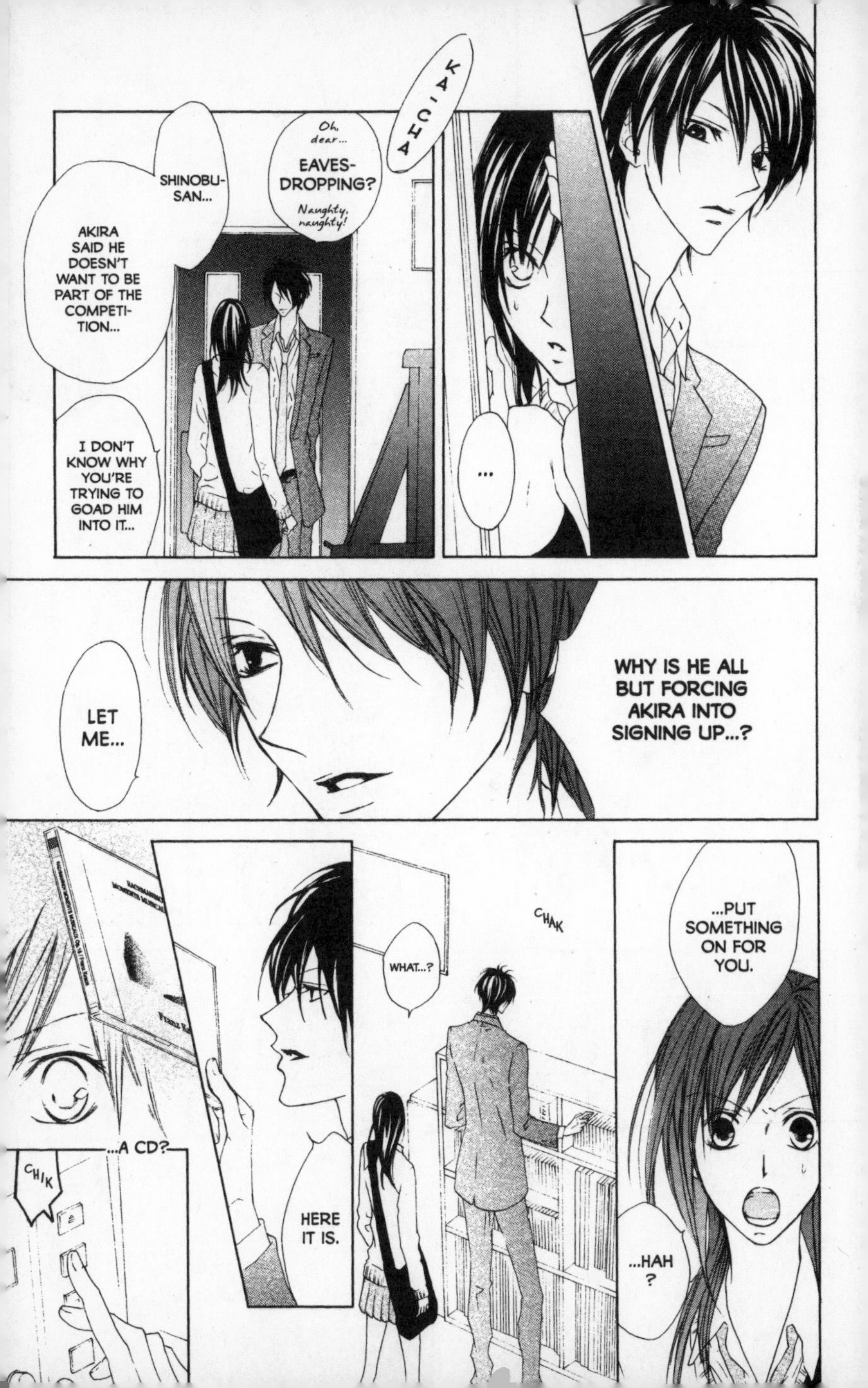
KA-CHA
...
Oh, dear... EAVES-DROPPING? Naughty, naughty!
SHINOBU-SAN...
AKIRA SAID HE DOESN'T WANT TO BE PART OF THE COMPETITION...
I DON'T KNOW WHY YOU'RE TRYING TO GOAD HIM INTO IT...
WHY IS HE ALL BUT FORCING AKIRA INTO SIGNING UP...?
LET ME...
...PUT SOMETHING ON FOR YOU.
...HAH ?
CHAK
WHAT...?
HERE IT IS.
...A CD?
CHIK

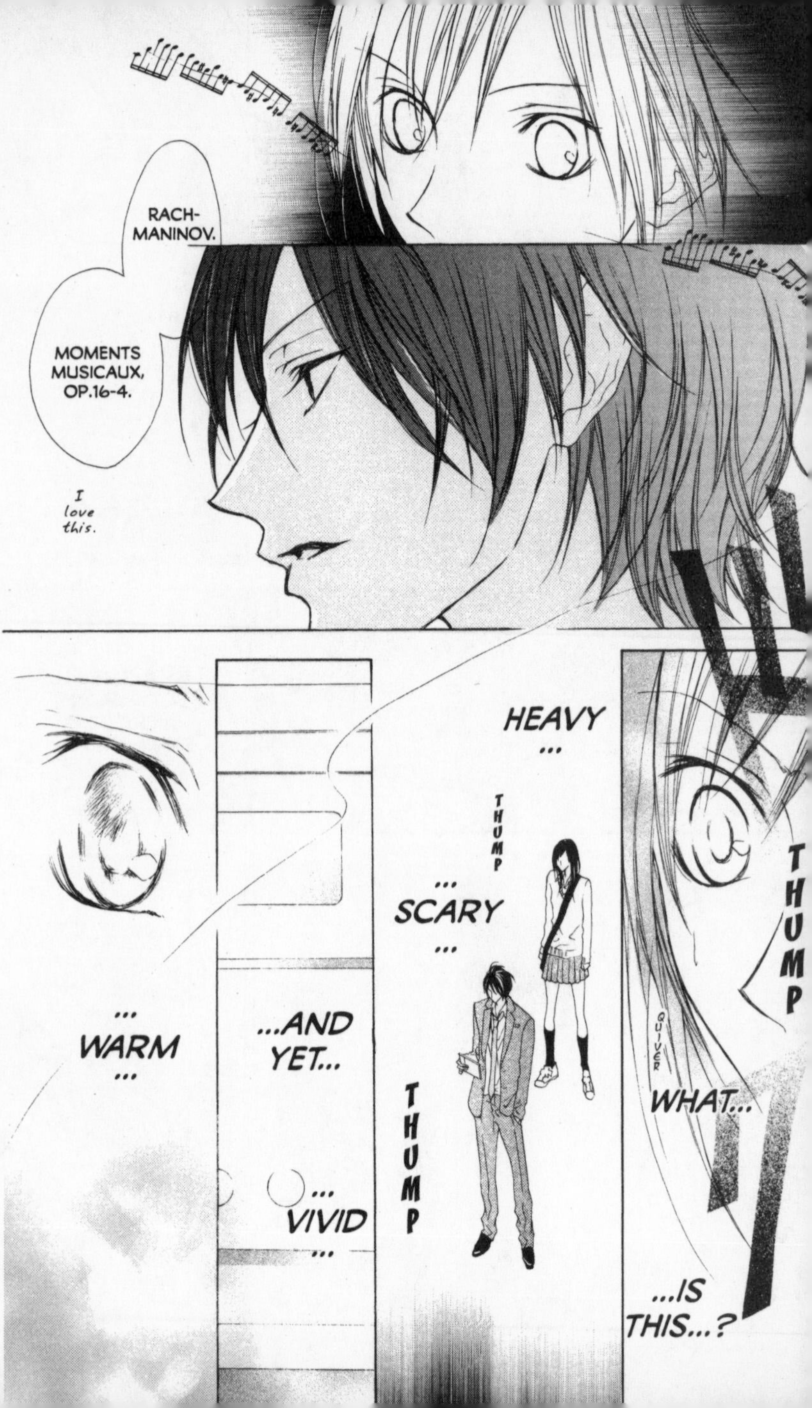
RACH-MANINOV.
MOMENTS MUSICAUX, OP.16-4.
I love this.
THUMP
QUIVER
WHAT...
...IS THIS...?
HEAVY ...
THUMP
... SCARY ...
THUMP
...AND YET...
... VIVID ...
... WARM ...

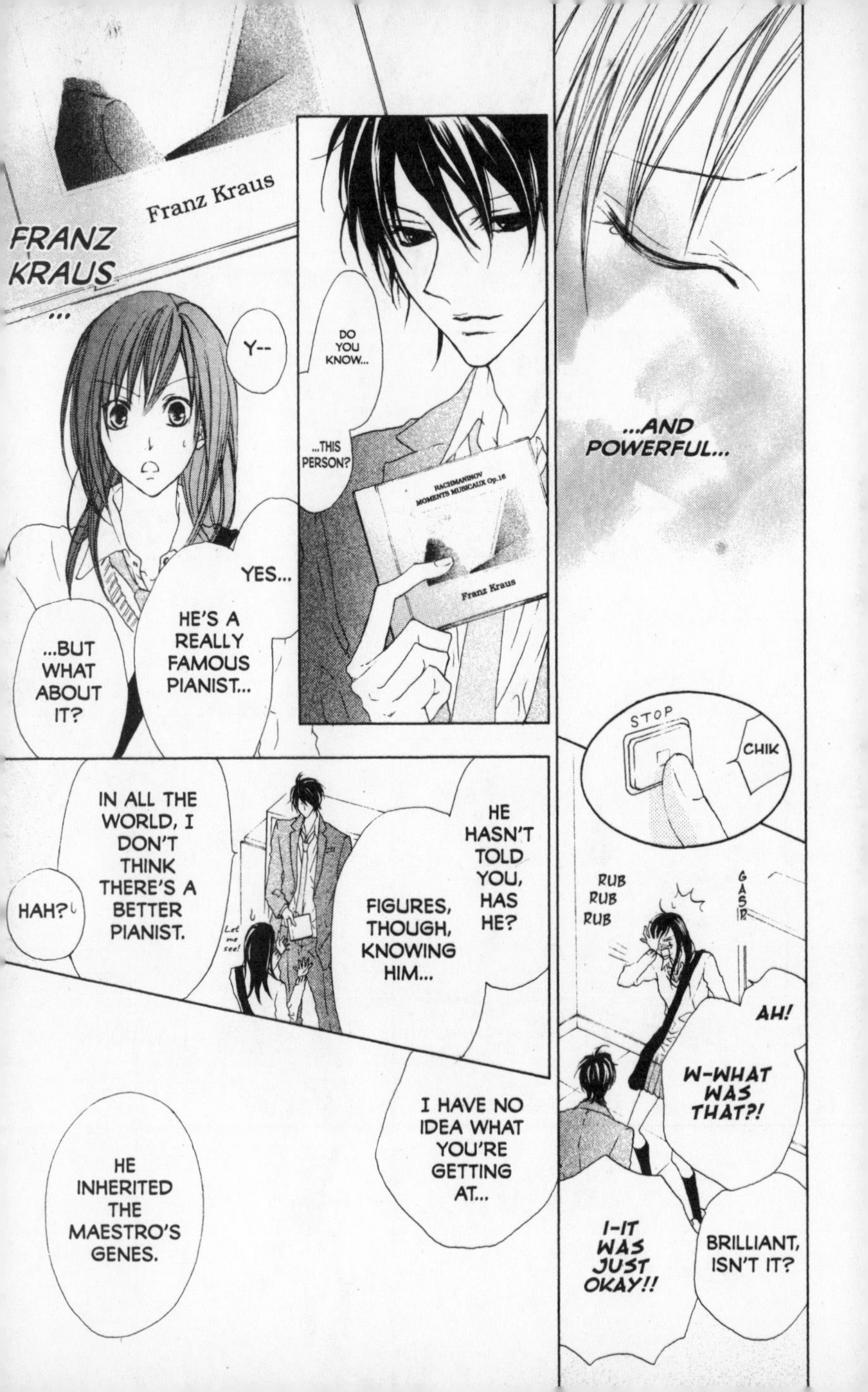

...AND POWERFUL...
STOP
CHIK
RUB
RUB
RUB
GASP
AH!
W-WHAT WAS THAT?!
BRILLIANT, ISN'T IT?
I-IT WAS JUST OKAY!!
RACHMANINOV
MOMENTS MUSICAUX Op.16
Franz Kraus
DO YOU KNOW...
...THIS PERSON?
Franz Kraus
FRANZ KRAUS ...
Y--
YES...
HE'S A REALLY FAMOUS PIANIST...
...BUT WHAT ABOUT IT?
HE HASN'T TOLD YOU, HAS HE?
FIGURES, THOUGH, KNOWING HIM...
Let me see!
IN ALL THE WORLD, I DON'T THINK THERE'S A BETTER PIANIST.
HAH?
I HAVE NO IDEA WHAT YOU'RE GETTING AT...
HE INHERITED THE MAESTRO'S GENES.

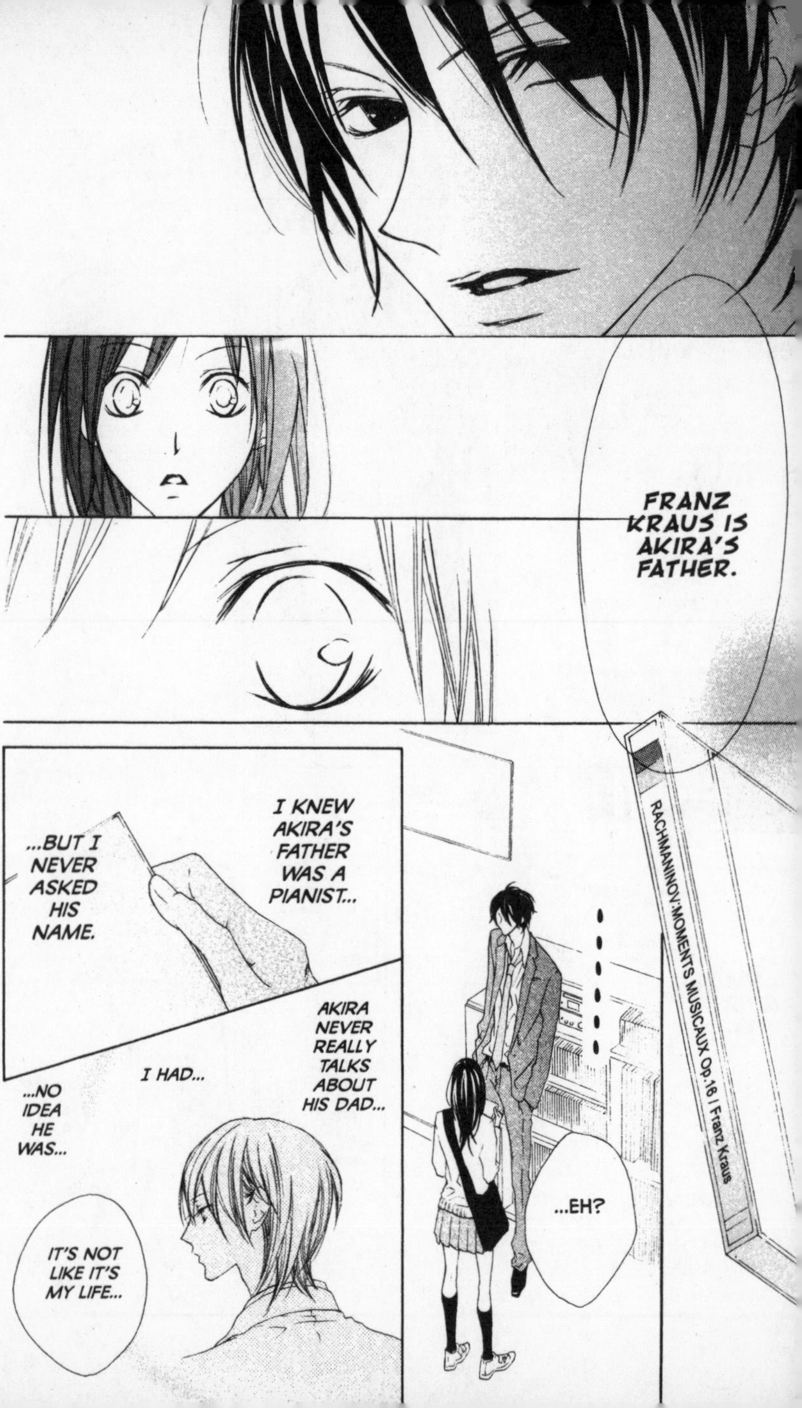
FRANZ KRAUS IS AKIRA'S FATHER.
RACHMANINOV:MOMENTS MUSICAUX Op.16 | Franz Kraus
......
...EH?
I KNEW AKIRA'S FATHER WAS A PIANIST...
...BUT I NEVER ASKED HIS NAME.
AKIRA NEVER REALLY TALKS ABOUT HIS DAD...
I HAD...
...NO IDEA HE WAS...
IT'S NOT LIKE IT'S MY LIFE...

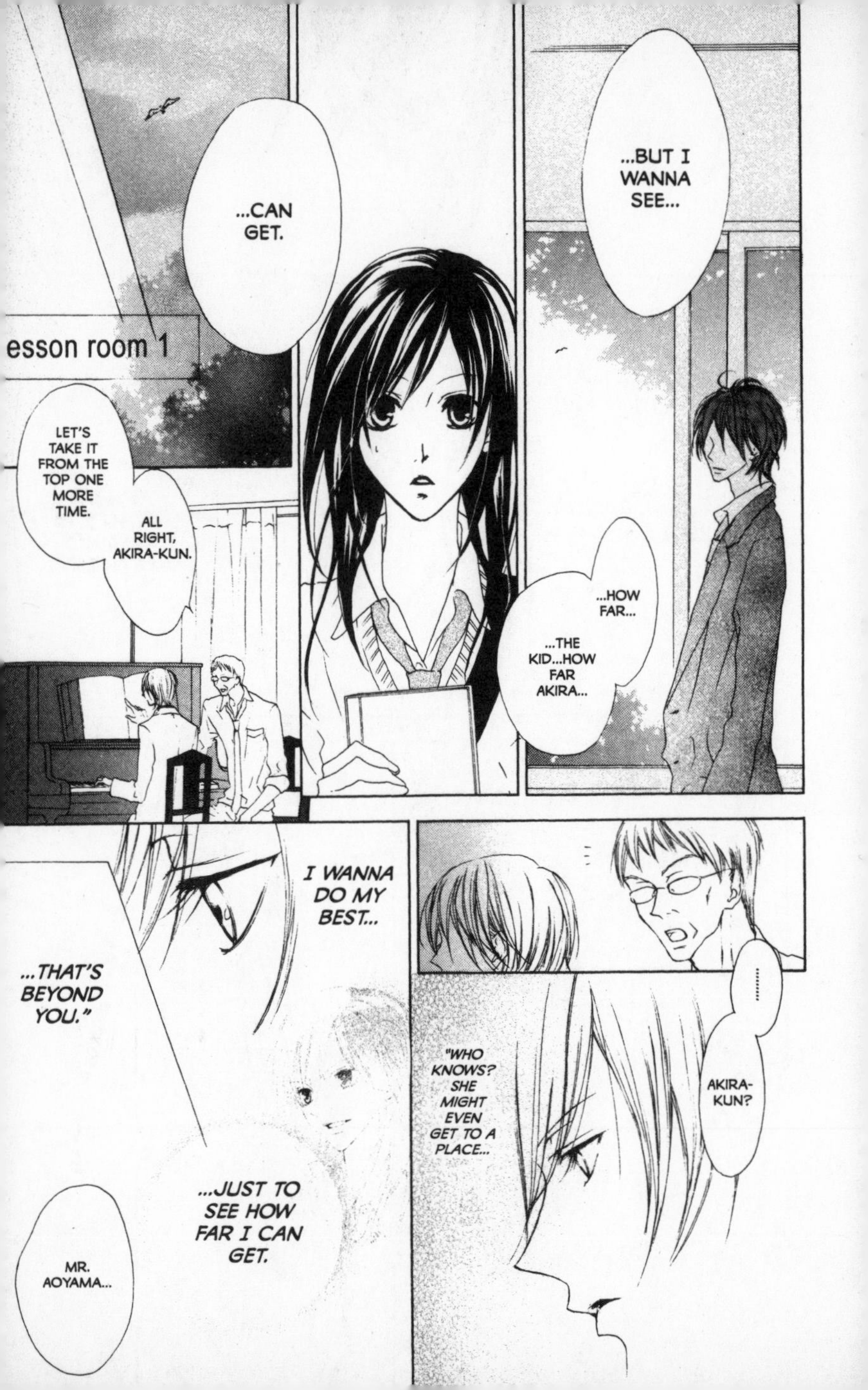
...BUT I WANNA SEE...
...HOW FAR...
...THE KID...HOW FAR AKIRA...
...CAN GET.
esson room 1
LET'S TAKE IT FROM THE TOP ONE MORE TIME.
ALL RIGHT, AKIRA-KUN.
......
AKIRA-KUN?
"WHO KNOWS? SHE MIGHT EVEN GET TO A PLACE...
I WANNA DO MY BEST...
...THAT'S BEYOND YOU."
...JUST TO SEE HOW FAR I CAN GET.
MR. AOYAMA...

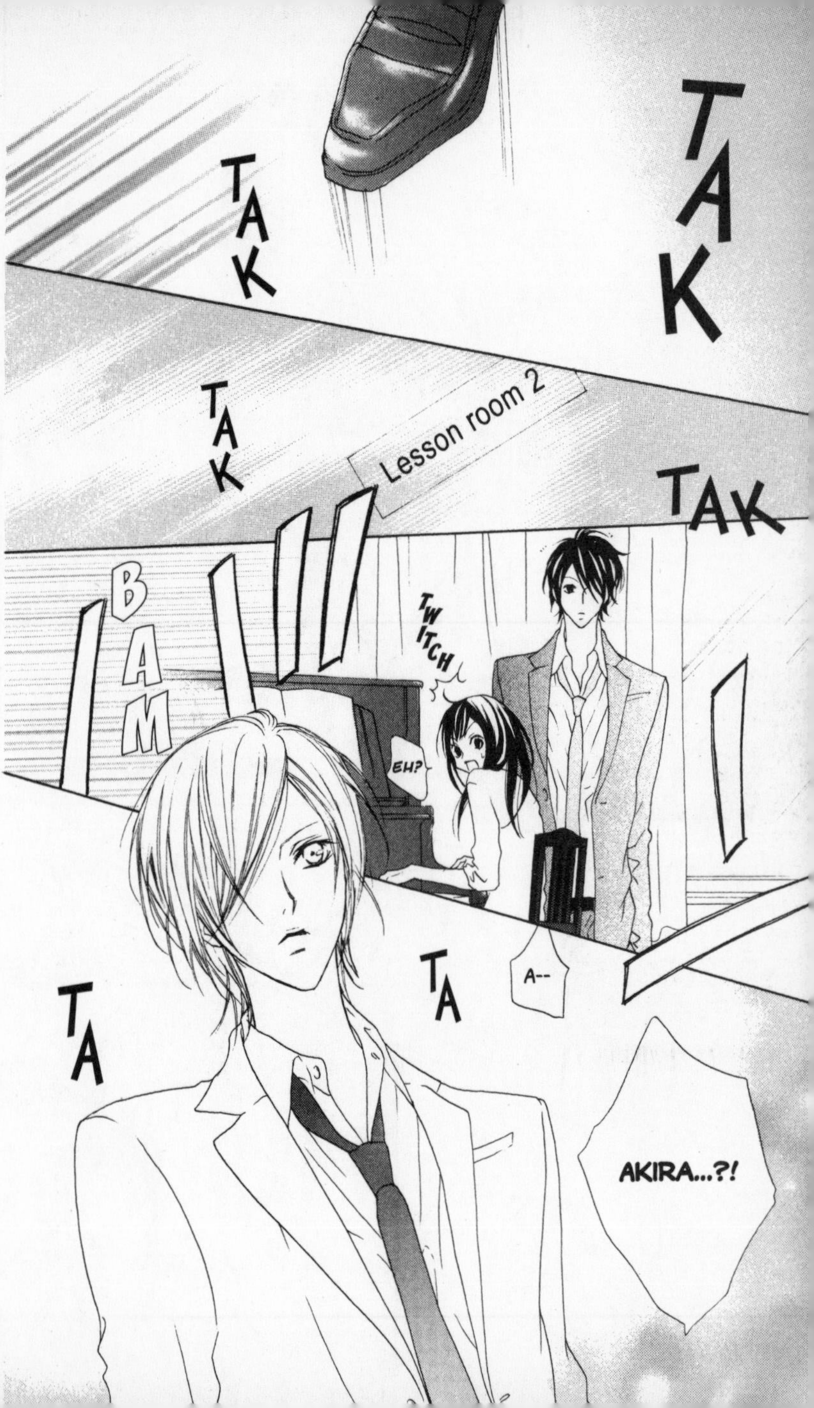
TAK
TAK
TAK
TAK
Lesson room 2
TAK
BAM
TWITCH
EH?
A--
TA
TA
AKIRA...?!

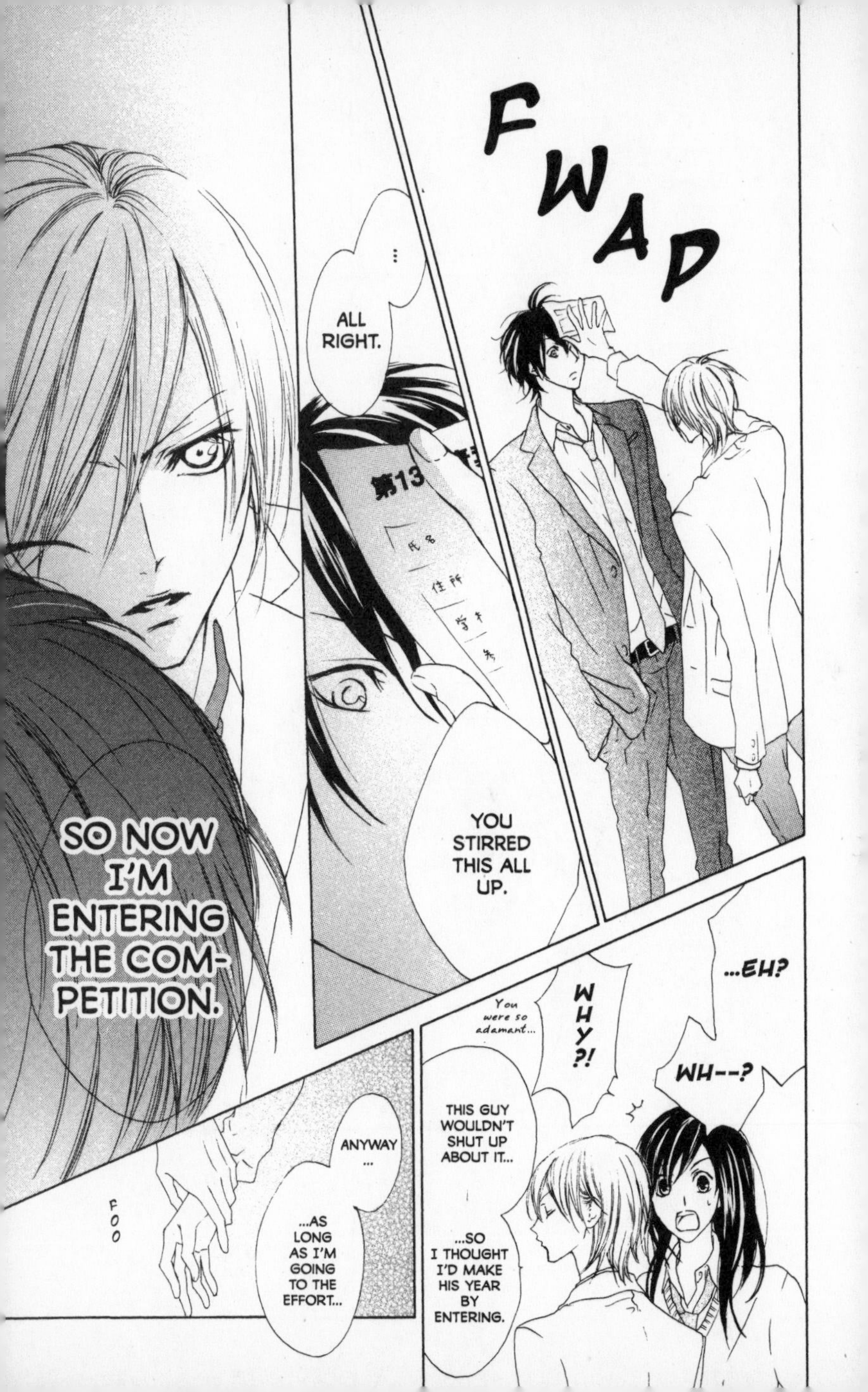

FWAP
...
ALL RIGHT.
YOU STIRRED THIS ALL UP.
SO NOW I'M ENTERING THE COM-PETITION.
...EH?
WHY?!
WH--?
You were so adamant...
THIS GUY WOULDN'T SHUT UP ABOUT IT...
...SO I THOUGHT I'D MAKE HIS YEAR BY ENTERING.
ANYWAY...
...AS LONG AS I'M GOING TO THE EFFORT...
FOO

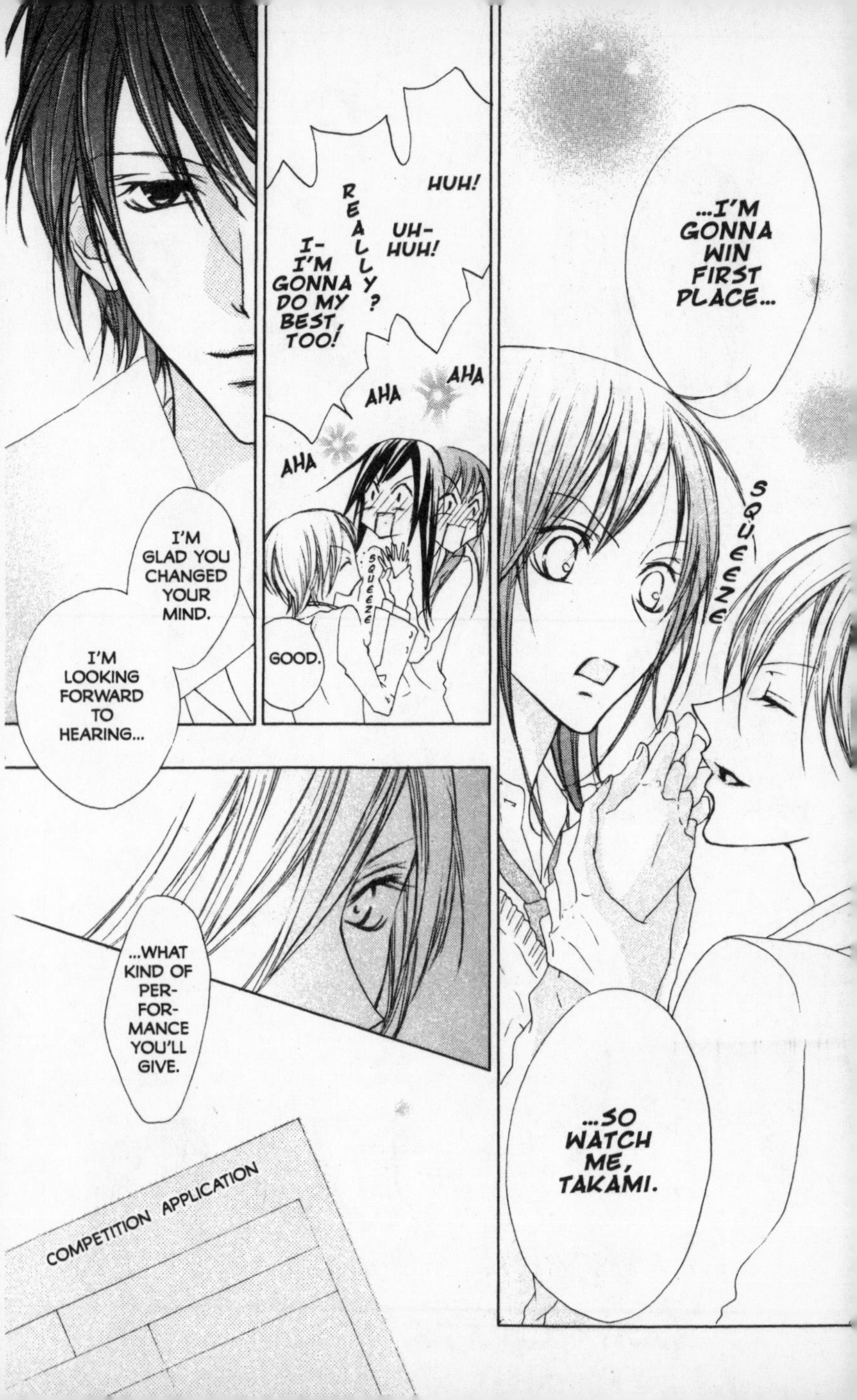
...I'M GONNA WIN FIRST PLACE...
SQUEEZE
...SO WATCH ME, TAKAMI.
HUH!
UH-HUH!
REALLY?
I-I'M GONNA DO MY BEST, TOO!
AHA
AHA
AHA
SQUEEZE
GOOD.
I'M GLAD YOU CHANGED YOUR MIND.
I'M LOOKING FORWARD TO HEARING...
...WHAT KIND OF PER-FOR-MANCE YOU'LL GIVE.
COMPETITION APPLICATION

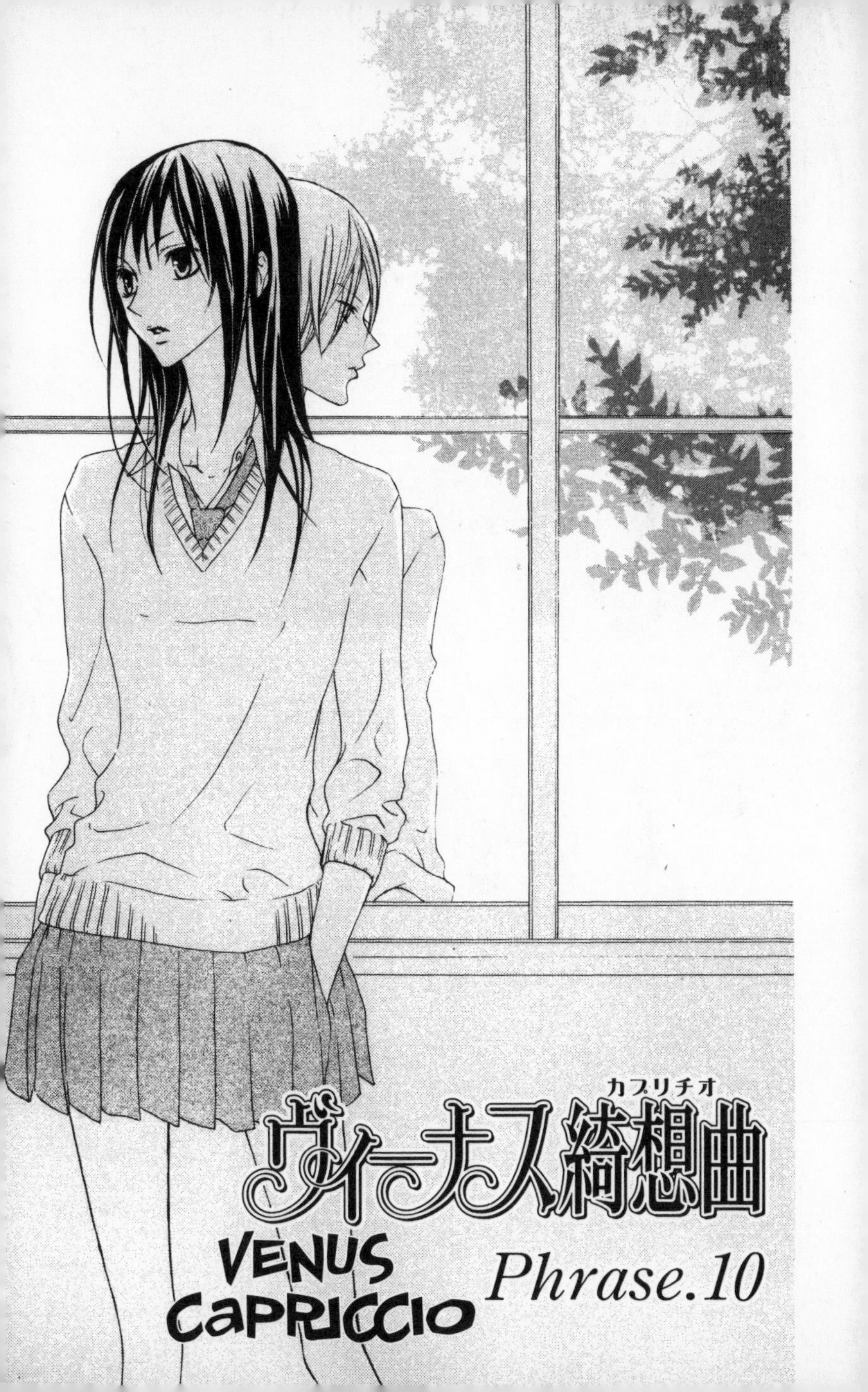
ヴィーナス綺想曲（カプリチオ）
VENUS CaPRICCIO
Phrase.10

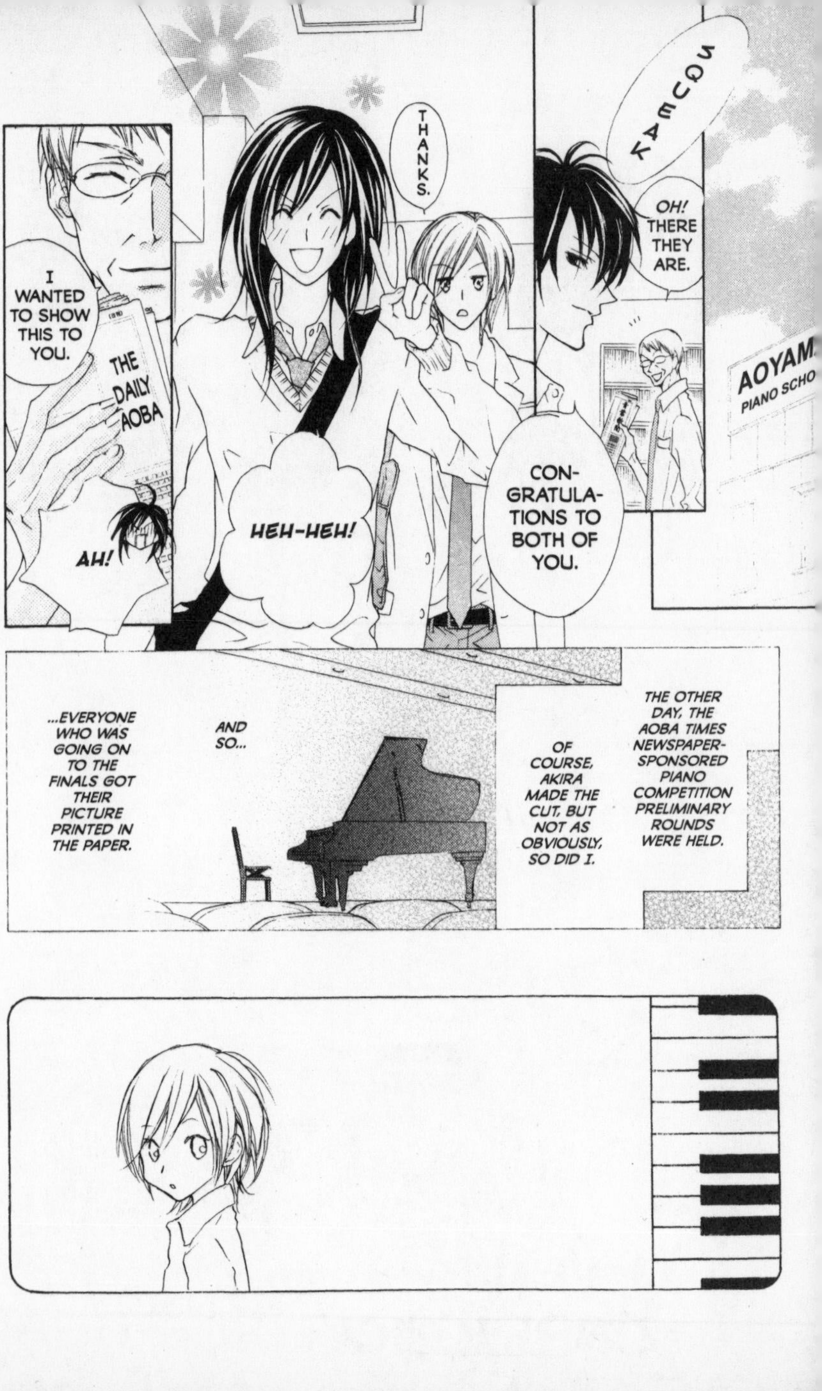
SQUEAK
AOYAMA PIANO SCHO
OH! THERE THEY ARE.
CON-GRATULA-TIONS TO BOTH OF YOU.
THANKS.
HEH-HEH!
I WANTED TO SHOW THIS TO YOU.
THE DAILY AOBA
AH!
THE OTHER DAY, THE AOBA TIMES NEWSPAPER-SPONSORED PIANO COMPETITION PRELIMINARY ROUNDS WERE HELD.
OF COURSE, AKIRA MADE THE CUT, BUT NOT AS OBVIOUSLY, SO DID I.
AND SO...
...EVERYONE WHO WAS GOING ON TO THE FINALS GOT THEIR PICTURE PRINTED IN THE PAPER.

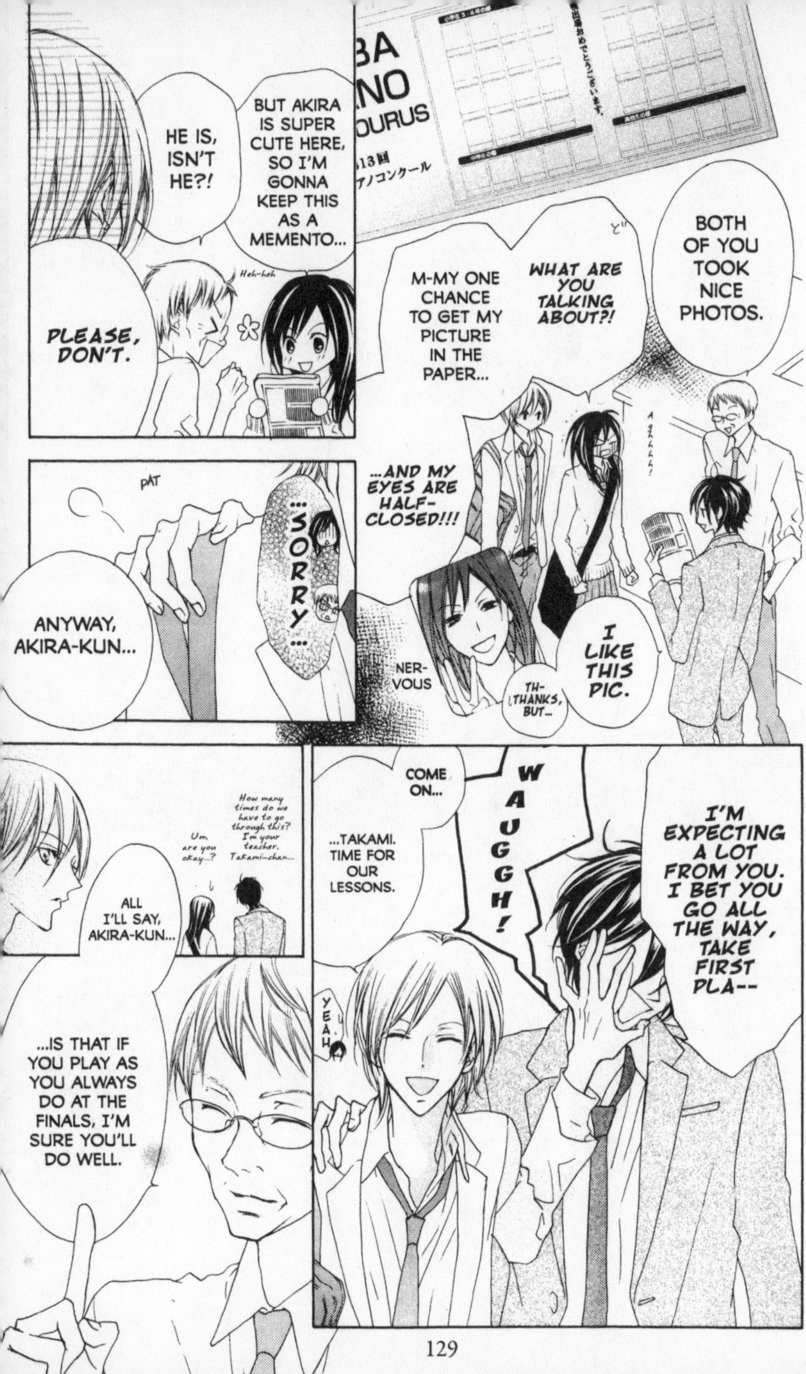
BOTH OF YOU TOOK NICE PHOTOS.
WHAT ARE YOU TALKING ABOUT?!
M-MY ONE CHANCE TO GET MY PICTURE IN THE PAPER...
...AND MY EYES ARE HALF-CLOSED!!!
Agghhh!
I LIKE THIS PIC.
TH-THANKS, BUT...
NER-VOUS
BUT AKIRA IS SUPER CUTE HERE, SO I'M GONNA KEEP THIS AS A MEMENTO...
HE IS, ISN'T HE?!
Heh-heh
PLEASE, DON'T.
PAT
...SORRY...
ANYWAY, AKIRA-KUN...
I'M EXPECTING A LOT FROM YOU. I BET YOU GO ALL THE WAY, TAKE FIRST PLA--
WAUGGH!
COME ON...
...TAKAMI. TIME FOR OUR LESSONS.
YEAH
How many times do we have to go through this? I'm your teacher, Takami-chan...
Um, are you okay...?
ALL I'LL SAY, AKIRA-KUN...
...IS THAT IF YOU PLAY AS YOU ALWAYS DO AT THE FINALS, I'M SURE YOU'LL DO WELL.

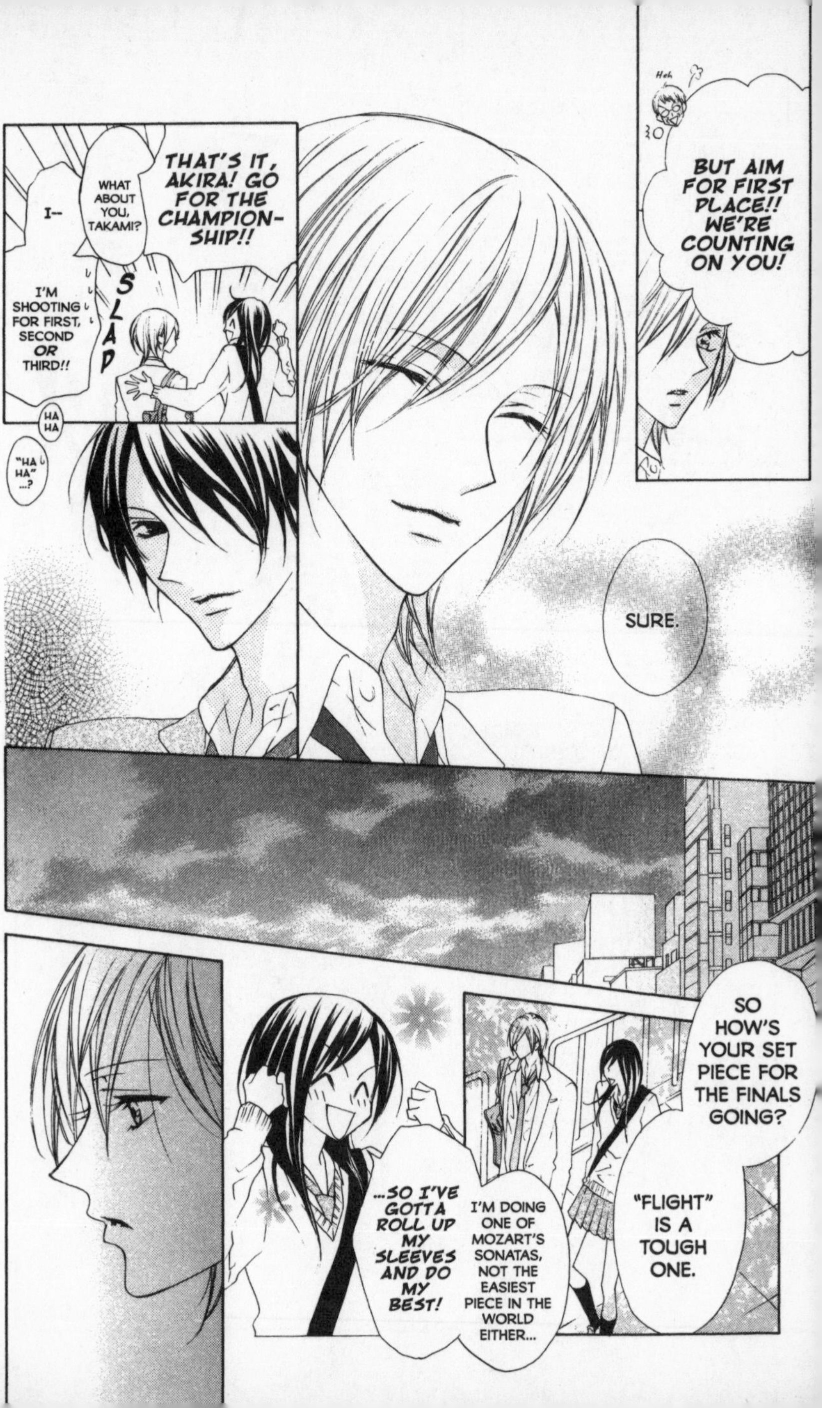
Heh
BUT AIM FOR FIRST PLACE!! WE'RE COUNTING ON YOU!
THAT'S IT, AKIRA! GO FOR THE CHAMPIONSHIP!!
WHAT ABOUT YOU, TAKAMI?
I--
SLAP
I'M SHOOTING FOR FIRST, SECOND OR THIRD!!
HA HA
"HA HA" ...?
SURE.
SO HOW'S YOUR SET PIECE FOR THE FINALS GOING?
"FLIGHT" IS A TOUGH ONE.
I'M DOING ONE OF MOZART'S SONATAS, NOT THE EASIEST PIECE IN THE WORLD EITHER...
...SO I'VE GOTTA ROLL UP MY SLEEVES AND DO MY BEST!

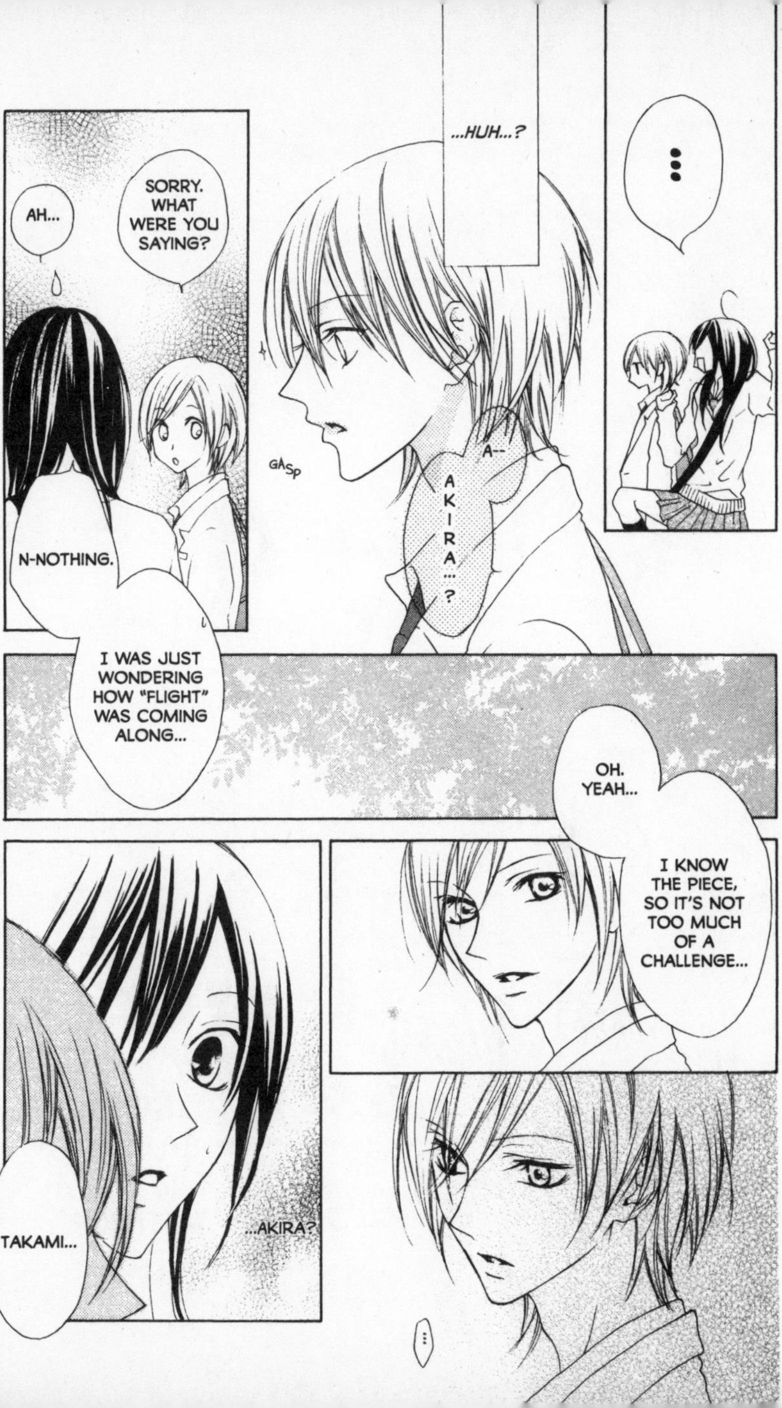
...
...HUH...?
GASP
A-- AKIRA...?
SORRY. WHAT WERE YOU SAYING?
AH...
N-NOTHING.
I WAS JUST WONDERING HOW "FLIGHT" WAS COMING ALONG...
OH. YEAH...
I KNOW THE PIECE, SO IT'S NOT TOO MUCH OF A CHALLENGE...
...
...AKIRA?
TAKAMI...

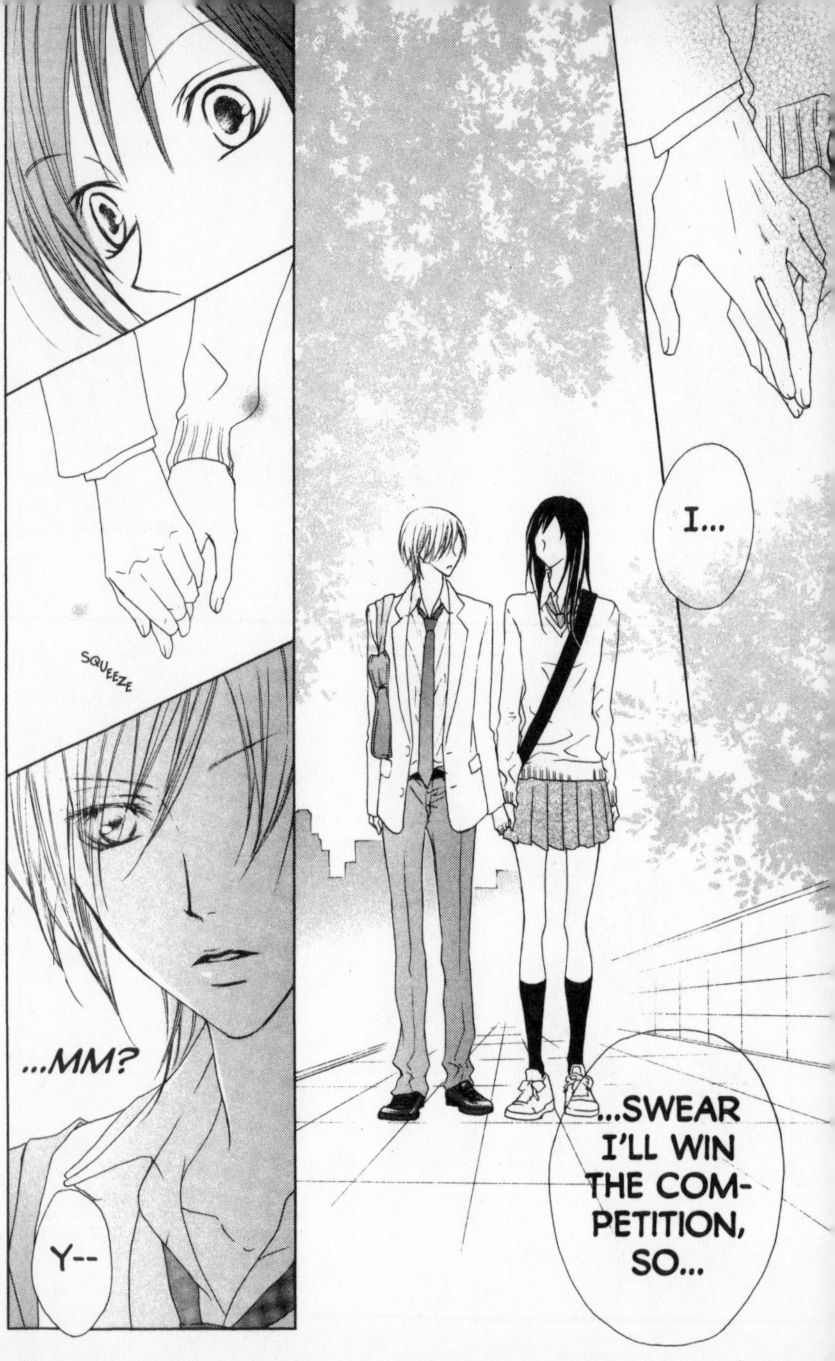
I...
...SWEAR I'LL WIN THE COM-PETITION, SO...
SQUEEZE
...MM?
Y--

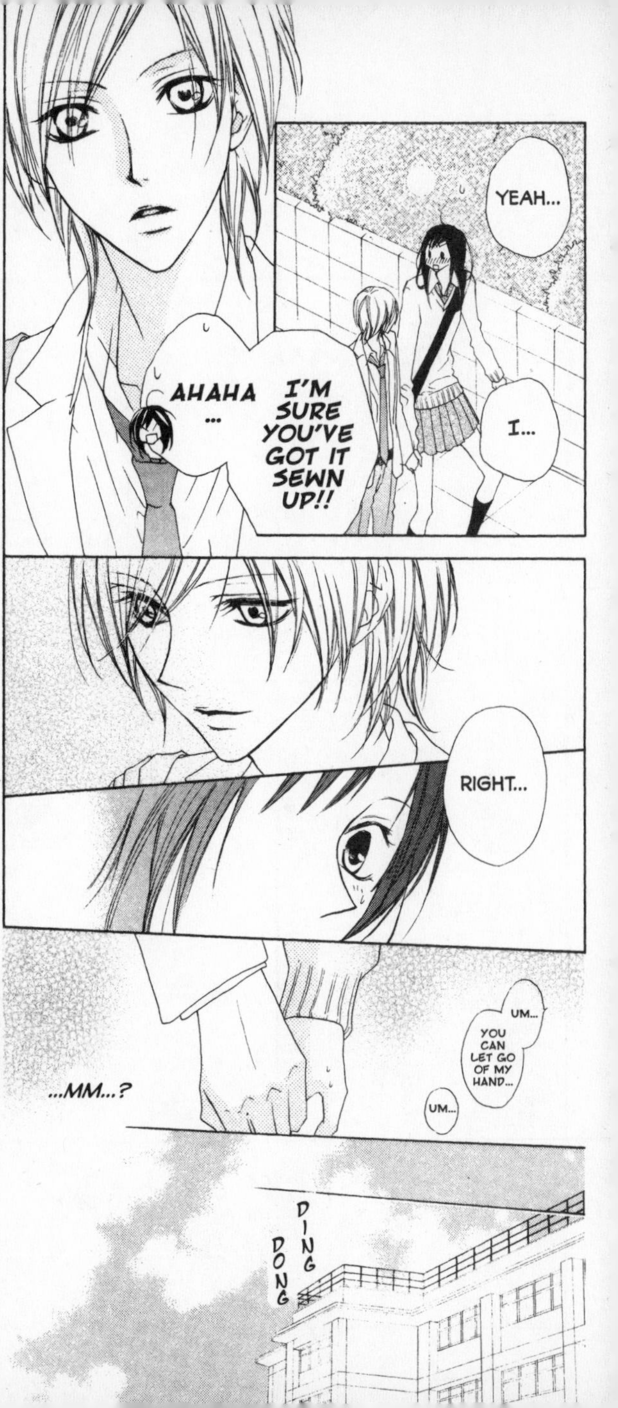
YEAH...
I...
AHAHA ...
I'M SURE YOU'VE GOT IT SEWN UP!!
RIGHT...
UM...
YOU CAN LET GO OF MY HAND...
UM...
...MM...?
DING
DONG

5

NOT THAT THIS HAS ANYTHING TO DO WITH THE STORY, BUT WHENEVER MY LITTLE SISTER (RIGHT NOW, A FRESHMAN IN HIGH SCHOOL) IS AROUND, I GET THE URGE TO SKETCH.

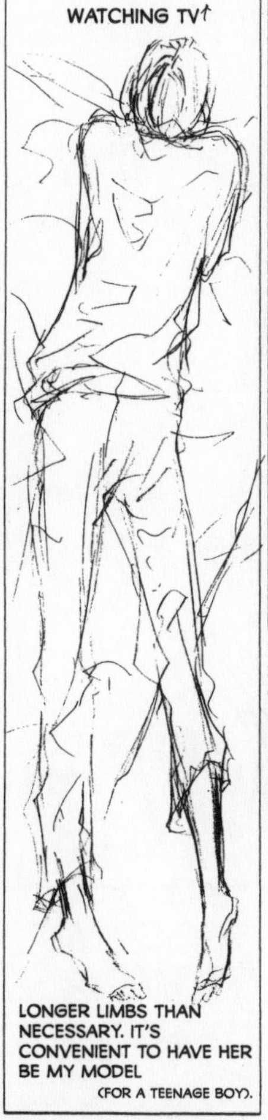
WATCHING TV↑

LONGER LIMBS THAN NECESSARY. IT'S CONVENIENT TO HAVE HER BE MY MODEL (FOR A TEENAGE BOY).

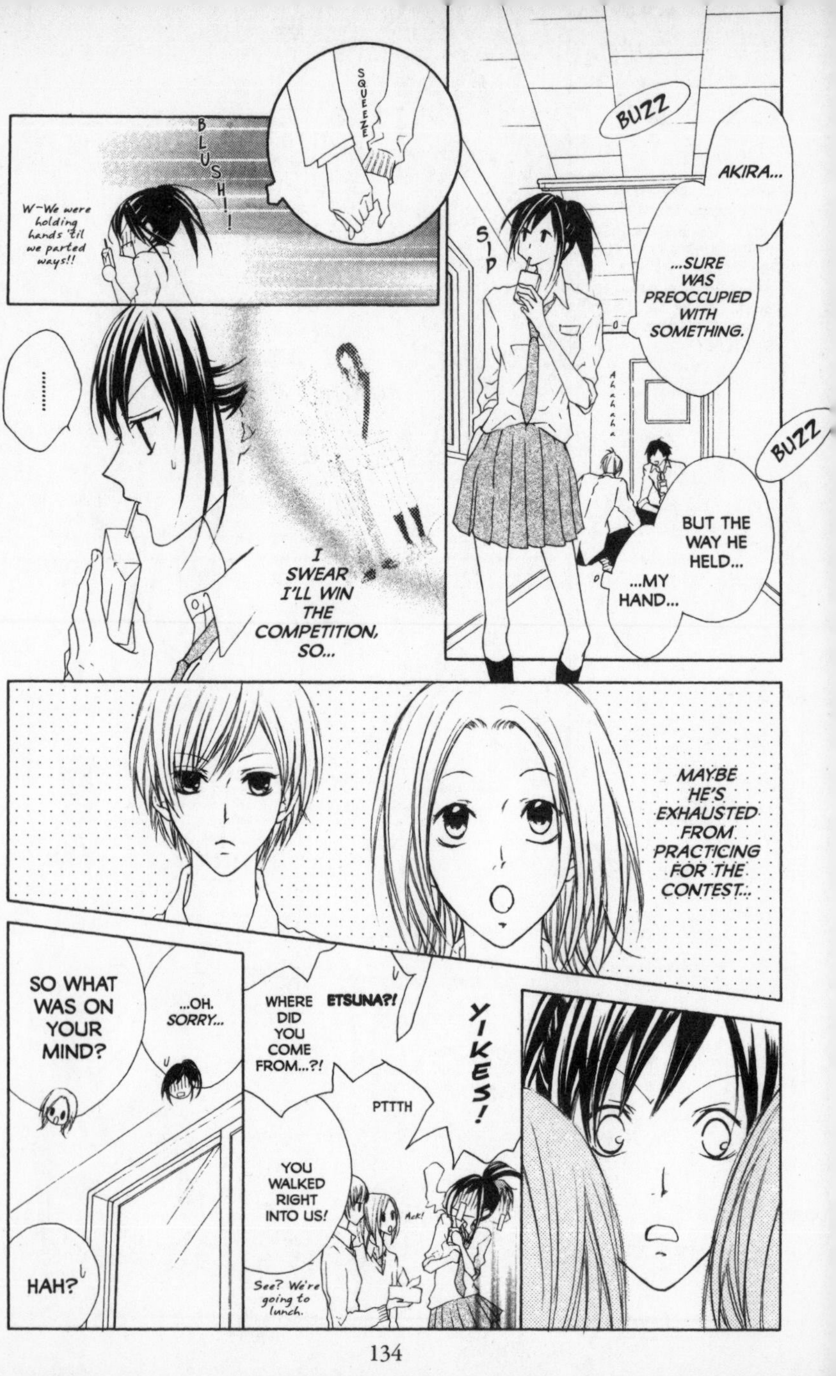
BUZZ
AKIRA...
...SURE WAS PREOCCUPIED WITH SOMETHING.
SIP
Ahahaha
BUZZ
BUT THE WAY HE HELD...
...MY HAND...
SQUEEZE
BLUSH!!
W-We were holding hands 'til we parted ways!!
......
I SWEAR I'LL WIN THE COMPETITION, SO...
MAYBE HE'S EXHAUSTED FROM PRACTICING FOR THE CONTEST...
YIKES!
ETSUNA?!
WHERE DID YOU COME FROM...?!
PTTTH
YOU WALKED RIGHT INTO US!
Ack!
See? We're going to lunch.
...OH. SORRY...
SO WHAT WAS ON YOUR MIND?
HAH?

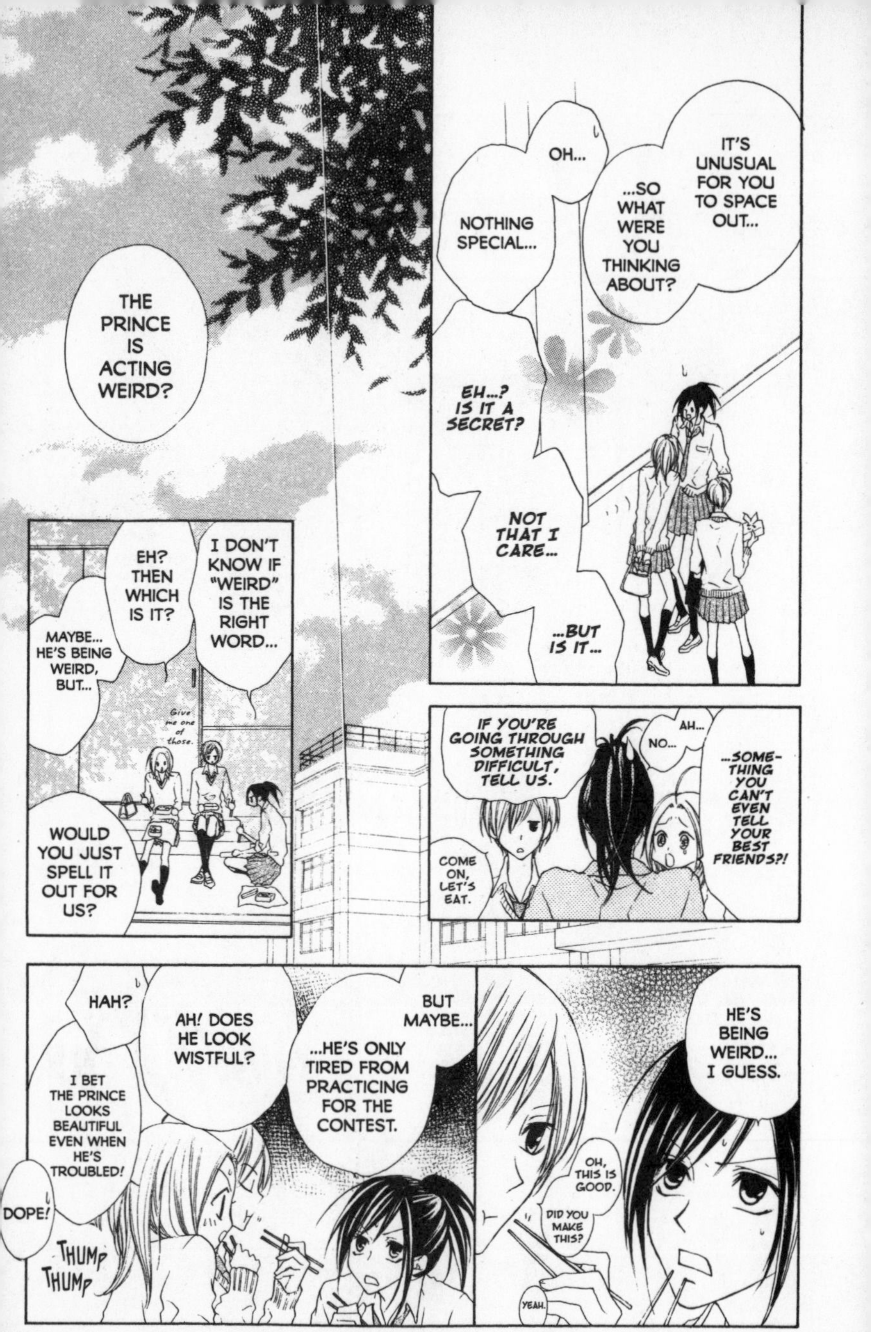
IT'S UNUSUAL FOR YOU TO SPACE OUT...
...SO WHAT WERE YOU THINKING ABOUT?
OH...
NOTHING SPECIAL...
EH...? IS IT A SECRET?
NOT THAT I CARE...
...BUT IS IT...
IF YOU'RE GOING THROUGH SOMETHING DIFFICULT, TELL US.
AH... NO...
...SOMETHING YOU CAN'T EVEN TELL YOUR BEST FRIENDS?!
COME ON, LET'S EAT.
THE PRINCE IS ACTING WEIRD?
I DON'T KNOW IF "WEIRD" IS THE RIGHT WORD...
EH? THEN WHICH IS IT?
MAYBE... HE'S BEING WEIRD, BUT...
Give me one of those.
WOULD YOU JUST SPELL IT OUT FOR US?
HE'S BEING WEIRD... I GUESS.
OH, THIS IS GOOD.
DID YOU MAKE THIS?
YEAH.
BUT MAYBE...
...HE'S ONLY TIRED FROM PRACTICING FOR THE CONTEST.
AH! DOES HE LOOK WISTFUL?
HAH?
I BET THE PRINCE LOOKS BEAUTIFUL EVEN WHEN HE'S TROUBLED!
DOPE!
THUMP THUMP

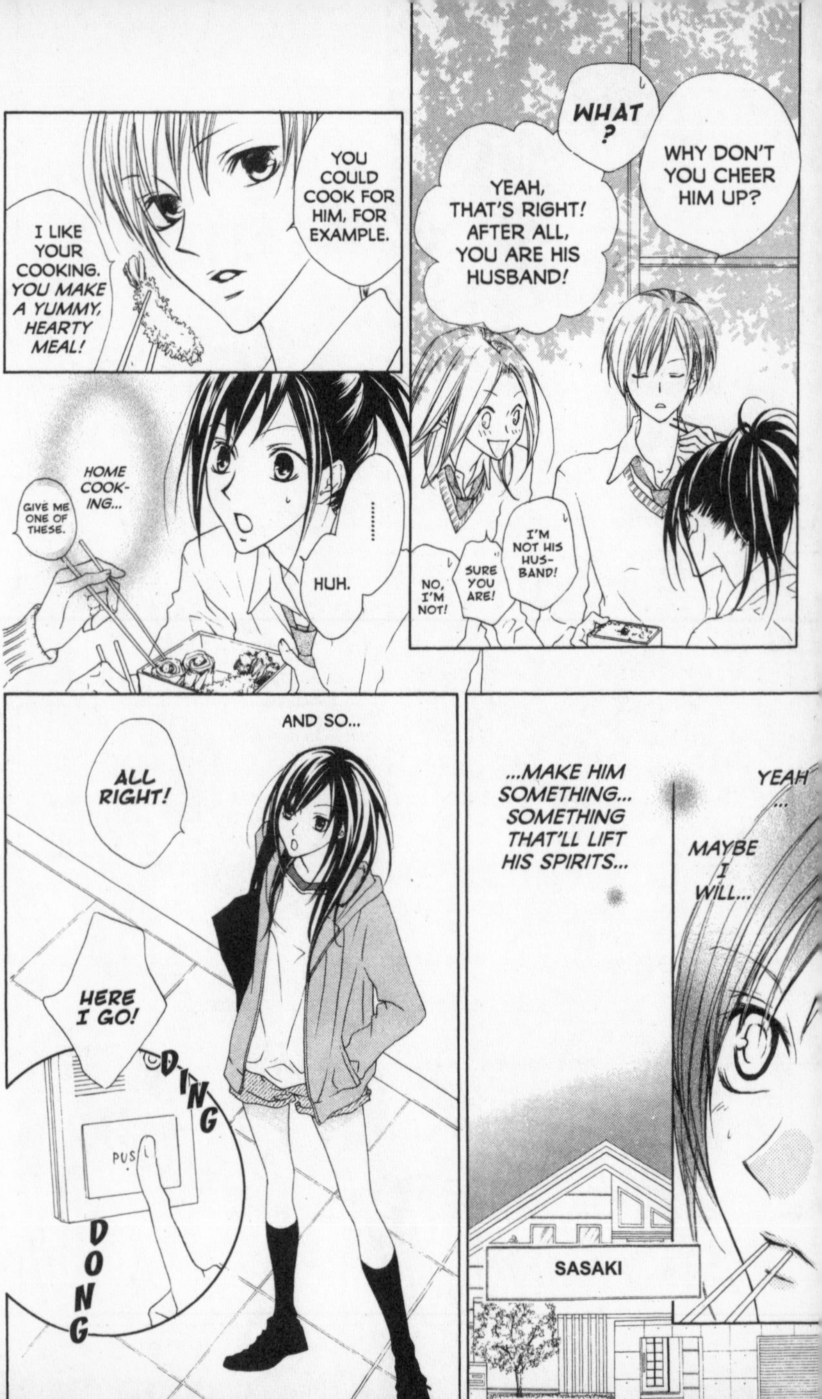
WHY DON'T YOU CHEER HIM UP?
WHAT?
YEAH, THAT'S RIGHT! AFTER ALL, YOU ARE HIS HUSBAND!
I'M NOT HIS HUSBAND!
SURE YOU ARE!
NO, I'M NOT!
YOU COULD COOK FOR HIM, FOR EXAMPLE.
I LIKE YOUR COOKING. YOU MAKE A YUMMY, HEARTY MEAL!
......
HUH.
HOME COOKING...
GIVE ME ONE OF THESE.
YEAH... MAYBE I WILL...
...MAKE HIM SOMETHING... SOMETHING THAT'LL LIFT HIS SPIRITS...
SASAKI
AND SO...
ALL RIGHT!
HERE I GO!
DING DONG
PUS

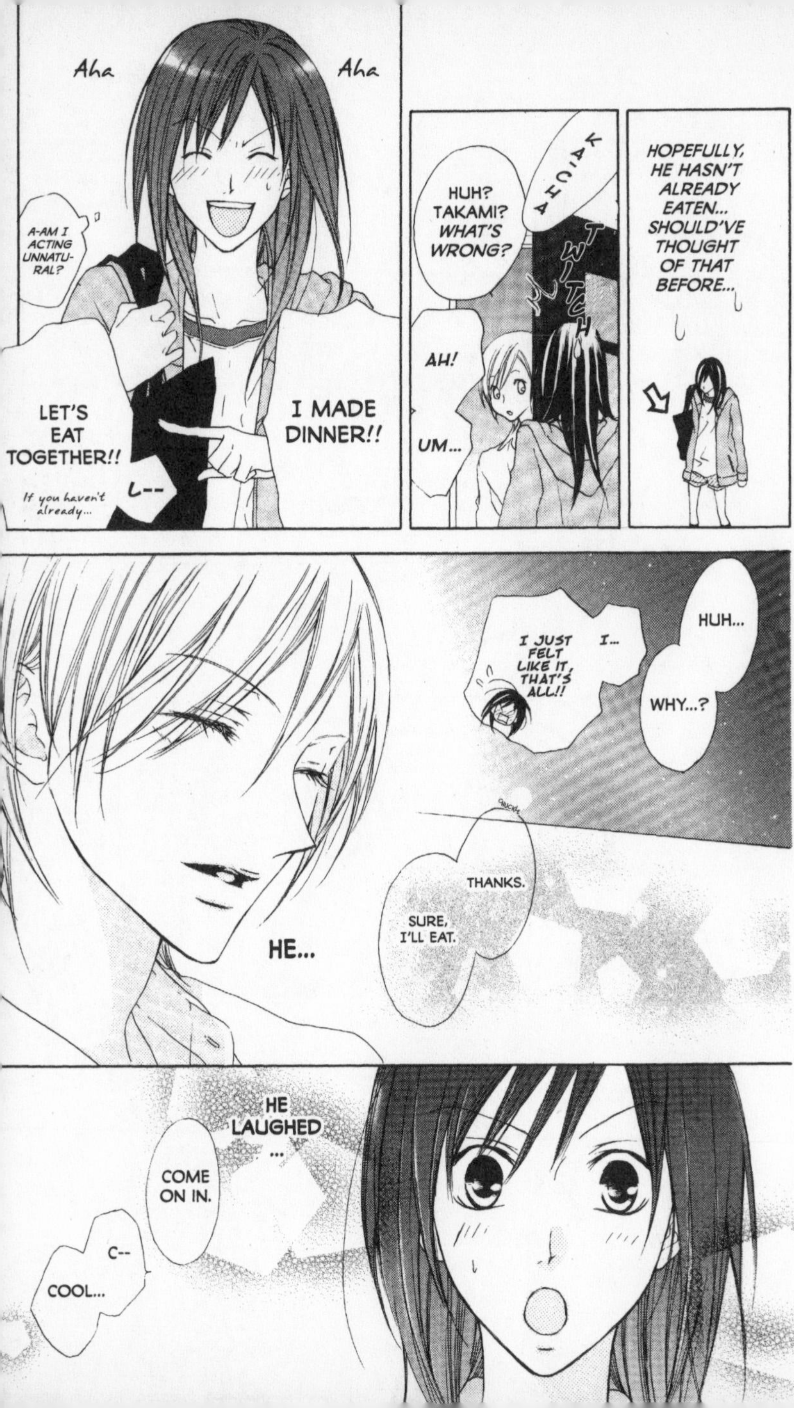
HOPEFULLY, HE HASN'T ALREADY EATEN... SHOULD'VE THOUGHT OF THAT BEFORE...
KAICHA
HUH? TAKAMI? WHAT'S WRONG?
TWITCH
AH!
UM...
Aha
Aha
A-AM I ACTING UNNATU-RAL?
I MADE DINNER!!
LET'S EAT TOGETHER!!
L--
If you haven't already...
HUH...
WHY...?
I...
I JUST FELT LIKE IT, THAT'S ALL!!
THANKS.
SURE, I'LL EAT.
HE...
HE LAUGHED ...
COME ON IN.
C--
COOL...

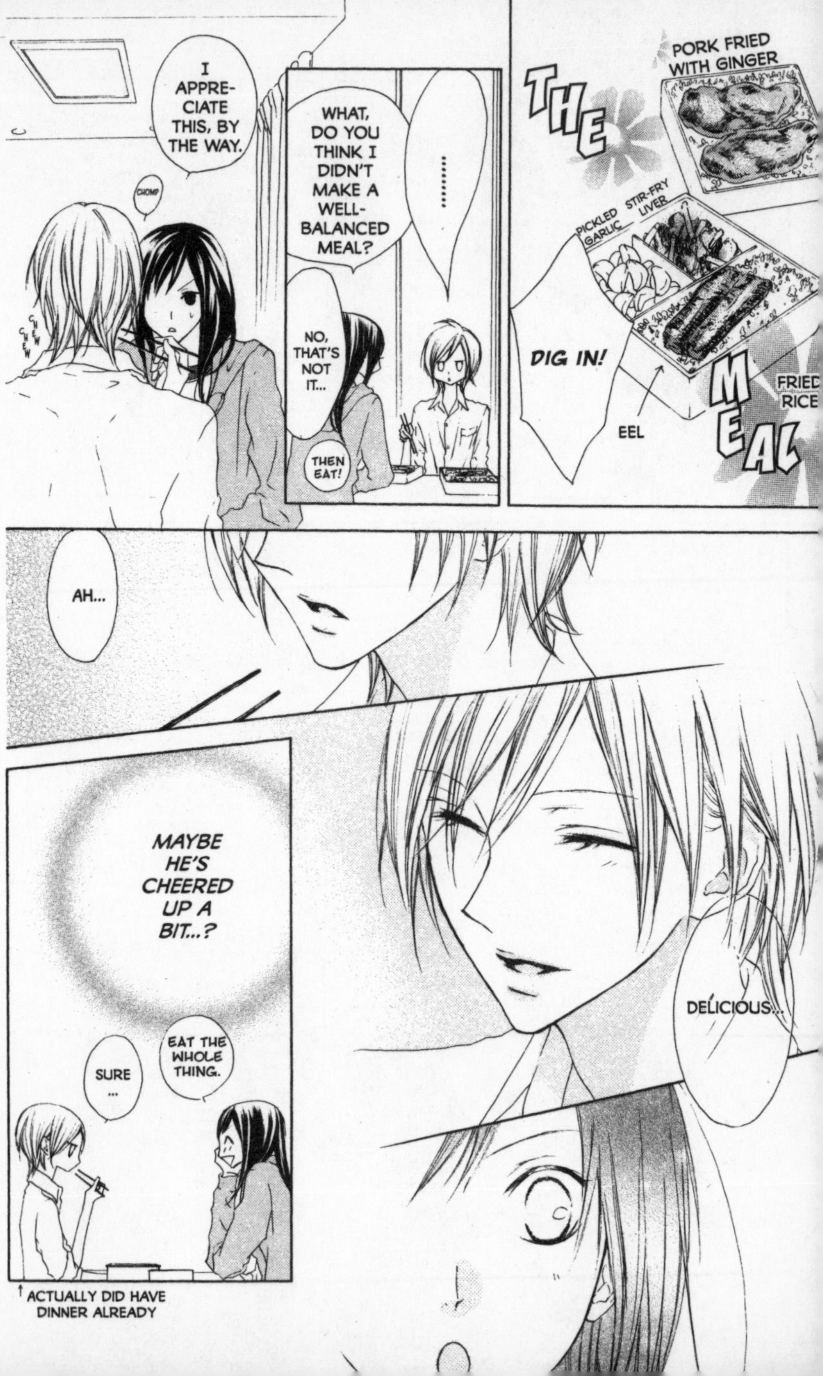
THE MEAL
PORK FRIED WITH GINGER
STIR-FRY LIVER
PICKLED GARLIC
FRIED RICE
EEL
DIG IN!
WHAT, DO YOU THINK I DIDN'T MAKE A WELL-BALANCED MEAL?
......
NO, THAT'S NOT IT...
THEN EAT!
I APPRECIATE THIS, BY THE WAY.
CHOMP
CHEW CHEW
AH...
DELICIOUS...
MAYBE HE'S CHEERED UP A BIT...?
EAT THE WHOLE THING.
SURE...
↑ ACTUALLY DID HAVE DINNER ALREADY

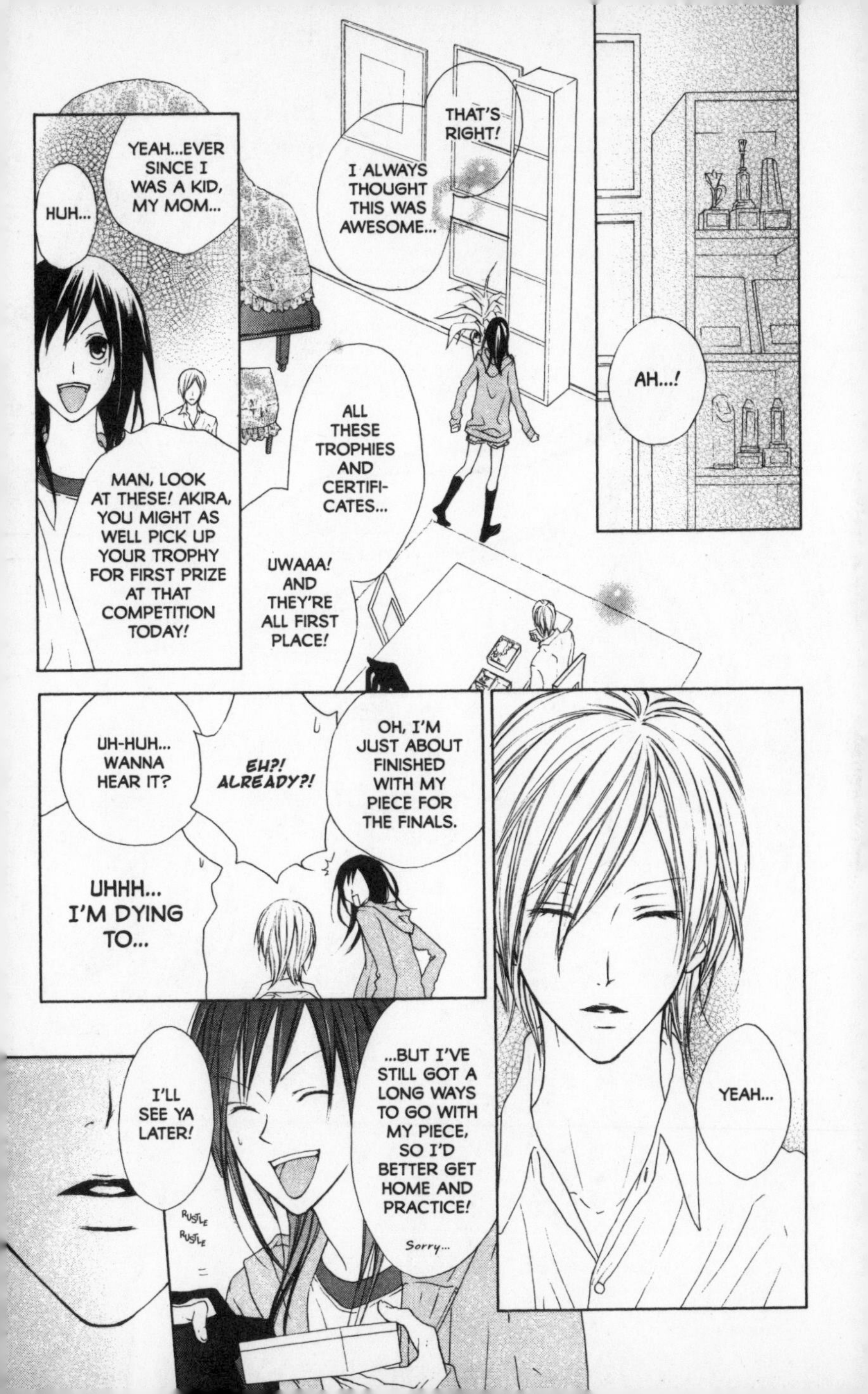

AH...!
ALL THESE TROPHIES AND CERTIFICATES...
UWAAA! AND THEY'RE ALL FIRST PLACE!
THAT'S RIGHT!
I ALWAYS THOUGHT THIS WAS AWESOME...
HUH...
YEAH...EVER SINCE I WAS A KID, MY MOM...
MAN, LOOK AT THESE! AKIRA, YOU MIGHT AS WELL PICK UP YOUR TROPHY FOR FIRST PRIZE AT THAT COMPETITION TODAY!
YEAH...
OH, I'M JUST ABOUT FINISHED WITH MY PIECE FOR THE FINALS.
EH?! ALREADY?!
UH-HUH... WANNA HEAR IT?
UHHH... I'M DYING TO...
...BUT I'VE STILL GOT A LONG WAYS TO GO WITH MY PIECE, SO I'D BETTER GET HOME AND PRACTICE!
Sorry...
I'LL SEE YA LATER!
RUSTLE
RUSTLE

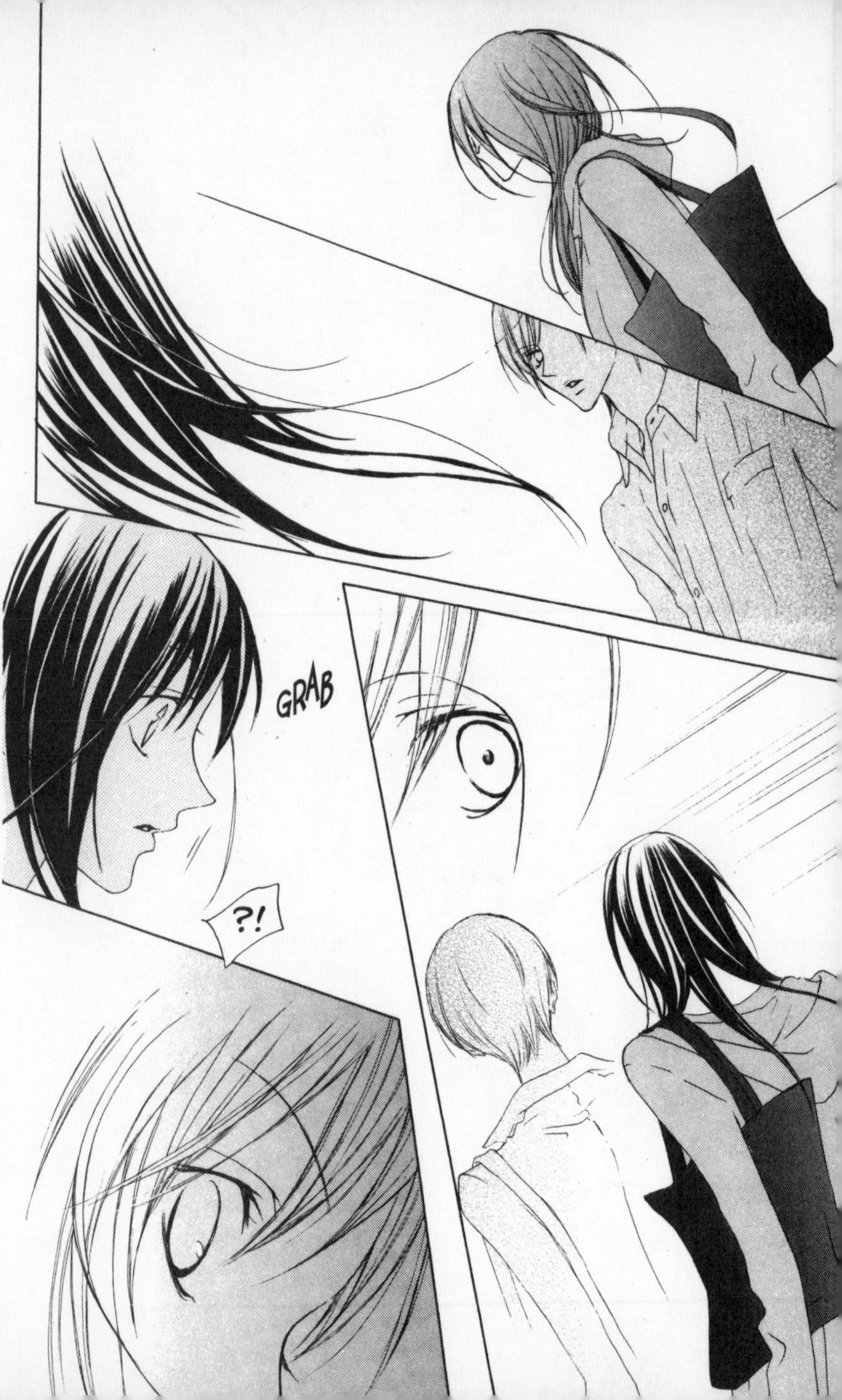
GRAB
?!

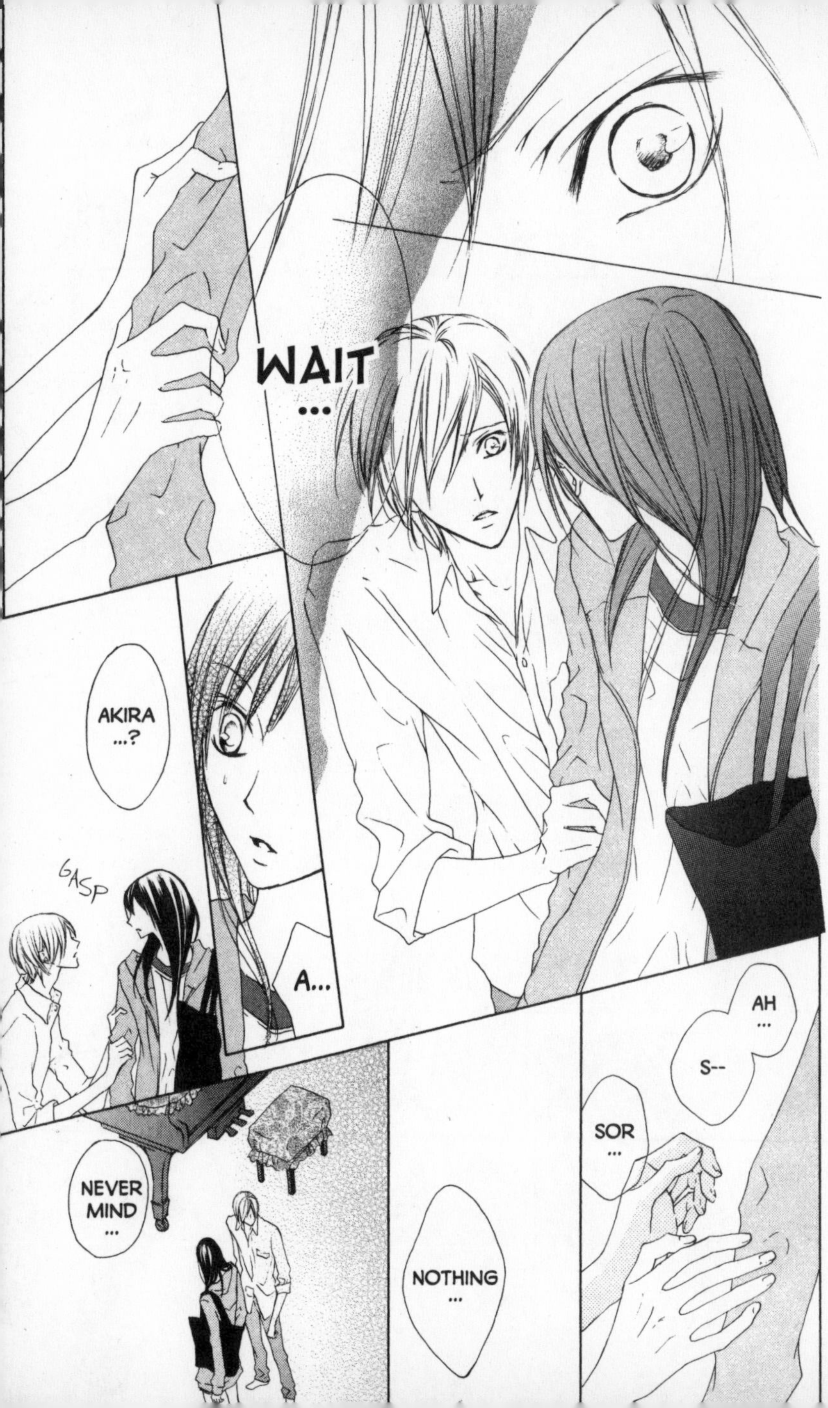
WAIT ...
AKIRA ...?
A...
GASP
AH ...
S--
SOR ...
NOTHING ...
NEVER MIND ...

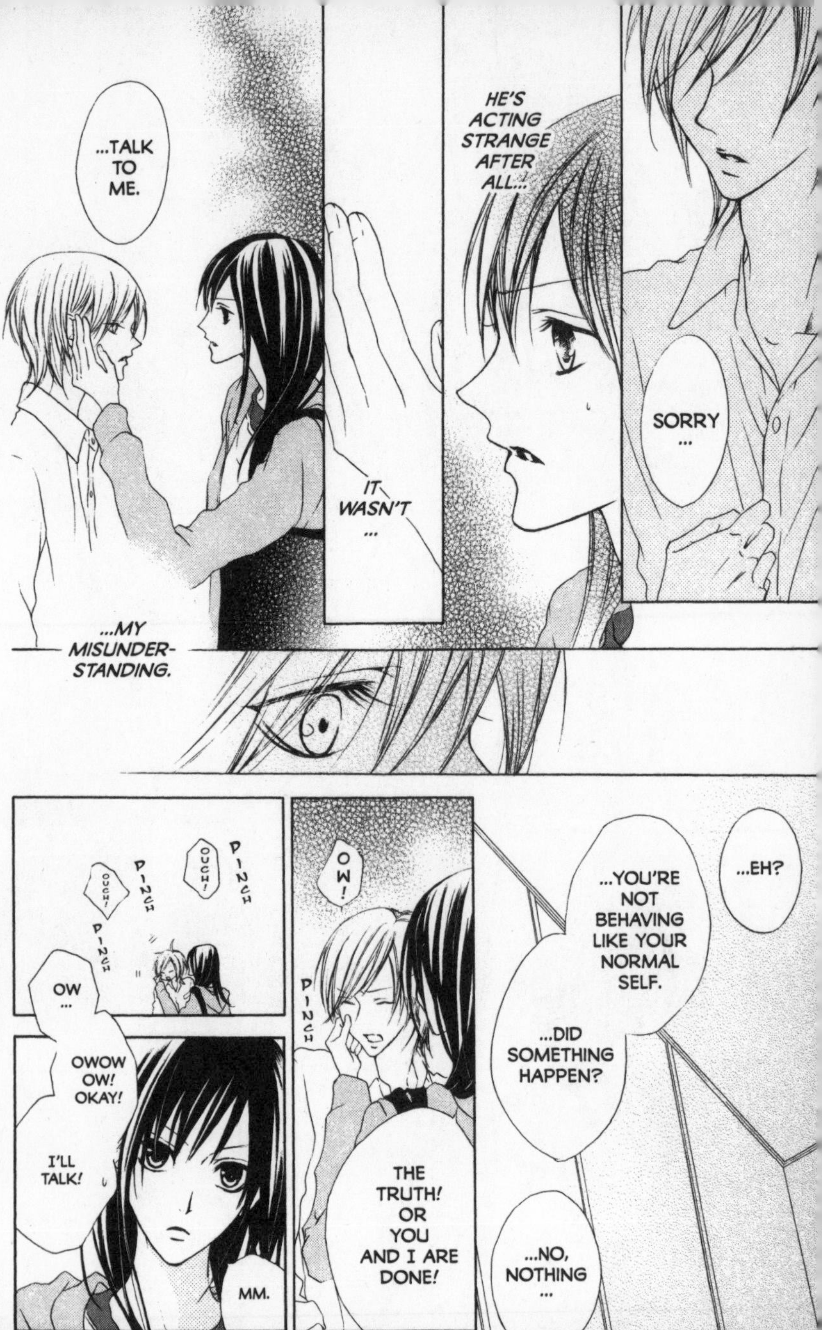

SORRY ...
HE'S ACTING STRANGE AFTER ALL...
IT WASN'T ...
...TALK TO ME.
...MY MISUNDERSTANDING.
...EH?
...YOU'RE NOT BEHAVING LIKE YOUR NORMAL SELF.
...DID SOMETHING HAPPEN?
...NO, NOTHING ...
OW!
PINCH
THE TRUTH! OR YOU AND I ARE DONE!
PINCH
OUCH!
PINCH
OUCH!
PINCH
OW ...
OWOW OW! OKAY!
I'LL TALK!
MM.

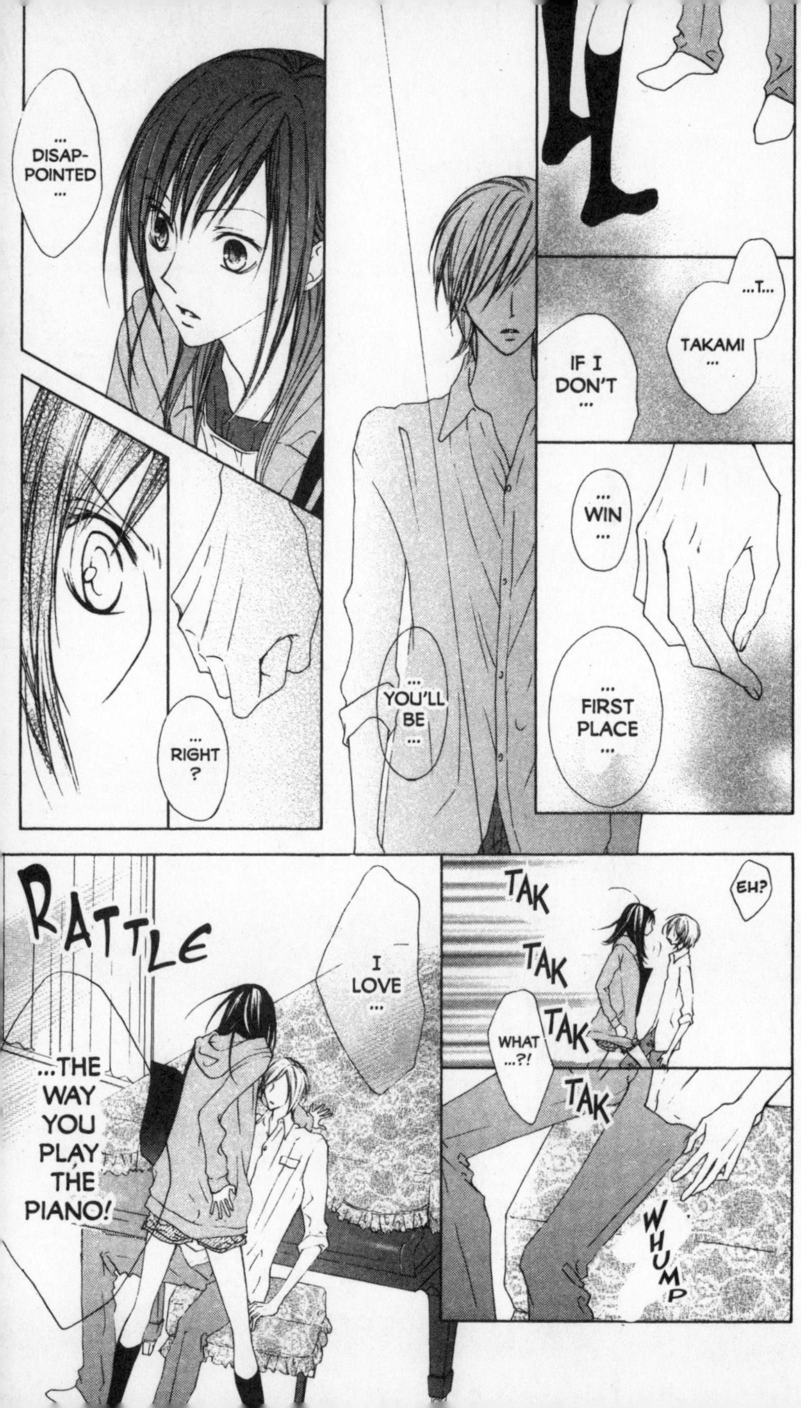
...T...
TAKAMI ...
IF I DON'T ...
... WIN ...
... FIRST PLACE ...
... YOU'LL BE ...
... DISAP-POINTED ...
... RIGHT ?
EH?
TAK
TAK
WHAT ...?!
TAK
TAK
WHUMP
RATTLE
I LOVE ...
...THE WAY YOU PLAY THE PIANO!

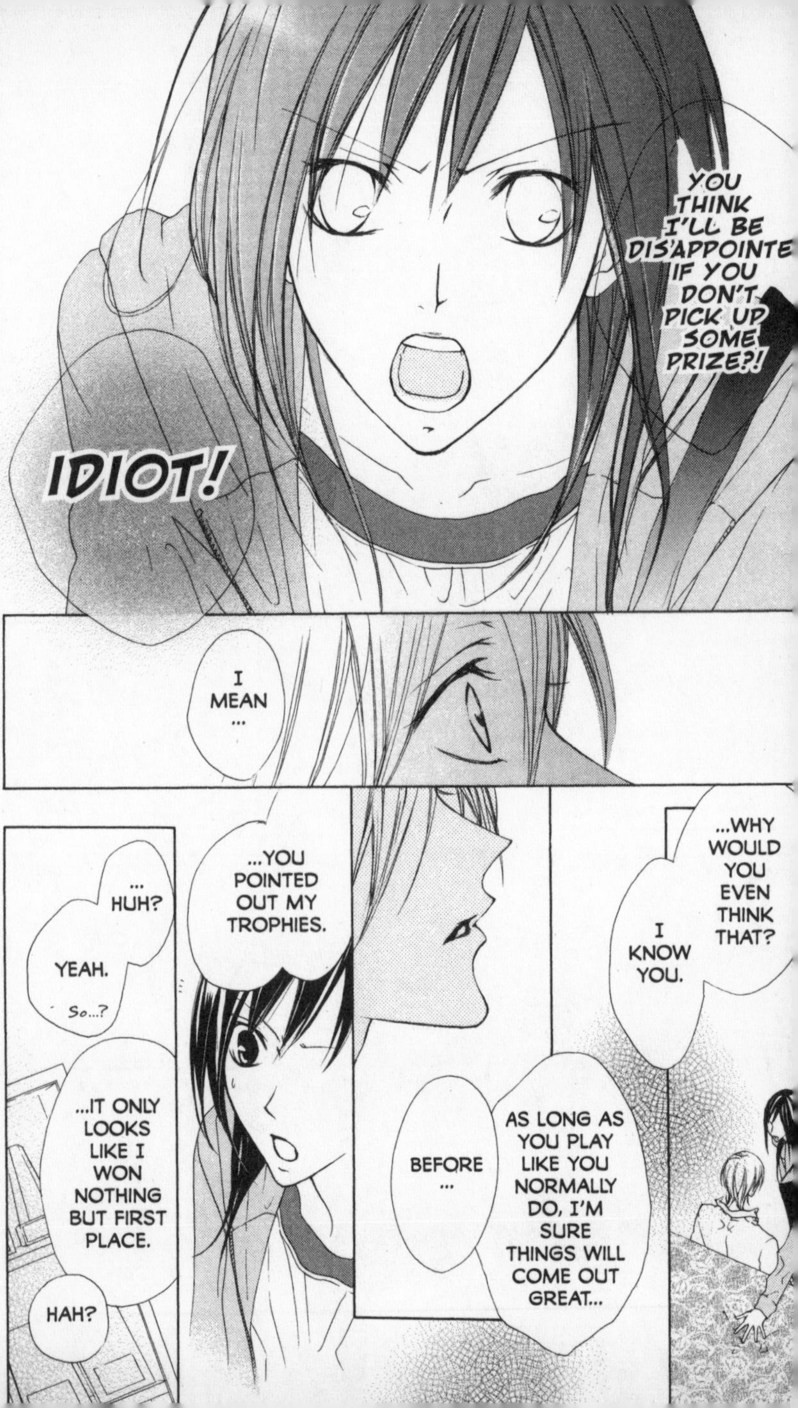
YOU THINK I'LL BE DISAPPOINTE IF YOU DON'T PICK UP SOME PRIZE?!
IDIOT!
I MEAN ...
...WHY WOULD YOU EVEN THINK THAT?
I KNOW YOU.
AS LONG AS YOU PLAY LIKE YOU NORMALLY DO, I'M SURE THINGS WILL COME OUT GREAT...
BEFORE ...
...YOU POINTED OUT MY TROPHIES.
... HUH?
YEAH.
So...?
...IT ONLY LOOKS LIKE I WON NOTHING BUT FIRST PLACE.
HAH?

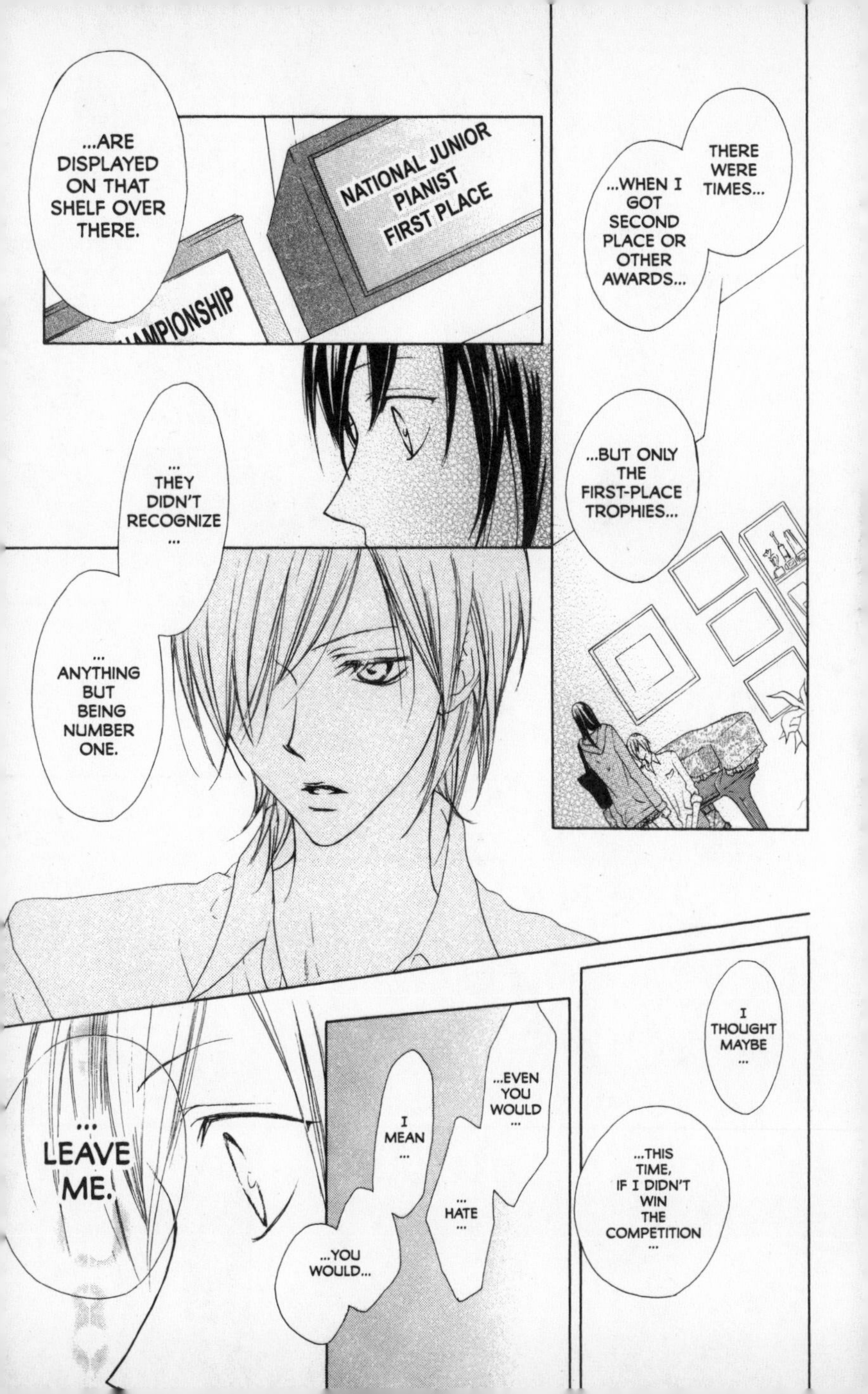
THERE WERE TIMES...
...WHEN I GOT SECOND PLACE OR OTHER AWARDS...
...BUT ONLY THE FIRST-PLACE TROPHIES...
...ARE DISPLAYED ON THAT SHELF OVER THERE.
NATIONAL JUNIOR PIANIST FIRST PLACE
... THEY DIDN'T RECOGNIZE ...
... ANYTHING BUT BEING NUMBER ONE.
I THOUGHT MAYBE ...
...THIS TIME, IF I DIDN'T WIN THE COMPETITION ...
...EVEN YOU WOULD ...
I MEAN ...
... HATE ...
...YOU WOULD...
... LEAVE ME.

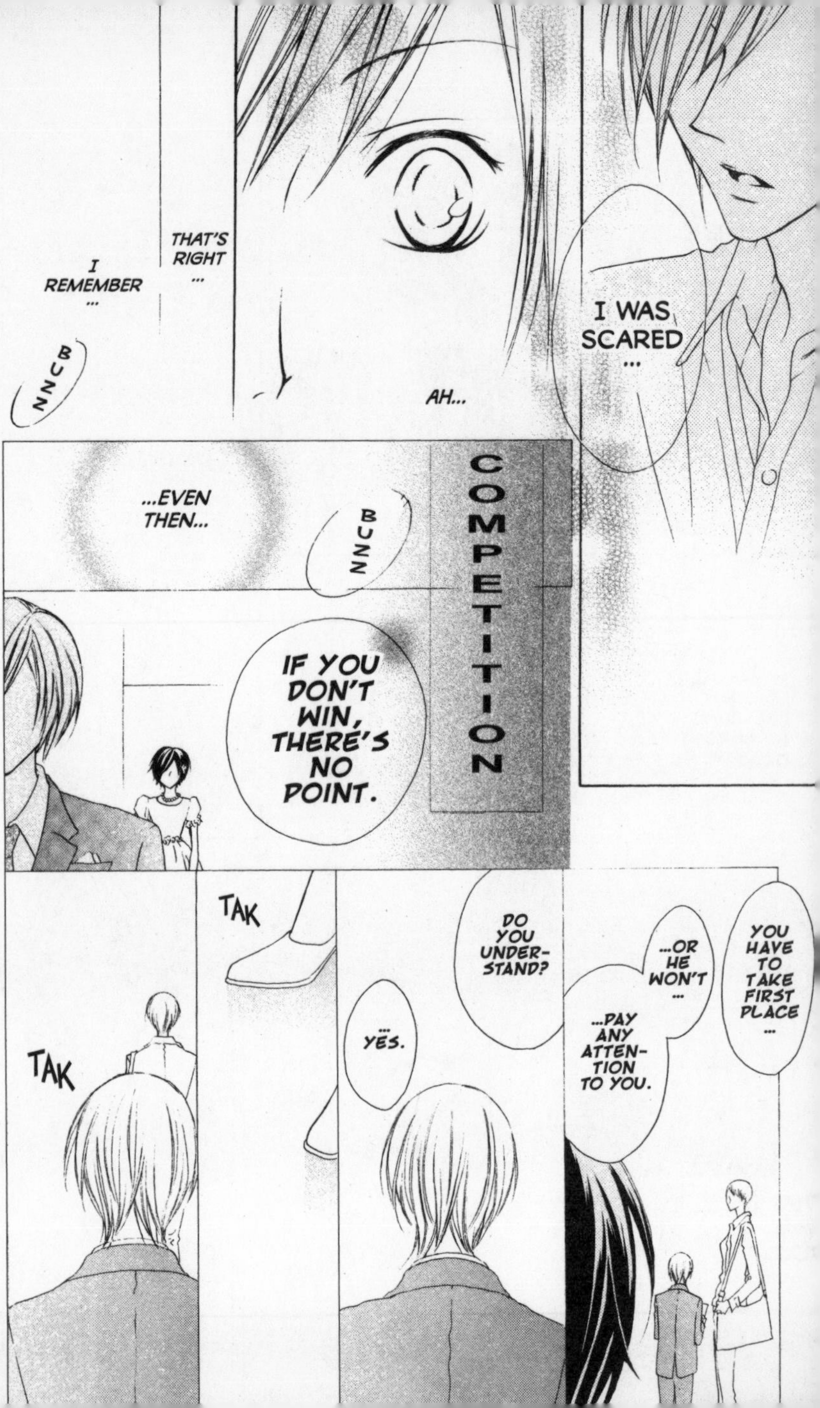
I WAS SCARED...
AH...
THAT'S RIGHT...
I REMEMBER...
BUZZ
COMPETITION
BUZZ
...EVEN THEN...
IF YOU DON'T WIN, THERE'S NO POINT.
YOU HAVE TO TAKE FIRST PLACE...
...OR HE WON'T...
...PAY ANY ATTENTION TO YOU.
DO YOU UNDERSTAND?
...YES.
TAK
TAK

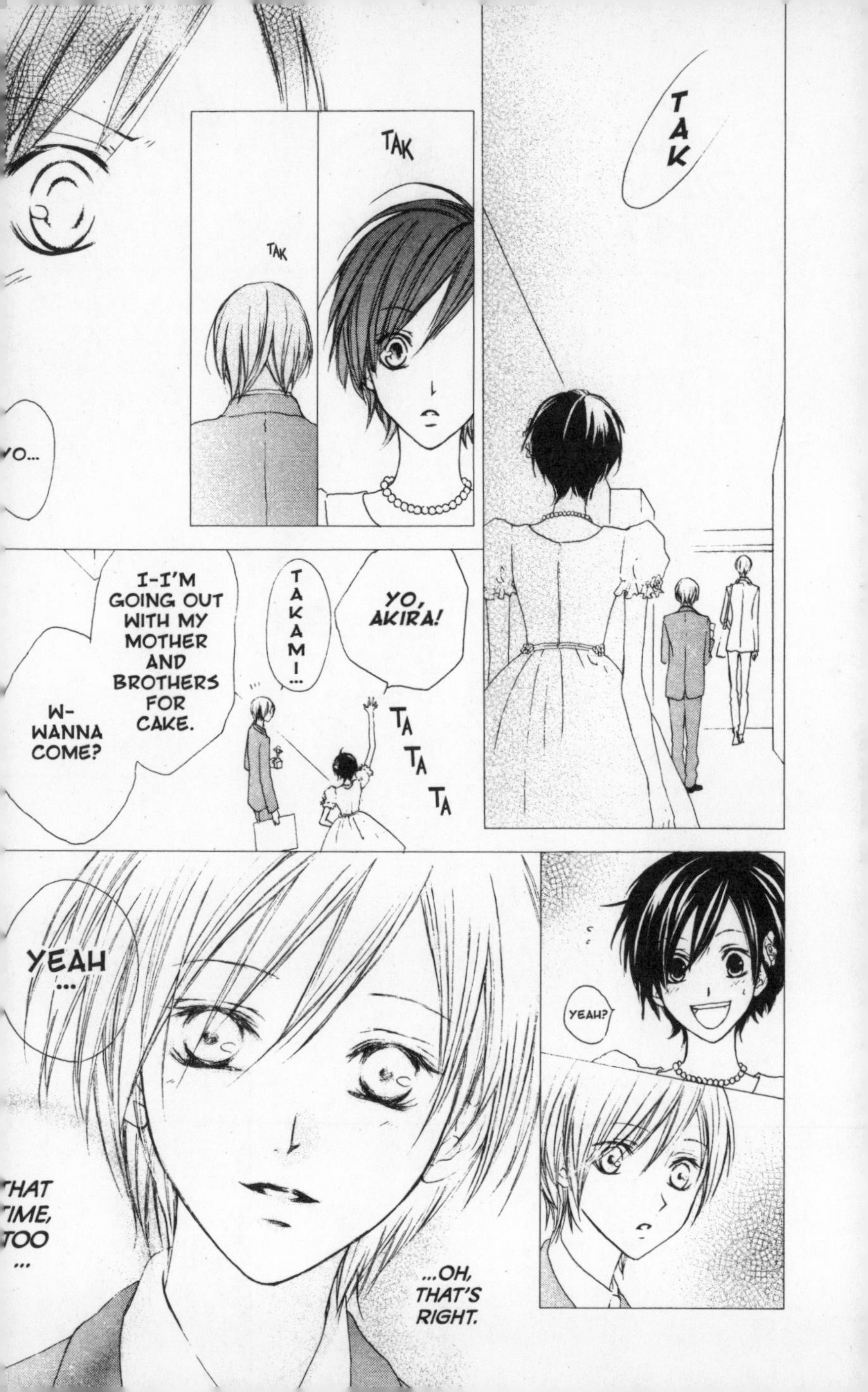
TAK
TAK
TAK
YO...
YO, AKIRA!
TAKAMI...
TA TA TA
I-I'M GOING OUT WITH MY MOTHER AND BROTHERS FOR CAKE.
W-WANNA COME?
YEAH?
...OH, THAT'S RIGHT.
YEAH...
THAT TIME, TOO...

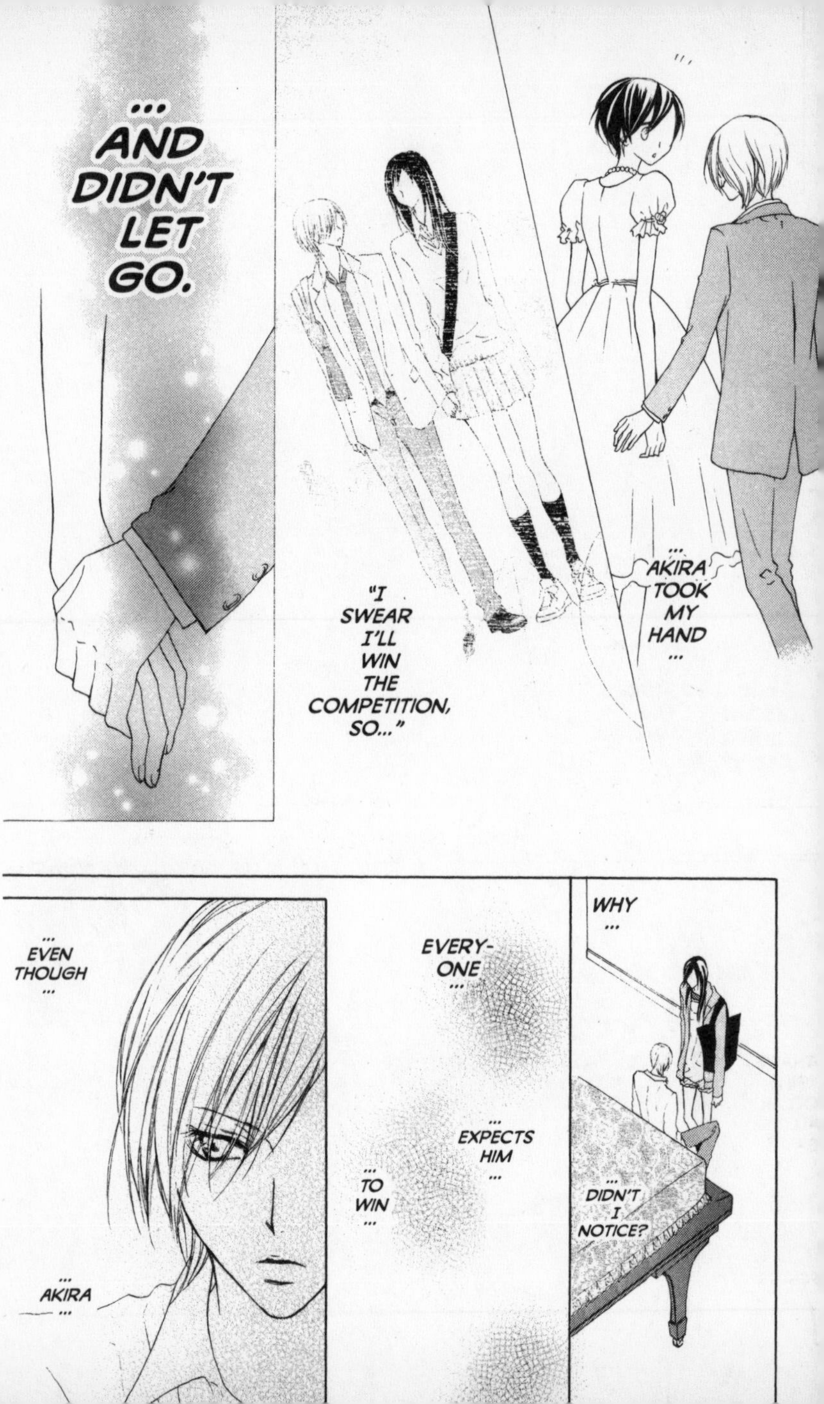
...AKIRA TOOK MY HAND...
"I SWEAR I'LL WIN THE COMPETITION, SO..."
...AND DIDN'T LET GO.
WHY...
...DIDN'T I NOTICE?
EVERY-ONE...
...EXPECTS HIM...
...TO WIN...
...EVEN THOUGH...
...AKIRA...

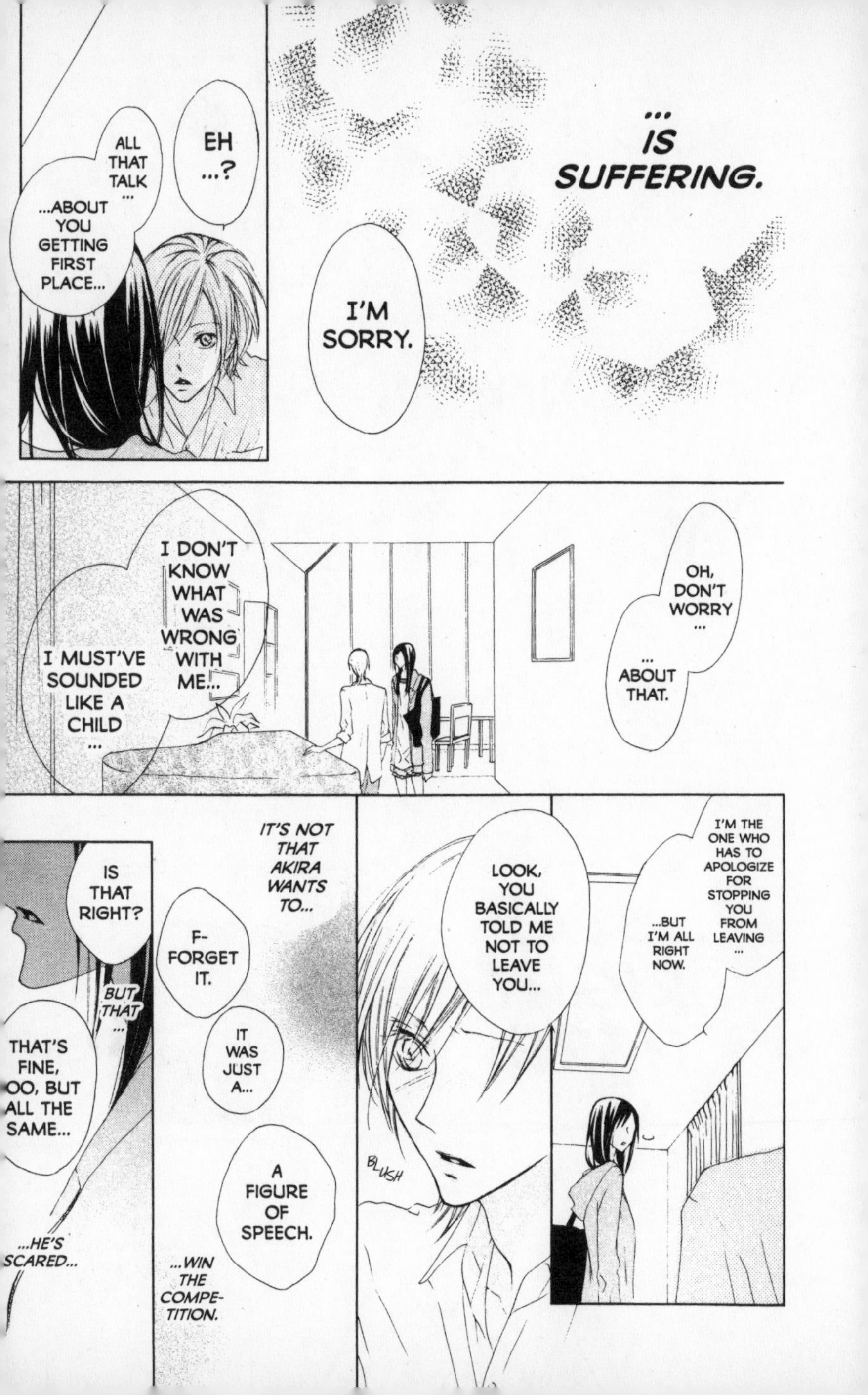

... IS SUFFERING.
I'M SORRY.
EH ...?
ALL THAT TALK ...
...ABOUT YOU GETTING FIRST PLACE...
OH, DON'T WORRY ...
... ABOUT THAT.
I DON'T KNOW WHAT WAS WRONG WITH ME...
I MUST'VE SOUNDED LIKE A CHILD ...
I'M THE ONE WHO HAS TO APOLOGIZE FOR STOPPING YOU FROM LEAVING ...
...BUT I'M ALL RIGHT NOW.
LOOK, YOU BASICALLY TOLD ME NOT TO LEAVE YOU...
BLUSH
IT'S NOT THAT AKIRA WANTS TO...
F-FORGET IT.
IT WAS JUST A...
A FIGURE OF SPEECH.
...WIN THE COMPETITION.
IS THAT RIGHT?
BUT THAT ...
THAT'S FINE, OO, BUT ALL THE SAME...
...HE'S SCARED...

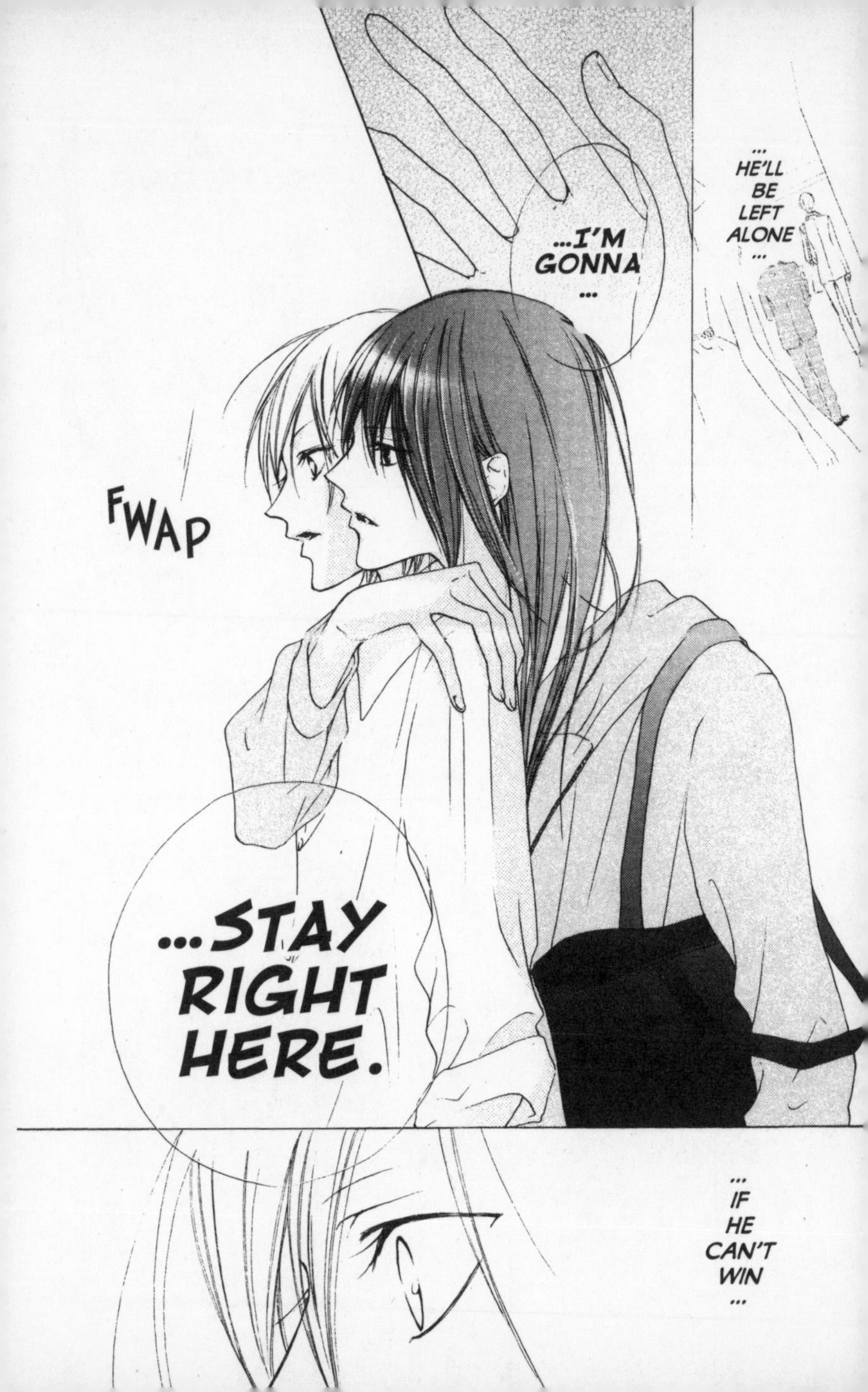
... HE'LL BE LEFT ALONE ...
...I'M GONNA ...
FWAP
...STAY RIGHT HERE.
... IF HE CAN'T WIN ...

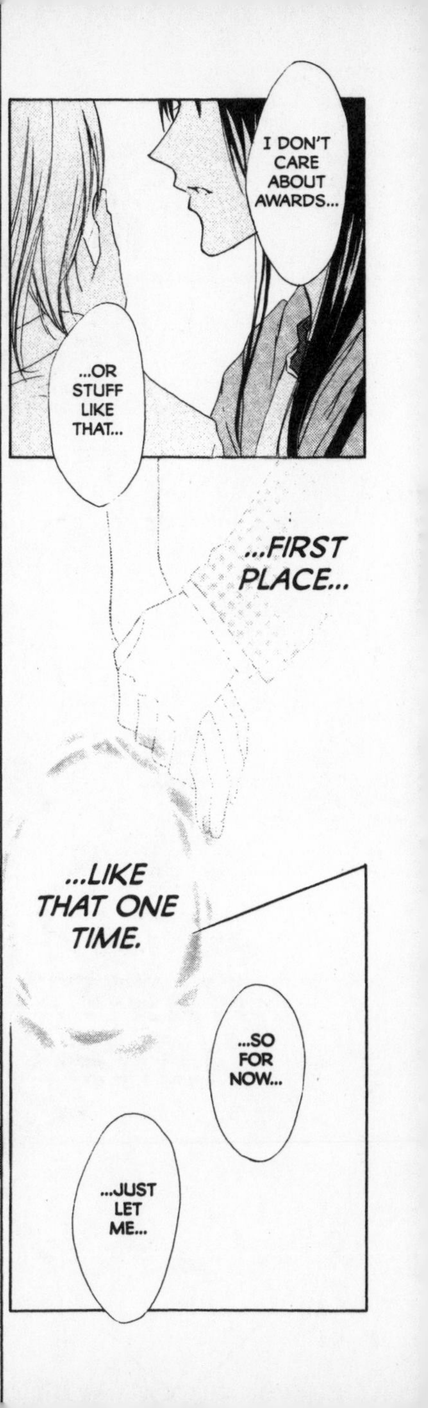
I DON'T CARE ABOUT AWARDS...
...OR STUFF LIKE THAT...
...FIRST PLACE...
...LIKE THAT ONE TIME.
...SO FOR NOW...
...JUST LET ME...

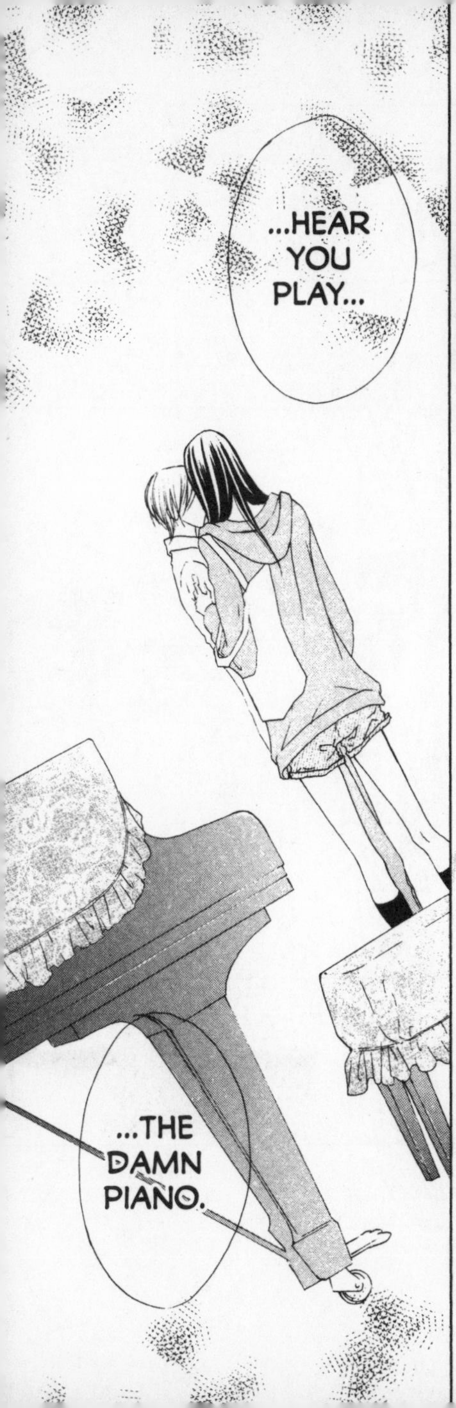
...HEAR YOU PLAY...
...THE DAMN PIANO.

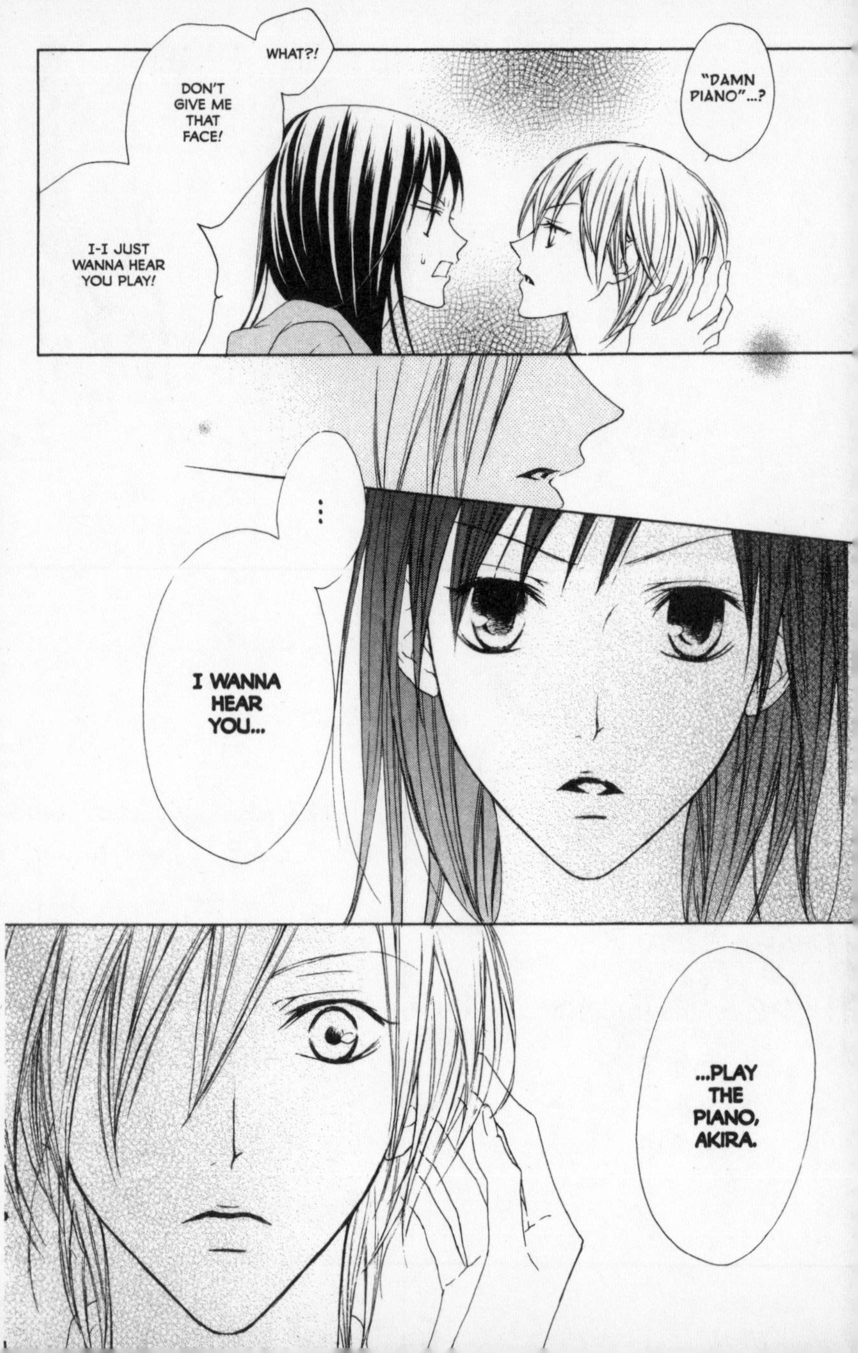
"DAMN PIANO"...?
WHAT?!
DON'T GIVE ME THAT FACE!
I-I JUST WANNA HEAR YOU PLAY!
...
I WANNA HEAR YOU...
...PLAY THE PIANO, AKIRA.

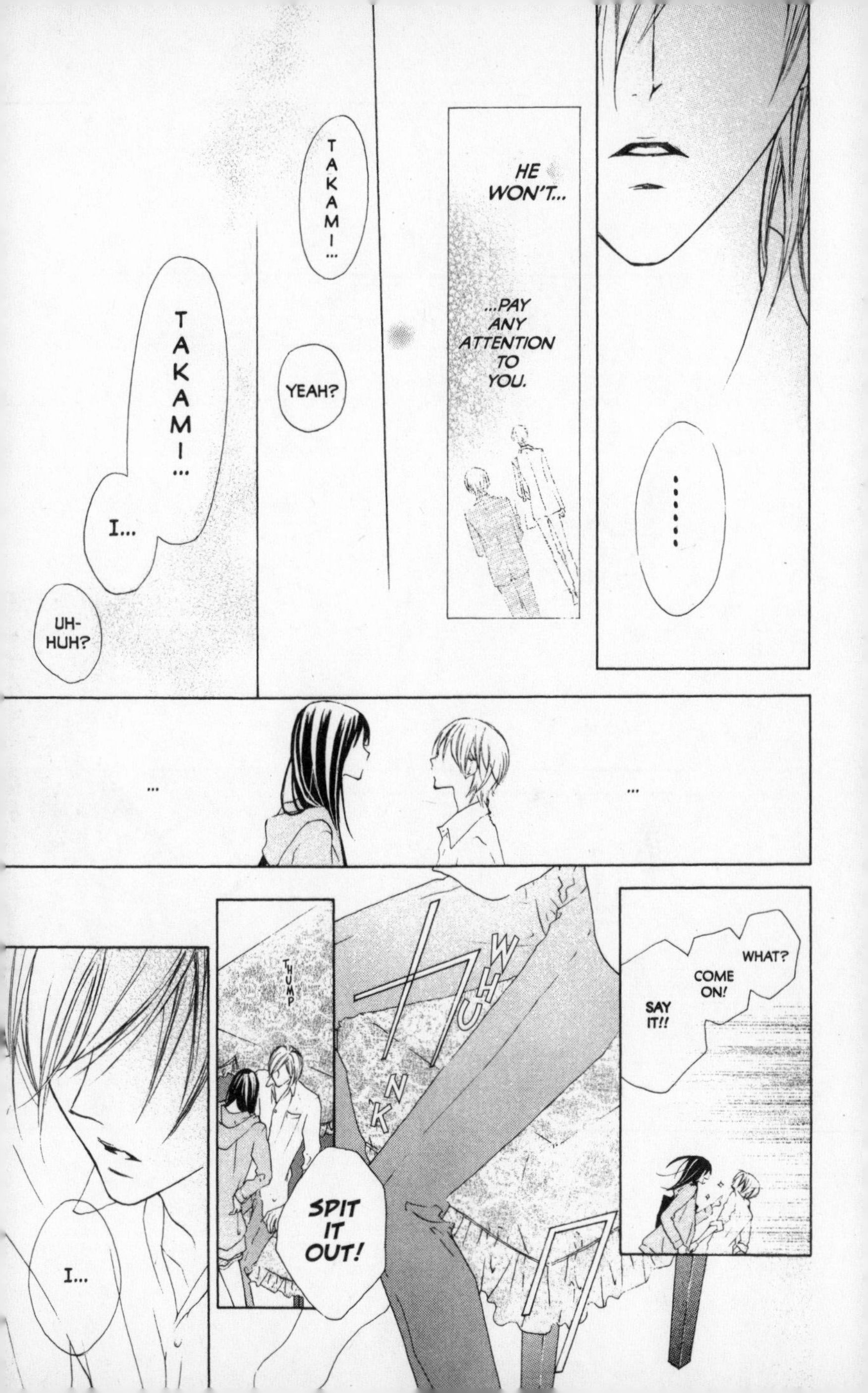
......
HE WON'T...
...PAY ANY ATTENTION TO YOU.
TAKAMI...
YEAH?
TAKAMI...
I...
UH-HUH?
...
...
WHAT?
COME ON!
SAY IT!!
WHUNK
THUMP
SPIT IT OUT!
I...

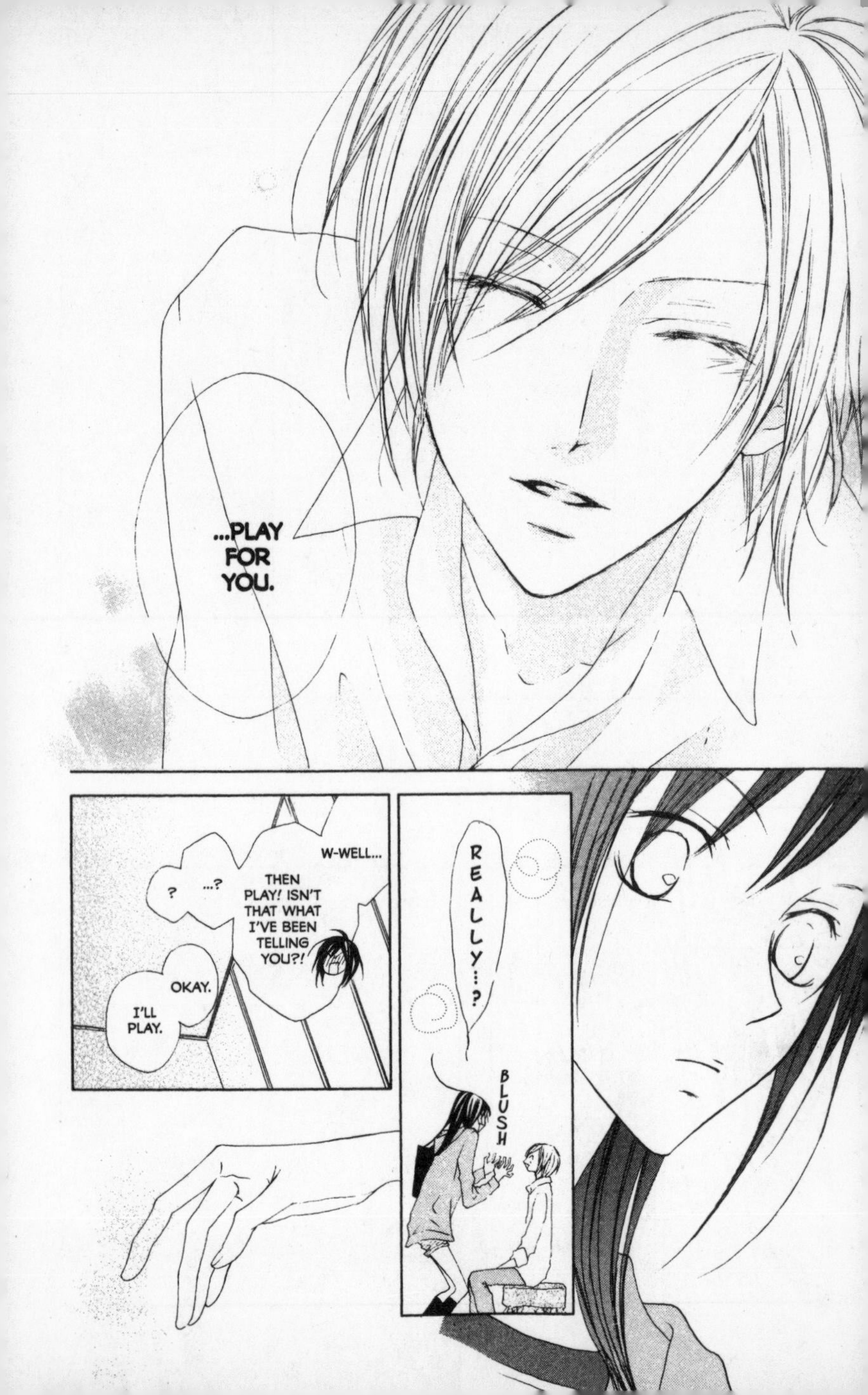
...PLAY FOR YOU.
REALLY...?
BLUSH
W-WELL...
THEN PLAY! ISN'T THAT WHAT I'VE BEEN TELLING YOU?!
? ...?
OKAY. I'LL PLAY.

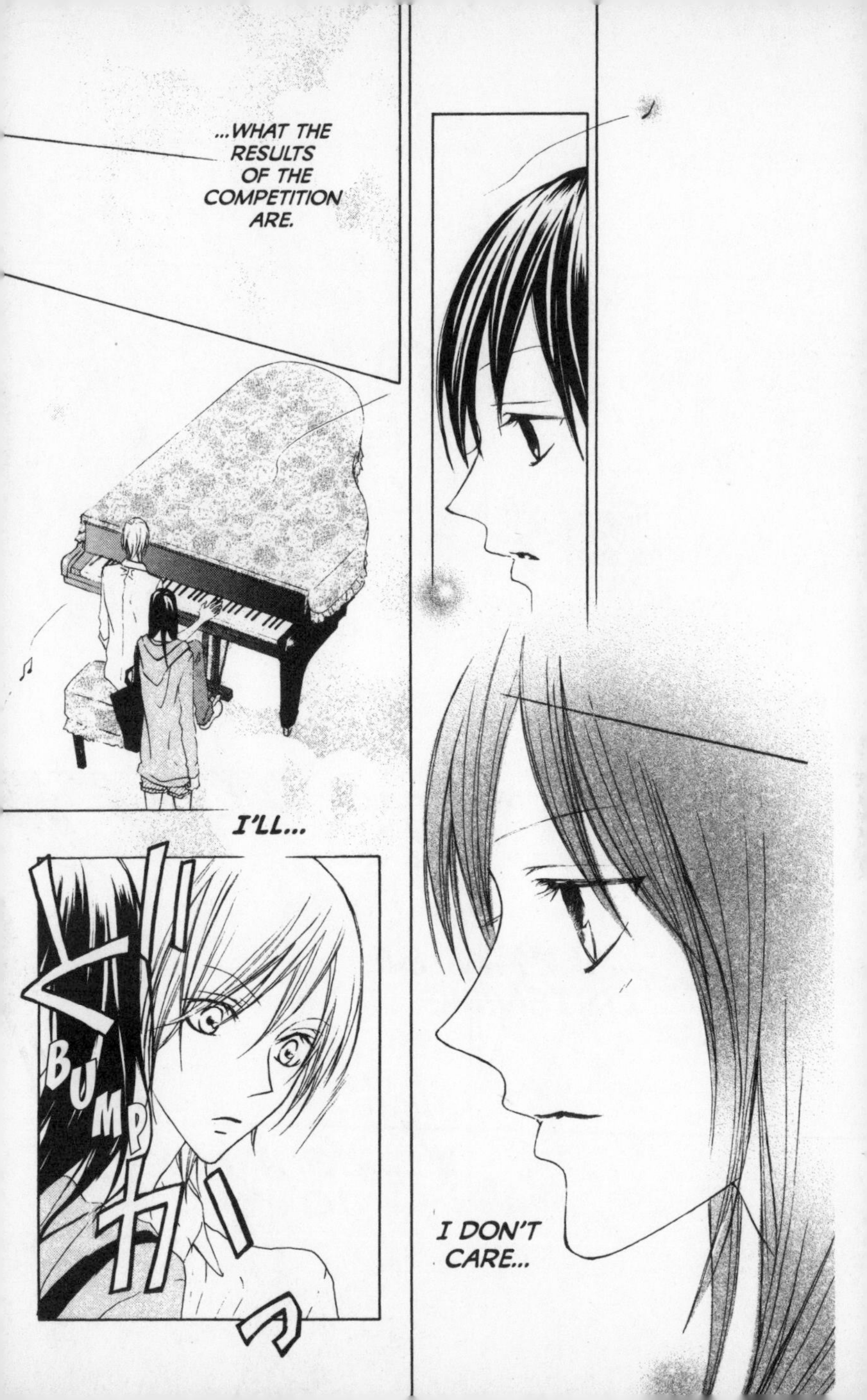
I DON'T CARE...
...WHAT THE RESULTS OF THE COMPETITION ARE.
I'LL...
BUMP

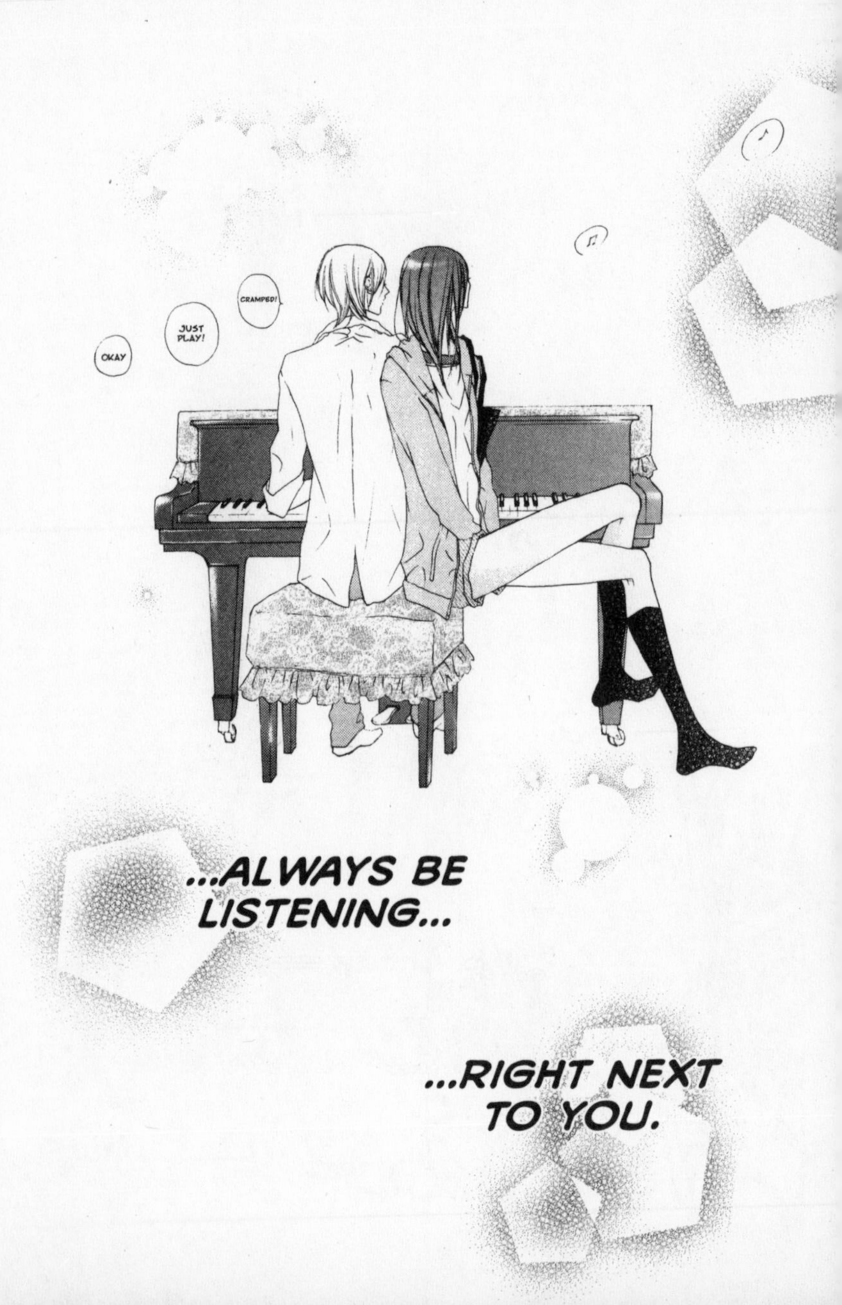
CRAMPED!
JUST PLAY!
OKAY
...ALWAYS BE LISTENING...
...RIGHT NEXT TO YOU.

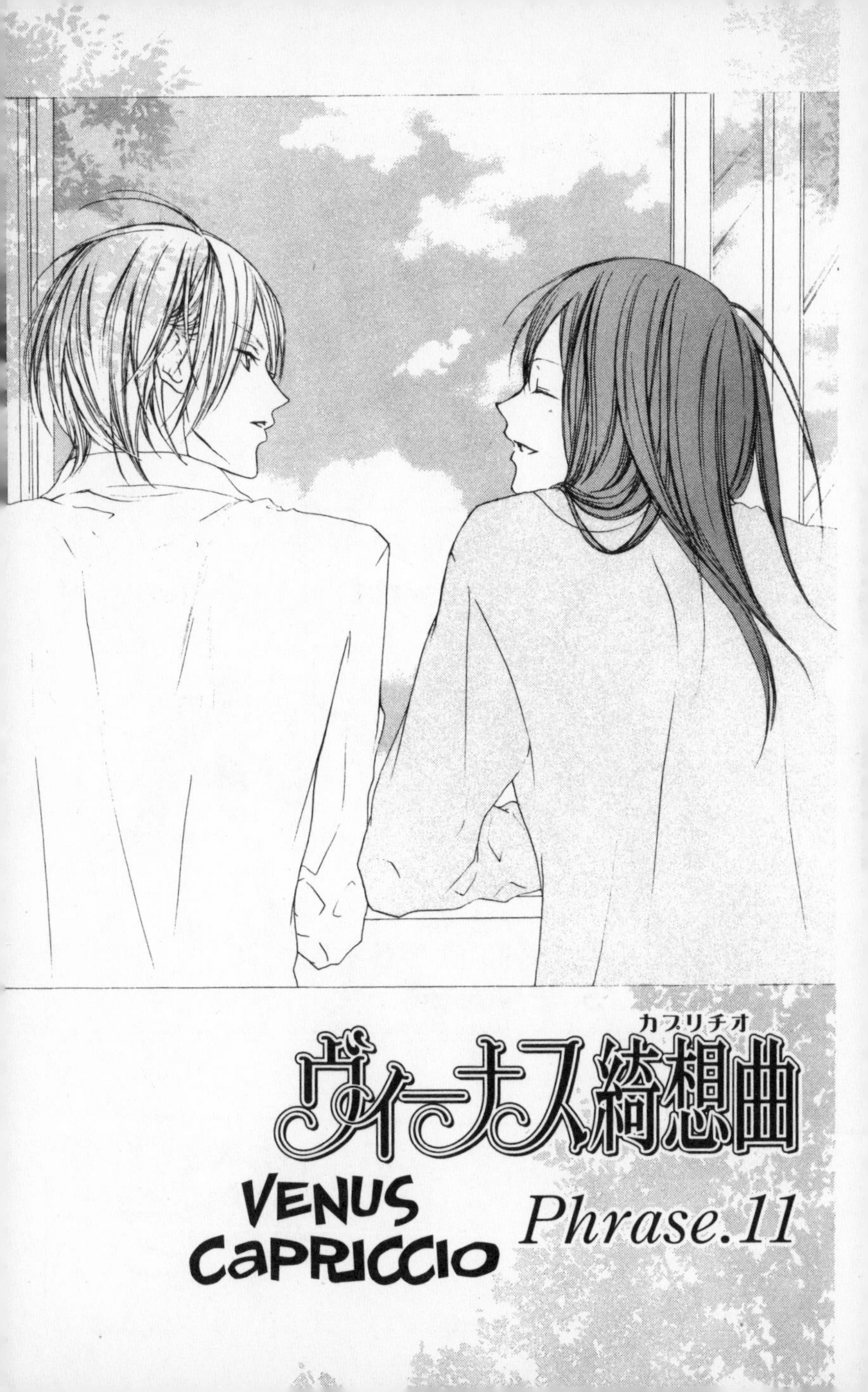
カプリチオ
ヴィーナス綺想曲
VENUS CaPRICCIO
Phrase.11

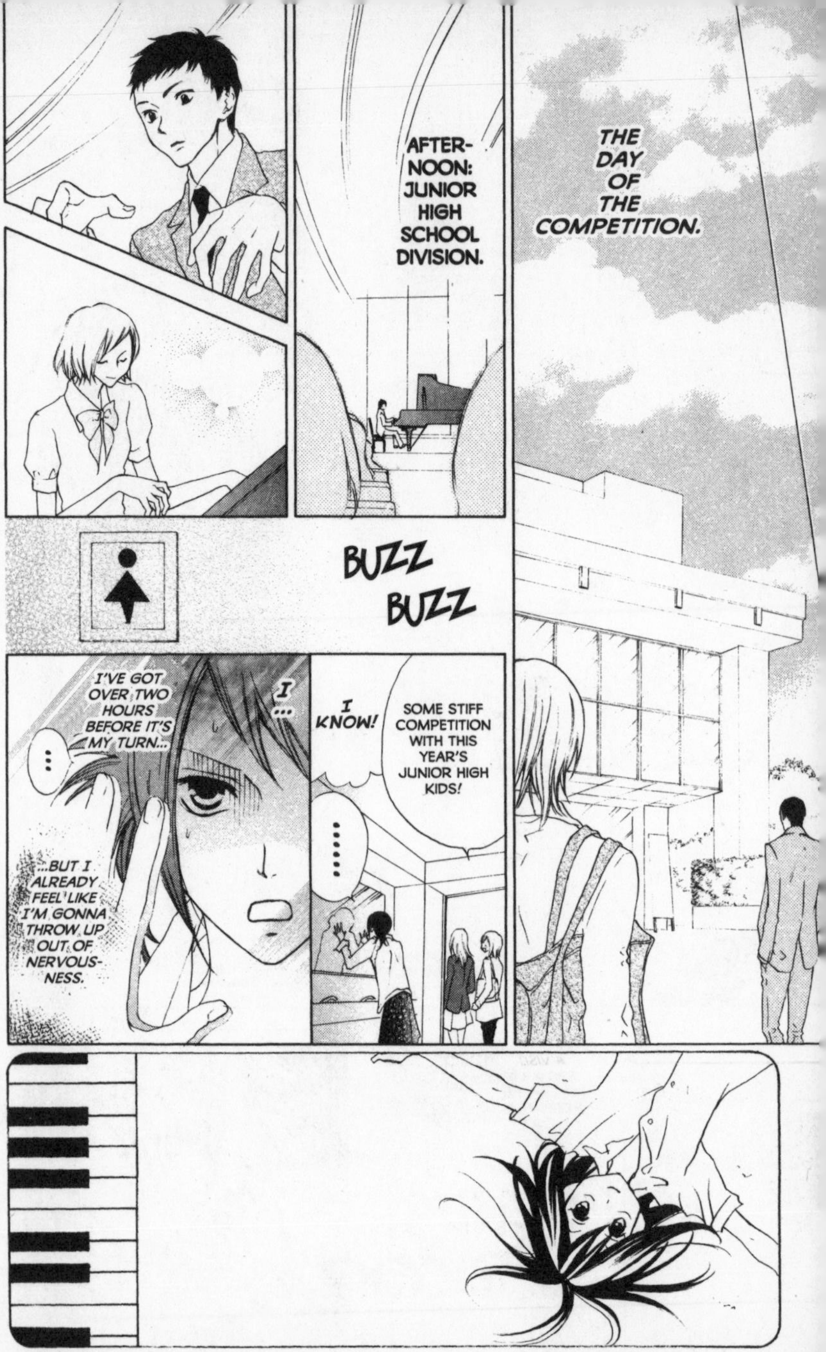
THE DAY OF THE COMPETITION.
AFTER-NOON: JUNIOR HIGH SCHOOL DIVISION.
BUZZ
BUZZ
SOME STIFF COMPETITION WITH THIS YEAR'S JUNIOR HIGH KIDS!
I KNOW!
......
I...
I'VE GOT OVER TWO HOURS BEFORE IT'S MY TURN...
...
...BUT I ALREADY FEEL LIKE I'M GONNA THROW UP OUT OF NERVOUS-NESS.

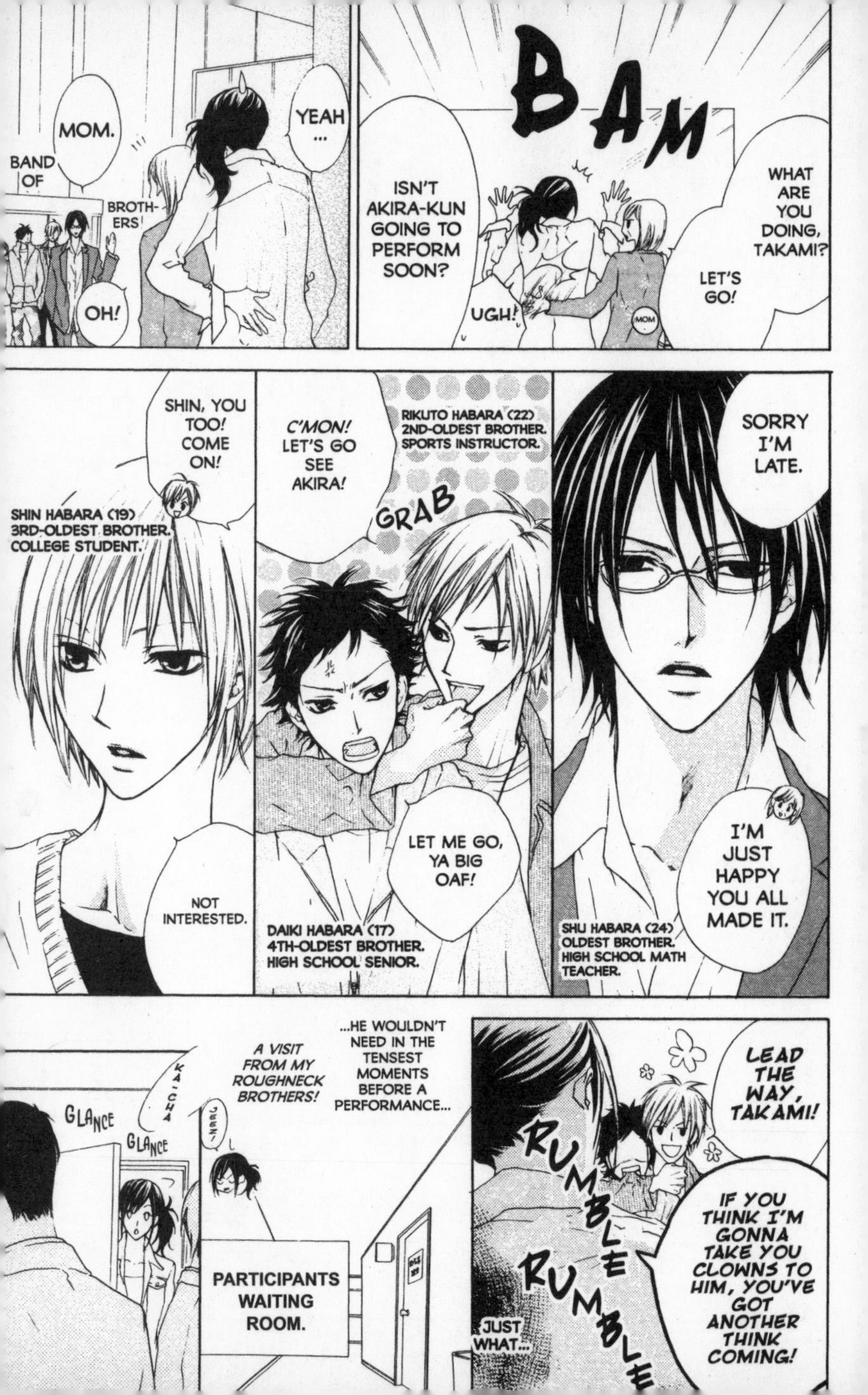
BAM
WHAT ARE YOU DOING, TAKAMI?
LET'S GO!
MOM
ISN'T AKIRA-KUN GOING TO PERFORM SOON?
UGH!
YEAH ...
MOM.
BAND OF BROTHERS
OH!
SORRY I'M LATE.
I'M JUST HAPPY YOU ALL MADE IT.
SHU HABARA (24) OLDEST BROTHER. HIGH SCHOOL MATH TEACHER.
RIKUTO HABARA (22) 2ND-OLDEST BROTHER. SPORTS INSTRUCTOR.
C'MON! LET'S GO SEE AKIRA!
GRAB
LET ME GO, YA BIG OAF!
DAIKI HABARA (17) 4TH-OLDEST BROTHER. HIGH SCHOOL SENIOR.
SHIN, YOU TOO! COME ON!
SHIN HABARA (19) 3RD-OLDEST BROTHER. COLLEGE STUDENT.
NOT INTERESTED.
LEAD THE WAY, TAKAMI!
IF YOU THINK I'M GONNA TAKE YOU CLOWNS TO HIM, YOU'VE GOT ANOTHER THINK COMING!
RUMBLE
RUMBLE
JUST WHAT...
...HE WOULDN'T NEED IN THE TENSEST MOMENTS BEFORE A PERFORMANCE...
A VISIT FROM MY ROUGHNECK BROTHERS!
KA-CHA
JEEZ!
GLANCE
GLANCE
PARTICIPANTS WAITING ROOM.

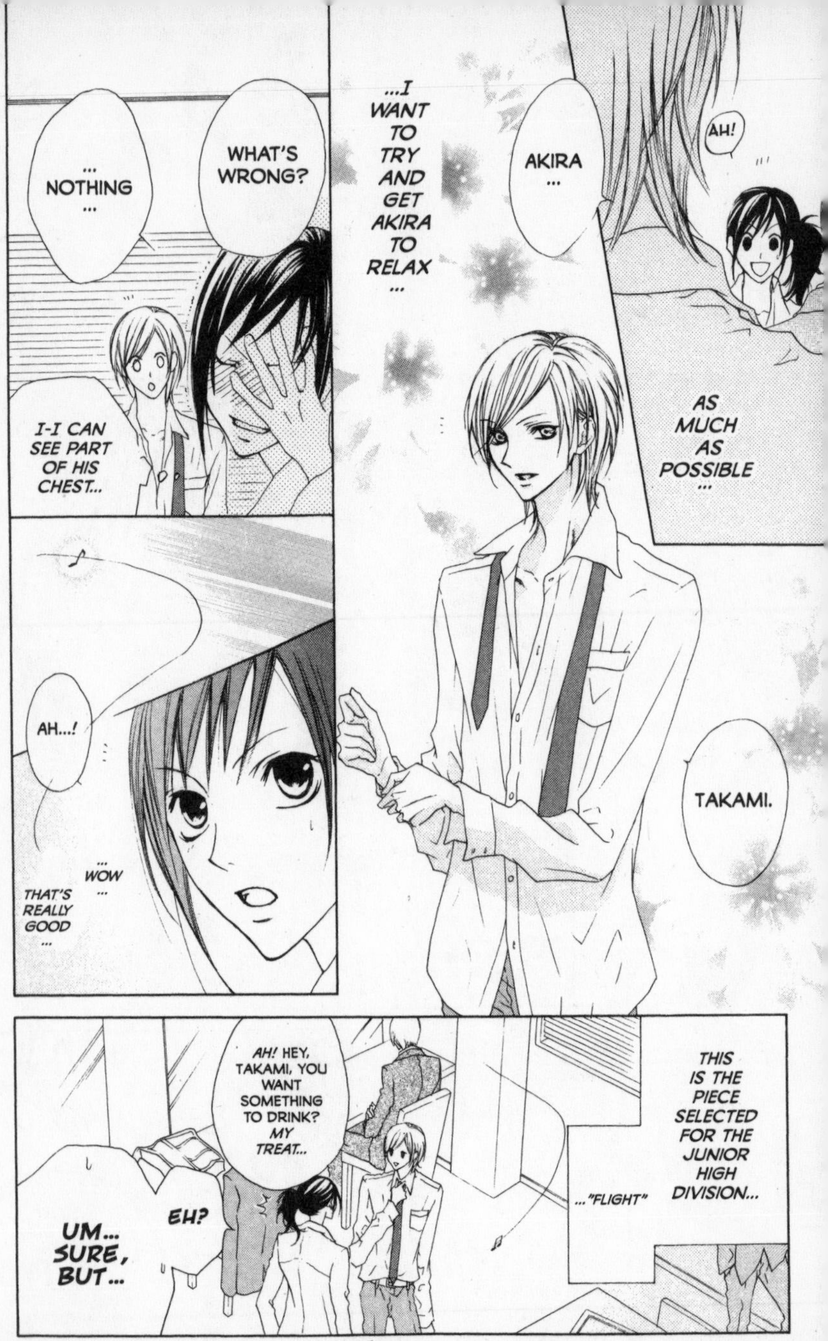
AH!
AKIRA ...
...I WANT TO TRY AND GET AKIRA TO RELAX ...
AS MUCH AS POSSIBLE ...
TAKAMI.
WHAT'S WRONG?
... NOTHING ...
I-I CAN SEE PART OF HIS CHEST...
AH...!
... WOW ...
THAT'S REALLY GOOD ...
THIS IS THE PIECE SELECTED FOR THE JUNIOR HIGH DIVISION...
..."FLIGHT"
AH! HEY, TAKAMI, YOU WANT SOMETHING TO DRINK? MY TREAT...
EH?
UM... SURE, BUT...

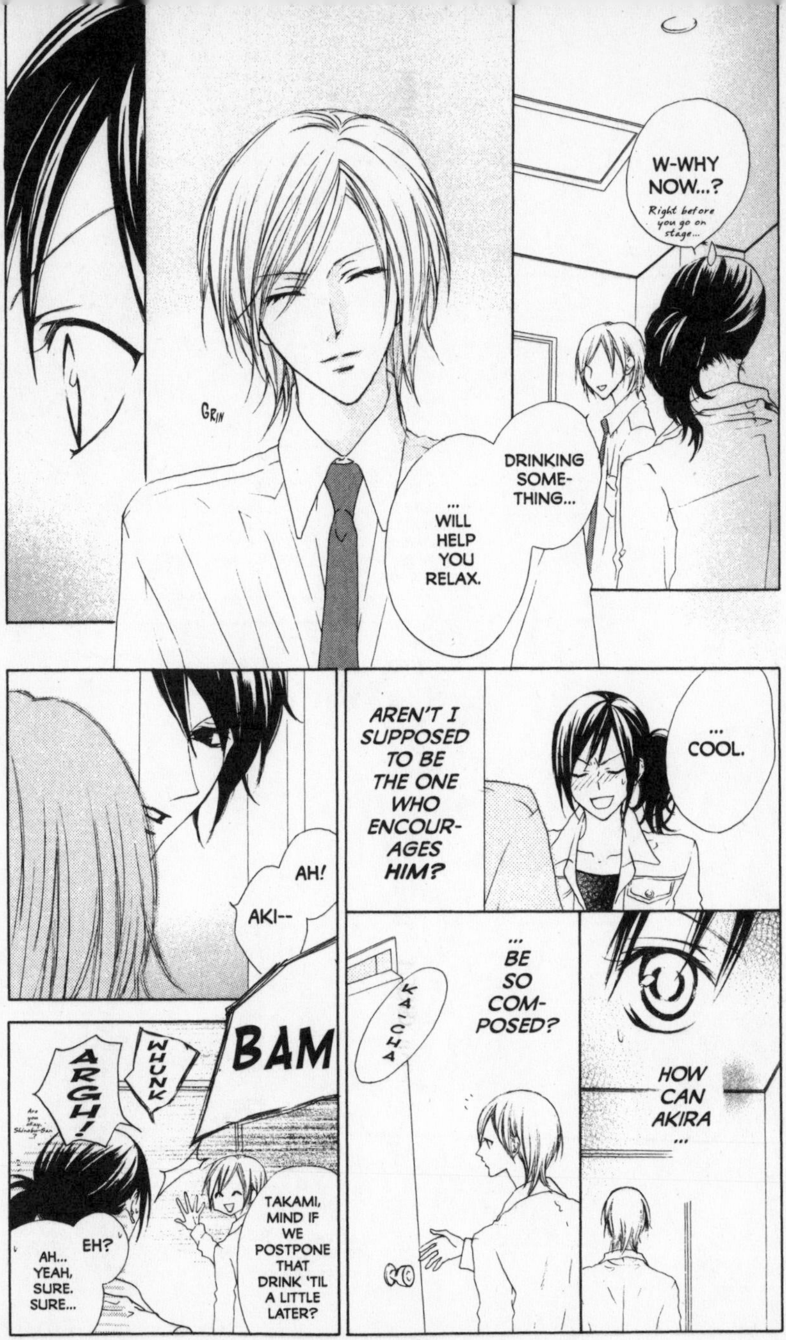
W-WHY NOW...?
Right before you go on stage...
DRINKING SOMETHING...
... WILL HELP YOU RELAX.
GRIN
... COOL.
AREN'T I SUPPOSED TO BE THE ONE WHO ENCOURAGES HIM?
AH!
AKI--
HOW CAN AKIRA ...
... BE SO COMPOSED?
KA-CHA
BAM
WHUNK
ARGH!
Are you okay, Shinobu-San ...?
TAKAMI, MIND IF WE POSTPONE THAT DRINK 'TIL A LITTLE LATER?
EH?
AH... YEAH, SURE. SURE...

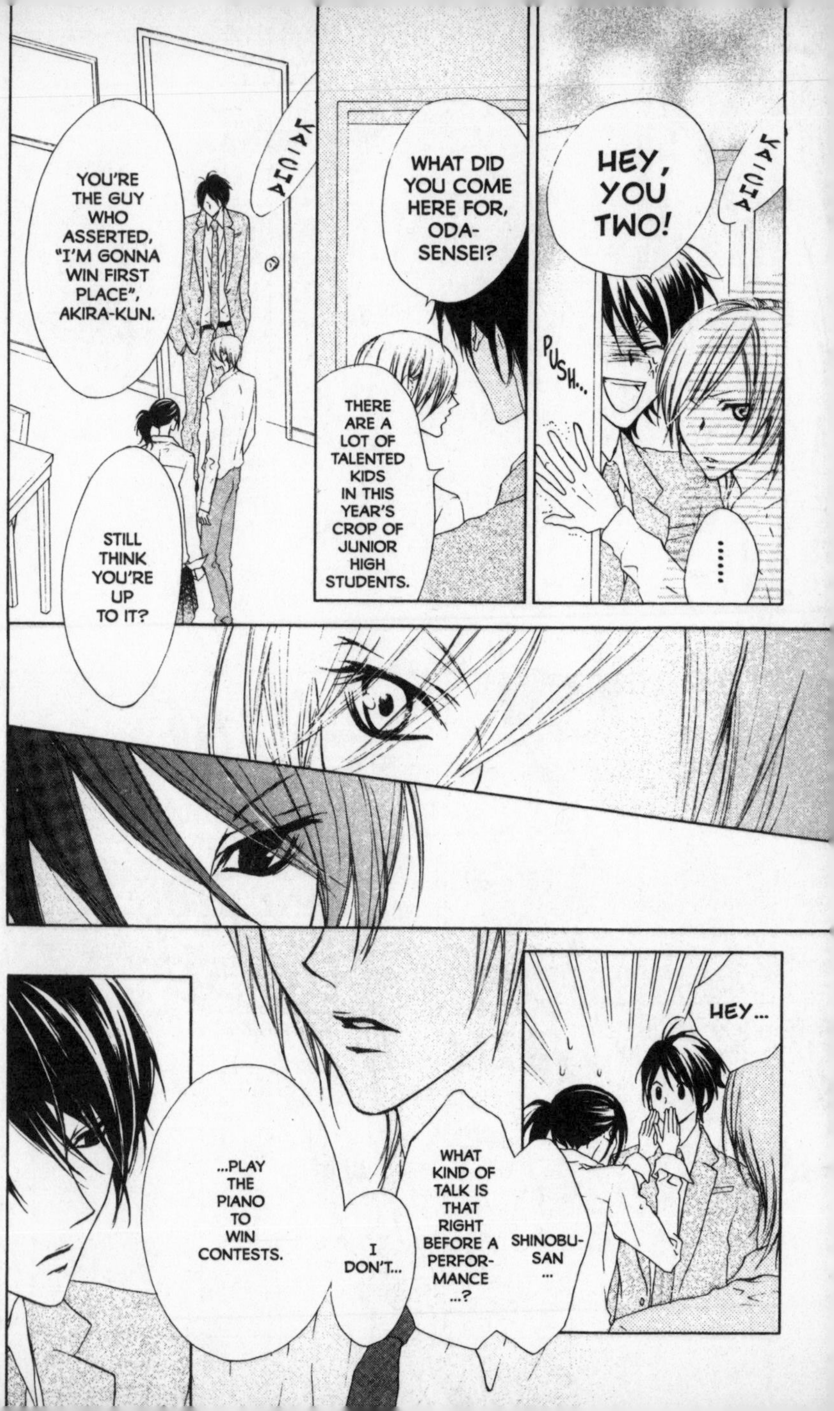
HEY, YOU TWO!
PUSH...
......
WHAT DID YOU COME HERE FOR, ODA-SENSEI?
THERE ARE A LOT OF TALENTED KIDS IN THIS YEAR'S CROP OF JUNIOR HIGH STUDENTS.
YOU'RE THE GUY WHO ASSERTED, "I'M GONNA WIN FIRST PLACE", AKIRA-KUN.
STILL THINK YOU'RE UP TO IT?
HEY...
SHINOBU-SAN ...
WHAT KIND OF TALK IS THAT RIGHT BEFORE A PERFORMANCE ...?
I DON'T...
...PLAY THE PIANO TO WIN CONTESTS.

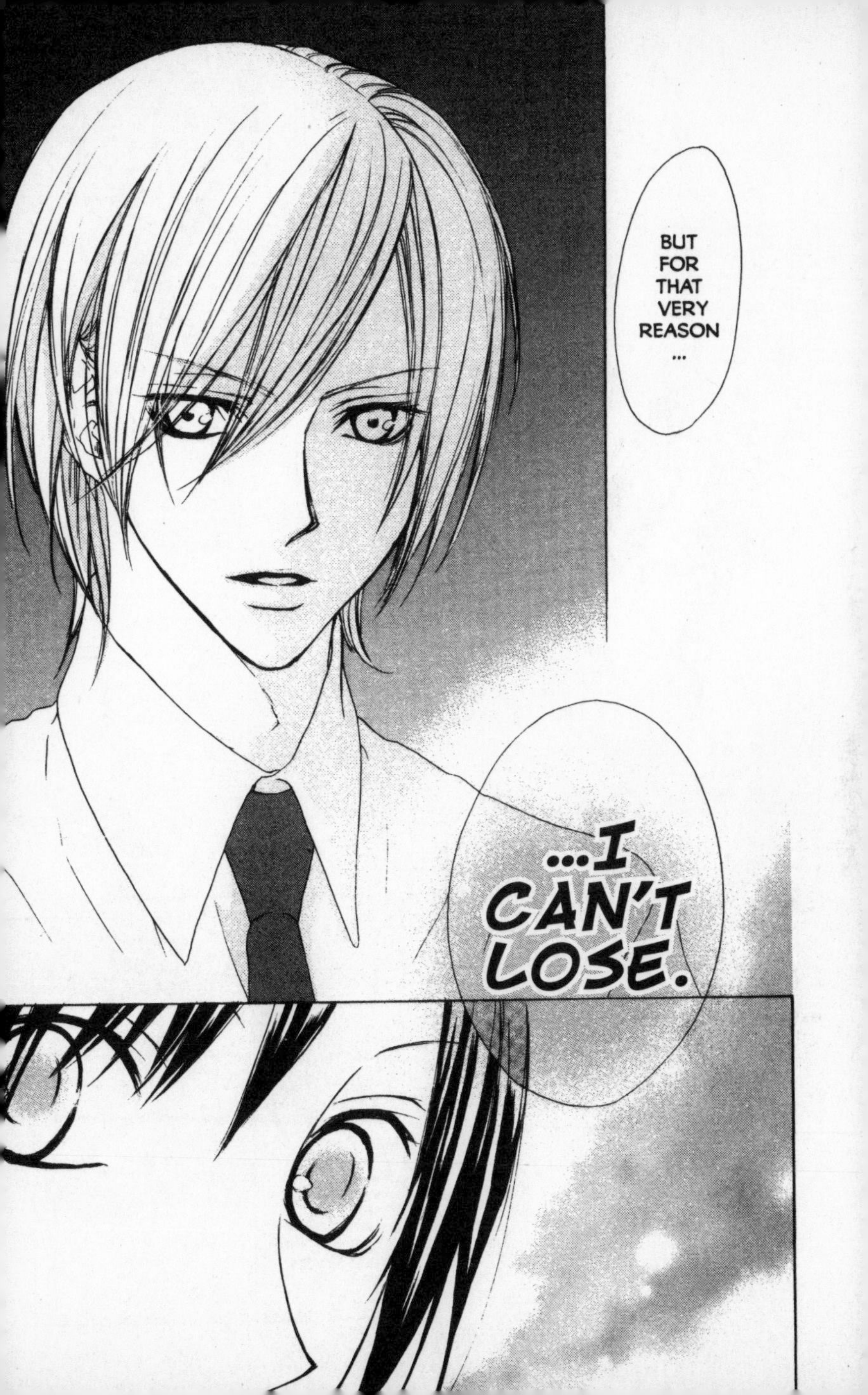
BUT FOR THAT VERY REASON ...
...I CAN'T LOSE.

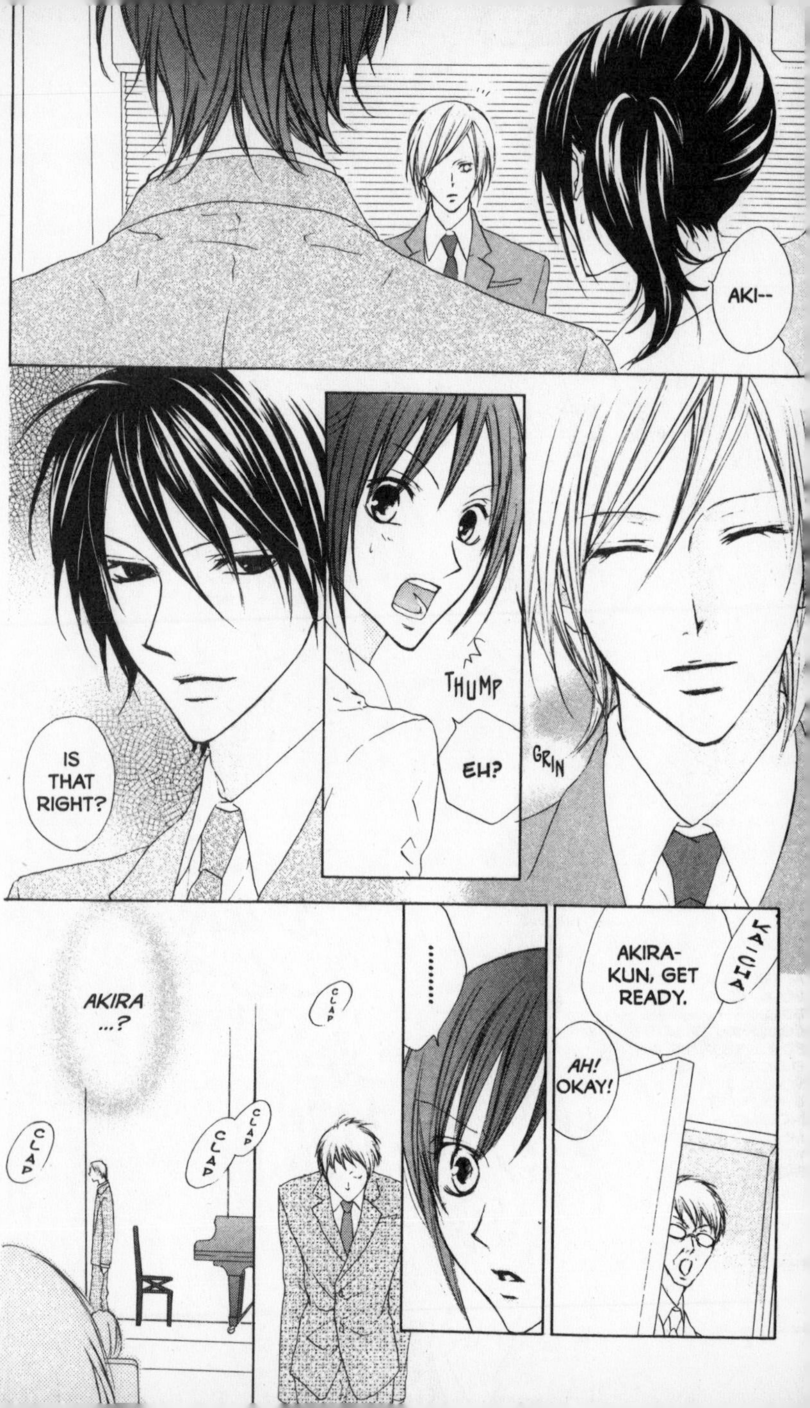
AKI--
GRIN
THUMP
EH?
IS THAT RIGHT?
KA-CHA
AKIRA-KUN, GET READY.
AH! OKAY!
....
CLAP
CLAP
CLAP
CLAP
AKIRA ...?

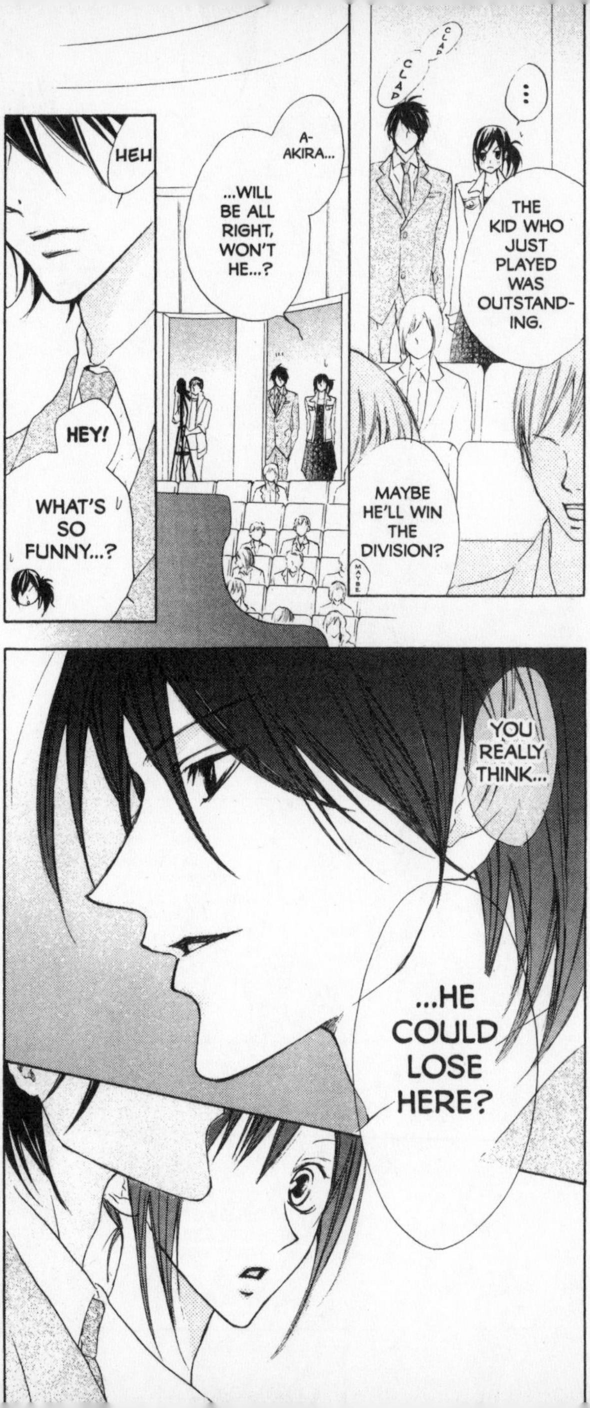
CLAP CLAP
...
THE KID WHO JUST PLAYED WAS OUTSTANDING.
MAYBE HE'LL WIN THE DIVISION?
MAYBE
A- AKIRA...
...WILL BE ALL RIGHT, WON'T HE...?
HEH
HEY!
WHAT'S SO FUNNY...?
YOU REALLY THINK...
...HE COULD LOSE HERE?

6

THE LAST COLUMN.

I HAD MORE SPACE THAN I KNEW WHAT TO DO WITH.

THANK YOU FOR READING THIS FAR!
AT THE BACK OF THE BOOK, YOU'LL FIND A BONUS MANGA THAT CONTINUES FROM THE BONUS STORY AT THE END OF THE FIRST VOLUME.
IF YOU'RE OF THE INCLINATION, BY ALL MEANS, PLEASE READ IT.
WELL, FOR NOW, FAREWELL.

THIS HAS BEEN NISHIKATA.

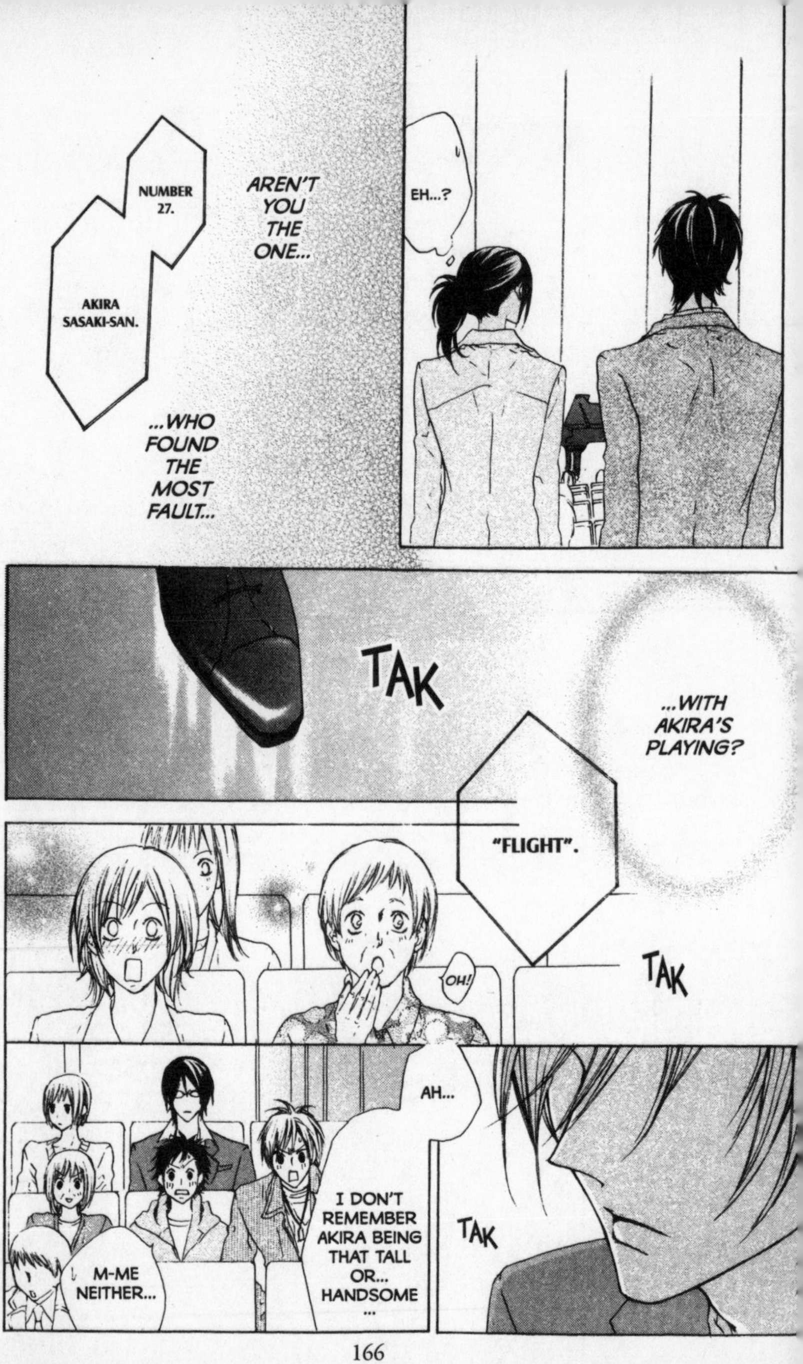
EH...?
NUMBER 27.
AKIRA SASAKI-SAN.
AREN'T YOU THE ONE...
...WHO FOUND THE MOST FAULT...
...WITH AKIRA'S PLAYING?
TAK
"FLIGHT".
TAK
OH!
TAK
AH...
I DON'T REMEMBER AKIRA BEING THAT TALL OR... HANDSOME ...
M-ME NEITHER...

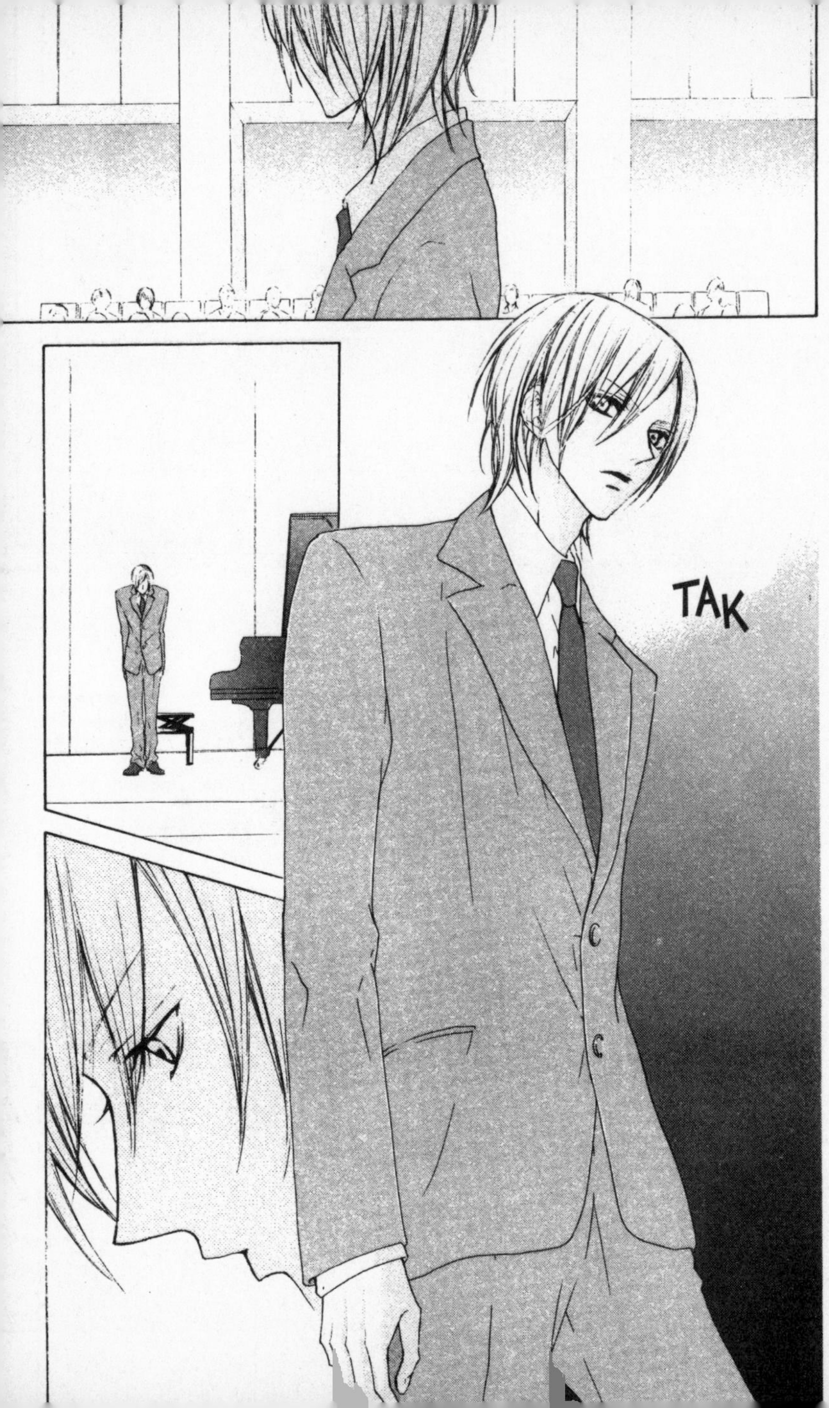
TAK

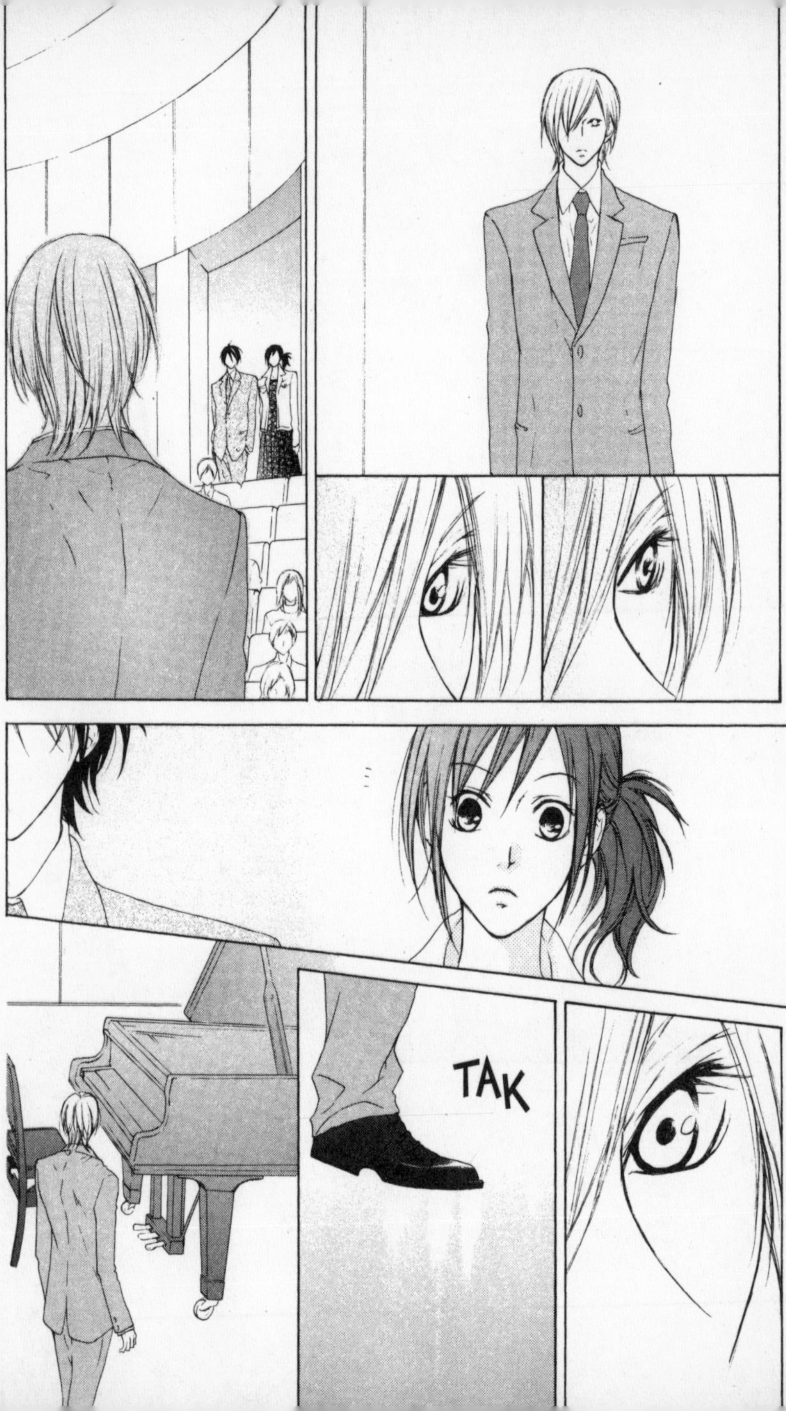
TAK

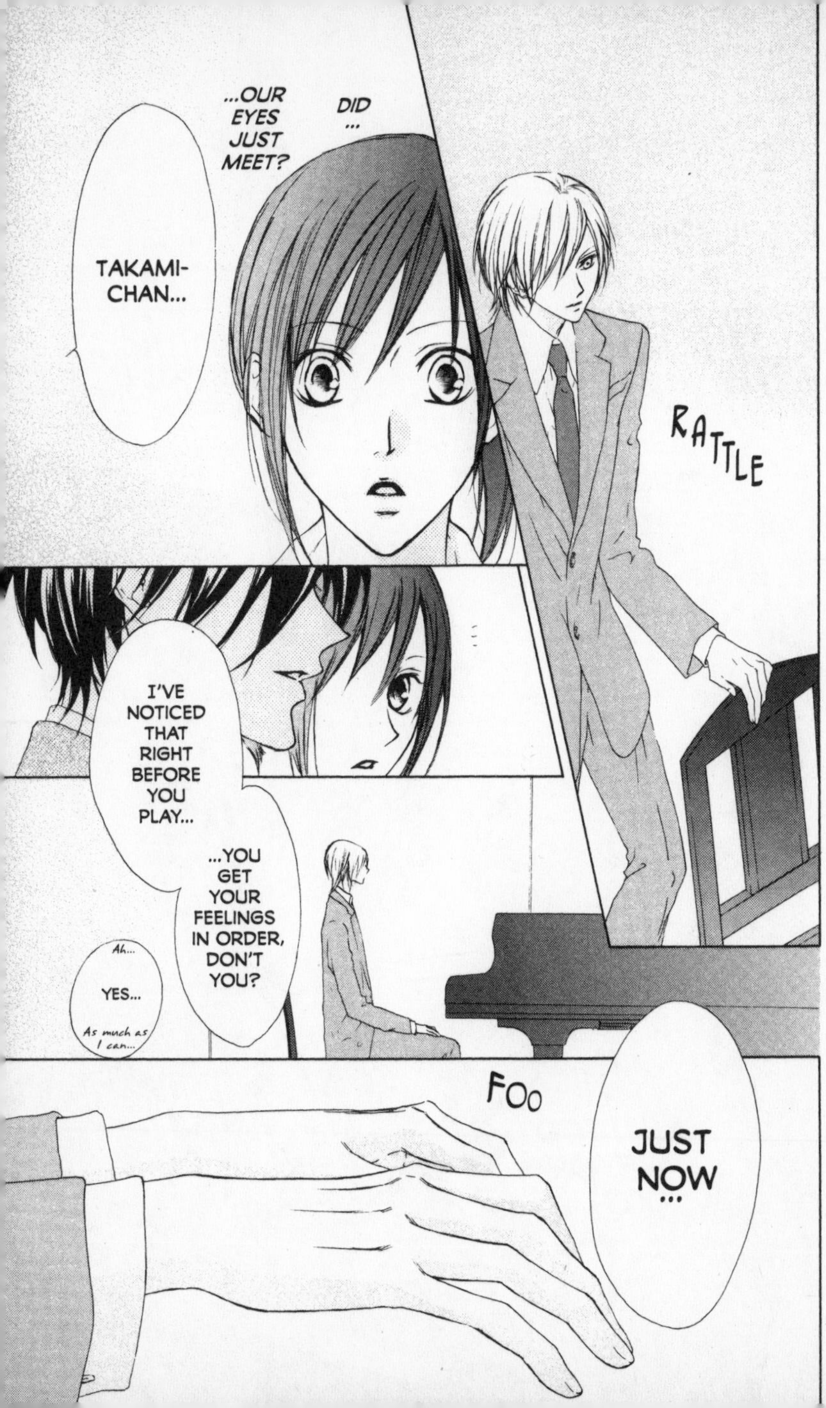

RATTLE
DID...
...OUR EYES JUST MEET?
TAKAMI-CHAN...
I'VE NOTICED THAT RIGHT BEFORE YOU PLAY...
...YOU GET YOUR FEELINGS IN ORDER, DON'T YOU?
Ah... YES... As much as I can...
JUST NOW...
FOO

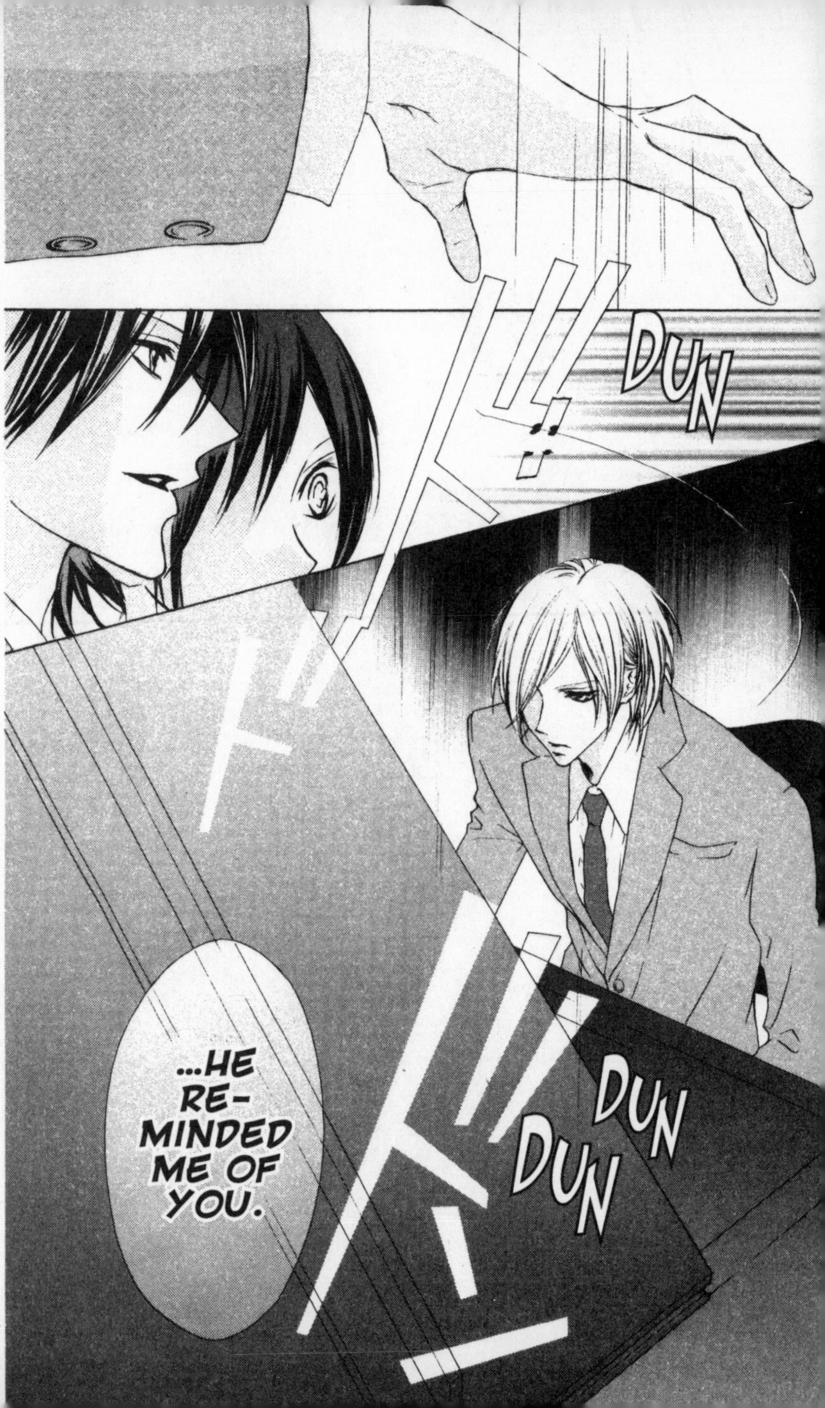
DUN
...HE RE-MINDED ME OF YOU.
DUN
DUN

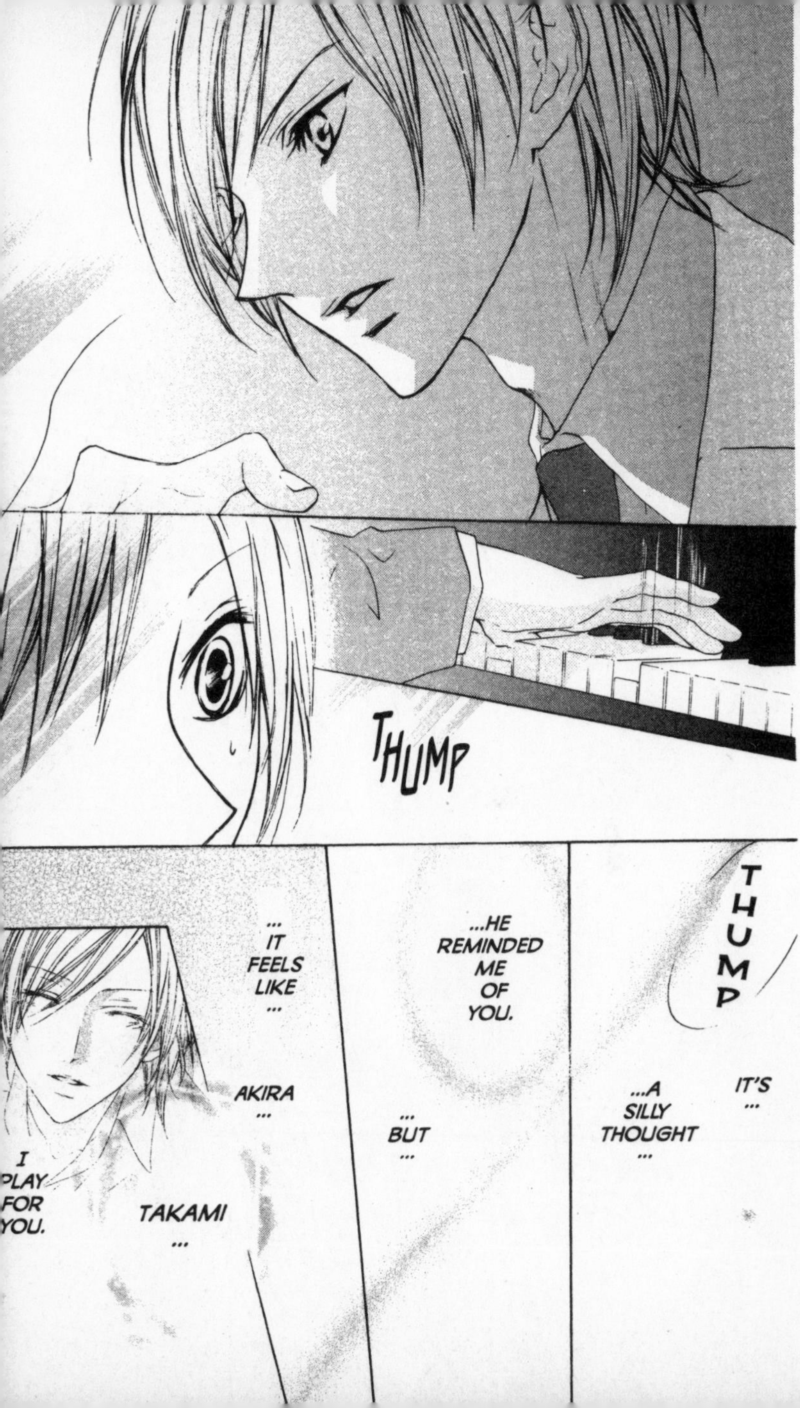
THUMP
THUMP
IT'S ...
...A SILLY THOUGHT ...
...HE REMINDED ME OF YOU.
... BUT ...
... IT FEELS LIKE ...
AKIRA ...
TAKAMI ...
I PLAY FOR YOU.

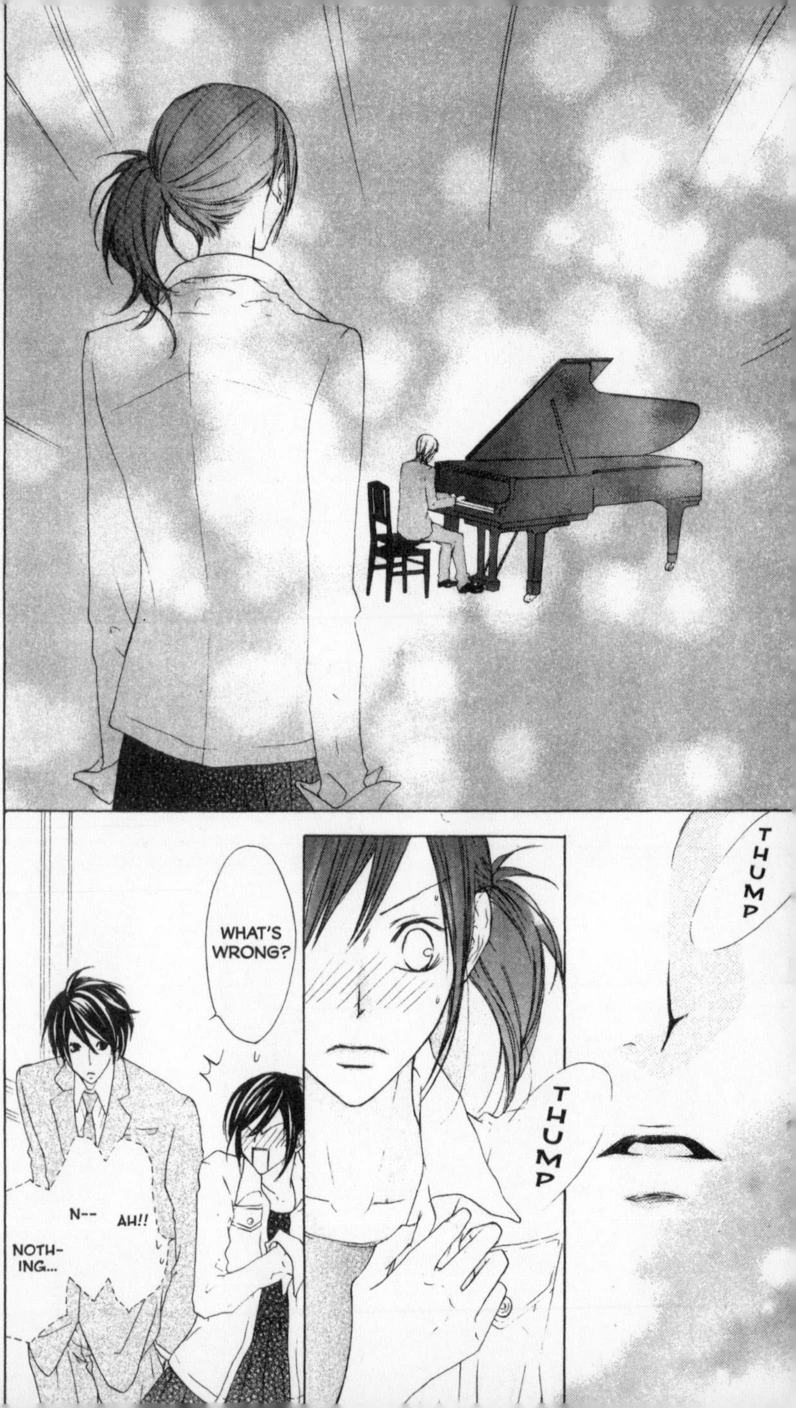
THUMP
THUMP
WHAT'S WRONG?
AH!!
N-- NOTHING...

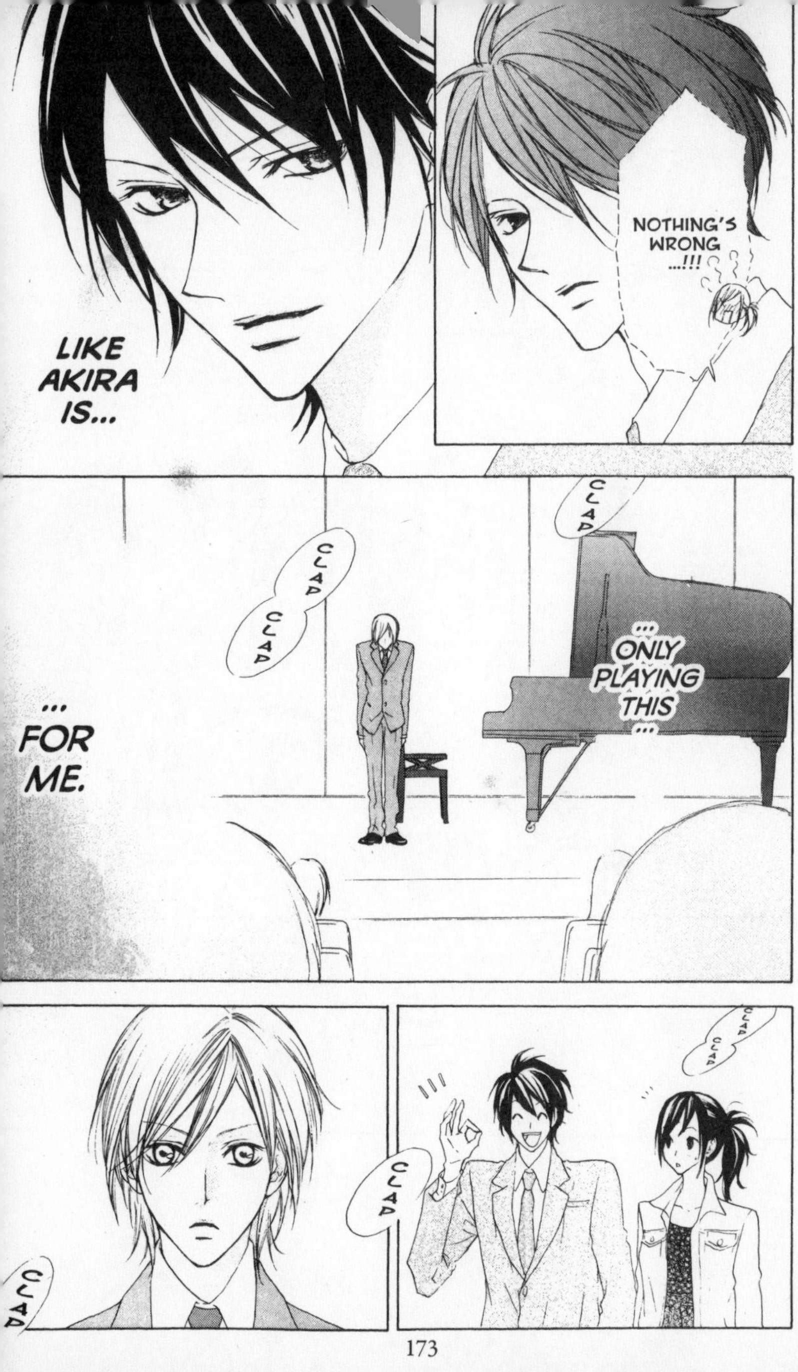
NOTHING'S WRONG ...!!!
LIKE AKIRA IS...
CLAP
... ONLY PLAYING THIS ...
CLAP CLAP
... FOR ME.
CLAP CLAP
CLAP
CLAP

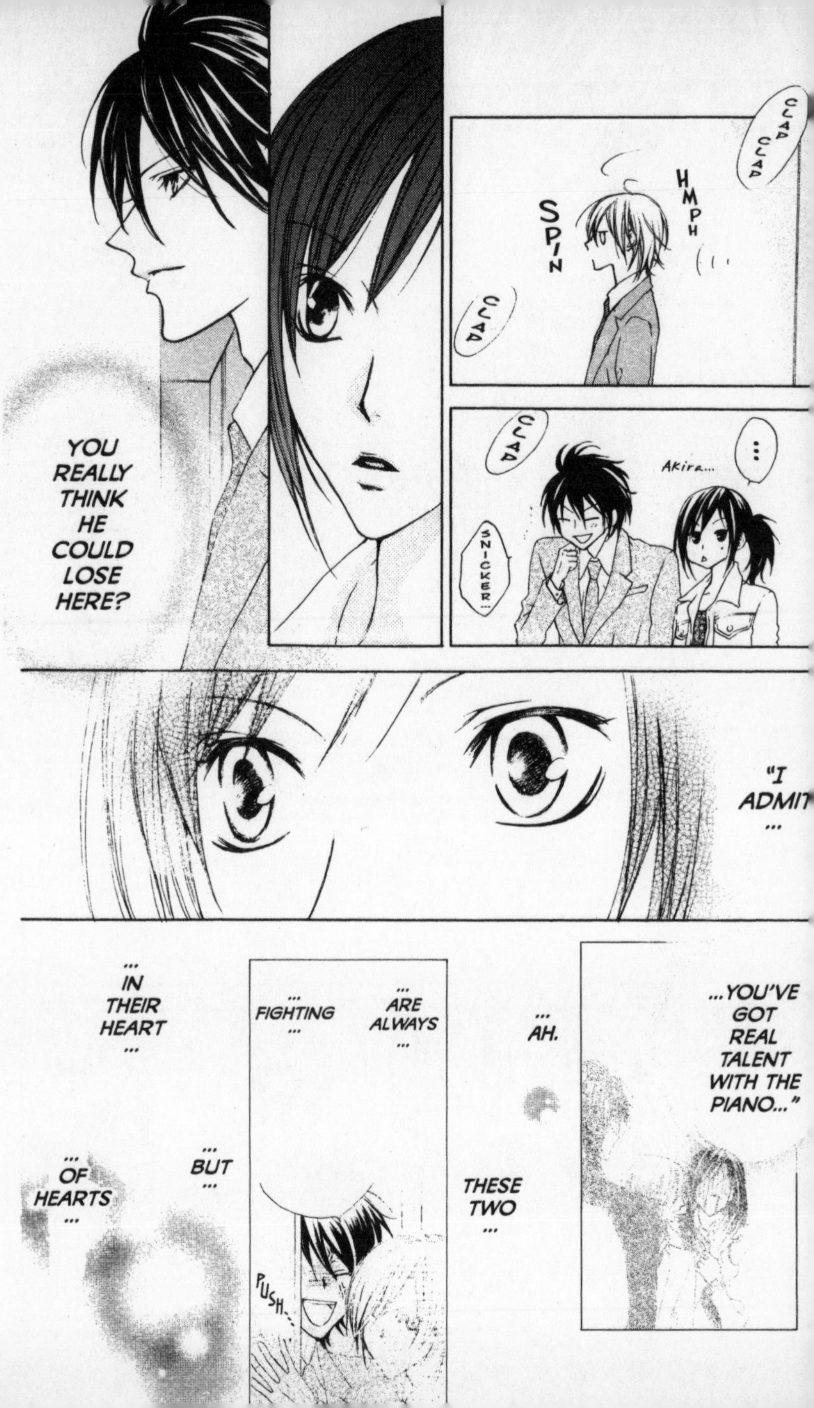
CLAP CLAP CLAP
HMPH
SPIN
CLAP
CLAP
...
Akira...
SNICKER...
YOU REALLY THINK HE COULD LOSE HERE?
"I ADMIT...
...YOU'VE GOT REAL TALENT WITH THE PIANO..."
...AH.
THESE TWO...
...ARE ALWAYS...
...FIGHTING...
PUSH...
...BUT...
...IN THEIR HEART...
...OF HEARTS...

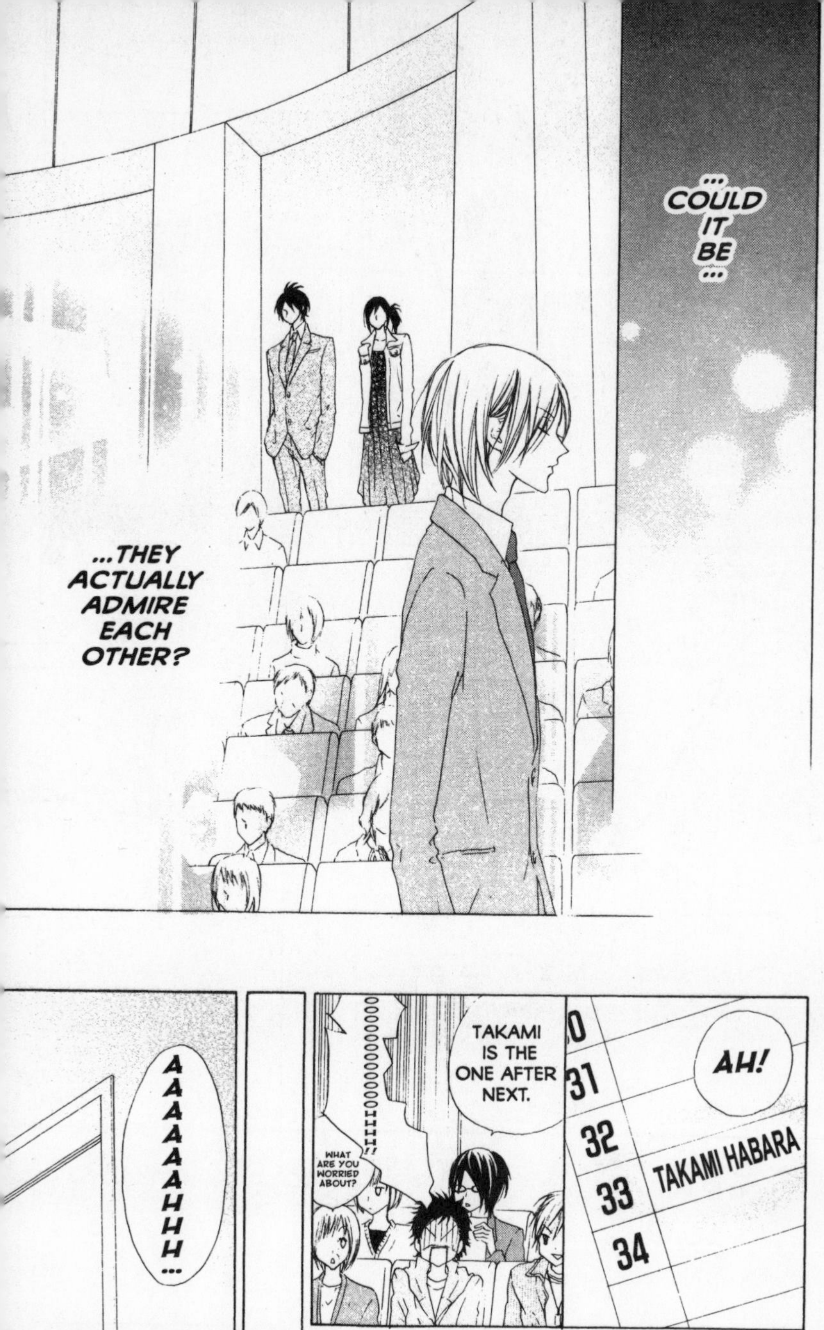
...COULD IT BE...
...THEY ACTUALLY ADMIRE EACH OTHER?
AH!
30
31
32
33
34
TAKAMI HABARA
TAKAMI IS THE ONE AFTER NEXT.
OOOOOOOOOOOOOOHHHH!!
WHAT ARE YOU WORRIED ABOUT?
AAAAAAAHHH...

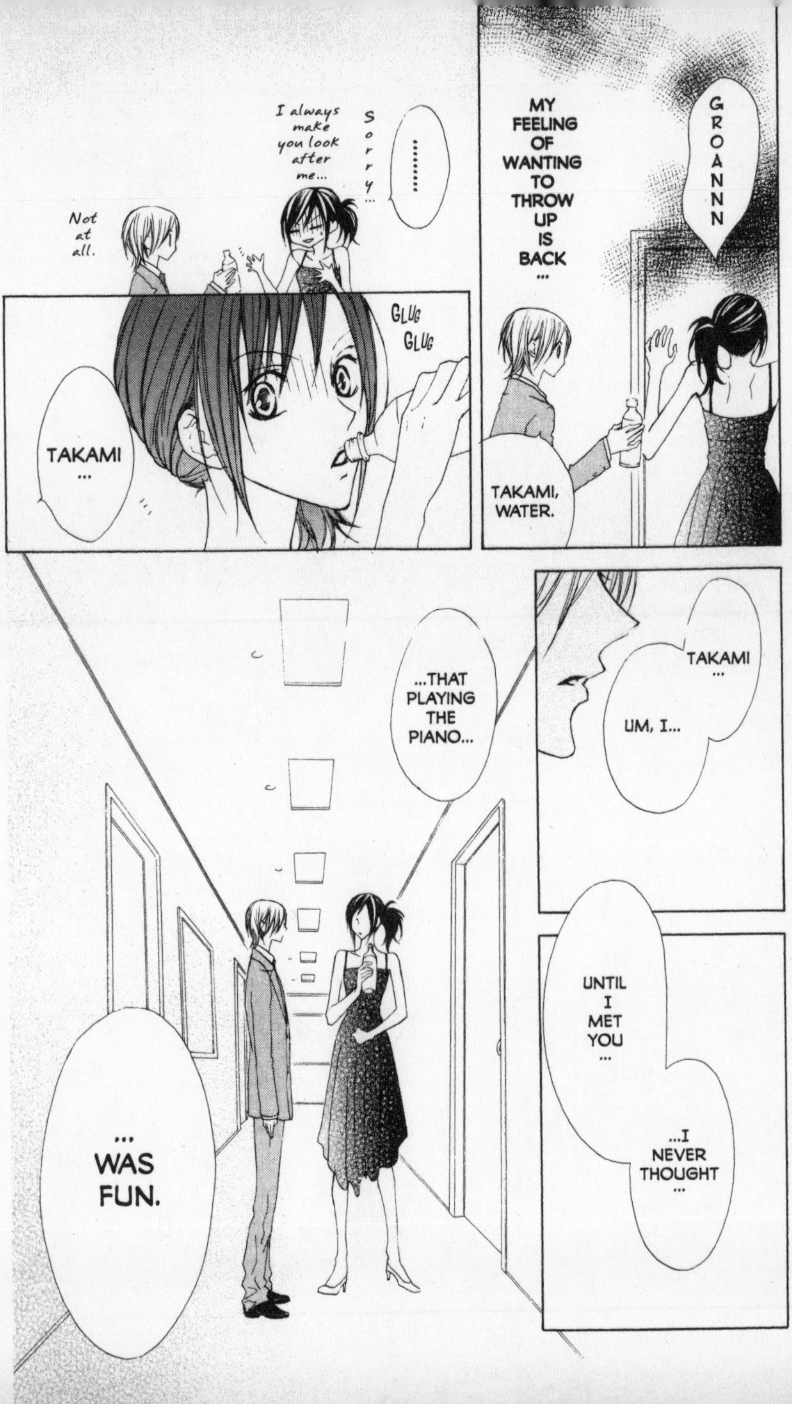
GROANNN
MY FEELING OF WANTING TO THROW UP IS BACK...
TAKAMI, WATER.
....
Sorry...
I always make you look after me...
Not at all.
GLUG GLUG
TAKAMI...
TAKAMI...
UM, I...
UNTIL I MET YOU...
...I NEVER THOUGHT...
...THAT PLAYING THE PIANO...
...WAS FUN.

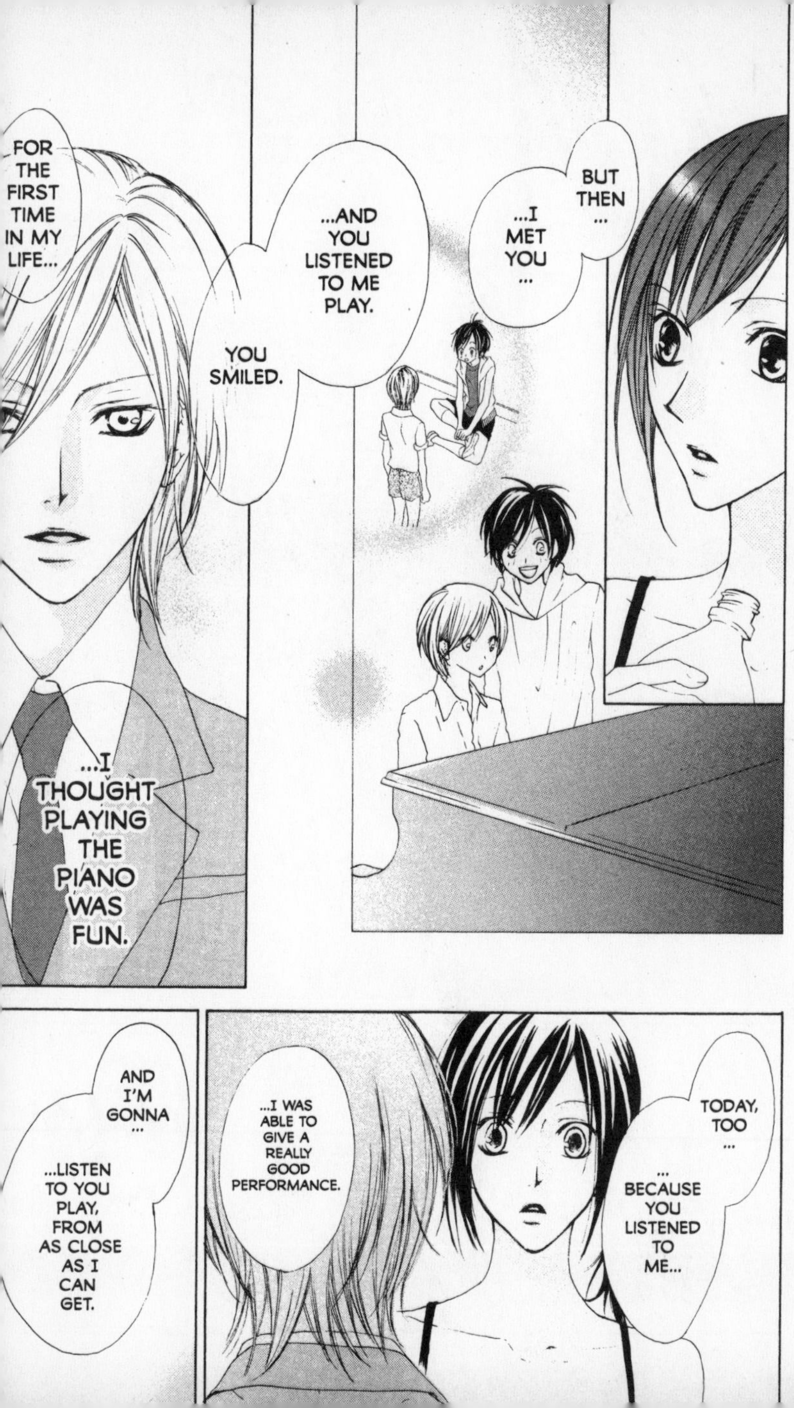
BUT THEN ...
...I MET YOU ...
...AND YOU LISTENED TO ME PLAY.
YOU SMILED.
FOR THE FIRST TIME IN MY LIFE...
...I THOUGHT PLAYING THE PIANO WAS FUN.
TODAY, TOO ...
... BECAUSE YOU LISTENED TO ME...
...I WAS ABLE TO GIVE A REALLY GOOD PERFORMANCE.
AND I'M GONNA ...
...LISTEN TO YOU PLAY, FROM AS CLOSE AS I CAN GET.

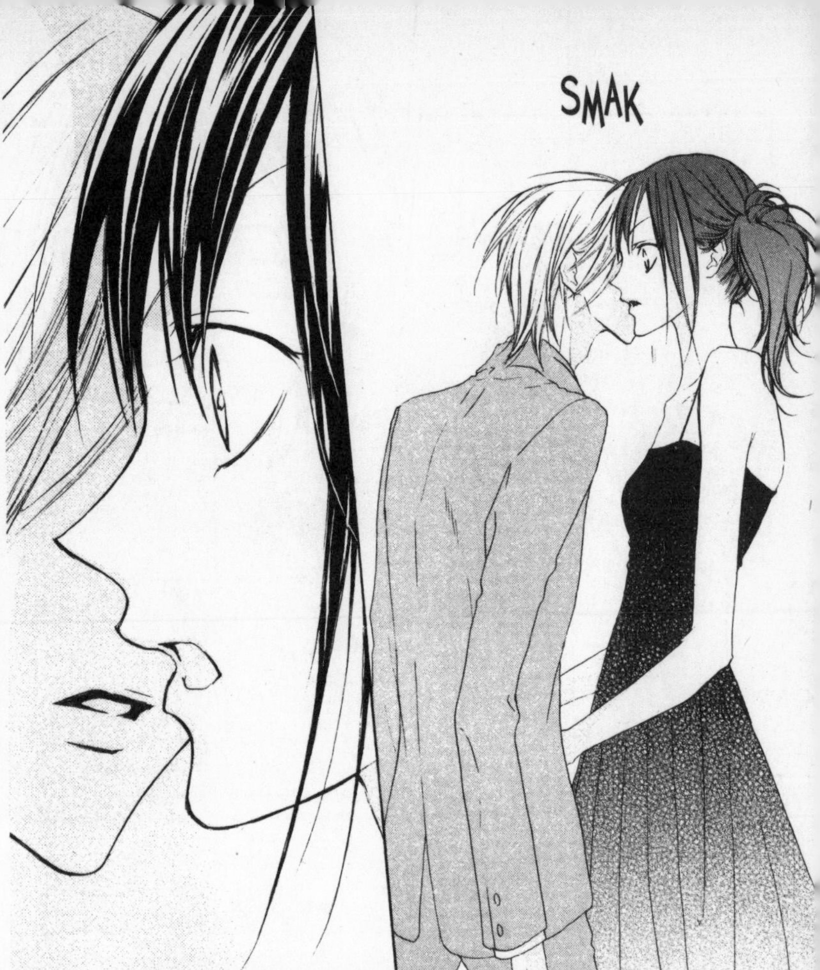
SMAK

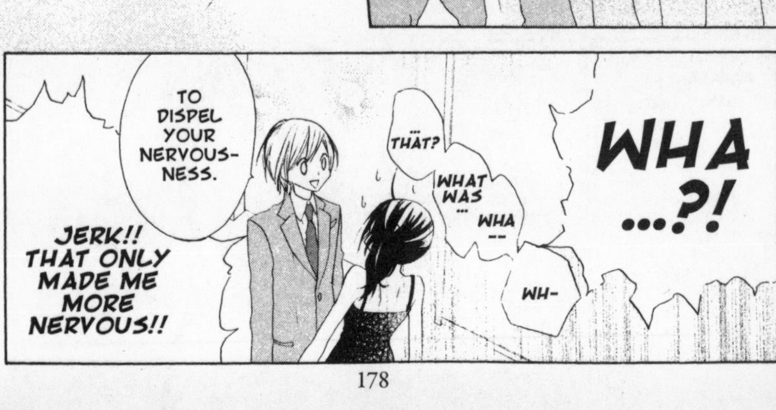
WHA ...?!
...THAT?
WHAT WAS ...
WHA --
WH-
TO DISPEL YOUR NERVOUSNESS.
JERK!! THAT ONLY MADE ME MORE NERVOUS!!

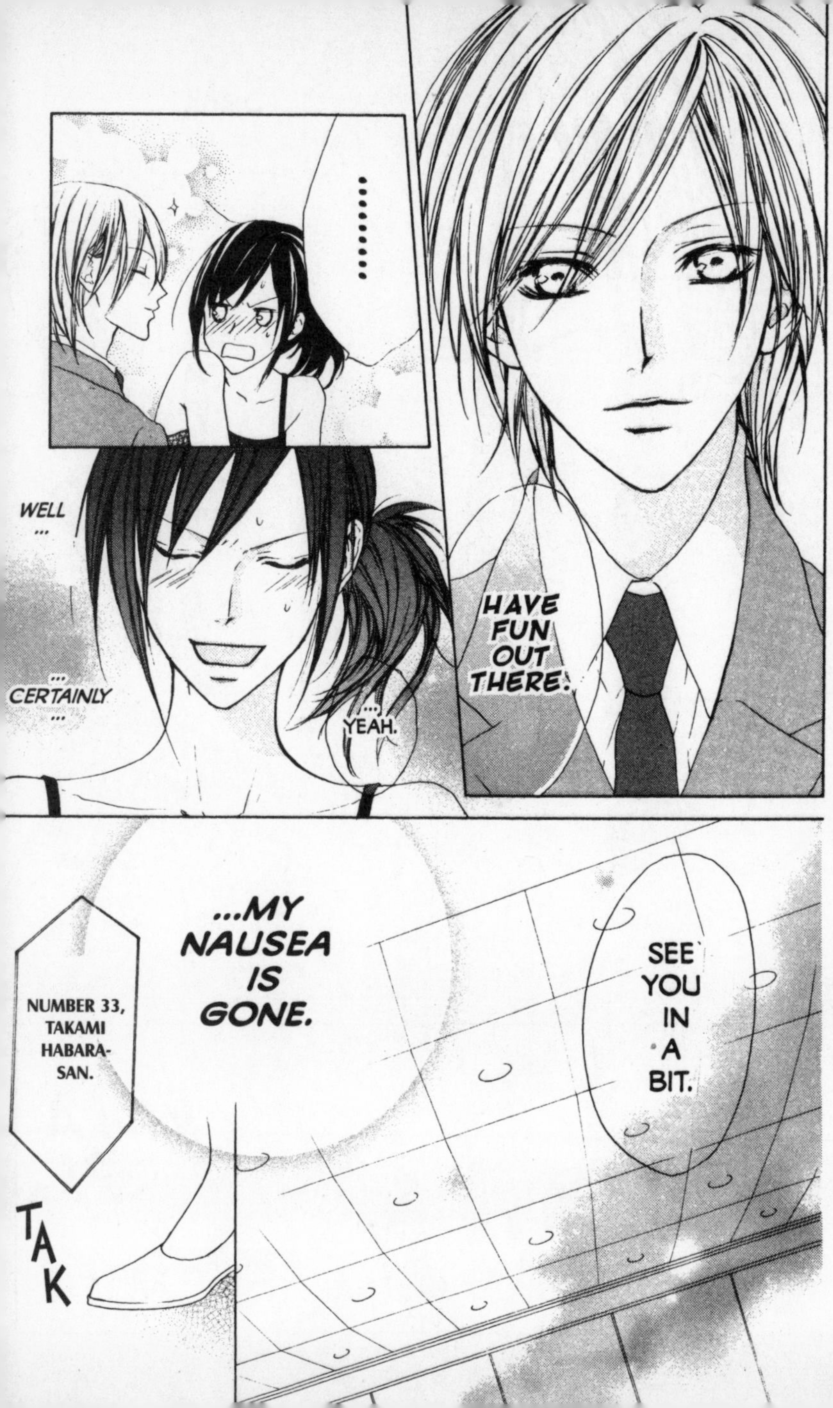
HAVE FUN OUT THERE.
......
WELL ...
... CERTAINLY ...
... YEAH.
SEE YOU IN A BIT.
...MY NAUSEA IS GONE.
NUMBER 33, TAKAMI HABARA-SAN.
TAK

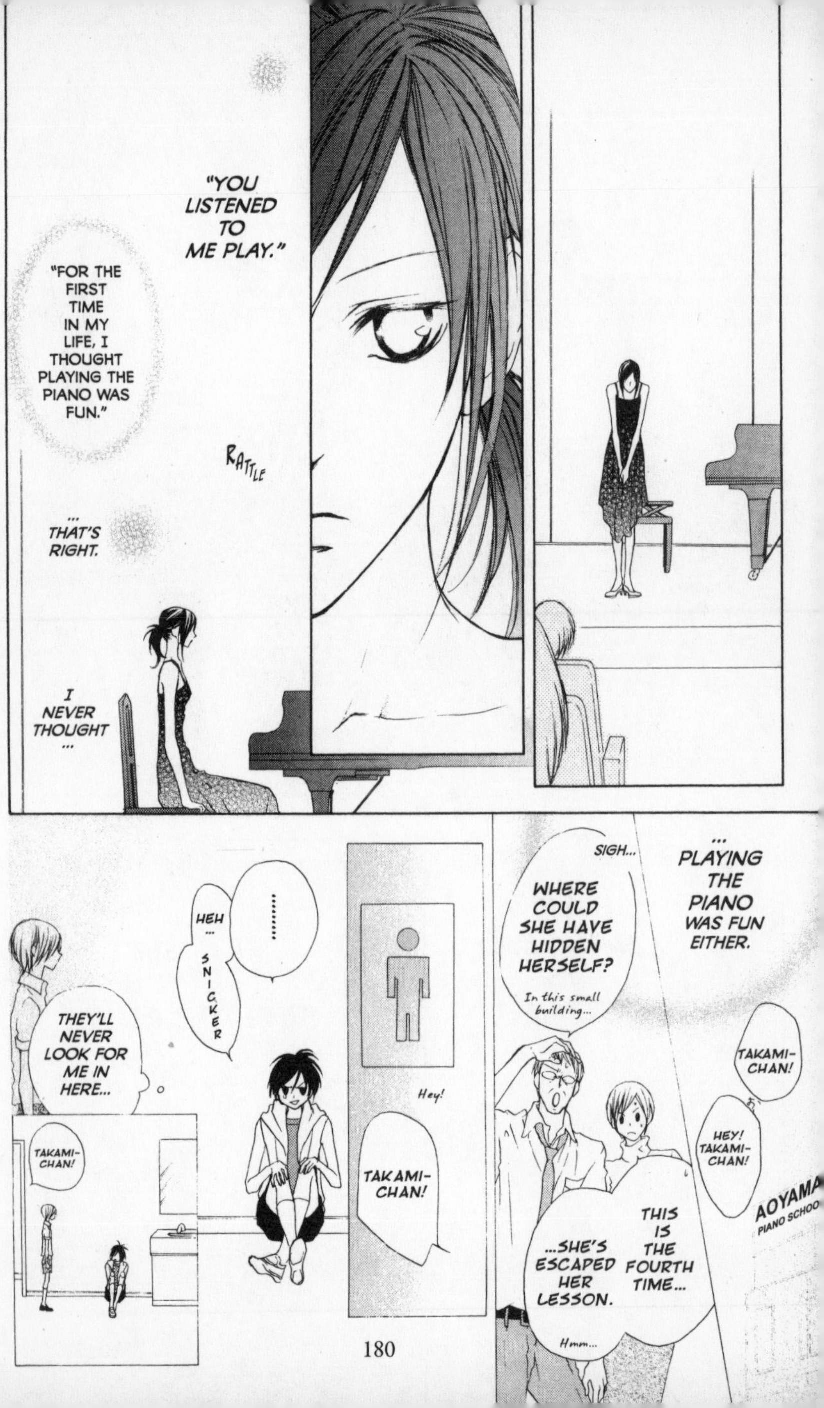
"YOU LISTENED TO ME PLAY."
"FOR THE FIRST TIME IN MY LIFE, I THOUGHT PLAYING THE PIANO WAS FUN."
RATTLE
... THAT'S RIGHT.
I NEVER THOUGHT ...
... PLAYING THE PIANO WAS FUN EITHER.
AOYAMA PIANO SCHOO
TAKAMI-CHAN!
HEY! TAKAMI-CHAN!
SIGH...
WHERE COULD SHE HAVE HIDDEN HERSELF?
In this small building...
THIS IS THE FOURTH TIME...
...SHE'S ESCAPED HER LESSON.
Hmm...
Hey!
TAKAMI-CHAN!
....
HEH ... SNICKER
THEY'LL NEVER LOOK FOR ME IN HERE...
TAKAMI-CHAN!

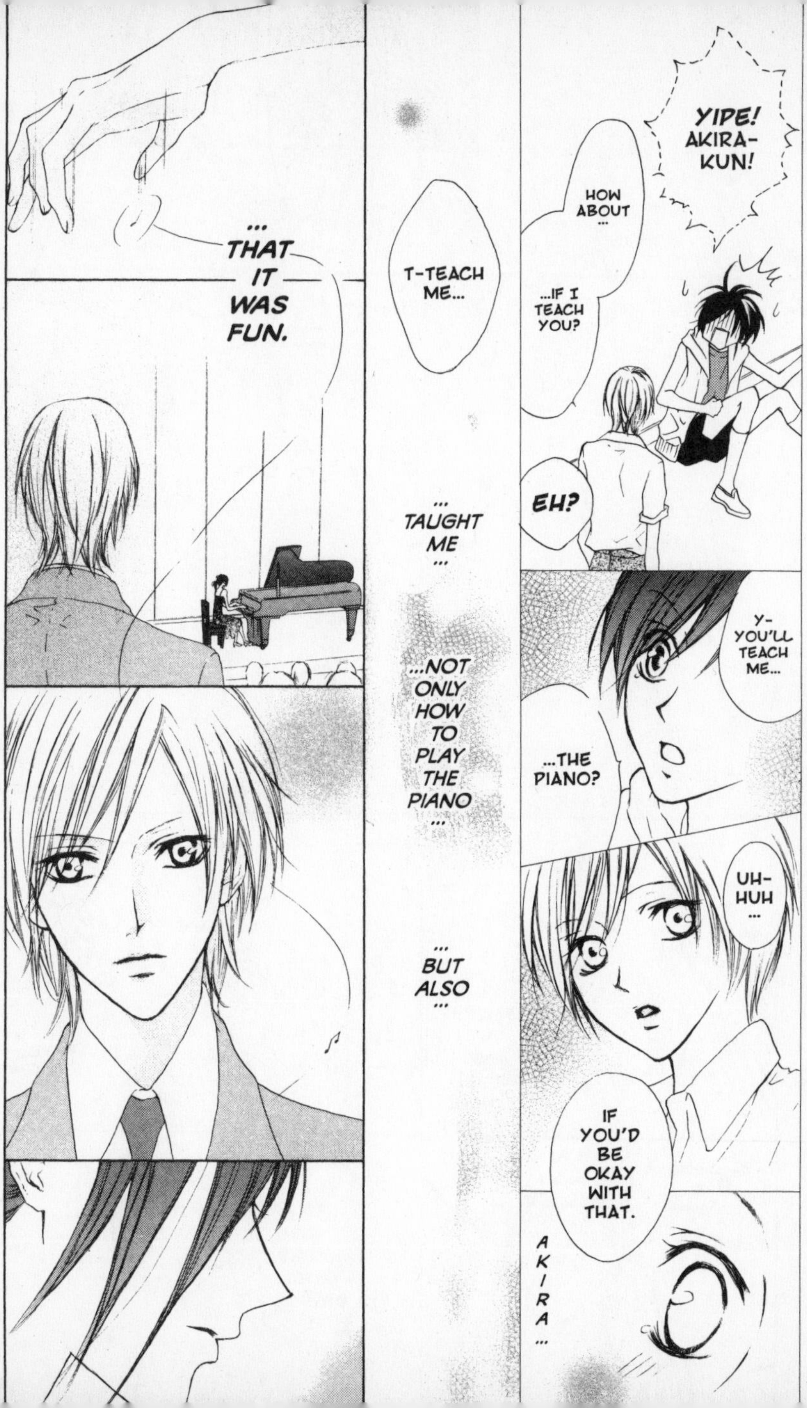
YIPE! AKIRA-KUN!
HOW ABOUT...
...IF I TEACH YOU?
EH?
Y-YOU'LL TEACH ME...
...THE PIANO?
UH-HUH...
IF YOU'D BE OKAY WITH THAT.
AKIRA...
T-TEACH ME...
...TAUGHT ME...
...NOT ONLY HOW TO PLAY THE PIANO...
...BUT ALSO...
...THAT IT WAS FUN.

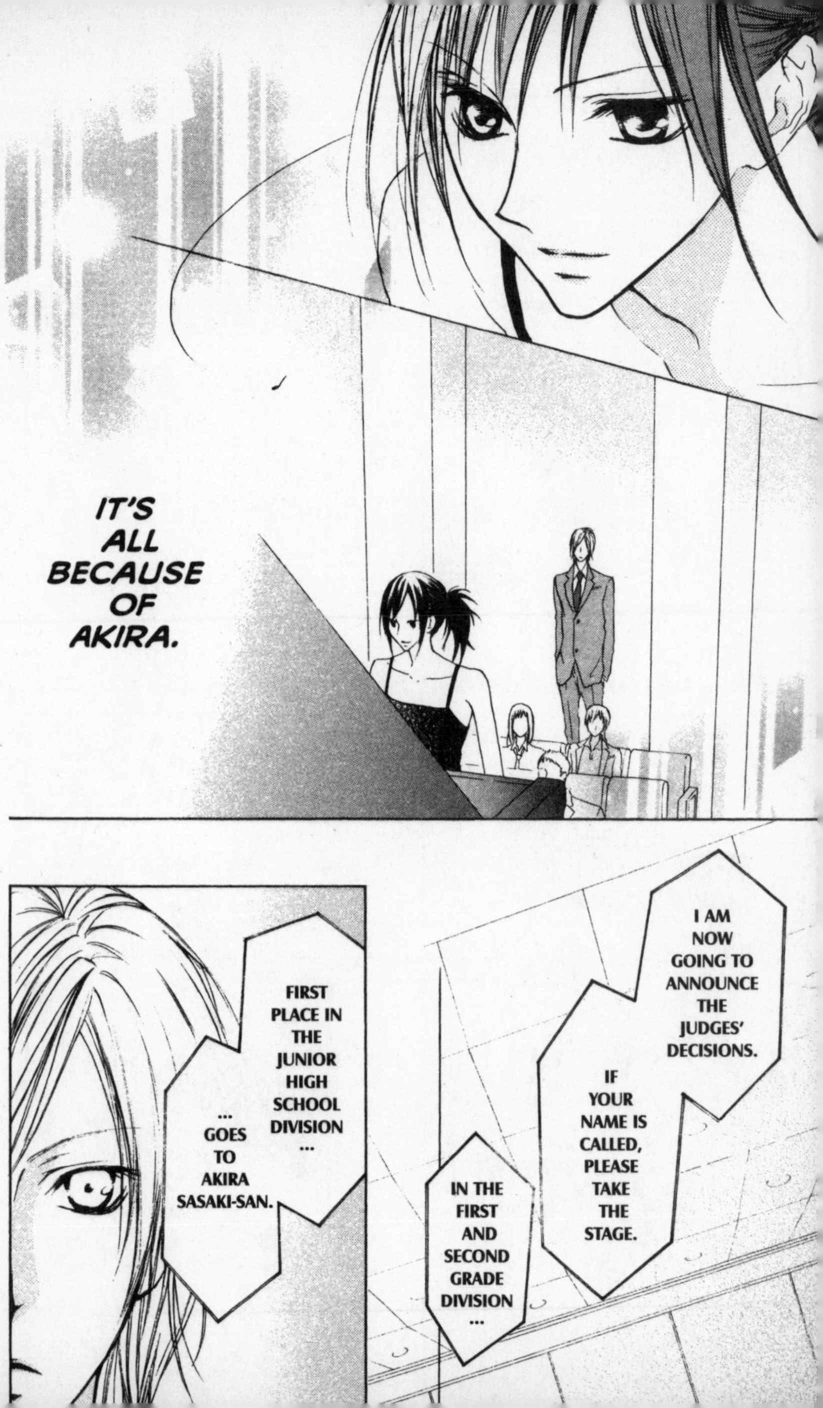
IT'S ALL BECAUSE OF AKIRA.
I AM NOW GOING TO ANNOUNCE THE JUDGES' DECISIONS.
IF YOUR NAME IS CALLED, PLEASE TAKE THE STAGE.
IN THE FIRST AND SECOND GRADE DIVISION ...
FIRST PLACE IN THE JUNIOR HIGH SCHOOL DIVISION ...
... GOES TO AKIRA SASAKI-SAN.

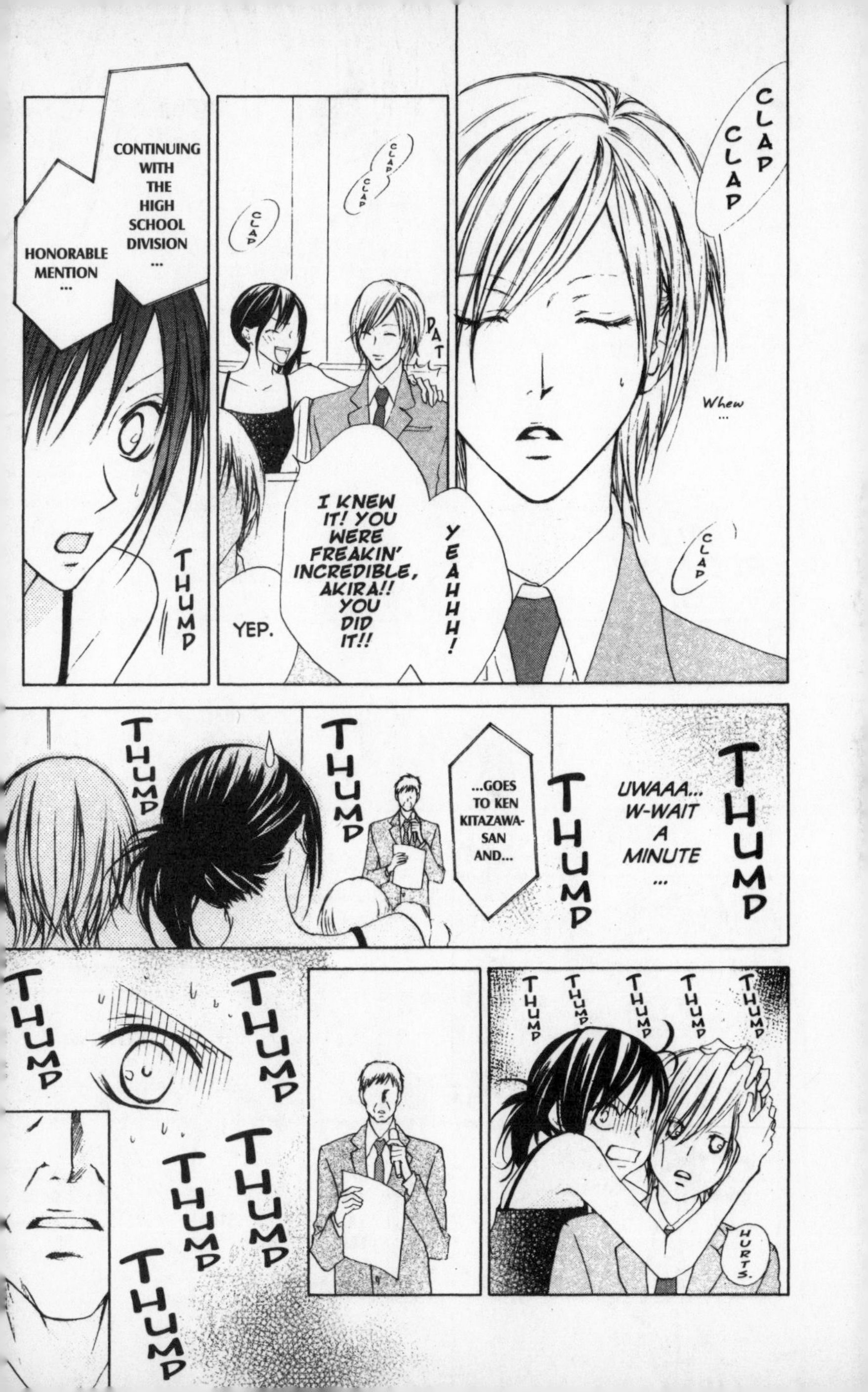
CLAP CLAP
Whew...
CLAP
CLAP CLAP
CLAP
PAT
YEAHHHH!
I KNEW IT! YOU WERE FREAKIN' INCREDIBLE, AKIRA!! YOU DID IT!!
YEP.
CONTINUING WITH THE HIGH SCHOOL DIVISION...
HONORABLE MENTION...
THUMP
THUMP
UWAAA... W-WAIT A MINUTE...
THUMP
...GOES TO KEN KITAZAWA-SAN AND...
THUMP
THUMP
THUMP
THUMP
THUMP
THUMP
THUMP
HURTS.
THUMP
THUMP
THUMP
THUMP
THUMP

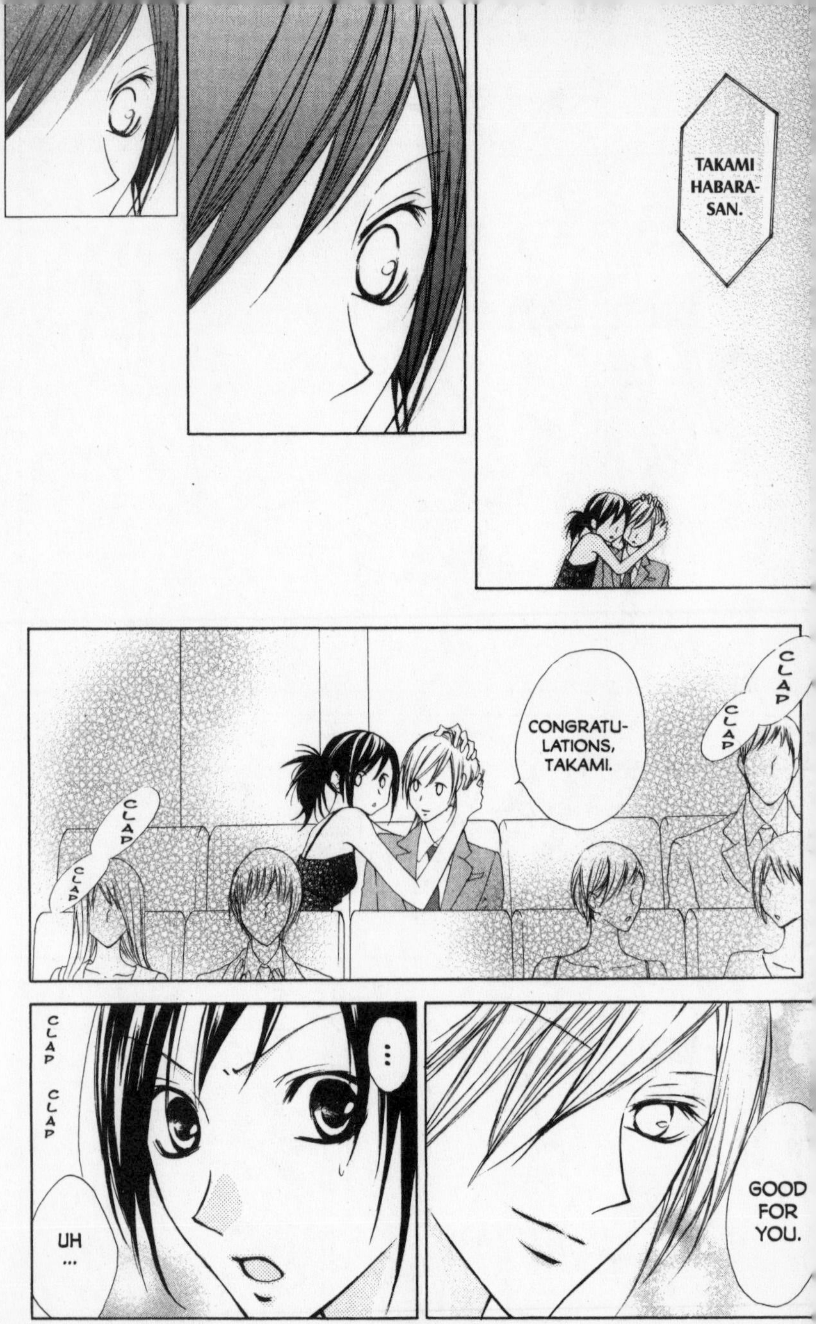
TAKAMI HABARA-SAN.
CLAP CLAP
CONGRATULATIONS, TAKAMI.
CLAP CLAP
GOOD FOR YOU.
...
UH ...
CLAP CLAP CLAP CLAP

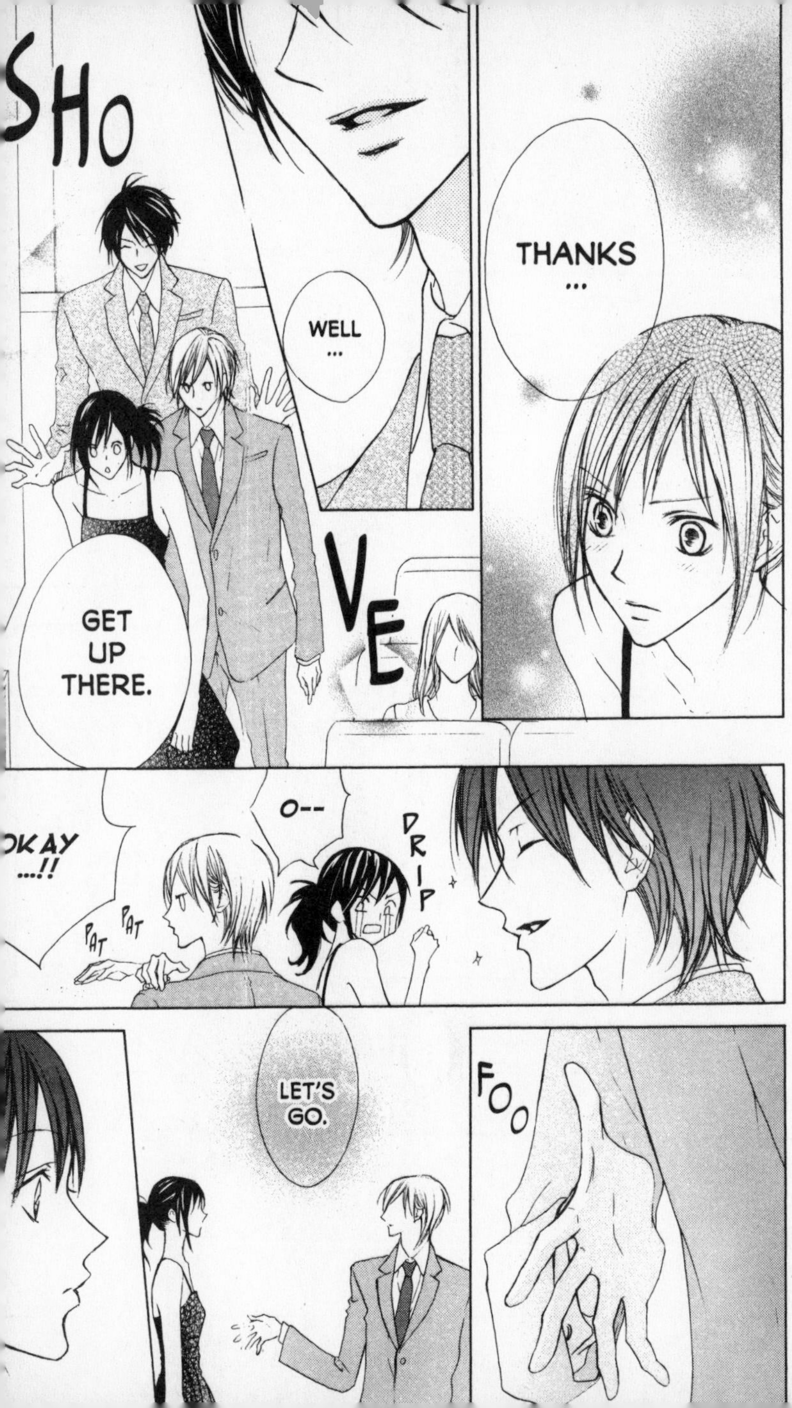
THANKS ...
WELL ...
SHO
VE
GET UP THERE.
DRIP
O--
OKAY ...!!
PAT PAT
FOO
LET'S GO.

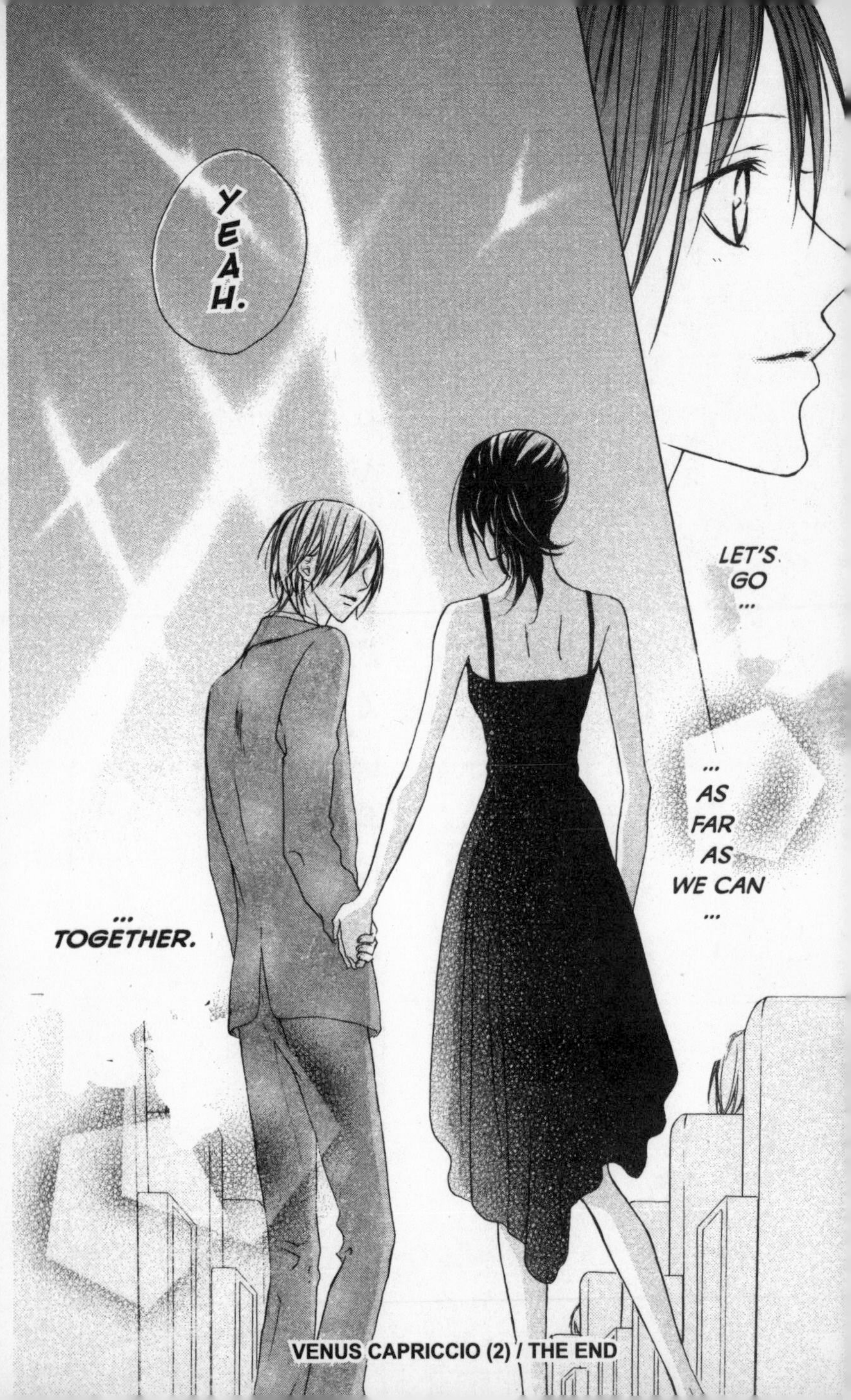
LET'S GO ...
... AS FAR AS WE CAN ...
YEAH.
... TOGETHER.
VENUS CAPRICCIO (2) / THE END

BONUS PAGES

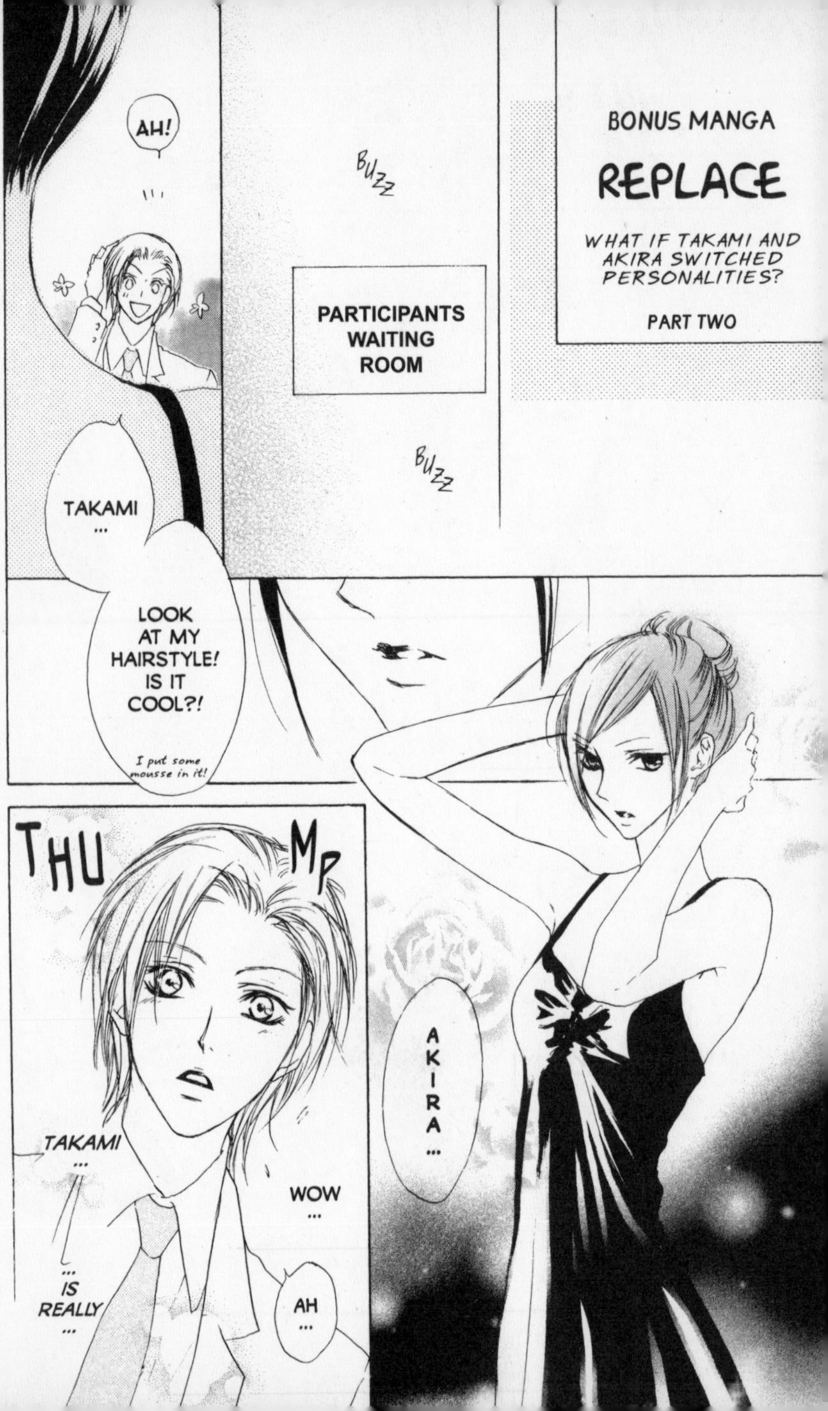
BONUS MANGA
REPLACE
WHAT IF TAKAMI AND AKIRA SWITCHED PERSONALITIES?
PART TWO
BUZZ
PARTICIPANTS WAITING ROOM
BUZZ
AH!
TAKAMI...
LOOK AT MY HAIRSTYLE! IS IT COOL?!
I put some mousse in it!
AKIRA...
THUMP
WOW...
AH...
TAKAMI...
...IS REALLY...

 **AFTERWORD**

THANK YOU FOR GETTING THIS FAR!

I WOULD NEVER HAVE BEEN ABLE TO COME OUT WITH
VOLUME 2 IF IT HADN'T HAVE BEEN FOR ALL YOU READERS,
THE SUPPORT OF MANY, MANY PEOPLE, AND THE TREASURED
LETTERS I GOT FROM A LOT OF YOU.

I'LL KEEP TRYING MY BEST FOR YOU!

 SPECIAL THANKS TO:

MY EDITOR, S-SAMA; KATORI-SAMA; TSUCHIYA-SAMA;
KOBAYASHI-SAMA
TSUKUDA-SENSEI; NAKAZAWA-SAN
(THANK YOU SO MUCH FOR ALL OF YOUR HELP!)

ALL OF MY FRIENDS AND PEOPLE I KNOW WHO
SUPPORTED ME

MY DEAR FAMILY

AND EVERYONE WHO PLAYED A PART IN GETTING
THIS BOOK PUBLISHED

IF YOU HAVE ANY THOUGHTS, OPINIONS, ETC.
YOU'D LIKE TO SHARE ABOUT THIS TITLE, PLEASE
SEND THEM TO ME CARE OF:

MAI NISHIKATA
C/O CMX
888 PROSPECT STREET
SUITE 240
LA JOLLA CA 92104

WELL, SEE YOU AGAIN SOMETIME!
THIS HAS BEEN NISHIKATA. MAY, 2007

BONUS PAGES / THE END

VENUS CAPRICCIO by Mai Nishikata © 2007 by Mai Nishikata. All rights reserved.
First published in Japan in 2007 by HAKUSENSHA, INC. Tokyo.

VENUS CAPRICCIO Volume 2, published by WildStorm Productions, an imprint of DC
Comics, 888 Prospect St. #240, La Jolla, CA 92037. English Translation © 2009. All Rights
Reserved. English translation rights in U.S.A. and Canada arranged with HAKUSENSHA,
INC., through Tuttle-Mori Agency, Inc., Tokyo. CMX is a trademark of DC Comics. The
stories, characters, and incidents mentioned in this magazine are entirely fictional. Printed
on recyclable paper. WildStorm does not read or accept unsolicited submissions of ideas,
stories or artwork. Printed in Canada.

DC Comics, a Warner Bros. Entertainment Company.

This book is manufactured at a facility holding chain-of-custody certification.
This paper is made with sustainably managed North American fiber.

Sheldon Drzka – Translation and Adaptation
MPS Ad Studio – Lettering
Larry Berry – Design
Sarah Farber – Assistant Editor
Jim Chadwick – Editor

ISBN: 978-1-4012-2062-4

THE SECRET IS OUT IN JANUARY 2010!

By Mai Nishikata. Akira and Takami join forces to help save the annual high school
chorus performance. Their teamwork is a huge success and after the concert Akira
finally tells Takami he loves her...but she doesn't seem to get it. He realizes that he
needs to take a more straightforward approach. When Takami flees her house after a
huge fight with her brothers and seeks solace at Akira's place while his parents are
out of town, the opportunity couldn't be more perfect. But when Akira makes his move,
the whole situation backfires!